The Cultural Dialectics of
Knowledge and Desire

The Cultural Dialectics of Knowledge and Desire

Charles W. Nuckolls

THE UNIVERSITY OF WISCONSIN PRESS

The University of Wisconsin Press
114 North Murray Street
Madison, Wisconsin 53715

3 Henrietta Street
London WC2E 8LU, England

5   4   3   2   1

Printed in the United States of America

Library of Congress Cataloging-in-Publication Data
Nuckolls, Charles William, 1956–
The Cultural Dialectics of Knowledge and Desire /
Charles W. Nuckolls.
350 p.   cm.
—Includes bibliographical references and index.
ISBN 0-299-15120-4 (cloth: alk. paper).
ISBN 0-299-15124-7 (pbk.: alk. paper).
1. Jalaris—Kinship.   2. Jalaris—Psychology.
3. Jalaris—Social conditions.
4. Cognition and culture—India, South.
5. Psychoanalysis and culture—India, South.
6. India, South-Social conditions.
I. Title.   II. Series.
DS432.J227N82   1997
306.4'2—dc20   96-18175

In formal logic a contradition is the sign of a defeat: But in the evolution of real knowledge it marks the first step in progress towards victory.

A. N. Whitehead,
Science and the Modern World

Contents

ix

Illustrations

Enrich reason with the powers of passion. Nowhere is the animating paradox of the modern era more clearly revealed than in this overweening desire to plunder passion, this contradictory urge to colonize the fecund chaos of unreason without destroying unreason's atavistic dynamism, this antagonistic compulsion to domesticate unreason *and* preserve the productive power of unreason's autarchic difference. Reason's need to dominate unreason without destroying the creative difference between itself and its unreasonable other is the paradoxical story told in all the guiding oppositions of the modern era, as allegorized, for example, in that infamous tale of the fundamental difference between mind and body, or in the opposition of culture and nature. This complementarity within contradiction, this necessity of zetetic opposition and antinomy is both the essence of paradox and the source of dialectic. It is also the dynamism of *The Cultural Dialectics of Knowledge and Desire.*

In this provocative work, Dr. Nuckolls proposes a "theory of paradox in culture" in which "culture is a problem that cannot be solved." Cultures are emergent systems that grow out of and mirror the dialectic of conflicting and competing desires within individuals, between individuals and culture, and within culture, but Dr. Nuckolls argues that conflicts in primary processes at the individual level are not resolved in higher order symbolic cultural syntheses and, conversely, that conflicts in cultural symbol systems are not simply reducible to conflicts in primary processes. Because cultures are emergent systems, they do not function according to the mechanics of the lower-level processes out of which they have emerged and consequently cannot directly motivate those processes. In other words, higher-level cultural symbols cannot be used as the sole explanation of individual behavior. Conversely, since lower-level microprocesses do not operate at the level of abstract symbolic cultural systems, those systems cannot be explained by reducing them to such processes. In place of either universalization or reductionism in which one level replaces, overcomes, or predominates over the other, Dr. Nuckolls argues that there is instead a dialectical relation in which different levels interact and mutually influence one another.

Dr. Nuckolls is here attempting to bring together two discourses that have formerly been rather at odds with one another—cognitive studies and psychoanalytic theory. He proposes a kind of dialectic between them that focuses on the preservation of their creative dissonance. Central to his argument is the idea that cultures are paradoxical. They contain intractable paradoxes that continue from generation to generation as sources of creative reinterpretation. He uses the same argument to facilitate a reconciliation between relativistic and objectivistic forms of explanation. The dialectical resolution of Weber and Freud, for example, is neither a reduction of one to the other nor a *via media* between them, nor even less of an *Aufhebung,* an overcoming of the difference by means of a new synthesis. His argument, moreover, is that forms of rationalizing are mediated by primary processes. Thus rational thought (Weber) and primary process thinking (Freud) are parallel and persistent. Reason does not overcome unreason; it needs unreason to provide it with goals. The idea of cultural goals is critical for understanding how different cultures can deploy incommensurable patterns of rationalization. Different goals cannot only entrain different forms of rationalization, they can make dissimilar cognitive demands for totalization, consistency, coherence, and generalizability and thus create quite different possibilities for the expression of cognitive dissonance.

In a further application of this relationship between reason and passion, Dr. Nuckolls finds the ideas of paradox and dialectic overtly theorized in a number of anthropological works but discussed most thoroughly in Gregory Bateson's *Naven*. Bateson's concepts of *ethos* and *eidos* are understood as exemplifying, respectively, the emotional and the rational orders of thought. Schizmogenesis is the means of establishing a temporary equilibrium between them, without subordinating them to a higher-order synthesis. The dialectical tension between ethos and eidos is *maintained* in relation to an equilibrium that is never permanent, but is forever being disturbed and reestablished.

Dr. Nuckolls applies the same reasoning to the paradoxical values of unity and separation in the kinship relations of the Jalari of South India, among whom he did his fieldwork. Jalari brothers cannot simultaneously fulfill the cultural goals of agnatic solidarity *and* personal independence, and brothers and sisters are similarly unable to meet the cultural goal of affinal solidarity expressed in cross-cousin marriage at the same time as they seek to cope with the competing goals of family and lineage solidarity.

Although these paradoxes are irresolvable in Jalari culture, they are none-theless the sources from which the Jalari draw explanatory principles for problematic behavior.

The Cultural Dialectics of Knowledge and Desire provides a strong im-petus to rethink the relationship between the competing discourses of psychological anthropology, and it will inevitably stimulate discussion of some of the intractable paradoxes that continue to constitute the *ethos* and *eidos* of anthropology. There, is however, a cautionary note. Dr. Nuckolls skates close to the abyss of postmodernism, for *a theory of paradox is itself a paradox since the paradoxical theorized is neither theory nor paradox,* just as *unreason reasoned is unreasonable because it is neither reason nor unreason.*

STEPHEN A. TYLER

Acknowledgments

This book tries to rescue the concept of culture from the wasteland into which it has been cast, by proving that it is a problem that cannot be solved. Is that a paradox? As I define it, yes, and that is what explains the dynamic power of culture both to organize itself in dialectical knowledge structures and to deeply motivate human action. This is not a new idea. It can be traced as easily to Weber and Freud as it can to Kant and Plato. Boas certainly held it, while Gregory Bateson and Victor Turner expressed it better and put it to better use. It could be called the cultural dialectics of knowledge and desire, and the theory of cultural dialectics to be presented here unites cognitive and psychoanalytic approaches to culture. It is unabashedly theoretical, and it touts anthropology as a science still capable of explanation.

It might already be apparent that this is an effort born of frustration, but "conflict" is a better word. Who has studied anthropology and not felt the conflict between the tendency to idealize and reduce it? Is culture a reality *sui generis,* as Durkheim said, or is it a mindful thing, understandable in terms of cognitive processes? Should individual action be considered primary, because it is more perceptually salient, or should priority be given to the shared symbols in terms of which action is expressed? Even the briefest exposure to the discipline is enough: We know that these are long-standing problems, with histories that can be traced to the very beginning of the field, and they are terribly frustrating. I claim that it is time to come clean and admit that the fundamental problems of the field are not problems in the first place, but solutions to problems whose precise nature remains hidden. Only an approach that does not avoid paradox, but positively revels in it, can achieve this vision.

This book seeks conflict and embraces contradiction, and it admits that a complete and consistent solution to any problem in cultural anthropology is certainly impossible and probably undesirable. Can there be a theory of

xviii   *Acknowledgments*

cultural paradox? We shall find out, but only by directly encountering the problems that give rise to our frustration in the first place.

The circumstances of dual-career academic couplehood do not recommend themselves in most regards, especially when spouses must commute across state lines and time zones to family and work. But in one, at least, I can say that I am thankful. When my wife, Janis Nuckolls, relinquished her teaching position at the Department of Anthropology at Indiana University and moved to the University of Alabama at Birmingham, to make my commuting to Atlanta more manageable, we both found a new and engaging set of colleagues. Most of this book was written in Birmingham, and I have enjoyed discussions with many of the Alabama faculty, including George Graham, Tom McKenna, and Chris Taylor. I thank them for providing us with an intellectual home, and for making life in Alabama interesting.

I am also very grateful to Stephen Tyler, for his comments; to Rick Shweder and Howard Stein, for pointing out, in different ways, the relevance of cognition and motivation to culture; to Gananath Obeyesekere and Sudhir Kakar, for their advice and the example of their work; to Gregory Schrempp, for demonstrating the relevance of the Kantian antinomies to cultural structures; to Drew Westen, for his pathbreaking efforts to eliminate the absurd antagonisms between cognitive psychology and psychoanalysis and to build a synthesis; to Bob McCauley and Tom Lawson, for their trenchant critique of cultural anthropology, and for reminding us that our sole claim to intellectual relevance is the concept we have very nearly lost; to Joe Elder, for sending me, quite arbitrarily, to Andhra Pradesh my first year in India; to Marshall Sahlins and David Schneider, for frustrating me in all my earliest efforts to understand meaning both culturally and psychologically; and to all the postmodernists, who, in their efforts to decompose culture and distribute its remains among other concepts—power, discourse, resistance—have forced the creation of new theories of culture.

My greatest debt is to the members of the Jalari caste community of coastal Andhra Pradesh. As friends and colleagues, they not only gave me interesting problems to think about but also solved many of them, with a warmth and good humor I only wish I could imitate. Only a few can be singled out for special mention: Teddi Pentayya and Desamma, Potti Puteyya and Ellamma, Ramulu Nukali, and Nolli Laksmanayya.

I single out for special attention my friend and colleague, M. V. Krishnayya, Professor of Philosophy at Andhra University (Waltair). Through the years, he has been a colleague and friend, a source of creative inspiration and a safe haven in times of stress. When I was sick, he got a doctor;

when I needed transportion to attend a midnight festival, he miraculously
supplied a car (nothing less, in fact, than the vice-chancellor's own 1965
Cadillac). To Krishnayya I owe more than I can possibly convey, and therefore, I thank him sincerely: *Santosham.*

I thank the Department of Anthropology, Emory University, and its
members, especially Fredrik Barth, Bobby Paul, Bradd Shore, and Carol
Worthman, as well as George Armelagos, Peggy Barlett, Peter Brown,
Don Donham, Carla Freeman, Marcia Inhorn, Mel Konner, Bruce Knauft,
Michele Lampl, Neil Smith, Debra Spitulnik, and Pat Whitten. Ron Bar-
nett, Alex Hinton, and Keith McNeal provided extremely helpful comments. For their colleagueship I also thank colleagues from other departments at Emory from whom I have learned much: David Carr, Robyn
Fivush, Rudy Makkreel, Dick Neisser, Paul Courtright, and Mike Toma-
sello. I am especially grateful to the dean, David Bright, for providing the
necessary time off for the completion of the work, both in this country and
in India.

Various institutions and agencies have provided financial support: The
American Institute of Indian Studies, the National Endowment for the
Humanities, the American Council of Learned Societies, the National In-
stitutes of Mental Health, the National Science Foundation, and the Char-
lotte W. Newcombe Foundation. A great debt of gratitude is owed to
Rosalie Robertson, senior acquisitions editor of the University of Wisconsin Press, and to Lisa Williams, copyeditor. I thank them most sincerely,
the first for liking this book enough to agree to publish it, and the second
for putting up with my manifold failures and shortcomings as a compiler
of notes and references.

I assume the reason most authors leave to the very end their expressions
of gratitude to family members is because they are the most important, and
also the hardest to write. At least that is true in my case. To my wife, Janis,
I owe nearly two decades of love and friendship, patience and resolve. At
the hottest time of the year, in early May, she did a complete survey of the
Jalari village, painstakingly compiling a complete record of house ownership and household activities for over 600 families. In 110° heat, that was
no small accomplishment, and I count it one of those great feats of spousal
self-sacrifice and virtue. That is especially so, since I never actually used any
of the data, being essentially illiterate in matters of demography and map-
ping. To my son, Will, I owe the great debt of having finally enlightened
me on a matter of fieldwork just at the moment he was born. Pentayya, my
closest Jalari informant and *anna* (older brother), told me a long time ago
that I would not grasp the meaning of patrilineal succession until I looked

into the face of my newborn son. I was twenty years old when he told me that, and I had no idea what he was talking about until sixteen years later, when I first held my son in my arms. Since then, I can honestly say that Will has opened up whole new vistas for me and enabled me to ask some new and better questions.

To my parents, Margaret Ann and William C. Nuckolls, I express gratitude for having permitted me to go to India in 1977, and then paid for the trip. On the way back, the travel agency went bankrupt and my return ticket was cancelled, so they then paid again. They didn't seem to mind. My great regret is that ill health prevented them from visiting my field site and meeting the villagers who also became family members. Still, they could see each other through photographs, and even came to know each other after a fashion. I am very grateful to my maternal uncle, Charles W. Rice, who in many ways lived up to Radcliffe-Brown's description of that role in another society: "male mother." He has helped me in ways that are quite beyond description, most of all in understanding and appreciating my own place of origin: Oklahoma.

Finally, I want to thank the reader for the effort he is about to make. This book is a work of theory, and it will make some people mad. Indeed, that is one of its purposes, but since a dialectic of the kind I am going to describe does not work without strongly opposed "value orientations," as Parsons called them, I count that a good thing. There is nothing mean-spirited in this, no critique that is merely for the sake of laying waste. In fact, if it works at all, my theory must lead to its own demise as the paradoxical dialectics at work within the discipline—pitting culture against mind, cognition against emotion, idea against material—reassert themselves in any attempted synthesis, like the one I propose in the pages that follow. To the person of utilitarian persuasion, the heir of Hobbes and Mill, and given to seeking the certainty of right answers, this must seem ridiculously perverse. But to the dialectician, the heir of Plato and Kant, it will come as no surprise, and the words of Hegel in *The Phenomenology of Spirit* will have a very familiar ring:

> This consciousness is therefore the unconscious, thoughtless rambling which passes back and forth from the one extreme of the contingent consciousness that is both bewildered and bewildering. It does not itself bring these two thoughts of itself together. At one time it recognizes that its freedom lies in rising above all the confusion and contingency of existence, and at another time equally admits of a relapse into occupying itself with what is unessential. It pronounces an absolute vanishing, but the pronouncement *is,* and this consciousness is the vanishing that is

pronounced. It affirms the nullity of seeing, hearing, etc., yet it is itself
seeing, hearing, etc. It affirms the nullity of ethical principles, and lets its
conduct be governed by these very principles. Its deeds and its words
always belie one another and equally it has itself the doubly contradictory consciousness of unchangeableness and sameness, of utter
contingency and non-identity with itself. But it keeps the poles of this its
self-contradiction apart, and adopts the same attitude to it as it does in
its purely negative activity in general. (Hegel 1977:125)

—Easter Sunday, Birmingham, Alabama, 1996

Introduction: Defining "Culture"

Throughout its century-long struggle for academic respectability, anthropology has regularly insisted on its unique role as the proprieter of 'culture.' Its variety of approaches and feuding factions notwithstanding, it is this proprietary claim that unifies anthropology to an extent sometimes unrecognized even by its own (post-modernist) practitioners. (Lawson and McCauley, "Who Owns Culture?")

One of the easiest ways to get in trouble in anthropology is to define a term, and the most difficult term of all is "culture." Since the purpose of this book is to make trouble, however, the best way to begin is with a definition of culture. I offer it for three reasons. First, cultural anthropologists do not have much to talk about if they stop talking about culture, and this is the danger, given the disintegration of the concept into competing notions of power, agency, and instrumentalism. Second, fear that the concept of culture presents an overly inclusive and homogeneous view is wrong and needs to be debunked. Third, the concept of culture is essential to anthropology as both an explanatory science and a method of interpretation, and we dispense with it at our peril.

Consequently, before even trying to say what I mean by the dialectics of knowledge and desire, let me spell out my ideas about culture and thus make it as clear as possible where I stand.

There is no doubt that many problems arise from confusion over the ontological status of culture. This has prompted many anthropologists, including Barth, to advocate that we substitute for culture a concept of "knowledge" (Barth 1995). In part this is due to the very size of the phenomenon, since "culture," whatever it is, does not possess the features that make it readily salient perceptually, as Lawson and McCauley (1990) have pointed out. Of course, there are natural phenomena that are difficult to characterize because of their scale, like the weather. In such cases scientists try to describe general principles, but given all the variables, any generalization can be upset fairly easily. The problem is worse in the case of culture since it is difficult to define any of its principles. "Systems of symbols and meanings," to use a once popular phrase, are not like steel balls rolling down an inclined plane.

By "culture" we cannot mean the sum total of all actions (mental, social, or otherwise) undertaken by individuals in all of their many differences. As Lawson and McCauley (1990) point out, all successful sociological (in the larger sense) accounts involve, to some extent, the construction and evaluation of hypotheses about idealized actors—whether by using statistical strategies to level out differences or by constructing ideal types in the Weberian sense. There is nothing unusual in this approach. All theories in science formulate idealized accounts of their objects of study. It is the purpose of theory to offer an abstract and generalizable account of the particularities which we encounter. Idealization is the consequence of this necessary abstraction, and not to be eschewed in any account claiming the status of an explanation. The question therefore has nothing to do with whether or not idealized abstraction is necessary, but rather with what types are best able to capture the range of phenomena which interest us.

Many anthropologists no longer accept the term "culture" as valid, at least not in the old sense, to describe the system of a connected whole. To an extent my argument can only contribute to the general skepticism, since the view taken here emphasizes conflict and contradiction over uniformity and consistency. *But this is not at the expense of giving up the idea of "system,"* which, properly understood, can be seen as internally contradictory. The difficulty with the term "culture," or "cultural system," as an abstract idealization is not that it is incapable of providing a sufficiently nuanced account, but rather that using it at all gives the appearance of defining borders and delimiting inclusivity. This is where we need to make some changes, before it is too late and "culture" ceases to be what cultural anthropologists talk about.

Here I wish to examine two modifications which in conjunction might be helpful. The first is the reconceptualization of culture as an *emergent phenomenon*. "Emergence" is a popular notion. It is not unusual to hear this term used by people trying to grapple with the unseen but evidently organized properties of Kroeberian superorganics, like society or culture. But what does it mean, if it is anything more than a convenient rhetorical device? That is what we will consider in a moment. The second modification is the idea of emergence itself as a relationship between a system and its parts. I will claim that "culture" sets up special problems for any emergentist theory and that these are best dealt with by defining the relationship between systems and their parts as dialectical.

All social theories derivative of Durkheimian sociology posit the exis-

tence of "society" as a real phenomenon whose properties cannot be reduced to the properties of its constituents. Is it ever appropriate to attribute
to society properties and principles which are exclusively its own? Over the
last decade or so, the answer has been that it is not. According to Heald,
"the old reified view of society has been abandoned" (1994:1) in favor
of a view which attributes primary importance to individual agency and
strategies of domination and resistance. Anthropologists have embraced
this perspective so completely that it is hard to remember what Durkheim
was trying to do or why anyone (then or since) would advocate studying
"society" or "culture" as a thing in itself.

The critique is not justified on intellectual grounds but accepted merely
as an epistemological stance. It is an a priori judgment which starts by attributing reality to some things and not to others, and does a disservice to
the view it allegedly replaces. Principled arguments in favor of considering
society or culture "real" and objectively exigent do exist and can be justified on philosophical as well as empirical grounds. Most of these arguments
are "emergentist" to some extent. And that is exactly the kind of argument
I shall make. My point is that it is time we considered the status of such
arguments, to find out whether or not they might still prove serviceable.

Emergentist perspectives refer to so-called secondary phenomena, like
biological life and consciousness, and to the claim that such phenomena
are at once *grounded in* and yet *emergent from* the underlying structure with
which they are associated. Alexander sums up the usual way in which the
emergentist argument is presented:

> Physical and chemical processes of a certain complexity have the quality
> of life. The new quality life emerges with this constellation of such
> processes, and therefore life is at once a physico-chemical complex and
> is not merely physical and chemical, for these terms do not sufficiently
> characterize the new complex which in the course and order of time has
> been generated out of them. Such is the account to be given of the
> meaning of quality as such. The higher quality emerges from the lower
> level existence and has its roots therein, but it emerges therefrom, and it
> does not belong to that level, but constitutes its possessor a new order of
> existence with its special laws of behavior. The existence of emergent
> qualities thus described is something to be noted, as some would say,
> under the compulsion of brute empirical fact, or, as I should prefer to
> say in less harsh terms, to be accepted with the "natural piety" of the
> investigator. It admits no explanation. (1920:46–47)

Putting the argument another way, what emergentism says is that once an
object or system attains a sufficient level of structural complexity, it thereby

acquires an emergent quality. This quality differs from typical macro-properties of complex wholes, such as the shape of a chair, which could be described as the resultant of the object's internal structural constituents. But the chair is not the emergent property of four legs, a back, and arm-rests, or even of the microproperties which constitute them. The difference is reflected in the fact that emergence introduces a change in the behavior of the object that possesses it, "such that processes internal to that object cannot be explained in terms of the laws that govern its micro-particles in the absence of such organizational complexity" (O'Conner 1994:92). In short, macroqualities that are not emergent, but only resultant, such as mass or size or shape, do not belong to the "higher levels" of that object's existence as Alexander's and other theories of emergentism conceive them.

While the argument for emergent properties possesses an intuitive ap-peal, it runs into trouble when we realize that it imposes a necessary dual-ism. As soon as objects or systems possess a certain complexity, they trans-late themselves into a new level of existence, exhibiting new properties that cannot be explained by reduction to the properties which constitute them. In other words, where there was one object or system before, now there are two: the thing before it became emergently complex, and the thing after it became emergently complex. Alexander even goes so far as to claim that emergent qualities cannot be predicted on the basis of microlevel laws and that the existence of laws involving them (i.e., emergent qualities) "admit[s] no explanation."

At this point, not only do we find that emergentism is dependent on a starkly defined substance dualism, but also that it has become somewhat mysterious. Its development cannot be explained, and its laws bear no nec-essary relationship to the laws which govern the nature of its constituents. This is not what scientific reasoning would lead us to expect. Yet Durk-heim was driven to adopt this approach, mainly for polemical reasons, in order to carve out a domain for himself and the new discipline he hoped to create. For a while (and for reasons I shall not go into) this approach did hold sway—reaching its zenith, probably, in the development of symbolic anthropology. It has passed from the scene today (even at Chicago), not be-cause emergentism is wrong but because the approach just described is not sophisticated enough to withstand the assault of the perspective that is most congruent with American common sense: methodological individualism.

Let us reexamine the central tenets of emergentism. First, an emergent property is to be inferred wherever the characteristic behavior of a whole could not, even in theory, be deduced from the most complete knowledge of the behavior of its components, taken separately or in other combinations, and of their proportions and arrangements in this whole. This is the quality which philosophers call *supervenience*. Second, an object or system possesses emergent properties if it is nonstructural, that is, not constituted by properties of the object's or system's parts. Third, emergent properties generate novel causal inferences irreducible to the microproperties on which it supervenes: it bears its influence in a direct, "downward" fashion, in contrast to the operation of a simple macroproperty, whose causal influence occurs via the activity of the microproperties that constitute it. A formal definition, summing up these features, has been put forward by O'Conner:

> Property *P* is an emergent property of an object *O* if:
> 1. *P* supervenes on properties of the parts of *O*;
> 2. *P* is not had by any of the object's parts;
> 3. *P* is distinct from any structural property of *O*; and
> 4. *P* has direct ("downward") determinative influence on the pattern of
>   behavior involving *O*'s parts. (O'Conner 1994:98)

A satisfactory account of emergence is possible when it assumes the stated form and when it avoids substance dualism and the resultant mystification. Failing these modifications, the emergentism of all post-Durkheim social theory is put at risk and, with it, the whole concept of culture as a reality that can be studied. Is it possible to rescue emergentist social theory from this fate?

Yes, it is. Let us consider how Michael Polanyi does it. He notes that a complex system works under the control of two distinct principles. Take a machine. The higher order one is the principle of the machine's design, and this *harnesses* the lower one, which consists in the physical-chemical processes on which the machine relies. The first and higher principle imposes what Polanyi refers to as "boundary conditions" on the second. That is, the structure of the machine, or organism, serves as a boundary condition harnessing the physical-chemical processes by which its organs perform their functions. The control of a system by irreducible boundary conditions, however, does not interfere with the laws of physics and chemistry:

> A system under dual control relies, in fact, for the operations of its
> higher principle, on the working of principles at a lower level, such as
> the laws of physics and chemistry. Irreducible higher principles are
> additional to the laws of physics and chemistry. The principles of
> mechanical engineering and of communication of information, and the
> equivalent biological principles, are all additional to the laws of physics
> and chemistry. (Polanyi 1968:1310)

Polanyi's approach to emergent properties, therefore, recognizes the higher levels of life as forming a hierarchy, each level of which relies for its workings on the principles of the levels below it, even while the system itself is irreducible to these lower principles.

An example suggested by Polanyi helps to explain the organization of his "dual principle" emergentism: language, and its various levels of organization, from the phonological to the semantic. The lowest level is the phonological, the actual production of voice; the second is the utterance of words; the third, syntax, the joining of words to make sentences; and the fourth, the semantic working of sentences into meaningful utterances. The principles of each level operate under the control of the next higher level. Phonology is shaped, but not determined, by vocabulary; a given vocabulary is shaped, but not determined, into sentences in accordance with a grammar; and the sentences are fitted together to form contextually meaningful utterances, in accordance with the needs of the situation. Thus each level is subject to dual control: 1) control in accordance with the laws that apply to elements in themselves, e.g., the speech production system of the human larynx; and 2) control in accordance with the laws of the powers that control the comprehensive entity formed by these elements (Polanyi 1968:1310–11). As Polanyi notes, "such multiple control is made possible by the fact that principles governing the isolated particulars of a lower level leave indeterminate conditions to be controlled by a higher principle" (1311).

The conclusion to be drawn from this example, and from the logic of dual control, is that although emergent properties are governed by principles which arise *sui generis,* just as Durkheim said, they also depend on principles which govern the operation of their constituents. The first order is related to the second order, and dependent on it, without being determined by it. To make the same point methodologically: We can descend to the components of a lower level by analyzing a higher level. In fact, that is necessary. But we cannot go in the opposite direction, because this involves an integration of the principles of the lower level, and such an integration is beyond our powers. There is nevertheless a relationship between the two movements which, in practice, describes the way in which explanation can succeed. Polanyi calls this the "from-at" conception of hierarchy.

When we attend only to the individual words on a written page, Polanyi notes, we do not grasp their connected meaning as constituents of a full utterance. We are simply looking *at* the words. When we attend to the utterance as a whole, however, we are looking *from* the words *at* their meaning. The reader therefore has a *from-at* knowledge of the words' meaning, while he has only a *from* awareness of the words he is reading. Comprehension means moving back and forth between these levels very quickly, possibly simultaneously. The fact that the higher levels shape and constrain the lower levels does not mean that the principles which govern the latter cease to be important. When examining any higher level, we must remain aware of its grounds in lower levels, and, in considering the latter, we must continue to see them as bearing on the levels above them. Polanyi refers to this as "the principle of stratified relations" (1968:1312).

The approach that Polanyi recommends, and that I intend to follow, preserves the concept of higher-order functional entities, like cultures, while at the same time allowing examination of their participating constituents. How does this work? When examining any higher level, where emergent phenomena reside, we must remain aware of its grounding in lower levels, and, turning our attention to the latter, we must continue to see them affecting the levels above them. Alternately detailing and integrating the phenomena on different higher and lower levels obviously possesses many dangers. It is not quite so dangerous to descend, since decomposition to the level of constituent members does not necessarily imply reduction of causal agency to the processes which operate at that level.

To say, for instance, that my coming to work this morning was dependent on the proper functioning of my kidneys is true, unless we make the mistake of reducing the cause of my decision to come to work to the functioning of my kidneys. The opposite danger, Polanyi warns, is far more real. The integration of terms at lower levels does not explain the form this integration takes, since there is usually far more indeterminacy in the system than this would allow. In other words, I can prove, at the risk of being trivial, that my coming to work depends on my kidneys, but I cannot prove that the proper functioning of my kidneys, in relationship to all the other organs and systems that constitute my body, resulted in the decision. In short, my mind harnesses the biophysical processes of organs at lower levels but is not determined by them in such a way that one could predict the integration of the former from the nature of the latter.

Now to the issue of "culture." All arguments for the ontological status of culture as a reality *sui generis* depend on the logic of emergent properties, i.e., on the nonreducibility of integrated systems to their constituent parts. Such arguments, good and bad, usually take the form of (stated or unstated) metaphors, as in:

—*Culture as Language:* Culture cannot be reduced to the actions of individual human beings, any more so than a language can be reduced to individual speech utterances. Culture is like grammar. It must be studied independent of its instantiations in individual experience.

—*Culture as History:* Culture is present before the individual and continues after his death. Culture is like history. It must be studied in terms of long-term forces and tendencies, independent of the discrete actions of individuals.

These are two of the arguments one hears, or used to hear, in defense of the idea that social reality cannot be reduced to the things which constitute it. But they are not really emergentist arguments, not in the true sense. Emergent properties are characteristic of a system that can be studied only as such, *as a system,* because the elements which constitute the system no longer exist as such. Water cannot be studied by considering the properties of either hydrogen or oxygen, because in combination these elements make up a different substance with properties unique to it. The same is true of many complex systems, from the brain to the stock market. Some properties are properties of systems only, not of the elements which constitute them. It is with respect to systems of this kind that emergentist arguments seem to work.

The first argument above, comparing culture to grammar, does not qualify as emergentist, because both of the systems in question — cultural and linguistic — are accessible only through their instantiation in individual performance. The second argument, comparing culture to history, also fails to qualify as emergentist, essentially for the same reason. This makes both language and history fundamentally different from other systems which are accessible only as systems under normal conditions, e.g., the human body. We do not encounter the human body as a collection of discrete and independent organs, with the option of viewing it from the perspective of the pancreas or the bladder. But that is exactly the way in which we normally encounter culture, as individual human beings with different roles and obligations which are socially defined. Such roles and obligations index the social whole and refer to a system which is larger than any of its constituent members. This provides the only basis for the inference that "culture" actually exists.

Following Lawson and McCauley (1990), my point is that culture is a system, *but a system different in kind from those that emergentist arguments generally consider.* The difference rests in the continuing relationship between culture as a set of institutionally located norms and the individuals who embody and enact these norms. The individual retains more of his phenomenal uniqueness in society than does an oxygen atom in water. The oxygen atom cannot choose to act, or not to act, in congruence with the properties of the whole which it helps to constitute; it cannot comment on that whole, nor can it exit the system without causing the system itself to break down. Human beings possess these capacities precisely because the system which they help to constitute is different from others.

This seems to be the stumbling block which arguments both for and against the utility of the culture concept have run into. On the one hand, arguments for the autonomy of the cultural system have a hard time explaining individual agency or desire except as direct instantiations of the cultural system. This makes them vulnerable to the critique that they ignore the degree to which people can creatively shape their own experience. On the other hand, arguments against the autonomy of the cultural system cannot easily explain the deeply shared and institutionally embedded values people who are members of the same culture seem to possess. To a certain extent, culture *is* manifestly language-like in having rules governing the formation of coherent actions and beliefs. Thus we are left in a muddle, caught between two perspectives, each of them untenable.

Let us cut to the heart of the matter and affirm, for argument's sake, that we would like to preserve the advantages of both perspectives, enabling us to talk about both cultural systems and individual autonomy at the same time. Is there a way to do that? There might be, if we pursue the insight of Polanyi's proposal that we view emergent properties as the result of a twin configurative process.

The laws governing the operation of constituent members of a system establish parameters for the system as a whole, without determining the system's content. Simultaneously, systems set boundary conditions for the working of the parts which make it up. This is right as far as it goes, and Polanyi's recommendation that we look both *from* the level of the system, to comprehend its parts, and *at* the parts themselves, to comprehend the working of the system, is valid. The problem is that he does not specify the relationship between the two more precisely, and this, in the matter of social or cultural systems, is what we need. I shall therefore explain what that relationship is, with a view to developing a new approach.

To say that a system cannot be reduced to its parts because the system is greater than the sum of its parts does not tell us anything about the relationship between the system and its parts. *The failure to specify this relationship is the weakness characteristic of most emergentist cultural theories* and of symbolic anthropology. In fact, most emergentist arguments create the impression that the relationship is pretty nonproblematic and that, once absorbed into the greater totality, whatever distinguishes individual elements ceases to be relevant. One is left to assume that such elements contribute to the formation of a seamless and internally consistent whole. That is the problem, contributing to a harmonious view of human social life, one in which political and religious institutions are mechanically reproduced. But what if constituent elements still possess enough of their individuality to remain distinct, and even in conflict with the totality they constitute? The relationship between them (the constituents) and the system might better be described as dialectical. A dynamic system of this kind would depend on continuing dialectical conflict, and compromise, between itself and the individuals which constitute it.

The idea that a cultural system is dialectical, made up of dynamic conflicts between the whole and its parts, is not new. Weber proposed a dialectic of person and culture in his work on the Protestant ethic and the spirit of capitalism. The system of ideas known as Protestantism defined a set of moral objectives, chief among which (in the ideal typical form) is certainty in one's own salvation. Of course, the question of salvation was already determined by God at the moment of conception. Nothing done in this life could alter it. Yet people worked hard in their callings, seeking certainty of their own salvation, because surely, if they were successful, it must mean that God intended them to be saved. Where did the motivation to seek certainty come from? It was not derived simply and directly from religious dogma, since the doctrine of predestination could have prompted a very different kind of response: fatalism. In fact, motivation combined fear of eternal damnation with the hope of God's reward. Without this combination, the cultural system could not have worked: A system which said of itself that all fear and hope were pointless nevertheless depended on fear and hope to motivate people to believe and to work.

Unfortunately, the dialectical features of Weber's argument have never been readily apparent, due mostly to Weber's own failure to spell them out. This has tended to contribute to a view—especially noticeable among Anglo-Saxon commenters—that Weber was an idealist of the worst sort, with no interest in mind or the pragmatics of everyday life (Mommsen 1987). The fact that this view represents a distortion, contradicted more than once by Weber himself, has been repeatedly emphasized (see Whimster and Lasch 1987). But it is really Obeyesekere, in his work on Sri Lankan ecstatic mediums, who has rescued Weberian dialectics and applied them systematically (Obeyesekere 1981, 1990). Weber himself probably could not have achieved this, given his peculiar distaste for psychology and his strongly moralist reaction to psychoanalysis (Mitzman 1985). The advantages of a psychoanalytic argument were therefore not apparent to him, even though the dialectic he proposed actually depended on a conflictual view of the psyche and its contents.

A self-avowed intellectual descendent of Weber, Obeyesekere (1990) explores what he calls "symbolic remove," the process through which symbolic forms existing at the cultural level are created and recreated through the minds of individuals. Symbols thus created are regressive because of their ontogenesis in individual development and unconscious processes. They represent and resolve important conflicts and thus become meaningful in personal experience. But such symbols are also "progressive," in that unconscious thought transforms the archaic motivations of early experience and looks forward to their realization in experience of the sacred. The further the transformation, the greater the "symbolic remove," as symbols are cut adrift from their moorings in unconscious conflict and develop relationships between themselves that are culturally determined. It is the concept of "symbolic remove" that makes it possible for Obeyesekere to overcome the limitations of traditional psychoanalytic interpretations, which can sometimes seem reductionistic, and thus achieve an elegant integration of depth psychology and hermeneutics.

For Obeyesekere, symbolization is dependent on a model of psychic conflict and thus has little in common with several post-Freudian theories (e.g., Lacan) in which the role of conflict is reduced. This is not done in simple or uncritical acceptance of Freud, however, but because "conflict"—the conflict motivated by desire—is the phenomenon which Obeyesekere considers basic. Take for example the institution of possession-mediumship in Sri Lanka. It goes without saying that it would not exist were it not for the existence of people who were motivated to experience possession. Thus the empirical question is straightforward: What do we have to know about these people in order to understand their experience of possession-mediumship? Many mediums are possessed by spirits who resemble, even to the mediums themselves, individuals to whom the mediums were ambivalently attached in life—mostly mothers, fathers, and primary caretakers. The experience of mediumship seems to represent the ambivalence, and also to resolve it by transformation of the dead individual into a spirit with whom the possessed individual can have a satisfying and productive relationship. If it were not for individual psychological conflict, therefore, and the fact that the possessing agencies both represent and resolve that conflict, the institution of possession-mediumship could not exist in the form that Obeyesekere describes.

What makes this view problematic (especially for Americans) is that it is so Germanic, with roots deep in Kant and Hegel, and especially Weber and Freud. With notable exceptions, it is not something most American anthropologists know a lot about or feel comfortable with, given the heavy penetration of the discipline in this country by reductive pragmatism and logical empiricism. Obeyesekere draws upon this Germanic heritage and achieves a remarkable synthesis, not only of Weber and Freud, but also, it must be said, of anthropology and Buddhism. For Obeyesekere, dialectical

xxxiv   *Introduction*

conflict is the truth of our human condition—one which we all share but which most of us tend to sweep under the rug. It is the virtue of psychoanalysis (and, of course, Buddhism) to have discovered this, and that of Obeyesekere to have devised a means of connecting the two, with great subtlety, in his work.

What I have tried to suggest, via Weber and Obeyesekere, is that culture is an emergent system, dependent on individual psychological conflicts for its motivation. The only way to represent this relationship analytically is by way of the concept of dialectic. Just how broadly can it be applied? Conflicting desires within the individual seek resolution in cultural symbols which act as compromise formations. There is thus a dialectic within individuals, made up of dynamic opposition between conflicting desires. There is also a dialectic operating between living individuals and the cultural system that informs them, providing integrations or resolutions in the form of cultural symbols. This second dialectic is what Obeyesekere terms *objectification* (1981). But the same dialectic can work to opposite effect, when individuals construct their own compromise formations and these achieve social acceptance, becoming collectively shared symbols. Obeyesekere calls this *subjectification* and identifies it as one of the mechanisms through which new cultural symbols are created. There is also a third dialectic, related to the earlier two but distinct from them, which operates in and through cultural symbols themselves. It is the level of *cultural dialectics*, and it is the subject of the analysis that follows in the remainder of this book.

I have considered the problem of "culture" at some length, because it is important at the outset to be clear. As I understand it, culture is a set of emergent properties, organized systematically and at three levels, all dialectically structured. At the lowest level it consists of individuals whose conflicted desires provide some of the motivation for internalizing cultural symbols. The second level is the psychosocial, and refers to the dialectics, both "objectifying" and "subjectifying," which connect individuals and cultures, making them mutually interdependent. The third level is the level of cultural dialectics, of symbols and their relationships to each other. Analytically, it is possible to talk about the three levels as if they were distinct. In reality, they are very tightly linked. The analysis at one level, when pushed to a certain point, inevitably transforms itself into the analysis of the other two. What all three share is the property of dynamic opposition. It is the motivational force which keeps them from becoming static or unchanging.

DIALECTICS AND THE HISTORY OF ANTHROPOLOGY

Dialectics are hardly unknown in anthropology or the social sciences in general, and it makes sense to consider the history, if only very briefly. There is no doubt that, for most of us, what we think of as "dialectical" reasoning has been completely preempted by Marx and "funneled down to us through the medium of his writings," as Robert Murphy says (1971:86). It is of limited utility, however, for reasons I will explain. Of more importance for my argument is the work of Boas, Benedict, Turner, and Bateson.

Marx himself called dialectics a "method of science" (Marx and Engels 1942:246), and their presence is evident in *Capital* in the frequent references to "contradictions," "antitheses," and "oppositions" which supply the springboard for further conceptual development. When Marx discusses the metamorphosis of commodities, he speaks in a very Hegelian fashion of contradictions and their resolutions:

> We see that the exchange of commodities comprises contradictory and
> mutually exclusive relations. The (wider) development of the commodity
> does not remove these contradictions but rather provides the form
> within which they can move. This is generally the method through
> which real contradictions resolve themselves. For instance, it is a
> contradiction that one body consistently falls towards another and just
> as consistently flies away from it. The ellipse is a form of motion within
> which this contradiction is both realized and resolved. (Marx 1970:
> 103–4).

Marx constructs an analogy between the way commodities circulate and the elliptical manner in which the planets revolve around the sun. Both express and make possible contradictory relations.

But Marx rarely used the word *dialectic* himself. It was Engels who extended the Marxist approach to the materialist philosophy of nature, and portrayed Marx (by then dead) as a social scientist using a post-Darwinian natural-science approach and applying "dialectics" to the relevant data from political economics. Today many Marxists question, and even deny, the relevance of dialectical thinking to Marx himself. Althusser insisted that dialectic is just a remnant of idealism and did not facilitate any of Marx's, or even later Marxism's, discoveries. Guillaumaud agrees and comments: "The 'dialectical laws'—are they or are they not laws of nature? If the answer is 'yes,' how do we explain their scientific sterility? . . . If the answer . . . is 'no,' this answer entails on the one hand an explicit disagreement with an Engels and a Lenin . . . and, on the other hand, an eradication of dialectic" (Guillaumaud 1980:85, 89–90, 93).

Lukacs, Ruben, and Schmidt also question the relevance of the dialectical approach, agreeing that dialectics were limited to Marx's intermittent summarizing of some results of research, most of his analysis not being developed according to any specifically dialectical methodology (Hudelson 1986).

To be sure, Marx's dialectic was complex and not easily classified. But he was not a dialectical philosopher or historian or social scientist or evolutionist in any of the usual senses; nor could it be said that *Capital* or any of his later works were history or natural history or political economics. In a sense, all of these characterizations are applicable. It is simply not the case that in any of them a dialectical approach is developed as such or shown to be applicable outside the confines of historical materialism.

It is a different matter when we consider the Marxian legacy reworked by members of the Frankfurt school, especially Adorno, Fromm, and Marcuse. Each struggled to extend orthodox Marxism to include consideration of the mechanisms which mediate ideological superstructure and socio-economic foundation. They all turned to psychoanalysis—not as surprising as it might seem, since most of the Frankfurt group underwent personal analysis at some point. (Adorno was one of the few exceptions.) Orthodox Marxism could not explain motivation except as a combination of basic drives (hunger, love, and so forth) which seek gratification and then undergo transformation through different forms of acquisitiveness in specific social conditions. If dialectical materialism functions in and through the shaping of human desires, then a theory of desire is called for, and a psychology of dialectical materialism is required. Merely to call it "false consciousness" or the mental inscription of inequality ("habitus" in Bourdieuian terms) is not sufficient. That is why members of the Frankfurt school turned to Freud early, despite the widely shared suspicion that Freud had absolutized the status quo and resigned himself to the necessity of a permanent elite.

The attempt to locate dialectics in a theory of society that is also a theory of mind and motivation did not result in a major synthesis, at least not until Marcuse's *Eros and Civilization* (1955). Adorno was the first to try, in his 1925 *Habilitationsschrift* (second dissertation), a work that begins as an idealist defense of Freud and ends as a Marxist critique—and which his dissertation adviser, Hans Cornelius, rejected. Adorno did not develop a coherent posture toward psychoanalysis until much later, when he tried to explain the psychological dynamics of bourgeois anti-Semitism. His argument makes heavy use of the concept of "projection." The ultimate target of social domination, Adorno says, is the worker, who because of his partial awareness cannot identify the true source of domination. The result is suppressed aggression: "the hatred felt by the led, who can never be satisfied economically or sexually, knows no bounds" (Horkheimer and Adorno 1972:173). Fascism exploits this deflection of aggression onto the Jews. Instead of rebelling against society, the workers consent to be led, while falsely projecting onto the Jews their own socially unacceptable (and hence potentially revolutionary) desires.

An interesting argument; but for Adorno it did not represent a synthesis of Freudian and materialist theory. In fact, what made Freud interesting for Adorno was the fact that psychoanalysis so completely represents the structure of the society that created it. Freud's instinct theory, for example, conceals the social origins of repression by pretending that they are biologically ordered and therefore inescapable and unchanging. Adorno argues that Freud was the product of his time and that "repression" was the signature formation of the bourgeois psyche. It is not as relevant to late capitalism, Adorno believed. Immediate gratification is the characteristic formation of the present, and it seeks realization not in anal possessiveness and sexual repression (the nineteenth-century syndrome) but in a consumerist ethos that treats all objects as fungible and disposable.

Ultimately, Adorno dispenses with Freud, probably because he viewed psychoanalysis as a kind of "positive" dialectics which could not achieve unequivocal fulfillment. To Adorno, this simply meant that it would lead to the reproduction of the socioeconomic system that requires critical transformation. There must be a "negative" dialectics, one that forever questions and never assumes an identity between thinking and its object. Negative dialectics is parasitic on nondialectical modes of thought because its role is to point out the contradictions. And it cannot end, because the world as it is conceptualized and the world as it really is never coincide. As with Kant, Adorno's antinomies remain unreconciled, but this is due not to the limits of reason but to reality itself and any possible mode of encountering it.

Dialectics for Adorno were a complicated business, and the last thing his philosophy leads to is systematic characterization. To a large extent, the similarity to Kant was intentional, since Adorno tended to locate the meaning of dialectical categories in cognition. He did not consider dialectical development an immutable law of history or nature, or as a process based simply and solely on the circumstances of class struggle. Dialectics always exist. By pushing them forward, and by exposing the contradictions which make and sustain them, the philosopher advances the development of dialectics to the point where categories self-destruct.

More than Adorno, Erich Fromm used psychoanalytic concepts to mediate the relationship between individual and society—even to the point of discussing hostility to authority in terms of the Oedipus complex. Fromm not only underwent analysis, like many Frankfurt school members, he became an analyst himself, having received training at the Berlin Psychoanalytic Institute under Theodor Reik. Fromm argued that the task of a psychoanalytically informed social theory was to understand unconsciously motivated behavior as an effect of the economic structure on basic psychic drives. This was the point he later developed in *Escape from Freedom,* although by then he had dispensed with classical Freudianism and developed a much more positive view of a future in which human beings were not only free from tyranny and authority and alienation, but free to experience basic human emotions and love for each other. This was the view, by the way, that seems to have led to Fromm's break with the *Institut für Sozialforschung* and to the ascent of Adorno, who advocated a more pessimistic view of human attainment more in keeping—Adorno thought—with Freud's view of human nature.

Moreover, Fromm believed that the dialectic between basic human desires and capitalist social structure must result in tensions so extreme that change becomes inevitable. The argument he makes is interesting, in light of its source: the mid-nineteenth-century German historian, Johann Bachofen, who figures prominently in the early history of anthropology because of his views on "primitive matriarchy." Fromm accepted Bachofen's assertion that the original human condition was matricentric, because maternal love was unconditional and less responsive to social dictates (Jay 1973). Patriarchal capitalism negates this condition but prepares the way for its return in depriving human beings more and more of this source of fulfillment. Fromm did not believe Freud could have come to this conclusion, due to his imprisonment by bourgeois morality and patriarchal values.

Like Fromm, Marcuse did not accept the nonidentity arguments of Adorno and Horkheimer, and therefore could be optimistic about the end of dialectics. But unlike Fromm, Marcuse did not dispense with some of the more classically Freudian concepts: drives, instinct, and the libido. There is a conflict between sexual craving and normative social structure, Marcuse claimed, such that the Oedipus conflict becomes the prototype for all conflicts between the individual and society. This is one of the dialectics which sustains social process, and the process itself depends not only on the tension which the dialectic creates but on its unceasing repression by institutions. Marcuse believed that there was a way to restore identity between desire and its objects and thereby eliminate repression and its social uses: nonrepressive re-eroticization of human relations to nature and the breakdown of sexual tyranny. "The altered social conditions," Marcuse writes, "would therefore create an instinctual basis for the transformation of work into play" (1955:215). Interestingly, like Fromm, Marcuse also turns to anthropology for support—in this case, to Mead's study of the Arapesh, whom Marcuse believes come as close as any human group can to realizing this emancipatory ideal.

More could be said about the contribution of Frankfurt school philosophers to the development of dialectics and the social explanation of motivation. But this is not a history lesson, and the purpose of the discussion is merely to set the stage. I want to prepare the way for the development of a new theory, to be built on the foundations which, admittedly, members of the Frankfurt group also share: Kant and Hegel, Weber and Freud. But to do that a quick look at dialectical theory in anthropology is necessary, to show what the theoretical synthesis I am touting might have to offer.

The most clearly dialectical approach in anthropology is structuralist, in the form articulated by Lévi-Strauss in studies that began with *The Elementary Structures of Kinship* (1969) and culminated in *The Jealous Potter* (1988). According to Lévi-Strauss, culture and nature exist as dialectical opposition, in constant dynamic tension with each other. Their opposition is mediated in the incest taboo, which does not resolve the opposition but transforms it so that it becomes the basis of social structure through the elaboration of different forms of exchange. Dialectical oppositions are basic to the development of social structure, prompting Lévi-Strauss to surmise that "duality, alternation, opposition and symmetry, whether expressed in definite forms or imprecise forms, are not so much matters to be explained, as basic and immediate data of mental and social reality which should be the starting point of any attempt at explanation" (1969:136).

Lévi-Strauss did not develop a concept of cultural dialectics, and ultimately the particularities of oppositions are less interesting to him than the universal oppositions which the particularities revealed. He never provided any systematic account of how the principles he proposed are able to specify or produce the symbolic-cultural materials in question. All myth is reducible to the resolution of the contradiction between nature and culture. This is assumed to be a constant, and reducible to formula: Nature : Culture :: Raw : Cooked. No meaning resides in the symbols of the myths themselves but in the code which generates them. The code is a set of basic terms that refer to fundamental dilemmas in the human condition and their possible resolutions, which the code can be used to represent through a variety of culturally specific transformations. The mind is a "bricoleur," who assembles together useful objects available in the surrounding world and uses them, representationally, to produce transformations on the basic code. The psychological process involved in this is essentially intellectualistic (Lawson and McCauley 1990), rather than emotional, and highly universalist in orientation.

It does not strike me, as it has others (e.g., Fox 1994), that a focus on universal dilemmas and their dialectics is misguided or uninteresting. The problem is that Lévi-Strauss never developed the idea into a theory. He defends structuralist oppositionality against the claim that it is all just a "gratuitous and decadent game" simply by saying that it represents one of the "profound organic truths" (Lévi-Strauss 1981:692). This is hardly sufficient. It has led people to reject Lévi-Strauss as just another intellectualist universalist, with no interest in psychological processes or the pragmatics and particularities of actual knowledge use. More to the point, although the possibility of doing so was implicit, the relationship between desire and knowledge was never specified except in the most preliminary fashion, with regard to the "archaic illusion" (Lévi-Strauss 1969).[1] Then it was dropped.

Victor Turner did not develop a theory of cultural dialectics integrating desire and knowledge, either, for that matter, but he came closer than anyone else—with the possible exception of Gregory Bateson. In one of his last papers, Turner spoke of his frustration with structural-functionalism of the Radcliffe-Brown and Gluckman type, which did not seem to illuminate symbols as anything other than tokens in the process of achieving or maintaining social integration. These, Turner said, were merely the "surface features" of symbol formation. (1978:571). At this point Turner could have been prompted to attend to the social pragmatics of symbol use, their negotiation and contestation in everyday life. That would have put him in league with some of today's cultural anthropologists, for whom symbols exist mainly to provide a means for transacting power relationships. But Turner dismissed the reduction of symbols to power and the play of cultural politics, writing that symbolic forms and patterns "cannot be directly ex-

---

1. In the chapter by the same name, Lévi-Strauss relates the logic of reciprocity to deeply psychodynamic processes, developed in childhood, including the need to identify with another and escape "the intolerable suspense of the arbitrary" (1969:87). Speaking of the desires implicit in gift-giving, Lévi-Strauss even goes so far as to remark that "all these attitudes reveal such a close analogy—except when pushed to its ultimate conclusions—between infant society and so-called primitive society that we cannot exempt ourselves from seeking reasons for them without running the risk of the most tragic mistakes (1969:87). One can only conclude that Lévi-Strauss was more persuaded by the exception he mentions than by pursuing the insight of the similarity between infantile and adult thought.

plained either by abstract structural principles or by factional or personal conflicts conducted with cognizance of those principles" (1978:571).

Turner encountered Freud in the early 1950s, and soon developed a new approach to the question "How do ritual symbols work?" Interestingly, this new approach takes the form of a dialectical theory not unlike Bateson's, but instead of "ethos" and "eidos," Turner speaks of the "orectic" and "ideological" poles of meaning (e.g., Turner 1967, 1974, 1975, 1978). The biological referents of a symbol constitute the orectic pole and include physiological phenomena, such as blood, sexual organs, coitus, birth, death, catabolism, "and so on" (1974:55). The ideological (also called "normative" or "semantic") pole incorporates normative values and moral facts, and refers to principles of social organization, such as matriliny, patriliny, kingship, gerontocracy, age-grade organization, sex-affiliation, and others. The drama of ritual action "causes an exchange between these poles in which the biological referents are ennobled and the normative referents are charged with emotional significance" (1974:55). The result of this exchange is a "cathartic effect, causing in some cases real transformations of character and of social relationships" (1974:56).

The orectic pole encompasses the domain of unconscious desires that are biologically and developmentally basic and related to fundamental processes such as sex and death. The ideological, or normative, pole refers to the social structures which organize human relationships, and thus to the organization of desires defined as orectic. The two are not the same, but one cannot exist without the other, and the relationship between them is dynamic and motivational. Is it also an opposition? Turner follows Freud in considering social structures to be limitations on basic desires, which seek "sublimation" in a socially sanctioned form. Not only does the opposition exist, therefore, it also constitutes the creative dynamic out of which ritual develops as both the representation and resolution of the basic opposition.

Turner's approach closely resembles Bateson's and depends on a similar attempt to relate cultural knowledge systems and the dynamics of desire. Turner explored the status of this relationship by studying the culturally constructed oppositions that the ritual system rationalizes. To name just a few: There is the characteristic Ndembu opposition between men and women, between novice's mother and tribeswomen in the rite of initiation, and between matriliny and virilocality. These oppositions differently invoke desires which conflict with each other and which therefore seek resolution in the sublimated forms offered by Ndembu rituals. This is not to say that ritual is the only means available for the resolution of structurally induced conflict. The inevitable fissioning of Ndembu villages that is prompted by the conflict between the rules of descent and residence is another. But ritual accommodates conflicting structures by resolving them in symbols which are multivocal and thus able to "speak" to conflicting structures equally. Turner's encounter with Freud inspired him to think critically about the necessary relation between knowledge and desire, and if he had chosen to give this relation a name, it could have been "dialectical."

Turner and Bateson both formulated theories readily identifiable as dialectical, and both rejected the monism characteristic of Humean social thought in preference for something distinctively Germanic. Bateson had read Hegel and Freud, and, whether or not the theory of schizmogenesis owes its origin to this encounter, the imprint of the post-Kantian tradition is evident. For Turner, the legacy of Freud is much clearer, although one suspects it might not have been so easily recognized if Turner himself had not openly admitted it in one of the last papers he wrote.

The legacy of German dialectical theory has descendants in social theory other than Bateson and Turner, including the founder of American anthropology, Franz Boas. This is not in the least surprising. After all, the only book Boas took with him to the field the first time was *Critique of Pure Reason.* Is Boasian anthropology implicitly Kantian, and does the approach I am advocating in fact represent a return to Boas? It is worthwhile to consider this question, since the history of cultural anthropology in the United States would have been different if the Kantian legacy in Boas had been continued and allowed to flourish.

Boas believed in the power of culture to mediate consciousness and that such mediations tended to form systematic wholes (e.g., Boas 1940:250, 256). These ideas were part of his Germanic heritage, as derivative of Goethe (whom Boas quotes extensively) as of Kant. To the extent Boas had a theory of culture as a systematic whole, it is a dialectical one, dependent on the dynamic combination of phenomena in opposition to each other. This is as true of the general as it is of the particular, of humans everywhere as well as of particular human cultures.

According to Boas, human beings are made up of competing impulses, the "aesthetic" and the "affective." The first is the desire for systematic orderliness in a cosmos governed by identifiable rules. It gives rise to science and the disciplines of discovery. The second refers to the desire of the individual to place himself in this cosmos and to develop some kind of satisfying orientation to it. This gives rise to the arts and cosmography. People and cultures vary in the extent to which they maximize one or the other. But both are present in each, and the movement of culture can be attributed to the interplay between the two (Boas 1940:639–47). Boas does not call this a dialectic, nor does he appeal to dialectical theory, but its imprint is evident.

The same is true of his analysis of individual cultures, which Boas emphasized must be historical. The reason is that each culture is a combination of characteristics but never static or uniformly consistent. It is true that the combination forms an integrated whole, but the integration "is not often so complete that all contradictory elements are eliminated" (Boas 1940:256). To understand the "curious breaks," as Boas called them, one must determine how contradictory elements influence each other in dynamic combination. This can be known only historically or by comparison to other cultures in which the "same" characteristics are differently organized.

Boas does not refer to the theory of cultural integration as dialectical, but it should be obvious that he had something very different in mind from the view that attributes to culture a simple, consistent quality. One sometimes hears Boasian anthropology described as if it were of this type, especially in the forms developed by Boas's own students, such as Benedict. But this is simply not so. Boas was neither a compiler of traits nor an imposer of cultural consistency. In his advocacy of the historical-comparative method, Boas was motivated by a concern for culture as a dynamic whole, composed of elements that might be in opposition to each other, and in their variety revealing the ways in which the "categories" of the human mind (a Kantian concept if there ever was one) might be elaborated.

Ruth Benedict was a more organized thinker, and her dialectical theory is easier to detect, especially in the book that made her famous, *Patterns of Culture* (1934). The most obvious sense in which this is true is in the relation between culture and the individual. Cultures elaborate tendencies inherent in the human psyche, becoming accepting and relaxed or anxious and paranoid, depending on how various traits have been combined. Culturally elaborated themes then react upon individuals, who differ in psychological makeup, some conforming to cultural themes and others rejecting them. The effect is a "back and forth" movement between culture and the individual, each conditioning the other, and in their interplay making the system they constitute change.

In *Patterns of Culture* there are repeated references to cultural "goals," the idea most reminiscent of the desire of unity which Kant, and especially Hegel, attributed to all systems of knowledge. There are many possible goals, which together constitute an "arc" of possibilities. The range of possibilities is not infinite, however, but in some sense determined by

the human condition. Cultures choose the ones which they wish to maximize, but the fact that as human beings we share the full range—if not in
actuality, then in creative potentiality—means that we can achieve mutual
understanding.

Some cultures, like the Zuñi and Kwakiutl, are so well integrated that
to apply a distinctive name characteristic of their mode of integration may
be adequate. Benedict adds, however, that "it would be absurd to cut every
culture down to the Procrustean bed of some catchword characterization"
(1937:228). Even in well-integrated cultures, competing tendencies and
goal orientations are present, giving rise to institutions whose purpose is to
compromise or mediate between them. Such is the case in Kwakiutl culture,
where matrilineal and patrilineal orientations conflict with each other. The
mode of inheritance neatly compromises the two competing social orders.
The Kwakiutl stress the right of the son-in-law to claim privileges from his
wife's father, these privileges to be held in trust for his children. The inheritance therefore passes matrilineally, but it skips a generation, thus "bringing the two antagonistic social orders into harmony" (Benedict 1937:228).
That is how a cultural integration, in the manner of a Hegelian transcendence, may be created in the face of fundamental conflicts.

In Boas the ideas of integration and conflict are first developed, while
in Benedict they are linked to form a concept of cultural goals and dialectics. Only in Bateson are all three ideas actually assembled, if not quite as
a theory, then as something pretty close. This is where we shall begin, in
chapter 1, and the rest of the book will be an attempt to refine and apply
insights that were, I think, originally Bateson's.

Part 1

The Dialectics of Paradox and
the Dynamics of Desire

Chapter One

The Synthesis of Cultural Cognition and Depth Psychology

The dialectical exercise is simple in the extreme, for it requires only that the analyst of society question everything that he sees and hears, examine phenomena fully and from every angle, seek and evaluate the contradiction of any proposition, and consider every category from the viewpoint of its noncontents as well as its positive attributes. It requires us to also look for paradox as much as complementarity, for opposition as much as accommodation. It portrays a universe of dissonance underlying apparent order and seeks deeper orders beyond the dissonance. (Robert Murphy, The Dialectics of Social Life*)*

The problem with most psychoanalytic approaches is that they reduce complex interactive phenomena to the workings of the dynamic unconscious and evaluate them according to the standards of the self-reflective ego. Discourse processes are trivialized and ethnocentric assumptions made about the value of cultural formations as responses to unconscious conflict. Psychoanalytic theory is thus open to the critique that it is overly reductionistic, interested only in universal "needs" and "wants" (D'Andrade 1992; Lutz 1988; Strauss 1992; White 1992).

The problem with cognitivist approaches is that they are informed by a perspective which reduces motivation to goal-directedness or to the play of environmental constraints and distributions of power. Emotions are tokens in complex social ciphers, to be "activated" and "negotiated" but never experienced at any level deeper than ordinary consciousness. This has left cognitivist theory open to the critique that it is overly mechanical (Holland 1992; Horowitz 1988; Westen 1992) and that the only motivation it considers is either covertly utilitarian or consumed with dynamics of power, hegemony, and resistance (Nuckolls 1995).

These are serious problems. They are sustained by each side's tendency to define itself in opposition. How, then, to resolve their real (not merely rhetorical) differences and integrate them, so that their strengths contribute jointly to an understanding of motivated knowledge?

This book is premised on the assumption that no theory of cultural knowledge is adequate which does not take into account the insights of cognitive theory and psychoanalysis. The two in combination provide a more powerful approach than either does individually, and the development of a combined approach is desirable and possible. The purpose of this book is to propose and test a synthesis. I tout this strategy not because it provides complete solutions—plenty of problems remain—but to break the impasse and chart a new direction.

The first problem is one of vocabulary. The terms *psychoanalytic* and *cognitivist* are labels of convenience, useful for discriminating (albeit roughly) between approaches that are Freudian, talking the language of the dynamic unconscious, and approaches that are "schema-theoretic," talking the language of information processing. Take Melford Spiro and Catherine Lutz, for instance: Is the first "psychoanalytic" and the second "cognitivist"? These are tricky labels, difficult to use, for while Spiro is unarguably psychoanalytic and does more than "talk" the language of depth psychology, Lutz is not an information-processing cognitivist. She makes use of the language of cognitive psychology, for a purpose which, ironically, considers any form of psychological explanation deeply suspect. When I speak of psychoanalysis and cultural cognitivism, therefore, I use these terms in a limited sense, to refer to psychodynamic approaches and those that focus on culturally variable knowledge structures (models, scripts, schemas) used in making inferences.

ETHNOPSYCHOLOGY AND THE WILL TO POWER

Ethnopsychology is a kind of cultural cognitivism and, according to Lutz, concerns itself with knowledge forms and processes and with "the way people conceptualize, monitor, and discuss their own and others' mental processes, behavior, and social relationships" (Lutz 1988:83). This is more or less the conventional definition, available in essentially the same form throughout the relevant literature (Black 1985; White 1990, 1992). The main problem with ethnopsychology is that the form such knowledge can take is severely limited by the kind of data that are considered relevant. "Words descriptive of self and other," writes Lutz, "constitute the primary elements from which ethnopsychological statements are built" (1988:85).

Words, however, appear in discourse, and their relationship to each other in sequence is governed by syntaxlike rules. In what makes up an ethnopsychology, then, a metaphor whose referent is language controls the search for rule-governed sequences. These sequences are taken to represent cultural knowledge. It is the social pragmatics of this knowledge—its "contestation" and "negotiation"—which constitute the subject matter of ethnopsychological inquiry in this form. There is an important difference, however, between using language as an information source and adopting descriptive linguistic models as models of thought and cognition. The problem is that the two are not the same. If sequences that resemble natural language are the structures which bear cultural knowledge—an empirical question—then this must be demonstrated with reference to what we know about memory. But such evidence is not usually cited in the work of those who study ethnopsychology, perhaps because of fears that psychological explanation could become reductionistic (e.g., Lutz 1988; Lutz and Abu-Lughod 1990; White 1992; White and Lutz 1992).

Even if language-like sequences do exist, the fact that they do does not rule out the existence of other structures, at other levels, such as the dynamic unconscious. Because deep structures are not sequential or governed by syntaxlike laws, they do not bear the characteristic resemblance to linguistic discourse that would make them detectable through the method Lutz and other students of cultural cognition adopt (but see Holland 1992; Hutchins 1987). In order to relate them, a new conceptual vocabulary must be developed which does not privilege linguistic knowledge or result in an overemphasis on discourse.

Lutz objects to the psychoanalytic explanation of motivation because it reduces discursive and intersubjective processes to mechanical, intrapsychic outcomes (1988:191). In part this reflects only the catechistic rejection of psychobiological universalism, a rhetorical stance which Strauss correctly labels a sacrament of the faith for students of "cultural models" (Strauss 1992:3). It is said that psychoanalysis is about universal "needs" and "drives." Ethnopsychology, on the other hand, demonstrates that cultural meanings and their social negotiation help to constitute meaning, not merely to name feeling states and emotions. Psychoanalysis is limited and culture-bound and must, we are told, be eschewed or simply passed over (e.g., Strauss 1992:2; White 1992:23).

This critique is wrong for three reasons. First, it is badly out of date, for while it is true that psychoanalysis was once limited to the discussion of "drives," this changed a long time ago, even before Freud died. Much more has been written about object relations (Mahler, Winnicott), ego defenses (Bion, Kernberg), self psychology (Hartmann, Kohut), and attitude ambivalence (Thompson, Zanna) than was ever written about drives. Second, even if not all needs and drives are universal, some undoubtedly are, so what is wrong with trying to figure out what they are and how they work cross-culturally? Third, psychoanalytic theory is more about the relationships between desires than about desires themselves, considered in the abstract, as "instincts." These relationships are what psychoanalysis evaluates using the language of repression, defense, compromise, and transference. This language provides insights into motivation which cultural cognitivism generally fails to deliver, mostly because its language of motivation continues to be unidimensional and ignores conflict.

Take the Ifaluk belief in malevolent spirits. The psychoanalytic account explains them as a projection of aggressive impulses and free-floating anxieties which the Ifaluk cannot express, due to a prohibition, and which they therefore must allocate to the world of spirits (Spiro 1953). The spirits are a socially acceptable vehicle for the expression of otherwise repressed emotions, emotions which, if they were given vent more directly, would make life on a small Pacific atoll exceedingly difficult. Spirit beliefs are thus functional. They do something that needs to be done to ensure the maintenance of psychological and social well-being.

The obvious logical rejoinder, and the one Lutz makes, is to point out the multiplicity of possible results if this were true. The Ifaluk do not lack projective targets, after all. They could have selected typhoons or foreigners, instead of spirits, as the vehicles of their projection. Surely this must weaken the psychoanalytic assertion that spirit beliefs serve to perform a projective function. Consequently, such beliefs must have some other significance, irreducible to the play of psychological forces. Why not, Lutz suggests, simply attend to what the Ifaluk say? They will tell us why spirits are significant. In his psychoanalytically informed study, however, Spiro never asserts that spirit beliefs exist *because* there are unconscious and repressed emotions which create such beliefs as a vehicle for their self-expression. Nor does he deny that other beliefs may serve the purpose of releasing aggression and anxiety equally well: "Belief in *alaus* [malevolent spirits] is not the only institution which could serve this vital function" (Spiro 1952:500 n. 14). Spirit beliefs, quite simply, are taken as given and, as such, available as a means through which a necessary function can be performed.

There is no principled theoretical reason for the ethnopsychological rejection of depth psychology. Nothing in the cognitivist account is threatened by it, and indeed, a much richer account of motivation could be developed if it were incorporated. So, why isn't it? More than anything else, it is the reluctance to acknowledge multiple levels, from the discursive to the psychodynamic, that characterizes the ethnopsychological critique of psychoanalysis. Such reluctance has its source in the suspicion of explanatory paradigms that are too obviously rooted in Western theory. Lutz does not present an argument to disprove the applicability of psychoanalytic theory. She even uses it herself when it is stripped of tell-tale references to its source (Nuckolls, in press). It is thus a distaste for Western-style explanatory theory which sustains the critique, and this, not because theory is wrong, but because it too obviously betrays its origins as a form of Western scientific explanation.

How did ethnopsychology, and cultural cognitivism generally, develop its slant on motivation, with its neglect of depth? The reason probably has to do with the way it developed—an accident of birth, if you will. Anthropological interest in cognitive processing arose at a time of rapid progress in the information sciences, especially artificial intelligence. Employing computer-based metaphors, schema-theoretic anthropology developed a language suitable for discussing cultural knowledge as a collection of programlike forms called "schemata," "scripts," or "models." This is where the problem of motivation begins, since computer-based models are notoriously weak when it comes to explaining *why* people instantiate their scripts. If culture consists of a repertoire of schemata, and social life of their activation and negotiation, then there must be something which provides direction and force. To put it simply: When do we activate models and why do we negotiate?

Lutz is mindful of this problem and, in acknowledging her debt to the cognitive tradition, questions the dispassionate and value-neutral description of knowledge structures. Some, like D'Andrade and Strauss, prefer to locate motives in the models themselves, as a kind of moral obligation (D'Andrade 1992:36), but for Lutz this is not culturally muscular enough. Her solution to the problem of dispassionate cognitivism—and her answer (at least implicitly) to the question of motivation—is to speak of "power."

"Power" is the force behind all action, permanent and irreducible, and it requires no definition. Motivation is the will to power. People who have less power seek to obtain more, just as people with more seek to maintain or increase what they already have. The transaction and negotiation of power within a hierarchy of dominance takes place through the resources culture makes available. One of these resources is the language of the emotions. That is why Lutz talks about it.

A good example is the Ifaluk emotion concept *fago* (love/sadness/compassion). Its function, Lutz tells us, is to ensure cooperation and harmonious relations among people crowded together on a tiny atoll. "*Fago* represents the emotional and ideological *product* of a society in which it is the rare individual who is separated either from others or from access to land" (Lutz 1988:152, emphasis mine). Lutz reduces an emotional complex to a form of social organization and tells us that the latter is the result of an adaptation to the environment. Could one say that *fago* helps people find a prosocial release for feelings that otherwise might prove disruptive? Interestingly, Lutz dismisses a similar argument by Spiro, which identifies these feelings with repressed aggression. She simply replaces aggression with "power."

Power is the desire of every individual for control over persons and things, and it is strongly influenced by the environment and the social organization of competition. Speaking of the problem of stratification and egalitarianism as competing tendencies on Ifaluk, Lutz mentions this dilemma and refers to power as a libido-like entity or force which must seek expression: "The character of the emotion *fago,* and its positive evaluation, provides an avenue for the exercise of power" (Lutz 1988:152). While D'Andrade (1995b) is correct to point out that this kind of argument bears a strong resemblance to Bentham, in fact it goes back further, to Thomas Hobbes and *Leviathan.* Lutz and Hobbes are utilitarian functionalists, defining knowledge as something to be used for the purpose of acquiring or maintaining power within a field of limited good. This does not seem like much of an improvement over a psychoanalytic account that talks of "drives" or "needs." In fact, power is a lot like the old-fashioned notion of psychic energy. It must exist and it must express itself. The only questions for the anthropologist (psychoanalyst or ethnopsychologist) are, what form does it take ("power" or "libido") and where is it going?

It is not difficult to see why "power" caught on in cultural cognitivism, rapidly becoming a master pretheoretical concept. That is because the will to power is a motivational construct well chosen to supply the needed force behind a cognitive-style theory of cultural knowledge. A rational theory of mind, after all, is compatible with a rational, Hobbesian theory of motivation, especially when both are subservient to a concept of culture that makes "politics" the root metaphor for social organization. This is *not,* I hasten to add, because a cognitive-style theory of cultural politics, or power-centric cultural anthropology, is wrong. Lutz is probably right about how emotions become tokens in the transaction of power relations. Right or wrong, however, it makes the critique of psychoanalysis less convincing, since the difference between the two is much less than it appears.

Ethnopsychology is no less reductionistic than the stereotype of psychoanalysis it criticizes. It explains emotion as the product of complex material circumstances and motivation as the will to power. Further, it is no less rooted in the Western conception of the self as an autonomous and bounded agent, for although Lutz speaks of the sociocentric conception of the self, power is still considered in individualistic Hobbesian terms (Nuckolls 1995, forthcoming). Power is what drives the system. "It is a theory in which there is only one real system, the power system" (D'Andrade 1995a:251). There is only a substitution here—of power for psychic energy, of politics for psychology—but no *solution* to what I consider a basic conceptual and empirical problem: how to develop accounts of cultural cognition which are not stunted and depthless.

CULTURAL SCHEMATA AND GOAL-DIRECTEDNESS

The type of cultural cognitivism being developed by D'Andrade (1991, 1992, 1995a) and Strauss (1992) is different from ethnopsychology—and better—because it acknowledges motivation but does not reduce it to power negotiations and the play of politics. Motives are considered culturally constructed goals, and goals are like normative imperatives, with the force of moral obligations. Thus we can speak of "marriage" in American culture as a set of knowledge structures organized with respect to the cultural goals they encode, e.g., "love," "happiness," "security." Goals represent superordinate knowledge structures, themselves organized by still higher goals, and linked via connecting propositions to clusters of knowledge structures and their goals. They are culturally variable and, although connected to the dynamics of power, not synonymous with them. Goals are not reducible to demographically induced structural imperatives, as motives tend to be in Lutz's account.

People do not blindly implement goal structures. Instead, they use them to achieve some end or purpose that is contextually defined. D'Andrade wants us to stop thinking of ends or purposes discretely, as "things" floating in psychic space. That is why he localizes them and relates them to larger structures which contain organized instructions and procedures for acting. This endows motives with situational variability, defining them as parts of an episodically organized whole which is sensitive to context. Goal-directed schema processing is a rationally construable process and, apparently, a fairly accessible one, explaining D'Andrade's statement that he and his colleagues had "no special difficulty" in identifying knowledge structures and the goals governing their application (D'Andrade 1992:225).

The problem with the language of "goals" is that it tends to make us think in terms of discrete and isolable aims which are relatively accessible.

Goals motivate action by "pulling" actors in a certain direction. This is consistent with the American common-sense understanding of behavior which always emphasizes the future, not the past, and directs people to formulate and pursue achievable goals. After all, the future is unknown and therefore open to change. Locating motives in goals preserves and enhances the American cultural model of the future as a place of boundless opportunity. The past is over and done with; any motives it provides only "push" us, perhaps in ways we would rather not go. Americans do not like to be pushed. That is why theories of motivation emphasizing past experience of whatever type (social, historical, psychoanalytic) are usually resisted.

The second difficulty is that when multiple goals are present, there is a tendency to treat them as hierarchically organized, thus preserving their identity as discretely bounded constructs. This is also consistent with the American common-sense view, but it puts at risk any understanding of motives as deeply conflicting. To anyone who has ever felt such a conflict, the fact that it can prove extremely motivating and emotionally provocative will come as no surprise. The problem is that conflict theories of motivation, of "ambivalence" and "compromise formation," are difficult to accommodate within the framework of unidimensional goals —a fact partly attributable to the development of goal theory by those whose models for understanding knowledge structures are (explicitly or implicitly) computer-based.

The third problem with goals is that they are easily described, too easily perhaps. D'Andrade comments positively on this feature: "It is a *relatively* straightforward task for an ethnographer to determine whether or not a schema has motivational force" (1995:233). Conscious schemata can be relatively easily solicited by direct inquiry of individuals. But it is hard to know what this means. Schemata may reflect false assumptions, cognitive biases, and concealed wishes, even if they are confidently entertained and consciously employed. How can we know if schemata as elicited are all there are, and that what appear to be organized and encapsulated knowledge structures really are that? To put it differently, what are the indications that schemata might contain elements that are outside ordinary awareness, and thus not regularly retrieved and replayed mentally?

More than once, D'Andrade cites Strauss's (1992) finding that among blue-collar workers in Rhode Island two cultural models or schemata could be detected: the "success" model, according to which one should maximize individual achievement, and the "breadwinner" model, according to which one should be prepared to sacrifice individual achievement for the well-being of one's family (D'Andrade 1991, 1992, 1995). The motivational force of the breadwinner model was stronger and affected career choices, while the less motivationally compelling success model tended to show up in interviews, in which the men simply voiced the dominant American ideology.

Strauss does not define "ideology" but implies that it represents a kind of official discourse which the interview easily elicits. This tends to simplify the relationship between discourse and deeply felt desire, as if the two are distinct and the latter best represented by nonideological "assumptions." The value of breadwinning is an assumption, according to Strauss, whereas the value of success is an ideology. Is this the kind of ideology Scheper-Hughes (1992) and others refer to when they talk about the specific forms of consciousness used to sustain or justify particular institutions or social practices? It is hard to tell. Therefore, let us consider the definition of ideology offered by the French psychoanalytic social theorists Janine Chasseguet-Smirgel and Bela Grunberger: "It is a system of thought which claims to be total, it is a historical and political interpretation whose (unconscious) aim is the actualization of an illusion, of illusion *par excellence,* that the ego and its ideal can be reunited by a short-cut, via the pleasure principle" (1986:15–16). Even an ideology has unconscious roots. It can be considered a projective system which ascribes the sources of human good and evil to such external factors as capitalism or communism rather than to desires whose conflictual dynamics are part of the human condition. Ideology does not simply inform discourse that deeper down is more strongly directed by unarticulated basic assumptions. It is a product of these assumptions, or more precisely, a projection from them of the problematic desires they represent. To consider ideology "only" a superimposition, as Chasseguet-Smirgel points out, is to accept *what ideology says about itself,* and to be misled.

No doubt values like "success" and "breadwinning" do function as goals which organize lower-level action schemata, the first less internalized than the other. Perhaps such goals can be elicited fairly easily by listening to what people say, especially when goals are congruent with the official social ideology. But is it also true that they are distinct and separate, and that for Strauss's informants it is the value of breadwinning, not success, which becomes motivating?

Fifty years before Strauss, Robert Lynd (of "Middletown" fame) found that Americans are highly ambivalent about precisely these values, and many others. In his book *Knowledge For What?* he listed twenty paired assumptions by which Americans live, noting that these run at once "into a large measure of contradiction and resulting ambivalence" (1939). For example:

1. Everyone should try to be successful.
   But: The kind of person you are is more important than how successful you are.
2. The family is our basic institution and the sacred core of our national life.
   But: Business is our most important institution, and, since national welfare depends upon it, other institutions must conform to its needs.
3. Honesty is the best policy.
   But: Business is business, and a businessman would be a fool if he didn't cover his hand.
4. Individualism, "the survival of the fittest," is the law of nature and the secret of America's greatness; and restrictions on individual freedom are un-American and kill initiative.
   But: No man should live for himself alone; for people ought to be loyal and stand together and work for common purposes. (Lynd 1939:60–62)

These value premises are widely and deeply held and not organized into sets of norms for one or another role in particular. They represent cases of cultural conflict. Lynd's findings are consistent with modern attitude theory, which questions the assumption that attitudes and roles are largely unconflicted and unidimensional. The fact that "success" and "breadwinning" represent contradictory ideals suggests the *possibility* that the two may conflict, not just rhetorically, but deeply and psychologically.

If success values are weakly internalized and "encapsulated," as Strauss claims, then conflict with the value of family support may not arise, and the language of psychoanalysis is irrelevant. But is the fact that Rhode Island men choose to put family obligations first the only, or even the best, evidence for the fact that success values were weakly internalized? The only factor presented in favor of this conclusion is occupational choice (Strauss 1992:210, 217). The world of work is deemed primary in deciding the question of model saliency. If Strauss had broadened her search, however, another picture might have emerged—one in which the value of success was strongly emphasized and the conflict between deeply internalized values of success and breadwinning, very powerful.

We can all think of instances in which we have held different beliefs about the same issue, or felt torn between two emotions or choices. The nature of these attitudes is different from what unidimensional attitude theory predicts. With the positive and negative aspects equally significant concerns, our attitudes pull us in different directions, and the result is a highly polarized evaluation; an "unstable dialectic" (Holmes and Rempel 1989:26). For the sake of argument, therefore, let us start from the hypothesis that success and breadwinning are deeply internalized knowledge structures and that they are in conflict with each other. What are the criteria by means of which we can judge this hypothesis?

A number of criteria can be considered and used to evaluate the relative consciousness or unconsciousness of specific schemata or scripts (see Singer and Salovney 1991). Realization that deeply held values conflict causes discomfort, prompting the creation of a defense, to keep the conflict from becoming overwhelming. One defensive strategy is projection. Because contradictory values cannot be reconciled, they are allocated to different external agencies or activities, which then "act out" these values independent of each other. Another possible outcome is splitting (Brook 1992). The person whose values conflict divides himself into two personae, each endowed with one or the other of the conflicting values. Testing these possibilities involves looking for data in places Strauss does not.

Consider the first, projection, and two of its expressions, movies and sports. The idea that forms of entertainment constitute projective systems is not new, but a staple of socio-psychoanalytic research (e.g., Kaplan 1990; Metz 1980, 1982; Rose 1976–77). Without more information, it is impossible to know to what extent Strauss's Rhode Islanders go to the movies, or which kinds they like. But one of the most popular themes throughout the United States is that of the rugged individual who makes it big (Stein 1985). The story begins with the hero in trouble, poor and on the verge of calamity. Through hard work and a little good luck, he triumphs and builds something (a machine, business, or political organization). The hero is intelligent and quick-witted and seizes all opportunities. Most importantly, he does not let the burden of family or community responsibility stand in his way. Examples of this hero genre include a variety of movies and television productions, such as *High Noon, The Story of Louis Pasteur, Alexander Graham Bell, Young Mister Lincoln, Ride the High Country,* "How the West Was Won," "The Virginian," *Star Wars,* and "Lifestyles of the Rich and Famous," to name but a few (Slotkin 1992).

Strauss might have found that her interviewees enjoy the spectacle of flamboyant individual success in fictional worlds that are far removed. In their own world, success of this kind is unachievable, and even unwanted, given their circumstances. They project the desire for individual success onto fantasy characters, who then act out the fantasy on the screen, safely removed from the real world and its workaday demands. That does not mean that the value of success or individual achievement is "encapsulated," or any less salient to everyday life, just because it appears in "fantasy" instead of in career choice. It has simply been projected someplace else.

Not only movie characters perform this function, certainly: famous coaches and sports stars can do the same thing. How much time do Strauss's informants spend talking about the brilliant achievements of the local players or competitively talking up the successes of one athlete over another? Do they create betting pools and wager on the outcome of major sporting events? If they do, then it could be in unconscious effort to realize a value which in working life they are not permitted, or are not able to express. We do not know. In any case, it would take more than an interview or two to find out, since fantasy material, unlike goal schemata, is not readily accessible or easy to interpret.

Now let us consider "splitting," which refers (among other things) to the ability of the ego to divide itself and separately act out conflicting values. The value of success is difficult to realize in the world of work, so instead men adopt an alternative nonwork persona in which this value can express itself. One avenue is participation in sports. Strauss's informant who spends his days toiling away as a mechanic at the Ciba-Geigy factory might express his desire for personal success in running marathons and, if he were good enough to win, would fulfill this desire in his role as part-time athlete. There are probably many similar examples—parachuting, hang-gliding, auto racing, skiing, mountain climbing, running—any one of which could provide an arena for acting out an alternative identity geared to personal success. Studies over the last ten years (all of them nonpsycho-analytic) support the conclusion that men who seek thrills and adventure in sports compensate in those activities for occupations that emphasize routine and cooperation (e.g., Hymbaugh and Garrett 1974; Kirkcaldy 1982; Straub 1982; Zuckerman 1971, 1979).

Another vehicle for the expression of alternative personae is religion. In his study of American fire-walking, Danforth (1988) finds that work in the everyday world offers few opportunities for individual expression or achievement. But the strength of value is strongly internalized, not encapsulated, and Americans experience the conflict between it and the breadwinner model very strongly. That is why some of them join fire-walking movements (see also Cox 1973; Needleman and Baker 1978; Tipton 1982). The goal is to achieve mastery over the fire, but more important, over one's own sense of fear. People who feel little sense of achievement or success in everyday life seem to feel it here, in a direct encounter with a material opponent that can be vanquished. The fire-walk organizers tell them that they should be able to transfer this new-found sense of mastery to their work back at the office. But one suspects that this is not often the case. Instead, fire-walking provides an arena in which to act out and revel in an alternative identity providing the possibility of immediate personal success.

Mainstream religious movements less exotic than fire-walking provide similar opportunities. Throughout the United States, there is increasingly less emphasis on traditional liturgy and more on expressions of personal religious fulfillment and spiritual attainment. What do Strauss's informants do in church? Recent studies in working-class communities have shown that men and women who are unable to succeed occupationally sometimes turn to charismatic Christian movements, in which praying and "witnessing" become domains for the exercise of personal achievement (Wuthnow 1976, 1979). Non-Christian movements and "New Age" cults—such as the neo-Buddhist *Soka Gakkai,* Satanism, the Hindu-American Society for Krishna Consciousness, Transcendental Meditation, Scientology, and the Unification Church—also provide domains for success and achievement, usually measured in terms of recruitment of additional members and advancement up the cult hierarchy (Gertlach 1974; McGuire 1988). So do a variety of cultlike business enterprises, from Amway to Mary Kay Cosmetics. Whether or not Strauss's informants participate in any of these is unknown because Strauss does not provide such information, preferring instead to concentrate on career choice as the sole indicator of model salience.

If Strauss's informants are conflicted, and build up defenses against the conflict, what happens when the defenses break down? Psychological ambivalence is the result of values that cannot be reconciled or of conflicts unsuccessfully defended against. It can arise when defenses are put under stress and manifests itself in a variety of ways, from a vague uneasiness to total incapacity and breakdown. One result can be alcoholism. As Stein (1985) points out, drinking functions as an "elixir of the return of the repressed" (Stein 1985:161), a socially marked release for men who use it as a vehicle for self-expression and social negativism. Men are expected to be rugged individuals, but society provides too few opportunities for expression, since most men work in settings that require cooperation and teamwork. How then to be a rugged individual and negate, at least temporarily, the values of personal responsibility and self-control?

Certainly, alcohol as a chemical has an effect, but that effect is to manifest what is sought after. Drinking and getting drunk provides an answer, giving men an arena for flamboyant atavistic display. It is the functional equivalent of Haitian voodoo, in which the passive individual in the guise of a horse undergoes possession by a rider who directs the horse to where he would not ordinarily go. Drinking epitomizes the culturally normative denial of dependability and responsibility, the values of the breadwinner. Afterward, everyone can claim that it was "only the bottle talking," and the drinker returns to his life as a cog in the machine. Culturally, "alcoholism" is a response to ambivalence, a compromise formation which both individuals and society employ to resolve (temporarily and partially) the conflict between the values of success and social responsibility. It permits the expression of both conscious independence and unconscious dependency, and, like any good compromise formation, balances the two by (1) attributing causes to the effects of ethanol rather than to the conscious intention of the self and (2) providing punishment in the form of a hangover attributed to overindulgence.

Do the men Strauss interviewed get drunk and act out fantasies of personal power, success, and aggrandizement? Are they then contrite, vowing never to do it again? And does the cycle almost always repeat itself? Once again, we do not know. But if so, one explanation might be that drinking is socially sanctioned compromise formation and helps men reconcile the ambivalence they feel over having to choose between the cultural models of success and breadwinning. Far from being distant from each other, success and breadwinning could be deeply interactive and conflicting, and the consequences of that interaction could strongly influence personal experience outside the domain of career choice.

If Strauss had not excluded the possible relevance of psychodynamic theory, she might have found that motives are not limited to goals and that interactions between multiple and conflicting motives have important consequences for culture and the individual. Making this kind of move does not put at risk any aspect of the goal-schematic account. But it would deepen it, forcing recognition that psychodynamic and cognitive processes mutually inform and constrain each other. In a contribution to a psychodynamically oriented book, D'Andrade himself raises this as a possibility, remarking in one of his concluding paragraphs that "interpretive networks appear to be constantly warped by various internal activations which 'push' the system toward certain relaxation states rather than others—often in conflict with the 'actual' external inputs" (1991:299). He even goes so far as to say that there may be an association between schemata and wishes. D'Andrade is surely right, but so far he has not chosen to elaborate on this thesis, preferring instead to develop the idea of schemas-as-maps-to-aid-in-achieving-goals (see D'Andrade 1992, 1995a).

The trick is to develop a way of talking about motivation that does not render it overly cognitive or reduce it to the invariant principles of the dynamic unconscious. As we have seen, the risks of the former are real, due mostly to the unnecessary polemical stance which excludes psychoanalysis. What of the latter? As I show in the next section, contemporary psychoanalytic theories of motivation bear little resemblance to the straw man attacked by the cognitivists in their formulaic statements of dismissal.

PSYCHOANALYSIS AND THE PROBLEM OF MOTIVATION

Overcoming the cognitivist bias against psychoanalysis requires more than a suggestion of its possible relevance to understanding blue-collar Rhode Islanders. It requires a demonstration that what psychoanalysis says about motivation and unconscious processes might be true. The best way to argue this point is to use the information which cognitive science and related disciplines themselves provide, and not rely, as psychoanalysts typically do, on easily dismissed clinical anecdotes. In a series of recent papers, the psychologist Drew Westen has attempted to do just that (Westen 1991, 1992, 1994), and I am indebted to his review of the literature for some of the evidence that follows.

As Westen points out, the first misconception is that psychoanalysis is synonymous with antiquated drive concepts, such as the drive for sex or the drive for hunger. The deficiencies of drive theory are not inherent in psychoanalytic models, however. In fact, most psychoanalytic theorists do not use words like "drive" at all anymore. Another misconception is that the concept of unconscious desires and wishes can be dispensed with because the only body of evidence which supports their existence is clinical and therefore too impressionistic to be useful. This is not the case. The literature on attachment, for example, demonstrates that people inhibit conscious access to representations of the self and others based on their affective qualities. For example, Shedler, Mayman, and Manis (1994) examined subjects in two studies who reported themselves to be free of psychological distress but whose descriptions of their early memories were rated as showing signs of psychological disturbance. These subjects were then "stressed" in ways (such as making them read aloud) that would be most stressful to people with a strongly developed unconscious defenses. The subjects who viewed themselves as healthy but showed signs of unconscious distress were significantly more reactive on the combined heart-rate and blood-pressure index. They also manifested many indirect signs of anxiety (stammering, sighing, etc.) which they were unaware of.

Let me stress once again that the researchers were not psychoanalysts, or even psychodynamically oriented psychologists. Nevertheless, the results of their study support a key psychoanalytic precept: Unconscious conflict motivates behavior, in ways that are inaccessible to consciousness due to the operation of defensive mechanisms, such as repression.

Other research on the relationship between repressive coping styles and health tends to support the same conclusion. Weinberger and Schwartz (1990) consider subjects who report low anxiety but have high scores on a scale measuring a combination of defensiveness, social desirability and overcontrol of affect. Subjects who repress report low levels of anxiety while demonstrating on various projective tests a high degree of physiological reactivity. Weinberger and his colleagues demonstrate that there is a link between repression and both cholesterol and asthma, and even uncovered an association between repressive strategies and vulnerability to cancer (Weinberger and Davidson 1994). The results confirm that inhibiting conscious access to one's emotions puts the heart and immune system under considerable stress, just as contemporary psychoanalytic theory would predict.

Westen (1994) notes that many of the abuse studies of repressed memory also confirm the existence of a dynamic unconscious which protects itself against conflict by defensive mechanisms, including amnesias. For example, Williams (1995) interviewed women who had been treated at a hospital for sexual molestation when they were children. She found that seventeen years after their documented abuse, 38% were amnesiac for the incident. Among a larger sample of adults reporting histories of childhood sexual abuse, about 60% identified some period during childhood in which they were amnesiac for the abuse (Briere and Conte 1993). Another study discovered that almost 20% of women treated for substance abuse who acknowledged a history of childhood abuse also reported periods of amnesia for the events (Loftus 1992). This is typical of the sufferers of abuse. Most tend to have gaps of months or years, and the memories they do recall come to them only as flashbacks or in physical form (such as the sensation of gagging) or in dreams. The mechanism which accounts for these phenomena is defensiveness, created by the intense desire to forget traumatic episodes involving close attachment figures (usually parents) and the ambivalence these episodes triggered.

A somewhat different outcome arises if conflicting but mutually unfulfillable desires result not in amnesiac repression but in compromise formation. A compromise formation is a thought, feeling, or action that represents an accommodation of some kind among multiple motives, such as the desire to maintain self-esteem, to obtain gratification, and to respond to moral imperatives. Kunda and Sanitoso (1989) showed that subjects induced to theorize that a given trait (extroversion or introversion) was conducive to academic success soon viewed themselves as characterized by higher levels of that trait. These changes in self-concepts were constrained to some extent by prior self-knowledge. The subjects were mostly extroverted to begin with and viewed themselves as less extroverted when they believed introversion to be more desirable, but they still viewed themselves as extroverted. The authors of the study do not refer to the change in self-concepts as a compromise formation prompted by the motivation to resolve competing expectations. Indeed, no reference is made to the vast psychoanalytic literature on compromise formation. The results of their study nevertheless confirm that reasoning motivated by unconscious conflict can lead to changes in the construction of self, a classic tenet of psychoanalytic theory.

Finally, there is evidence that currently imposed goals bias reconstruction of one's past behavior. Subjects led to believe that tooth-brushing (Ross, McFarland, and Fletcher 1981) or caffeine consumption (Sherman and Kunda 1989) was bad for their health reported having performed those actions in the recent past less frequently than did subjects led to believe that the same behaviors were good for them. These studies demonstrate that people can reconstruct memories to achieve satisfying accommodations between self-concept and induced expectation, another indication that a mechanism like compromise formation is at work.

In reviewing the literature on motivated reasoning, Kunda (1990) proposes that when one wants to draw a particular conclusion, one feels obligated to construct a justification for that conclusion that would be plausible to a dispassionate observer. "In doing so," she says, "one accesses only a biased subset of the relevant beliefs and rules" (Kunda 1990:493). Motivated reasoning is mediated by biased memories and constrained beliefs. In considering the mechanisms that could account for this, Kunda concludes: "The existence of constraints . . . may reflect a compromise between a desire to espouse new attitudes and an opposing desire to maintain current ones" (1990:493). All the studies she considers support the hypothesis that biased memory retrieval and belief construction represent compromise formations centered on concepts of the self. This is more or less what psychoanalytic theory would predict.

Finally, let us consider empirical support for another important psychoanalytic concept: transference, the process whereby a relationship pattern established in childhood becomes a recurrent schema for shaping later re-lationships. Luborsky and his colleagues (1991) reduced the concept to testable hypotheses. The data consist of narratives about relationships with other people or the self that are spontaneously told during psychotherapy sessions as well as elicited during relationship anecdotes. To test the data, judges read the transcript of a session, especially the relationship episodes, and identify three components: 1) the patient's main wishes, needs, or in-tentions toward the other person in the narratives; 2) the responses of the other person; and 3) the responses of the self. Through systematic studies (Crits-Christoph et al. 1988; Bond, Hansell, and Shevrin 1987; Levine and Luborsky 1981) it is known that this selection can be done reliably. Each of the three types of components is counted in terms of the frequency with which it appears in different relationship episodes. The highest frequency for each of the three types of components constitutes the transference.

Luborsky and his colleagues found that, based on their examination of patient narratives, there is usually a central relationship pattern across many relationship episodes. This kind of pervasiveness is consistent with Freud's (1912) view of the nature of the transference template. Second, they found that the pattern for patients is distinctively different. One man's pattern, for example, was focused on the conflict between his wish for as-serting autonomy and his resistance of domination, with the symptom of anxiety and social phobia as a consequence. Another man's pattern was focused on the wish for a close love relationship versus an opposite wish for distance, with guilt about his behavior (Luborsky et al. 1991:191). Third, with regard to consistency over time, the investigators found that their patient-subjects were very consistent in the kind of relationship patterns they mapped on different situations. The trend toward high consistency also fits with Freud's observations. Finally, with regard to Freud's obser-vation that the transference pattern is out of awareness, the study showed that this was true and that patients resisted therapists' efforts to make it conscious.

More evidence from the nonpsychoanalytic experimental literature could be adduced (see Horowitz 1988, 1991; Singer 1990), but by now the point should be clear. Freud was right about a lot of things. The uncon-scious exists; its conflicts are motivating; and its mechanisms—repression, compromise formation, and transference—have consequences for what we say, think, and feel. There is no need to rely exclusively on the testimony of psychoanalysts for this, on reports which begin "I once had a patient," when research in cognitive and social psychology now points to the same conclusions. Only a principled neglect of this literature can explain anthropologists' ritual disavowals of all things Freudian as if they represent magical thinking or vestiges from the distant past.

TOWARD A SYNTHESIS

In a brief but brilliant paper, Hutchins (1987) showed that a Trobriand myth functions as a disguised representation of repressed thoughts and fears concerning relations between the self and a deceased relative. He described mythic schemata as a series of episodic scenarios, but instead of ignoring motives, or locating them as "goals" in the schemata themselves, he uses the language of the dynamic unconscious to show that schemata selectively distort repressed motivational schemata. The value of Hutchins's analysis is in demonstrating that cognitive schemata and psychodynamic processes are related, but unfortunately, no unified theory is presented.

To construct a unified theory, the concept of the "schema" needs to be rebuilt, to take into account dynamic processes. Here is what I propose:

1. Schemata summarize past experiences into holistic, composite forms, thus allowing incoming information to be measured against the existing composite for "goodness of fit." Incoming information may be distorted or partially deleted, in order to achieve this fit, thus explaining some of the "errors" or "gaps" in remembered accounts. Schemata enable rapid perception, as information is assimilated to the existing composite, but they also lead to patterned and recurrent distortions.

2. Multiple schemata may be applied simultaneously and unconsciously to the interpretation of information. Multiple parallel channels operate in unconscious information processing, but conscious thought tends to proceed in one or only a few of these. As a result, there may be competition for priority among these multiple schemata.

3. Conscious reflection on schemata is possible, especially when schemata are given symbolic representation in words, signs, or gestures. This may facilitate changes in how the schemata are used in appraisals, decision, and negotiations of meaning, leading to changes that can construct new schemata or that integrate old ones (see Horowitz 1988).

Let us posit the existence of a repertoire of relational schemata which contains archaic components, many formed in childhood, that can never be erased. Such early schemata of self and others are constrained by mature concepts of self which contain and integrate immature self schemata.

Nevertheless, in a kind of parallel processing, earlier forms continue an unconscious appraisal of current events, possibly following primitive association and the logic of the "primary process." The link between the dynamic unconscious and cognitive schematic could then be stated as follows: *Access to conscious symbol systems, including cultural images, words, and action scenarios, might occur only through the information organized by unconscious schemata, such that to instantiate one is to instantiate the other.*

Unconscious relational schemata conflict, either because they represent mutually unfulfillable desires, or because the desires they represent are opposed by mature thought and culturally normative demands. Such schemata are what Luborsky and his colleagues (1991) refer to as "core conflictual relationship themes." If higher-order knowledge structures are accessible only by activating lower ones, in the dynamic unconscious, then it is possible that higher-order structures reproduce in their form and function the conflicts of the lower-order relational structures. There is a relationship between the conflicts of unconscious and conscious knowledge structures, but it is not necessary to say that unconscious conflicts produce, give rise to, or directly create conscious structures or cultural formations which then exist only to manifest or resolve underlying conflicts. Nevertheless, it could be true that unresolvable conflict at the level of deeply unconscious motivational schemata produces ambivalence and the need to deal with it through repression or compromise. Cultural knowledge structures might exist which both reproduce conflicts and attempt to resolve them, in a mutually reinforcing way, foregrounding the theoretical importance of *ambivalence* and *compromise formation* in constructing such structures.

Here we are on the verge of an insight Gregory Bateson formulated a long time ago. Bateson pointed out that there are cultural problems that cannot be solved, such as alcoholism or the political opposition between Palestinians and Israelis (Bateson 1972; see also Volkan 1991, 1994; Stein and Apprey 1985, 1987, 1990). What is the nature of these problems? Far from being merely secondary or derivative, such problems might be fundamental to what we call "culture." Where each generation transmits to the next its unresolved problems, there exists a continuity between generations that goes by the name *culture.* That is because they are not problems, but *solutions* to problems that are covert and intractable. Such problems are paradoxes, and what we need to follow Bateson's insight is *a theory of paradox in culture.*

The theory I shall propose comprehends cognitive structures and deep motivations as dialectical realizations of cultural paradox, and as necessarily related. Cognitive elements are those that regulate or resolve thoughts and feelings for defensive and adaptive purposes, although they cannot be reduced to them. Dynamic elements are the underlying representations, mixed with desires and fears, that must be regulated or resolved. Foremost among these are symbolizations of self and others. In creating this synthesis it is essential that we return to Weber and Freud.

Chapter Two

Culture as a Problem That Cannot Be Solved

The counter-thrust brings together, and from tones at variance comes
perfect attunement, and all things come to pass through conflict.
(Heraclitus, The Fragments 75)

WEBER AND FREUD

In the history of ideas, it can only be natural that we speculate on the consequences that might have followed if Weber and Freud had assimilated each
other's ideas. It might have forestalled decades of antagonism between the
disciplines they helped to create. Would the result have been a psychodynamic *Verstehensoziologie* or a psychoanalysis informed by the theory of
rationalization? This chapter is not an exercise in historical speculation,
nor is it a fantasy on the theme of what might have been.[1] It is motivated by
a question that is now at the center of the debate about mind and culture,
knowledge and motivation (D'Andrade 1991, 1992, 1995; D'Andrade and
Strauss 1992). How is cultural knowledge organized and how does it become emotionally compelling?[2]

The synthesis of Weber and Freud will proceed by stipulating the points
of correspondence between the theory of knowledge Weber called "rationalization" and a key component of the psychoanalytic theory of motivation, which Freud called "ambivalence." Both concepts are fundamentally
dialectical and depend on a dialectical view of social and psychological

1. Early on, Karl Jaspers, Weber's colleague and student, saw the potential of such a synthesis, and even suggested a rudimentary outline in 1913 in his *Allgemeine Psychopathologie*.
   But it was never fully formulated, and even Jaspers himself abandoned it as he began to
   develop a new approach, "existentialism."
2. For recent assessments of the field, foregrounding this question, see D'Andrade and Strauss
   (1992), Shweder (1991), and Stein and Apprey (1990).

realities. It is in the recognition of this fact (and what follows from it theoretically) that a synthesis of the two can be achieved. I do not claim that Weber and Freud would have agreed with the synthesis, or with the application, but only that the theories of the two are more powerful in synthesis than either is individually.

But first, what is a dialectic? A literal rendering from the Greek root defines it as a conversation back and forth, leading to development through various and apparently contradictory stages. More generally, it refers to a concept of knowledge and reality which differs from others in a particular kind of openness—a dialectical openness which preserves the tension between absolute and the relative, contingent and universal, mind and society. A dialectical system embraces the whole to which a problem belongs. Instead of dividing something up and considering it piecemeal— analytically—the dialectic totalizes, by seeking to characterize the relationship between disparate parts.

This relationship between parts is usually one of paradox. No doubt this must appear strange. We are accustomed to thinking of paradox as a source of vexation, and of any knowledge system based on paradox as impossible. Kant agreed, and considered dialectics to be infringements of the limits of reason precisely because of the fact that all dialectics begin in paradox. His favorite examples of paradoxical dialectics were the "antinomies," conflicts between equally demonstrable propositions, such as:

1. The world has a beginning (*thesis*), yet it is infinite in time and space (*antithesis*);
2. Everything is simple (*thesis*), yet it is also composite (*antithesis*);
3. There are in the world "causes through freedom" (*thesis*), yet there is no freedom, for all is nature (*antithesis*); and
4. In the series of world-causes there is a necessary being (*thesis*), yet nothing is necessary, for all is contingent (*antithesis*).

The four antitheses each present a potentially infinite regress, and the four theses each present an idea that terminates the infinite series. The result is that one can go back and forth, between arguments advanced on both sides of the antinomy, forever—with no end. That is the very essence of a dialectical movement, with paradox at its core.

If we pursue the systematic but contradictory objectives of the paradoxical antinomies, as reason seems to compel us to, we end up in dialectics, infinitely prolonged attempts to resolve the opposition which constitutes them. Does this not result in knowledge which is invalid? Kant emphasized that although reason produces contradictions, reason can be tested against experience, hence the only danger is to assume in advance of experience that ideas are true or false. This is what is meant by using the ideas "regulatively," to direct the course of our inquiry, but not to confuse the apparent goals of inquiry with reality itself. Generally speaking, however, we do not recognize the oppositions Kant identified as paradoxes, nor do we understand them as heuristic guides, as Kant prescribed. We think of them as real.

Dialectical Knowledge Systems and Paradoxical Antinomies

The antinomies are not just philosophical puzzles, invented by a man whose experience never transcended the boundaries of his native Königsberg. We can find evidence of them, and the dialectics they sustain, in modern physics. For example:

1. *The Theory of the Universe, Its Size and Age:* Astrophysicists assert that the universe is infinite, yet bounded and perhaps even circular. It cannot be both. Yet arguments can be made on both sides, with important consequences for the development of research programs. We know this because there are astrophysicists who study problems framed in terms of one side or the other. These inquiries are based on the paradox, derivative of the antinomy Kant calls "quantity," and permanently unresolvable in the terms expressed.

2. *The Theory of Matter.* Matter is divisible into constituent parts, and these constituents are also divisible, but physics is driven (partly) by the search for fundamental particles. Matter cannot be both fundamental and infinitely divisible, however, and this is what makes the physics of matter necessarily paradoxical. We know this because each new advance in particle physics is followed by another, in which yet another "fundamental" particle, like the proton or the electron, is shown to be made up of smaller particles, called quarks. Kant called it the antinomy of "quality."

3. *The Uncertainty Principle:* A fundamental paradox of quantum physics is presented in the "Copenhagen Interpretation" of Bohr and Heisenberg, which states that an observing system alters the observed system, so that "objective reality" is always influenced by our subjective interpretive procedures. Heisenberg concluded that the certainty produced by the observing system about position or time in subatomic particle physics would generate uncertainty in the measurement of momentum or energy, and vice versa. How can we know something which is changed by the very process of knowing? This is a paradox. Even though many physicists, including Einstein, were disturbed by the paradoxical status of this statement, they still accepted quantum theory and found it creatively stimulating.

4. *The Theory of Light:* In accord with Bohr's complementarity principle,

the same physical reality may be interpreted as either a particle or a wave at different times or from different points of view. Yet it cannot be both. This is paradoxical, but no less creatively stimulating for that, as research on light (treating it either as wave or particle) reveals.

Whether or not physicists resolve these muddles is less important than the inquiry paradoxical oppositions provoke and sustain in new theories of knowledge. The point is that there can be no end to these problematics, *and need be none,* for the process of inquiry to continue productively. This does not justify the leap to the conclusion that "reality is paradoxical," although we can point to it as support for the hypothesis that many forms of science (from subatomic physics and cosmology to anthropology and psychology) invariably yield paradoxical second-order results. Mindful of the same risk, Kant himself said that although reason produces contradictions, reason can be tested against experience; hence, the only danger is to assume in advance of experience that categories are true or false.[3]

Dynamic Paradox and Goal-Directedness

What makes anyone want the knowledge that is generated in the dialectical elaboration of unresolvable paradox? There has to be a goal. A dialectic begins with a standard or goal, and by virtue of the fact that effective existence cannot meet this standard, a contradiction is generated that is productive of dialectical movement. The Hegelian notion of the dialectic is thus ontological and in three parts: We begin with an inadequate realization of the goal; second, we have some very basic notions of what the goal is, including at least some of its critical properties; and finally, there is the standard or goal itself. The first step in a Hegelian dialectical movement reveals that a concept is incomplete, inconsistent, or otherwise inadequate by the standards which it seeks to realize. The second step is the postulation of an alternative form, which is a "determinate negation" of the first in the sense that its form duplicates that of the term it negates. It is a logical opposite. The idea is that every concept or form contrasts itself with an opposite—black and white, particular and universal, etc. When one form has been exhausted, the most "natural" move is to its opposite, "just as an

3. As Kemp Smith, translator of the *Critique of Pure Reason,* remarks. "As the sole legitimate function of the Ideas is that of inspiring the understanding in its empirical employment, they must never be interpreted as having metaphysical significance. As the ideas exist solely for the sake of experience, it is they that must be condemned, if the two really diverge. We do not say 'that a man is too long for his coat, but that the coat is too short for the man.' It is experience, not Ideas, which forms the criterion alike of truth and reality" (Kemp Smith 1984:430).

eye that is tired of light leaps to the shade, an eye that is jaded with green tends to see a reddish after-image, and so on" (Solomon 1983:231).

A dialectic therefore consists of a goal or standard toward which the development of concepts is directed but which it pursues through the clash of paradoxically related opposites, representing an inadequate fulfillment of the goal. A dialectic is the movement of thought directed by the coming together of these three parts in a process of development, wherein goals and their attempted fulfillments clash with each other in contradiction. In Kant's view, opposites confront each other and in their confrontation new forms of knowledge arise, but this is never given the character of a dialectic proper. In Hegel, a richer account of goal-directed dialectical movement is given, although it is put at the service of Hegel's metaphysical conception of *Geist,* which develops in only one direction: toward greater freedom, receptivity, and openness.

Paradoxical Dialectics in Social Theory

What I take to be useful in the Kantian-Hegelian concept of dialectics is this: Knowledge systems are fundamentally antinomian, founded on paradox, and dialectical. In the attempt to overcome contradiction and achieve the goal, new knowledge structures are generated in moments of integration. Since the goal cannot be reached, however, such moments are temporary, as oppositions once more assert themselves. Temporary integrations create new knowledge structures of paradox, and the whole process begins all over. Of what use is this conception of knowledge to social theory? We must now consider how Weber and Freud develop dialectics, Weber in the concept of "rationalization" and Freud in "ambivalence." Then we will be in a position to synthesize them, and apply the synthesis to the understanding of a cultural knowledge system.

FROM KANT TO WEBER: THE PARADOXICAL-DIALECTIC
OF RATIONALIZATION

Weber defined "rationalization" in different ways, using it in his early work to refer to the maximization of the effectiveness of action in the pursuit of predetermined goals. In his later work, however, he strongly emphasized the fact that different activities could be rationalized in different directions, depending on worldview.[4] As value standpoints become increasingly ex-

---

4. From *The Protestant Ethic and the Spirit of Capitalism,* written around 1904, to his death in 1920, Weber became increasingly interested in the different "value standpoints" from

plicit and their implications for action developed and made more rational, they also become more distinct as the objectives toward which progress in a particular domain (e.g., religion, music, explanation) is directed. The logic which governs this process is always of a certain kind, one Weber called Eigengesetzlichkeit or "inner logic," a term with strong Kantian resonances (Mommsen 1987). Weber's insight was not only that unique value intensifications and processual logics exist for diverse domains, but also that they are dialectically determined, and ultimately, paradox-based.

Let us see how this works in one of Weber's studies. In the *Sociology of Music,* Weber tries to describe the conditions for the development of Occidental music. His central question is this: Why did polyphonic and harmonic-homophonic music, as well as the modern tonal system, develop only in the Occident, in spite of the fact that polyvocality was fairly widespread? Weber demonstrates that the development of Western music is premised on a theory of music that foregrounds the principles of harmony and tonality, whereas everywhere else the principle of melodic distance is the most widely practiced. Western musical theory thus led to the development of a harmonic chord system as its "goal" and therefore took the form of a "rationally closed unity" (Weber 1958a:6).

The problem is that this system, with its culturally specific goal, is internally contradictory. The demand for consistency which musical theory makes cannot be fulfilled, and this becomes increasingly apparent. Thus "unavoidable irrationalities" arise that disturb this rationally closed unity. Such events in turn trigger new processes of rationalization directed to the end of overcoming inconsistency. The significance of the breaking through of rational inconsistencies provides the dynamic for development toward the culturally defined goal of harmony and totality. This is a dialectical movement in the sense I earlier described, even though Weber does not call it that or refer to dialectical theory.

Let us examine this argument more closely. The harmonic chord system, according to Weber, was bound to come up against several "irrational" obstacles in its development, in pursuit of its goal. In meeting these obstacles, musical theory was able to create a "greater variety of tonalities," which did not permanently resolve the oppositions, but did temporarily integrate them. Since Western music is rationalized according to harmonic chords, the octave had to be divided up into unequal tonal steps. The result was a

---

which knowledge systems could be rationalized. This interest reached its fullest development in his studies of the great world religions Hinduism and Judaism, and in his much neglected study of musical traditions.

series of notes and semitones that were different from each other, due to a strict application of the "harmonic" principle of division. This situation might have remained as it was, were it not for the fact that this inconsistency led directly to other difficulties and to the "infringement" of other "demands" in the theory of music.[5] There were other inconsistencies, too. With each inconsistency, a movement to resolve it resulted in the development of musical theory, and so on, to the present, when, presumably, the same force is still at work.

Weber used music as a test case for ideas that he was developing in the sociology of religion. The connection is the finding that a similar dialectical logic, or process of rationalization, governs both. The more knowledge systems follow the demand for consistency (a culturally specific goal), becoming more systematic in their own terms, the more likely they are to come into conflict with their own principles. This conflict, in turn, leads to compromises or the combination of elements that contradict each other, resembling what Hegel called supersessions (*aufheben*). Formation of dialectical compromises is the essential characteristic of most historical configurations. In the introduction to the *Sociology of Religion,* Weber says:

> Neither religions nor people are open and shut cases. They were historical configurations, and not logical or psychological constructions that were free of contradictions. Oftentimes they harboured a multitude of motives which, if they were all affirmed consistently and at the same time, would obstruct each other or even collide head-on. That they were "consistent" with each other was the exception, not the rule. (1991:291).

Weber believed that consistency is nevertheless a "dictate" of human thought, and as such, it must have a historical impact. How, then, do religious systems change through time? Weber proposed that for each system a dynamic tension exists between "the power of prophetic charisma" and "the enduring habits of the masses" (1993:79). These two influences oppose each other, dialectically. It is the role of religious specialists to attempt

---

5. As Schluchter notes: "One difficulty, for example, arose when the 'natural' leading note of the major scale had to be created 'artificially' for the minor scale in order to produce a dominant seventh chord for this particular key. This was achieved by raising the seventh note (transition from pure to a harmonic major). Yet this, in turn, led to a further problem; the tonal steps adjacent to this key became too large to satisfy harmonic sensibilities. The problem was solved by a reduction of these tonal steps (melodic minor). Meeting the demands of the major scale with this construction thus 'forcibly' led to a deviation from the pure principles of harmony (Schluchter 1987:93–94).

to systematize these oppositions, and thus to rationalize them, causing the religion as a system to develop.

More important to Weber was the paradox of ethical values within religious systems. Weber identified two internally consistent types: the ethic of responsibility and the ethic of conscience, each understandable in its own terms but in constant tension with the other. The ethic of responsibility advocates action with regard to consequences while the ethic of conscience demands that action be taken with respect to imperatives. No amount of argumentation can overcome this tension, and this, for Weber, was one of the "driving forces of all religious evolution" (1993:123) and of what we might choose to term "religious dialectics."

Irreconcilable oppositions of the sort Weber identified in music and religion inform his description of the two types of rational action, and of formal and material rationality. Efficiency may conflict with justice, precise calculation may detract from achieving an objective. Distributive justice may oppose production, while economic rationality may generate inequality. As Weber put it when discussing money calculation in relation to property distribution: "Formal and substantive rationality, no matter by what standard the latter is measured, are always in principle separate things, no matter that in many (and under certain very artificial assumptions even in all) cases they may coincide empirically" (Weber 1968:108).

For Weber, paradoxes were at the center of the debates about capitalism and socialism. All were ultimately unresolvable due to the manner in which they had been defined. But with each attempt at resolution, a new development took place. History is a fundamentally dialectical process involving the movement of paradoxically related oppositions, through repeated (but partial) integrations, toward a cultural defined goal that can never be reached. This provides part of the dynamic for change—the part Weber termed "inner"—and acts in combinations with other influences, economic and ecological (which he termed "outer") to produce historical development.

One cannot know the rationality of a system without knowing the values or goals which that system upholds and directs itself to. No prediction can be made about what those values will be: They can be anything. But Weber himself was concerned with two variations: Oriental and Occidental religious values, and the knowledge systems they inform.

Framed in these terms, the comparison to Oriental religion reveals that in the case Weber found most illuminating, classical Hinduism, values provided a completely different goal for rationalization: world rejection, as opposed to world mastery. A progression in the development of this value had taken place, resulting ultimately in the Upanishadic conception of karma: a completely rationalized ethical position which formally related cause and effect. This is what made it comparable to Calvinism. In terms of rational consistency the doctrines of predestination and karma were very much the same, even though they led in different directions—the first toward the goal of world rejection, the second toward the goal of world mastery. What this means is not simply that the content of action described as rationalized may be different depending upon whether we are examining a legal or religious value sphere, but that the *direction* which rationalization takes may also be different. It is impossible to understand the structure of knowledge without understanding the *directive goals* in terms of which it is rationalized. Since values have an irrational aspect, they must be examined with the instruments appropriate to that domain.

This is the problem. Even though Weber spoke often of "needs" as the basis of rationalization, i.e., the "need" for order, he never pursued this insight very far. This left "needs" without any basis in human experience. At worst, Weber can be accused of recapitulating the evolutionary assumption of the innately human drive to reason that only Western man successfully embodies. More fairly, and, I think, more accurately, one can see Weber on the brink of an important insight, one which he never quite comes to—the insight that would have led him to a much deeper engagement with Freud.

Weber was writing at a time which has been called "the recovery of the unconscious" (Hughes 1958:105). Weber cited Karl Jaspers's *Allgemeine Psychopathologie* (1965) on the first page of *Economy and Society,* later acknowledging that the kind of psychology Jaspers represents, "which employs the method of subjective understanding," could provide "decisively important services" (1968:19). The time was ripe for Weber to recognize the affinities between his own view and that of the psychologists of the unconscious. Quite clearly, his thinking took him a long way beyond the idea of purposive rationality or means-end thinking. But the link was never made, possibly because of Weber's personal animosity toward one of Freud's less distinguished disciples, Otto Gross. It is therefore to Freud that we must turn to see the Kantian philosophy of dialectical paradox reworked in a form that makes it serviceable as a theory of motivated knowledge.

FROM KANT TO FREUD: THE PARADOXICAL-DIALECTIC OF AMBIVALENCE

The theory of rationalization exposes oppositional dynamics and reveals the cultural goals toward which they are directed. This is extremely useful, but incomplete, since it does not comprehend deep motivation or emotional orientation. We must turn to Freud, not only because he offers an account of motivation, but also (and mainly) because his account of motivation is congruent with Weber's. Both are conflict-based, based on the dynamic power of paradox to motivate the development of dialectical systems. The difference is that whereas Weber chose to examine this process socially, Freud related it to the dynamics of unconscious desires.

Around 1910 Freud introduced the concept of "ambivalence" (crediting Bleuler) to describe the mingled emotional experiences of unconscious thought. All intimate relationships, he argued, produce some degree of it, from children's identification with parents to clients' transference with analysts (Freud 1950, 1960, 1965, 1966). The prototypical ambivalence-generating experience is the Oedipal. A child loves a parent of the same sex, but hates him (for Freud the child of exemplification was always male) because of competition for the love and attention of the parent of the opposite sex. The ambivalence is resolved in the process through which the child identifies with the same-sex parent and, in the case of the boy, incorporates the moral authority of the father as his own superego.

Identification does not actually dispel ambivalence, because the mind is permanently divided between conflicting entities, the one a repository of instinctual urges and inner desires (id) and the other a guardian of moral right and imposer of restraint (superego). The competition between them helps to constitute a mediate entity, the ego, which must attempt to balance the interests of the two sides so that life is lived realistically. Ambivalence is the sensation of this inner tension, which the ego attempts to resolve. The varieties of resolution are multiple, involving compromises and displacement, and continuous in one form or another, since the oppositional conflicts that call them into being cannot be resolved in most cases, at least not in any ultimate sense.

The vision of the mind as a locus of conflict between opposing entities gradually came to assume great importance for Freud, as he transformed the opposites first into "principles" (pleasure vs. reality) and then into elemental forces (life and death, Eros and Thanatos). Life was drawn to both, but could be lived only ambivalently, somewhere in the middle, if it were not to drift into pathology or perversion. It is known that Freud reported to his friend Lou Andreas-Salome as early as 1919 that he was reading Schopenhauer, the philosopher whose skeptical view of human nature did not attract much attention until late in the nineteenth century (Gay 1988). This is significant, because Schopenhauer was a Hegelian and may have inspired Freud with a deeper appreciation for dialectical theory.

Indeed, the Hegelian "tone" to his writing is not difficult to detect,

for when Freud speaks of the instincts turning into each other he recalls
Hegel's sense of the dialectic. In *Beyond the Pleasure Principle,* Freud states:

> In the obscurity that reigns at present in the theory of the instincts, it
> would be unwise to reject any idea that promises to throw light on it. We
> started out from the great opposition between the life and death
> instincts. Now object-love presents us with a second example of a
> similar polarity—that between love (or affection) and hate (or aggres-
> siveness). If only we could succeed in relating these two polarities to
> each other and in deriving one from the other! (1961a:47)

Of course Freud did relate them, showing that love was often mixed with
aggression and that aggression often had as its object a desire to unite with
the object, albeit regressively and by force.

Freud was thinking dialectically, and if not directly reliant on Kant for
this insight, he certainly borrowed on the tradition Kant began. It is interesting how much that is specific to Freud's argument—I refer mainly to
the concept of ambivalence—Kant *himself* actually anticipated. It is worth
pausing for a moment to consider this point more closely.

If knowledge is built up through the interplay of contradictions, toward
what is this process directed and how is it propelled? The answer, for Kant,
was a combination of discomfort and desire: the discomfort that results
from the contemplation of contrarieties and the desire to experience the
pleasure of their resolution in some kind of unity. This process was assumed
to be natural, grounded in the very nature of the ideas themselves and thus
independent of psychological reality or the facts of human existence. It is
necessary for reason, however embodied, to seek to unify concepts in a
way that both preserves and abolishes them, thereby avoiding their self-
contradictoriness. For Kant, unity and generality are thus the goal toward
which dialectical reason is directed, and movement toward this goal is propelled by necessity itself, which has no basis other than that it *is.*

In Kant one finds a strong anticipation of Freud in a theory of motivation which is sensitive to the *effect* of contradictory concepts on thought
and feeling. This is not something one finds in most of Kant's principal
works, in which he eschews all forms of psychology. It comes up mainly
in the very last work he published, *Anthropology from a Pragmatic Point of
View,* although there are anticipations in both the *Foundations of the Metaphysics of Morals* and *Critique of Judgment.* Like Freud, Kant challenged the
classical Greek view of happiness, which held that humans are capable of
achieving contentment. No increase in reason, in knowledge and its forms,
can create happiness. The problem is that "it is not his nature to rest and be

contented with the possession and enjoyment of anything whatever" (*Critique of Judgment,* section 83). Nothing can produce happiness because of "the inconsistency of his own natural dispositions."

This state is not merely an accidental or temporary one, Kant suggests, or one that can be removed by the increase of knowledge, because it is an essential aspect of the human condition. "Man feels in himself a powerful counterpoise against all commands of duty," and "from this a natural dialectic arises" (1990:405). This "natural dialectic" consists of the opposition between the two principles within man, the moral and the selfish. If either one were missing, we would not have a human being. The moral principle by itself would produce an angel and the self principle by itself would produce a devil. For Kant, there must be a dialectical relationship between these two contrarieties which cannot and must not be resolved.

In the *Critique of Judgment* Kant develops his theory of taste and aesthetic perception. The concept of dualities plays a significant role. The experience of the sublime, for example, is different from the experience of beauty because of the role oscillation plays. In the experience of the sublime, individuals are both attracted and terrified by some phenomenon or conception, as, for example, in viewing a deep crevasse and alternately approaching and stepping back from the edge. Kant presents this oscillation as the basic property of experience: ". . . the mind is not merely attracted by the object but is ever being alternately repelled, the satisfaction in the sublime does not so much involve positive pleasure as admiration or respect, which rather deserves to be called a negative pleasure" (section 23). Further: "The mind feels itself moved in the representation of the sublime. . . . This movement may (especially in its beginnings) be compared to a vibration, i.e., to a quickly alternating attraction toward, and repulsion from, the same object" (section 26).

Kant generalizes on his analysis of the sublime and makes the "vibration . . . quickly alternating attraction toward, and repulsion from, the same object" into an ordinary fixed property of human nature. In the *Anthropology,* this idea is developed still further (Kant 1974). Life is a movement between opposites; contradiction causes discomfort and pain; direction and movement result, but must end by recreating the oppositions that inspire them. Consider the following passages:

> To feel alive, to enjoy ourselves, is the same as to feel ourselves
> constantly impelled to leave our present state (which must therefore be a
> pain that recurs just as often as the present). (333)

> Pain is the spur of activity. (233)

> Enjoyment is the feeling of life being promoted, pain of its being
> hindered. But, as physicians have noted, life is a continuous play of their
> antagonism. (231)

> Contentment . . . is unattainable for man: he cannot attain it either from
> the moral point of view (being content with his good conduct) or from
> the pragmatic point of view (being satisfied with the well-being he tried
> to secure by skill and prudence). (234–35)

Clearly, we have come a long way from the "antinomies" which Kant first
considered logically necessary with no dependence on human feeling or
the facts of the human condition. But what is the relationship between the
two, between the "transcendental dialectic" and the "vibration" of opposites in human feeling?

As Kant moved from the consideration of "pure" reason to practical
and aesthetic judgment, he was forced to consider more and more of what
we would now call "psychological" processes. In doing so, he transformed
what were originally purely logical constructs, the antinomies, into human
feeling states with deep motivational content. The antinomies were psy-
chologized. Kant came as close as rationalist philosophy would allow to
formulating a theory of "ambivalence." It is therefore not surprising that
when Freud spoke of his enduring interest in philosophy, he referred specifically to his fascination with Kant (Gay 1988).

TOWARD A SYNTHESIS OF WEBER AND FREUD: DIALECTICAL
PARADOX AND THE RATIONALIZATION OF AMBIVALENCE

The theories of rationalization and ambivalence are differently realized
extensions, sociological and psychological, of the paradoxical-dialectical
theory formulated first by Immanuel Kant. Their synthesis can be stated,
briefly, as follows.

First, explanatory knowledge systems exist which are *dialectical*, made
up of oppositions and moved by the effort to resolve them. Second, dialectical knowledge systems are dynamic, directed to culturally defined objectives which act as *goals*. They are thus "rationalized" in one of the senses
in which Weber uses the term. Third, dialectical knowledge systems are
based on *paradox*. From this, two consequences follow. First, the process
of rationalization is directed to culturally defined goals which can never
be reached because the paradox which constitutes them is unresolvable.
That is why cultural knowledge systems possess continuity and remain
inherently problematic. Second, because unresolvable paradox generates

conflict, it becomes the basis of *cultural ambivalence*. Knowledge structures temporarily resolve ambivalence, but because they are temporary, the dialectical movement continues through repeated revision and reformulation.

To summarize: *Knowledge systems are paradoxical-dialectical systems, rationalized with respect to some goal, and motivated by the desire to resolve ambivalences which follow from the fact that they are paradoxical.*

What would a theory synthetic of Weber and Freud look like when applied to an explanatory system of some complexity? Three criteria must be fulfilled. *First*, it must be shown that the explanatory system framed in divinatory terms is a highly rationalized system, directed to a culturally defined goal that cannot be reached. *Second*, the system must be dialectically constructed and based on paradox, so that the process of rationalization consists of a constant back-and-forth action between contradictory opposites in search of temporary moments of resolution in pursuit of the culturally defined goal. *Third*, contradiction must be accompanied by conflicted emotional orientations and hence the cultural ambivalence which the divinatory system both represents and attempts to resolve. If these three criteria are fulfilled, then we shall conclude that the hypothesis is valid and that the explanatory system is a paradoxical-dialectical knowledge system.

ETHNOGRAPHIC CONTEXT

The following is a brief ethnographic overview, to orient the reader to the southeastern coast of India and the Telugu fishing village that is the subject of this research. It is worth keeping in mind Nadel's point that such an overview, if considered something easily within the ethnographer's grasp, is purely a myth (Nadel 1957:153). Without pretense of anything else, then, I begin with what the fishing village has looked like to me during the twenty years I have been working there.

Fishing villages dot the northern coast of Andhra Pradesh, one of the four southern Indian states where Dravidian languages are spoken. Jalaripet, a large fishing village near the large port city of Visakhapatnam, is on a bay that offers a good harbor and ideal protection from rough seas. Some people say that the bay is called Lawson's Bay after an eighteenth-century English pirate, John Lawson, who used it as a shelter between raids. Broad areas of sandy hills divide the habitations into three groups. The largest is Jalaripet itself, inhabited by members of the Jalari caste. The second, the northern, is a small Jalari village, Endada. At the northern extremity is Vada Vidhi, inhabited by members of another fishing caste, the Vada Bajilu.

To the north, east, and south are the weathered remains of a large

Fishing boats (*teppalu*) heading out into the Bay of Bengal

coastal plateau, now eroded into networks of hills and valleys and stripped of trees. The hills are known as the Eastern Ghats. They surround the fishing villages as well as the rest of an extensive coastal plain that extends for miles to the north and south. This broad expanse of flat land is occupied by Visakhapatnam, one of the three fastest-growing cities in India. The city began as a small port and minor trade town, developed by the British in the mid-seventeenth century as a factory and administrative center. It now fills the whole of the coastal plain, and its suburbs and satellites are expanding far beyond. The commercial sector is to the south, where the port and harbor are located, but the residential sectors have developed in all directions, most notably to the north, where the fishing villages are. Because the north is farthest removed from the polluted commercial and industrialized south, the city's wealthier and elite classes have settled there, conforming to a pattern begun by the British. Here, "slab" houses with compound walls topped with broken glass exist directly adjacent to the fishing villages, barely a stone's throw away from the Jalaris who have occupied their coastal hamlet for centuries. The site occupied by the fishing village is now prime commercial real estate, worth a fortune.

The principal Jalari village, Jalaripet, occupies a small piece of coastal

Fisherman

Preparing boat for departure

land. The population of the village is around 6,000. Houses are circular and built of compacted dirt reinforced with sticks interwoven to provide support up to a height of about six or seven feet. A center pole supports a roof made of a latticework of toddy tree trunks, split and tied with toddy rope fiber, and overlaid by layers of toddy leaves. The roof must be replaced every three or four years. Each house (*illu*) is surrounded by a wide porch (*gummam*). People spend considerable time on the porch because it is accessible to breezes and sunlight. Part of the porch is enclosed to make a small room that is accessible through a single door adjacent to the entrance of the main room. The small room is called the *pancotu*, or "workplace," a word with a double meaning, since the room is both a place both for making things and making love. The floors of the house and the outside porch are made of compressed dirt overspread with buffalo dung. The senior woman of the household resurfaces the floor every week and whenever there is a household ritual.

There are two kinds of houses. The *peddillu*, or "big house," is the residence of the head of a patrilineage group and the site for the group's rituals. The other kind of house is the *gadillu*, or "room house," occupied by adult male lineage members (probably the brothers of the headman) and

Fisherman

Out to sea

their families. The gadillu may be physically separate from the *peddillu,* but indistinguishable from it except for the absence of a spirit shrine, or *sadaru.* Or the gadillu may be connected to the big house, as a sort of additional room.

The interior of the big house is divided into two parts separated by a low wall extending across the middle, in front of the entrance, to a point about three-quarters of the way toward the opposite wall. The patriline senior and his family sleep and eat in the area in front of this wall, called the *ammavari goda* ("goddess wall"). Behind the wall is the *ammavari gadi* ("goddess room"), where the *sadaru* is located. The shrine is a low mound of whitewashed dirt in the corner of the goddess room, in an area least accessible to casual observation. Small clay lamps are placed on a series of dirt platforms, each representing one of the several patriline spirits, including goddesses (*ammavarus*) and ancestors (*pedda vallu*). On the wall behind the shrine there are one or more yellow-red circles painted with a combination of tumeric and *kunkum* (lamp black). Offerings to the spirits are made by applying a dot of the tumeric-*kunkum* mixture to each circle. A mat made of woven palm leaves hangs down from the rafter in front of the shrine to cover it from view. Other objects typically found nearby include colorful calendar pictures of the classical Hindu deities (which for the most part the Jalari cannot identify), boxes containing ritual implements, sacrificial swords and axes, braziers, and a peacock feather whisk. Also there is always a *cupa rayi*, or "seeing stone," a rough-hewn rock with a string attached at one end, and a *pasupu kommu* (tumeric root), used with the stone in performing a kind of divination. The seeing stone is the property of the lineage but operated only by the *dasudu*, a medium or shaman, who comes on invitation when family members are sick or unable to catch fish.

A room house differs from a big house only in lacking the central dividing wall and the goddess room, which the wall protects. Otherwise they are identical. Neither contains much furniture beyond the occasional rope bed, and sometimes a chair or two. Against the far wall, opposite the front door and near the entrance to the goddess room, there may be a wall shelf where precious objects, such as brass cups, are placed on display. Directly below this and in full view of anyone standing at the door are the family's storage vessels (for water and rice), made of clay, aluminum, or brass. Both the contents of the shelf and the vessels below are visible to visitors and indicative of the family's wealth. The village headman (*kula pedda*) has the largest number of these. In a society in which people regard with great suspicion any display of affluence, these are among the only symbols of prosperity present in the home.

Each house's territorial limit—the land area over which it has control—extends only a few feet beyond its porch, somewhat more if the house is a *peddillu* (to accommodate meetings and rituals) and somewhat less if the house is a *gadillu*. Common areas are few and confined to three places in or near the village: the beach, where men build boats and make nets; the main road, where women sit and sell vegetables and fish; and the compound in front of the village headman's house, where large village meetings are held.

The southern and northern borders of Jalaripet are marked by a sudden transition from inhabited to uninhabited space. In the latter area, full of creeping vines and tall grass, the Jalaris perform three vital functions: defecation, burial of the dead, and worship of the village-wide goddesses. The size of the uninhabited zone is now less than it used to be, due to encroachment by new housing developments. Yet what is left retains, for the Jalaris, a forbidding aspect. Children never go there, and adults are afraid to walk in it after dark or at noon—times when various malign spirits, including those of suicides and women who died in childbirth, are said to be active.

To the north, toward the Jalari burying ground, are the carved stone images of three village goddesses. Their names are unknown to the majority of villagers. Most of the year they are overgrown by vegetation and surrounded by piles of human waste, making them hard to reach. On their yearly festival days, the village *pujari* (priest) builds small palm-leaf huts for them. The huts are then allowed to collapse, and the area reverts to its usual desolation.

To the south, the land is broken by rolling sand dunes which conceal the only permanent goddess temples built by the villagers. One is the temple of the goddess Gatilamma, built in 1957 following the last cholera epidemic. The other, a temple to the goddess Ramanamma, was built in 1964 after an outbreak of smallpox. Both were constructed in the traditional South Indian style. There is a third temple near the beach, and very different from the other two. Dedicated to the goddess Mahankalamma, it is a small palm-leaf hut situated on top of a large mound of stones very near the beach. There is no central icon. No one remembers how long the temple has been there. On one side there is a flagpole called Gandhi Maharaja, the name some people say refers to the husband of the goddess.

There are no municipal water taps and only two wells for the entire village. Women who collect the day's water supply usually prefer to collect water from private taps in the adjacent suburbs, where wealthy house-owners charge them a fee. There are few public amenities. The government recently installed fluorescent tube lights along the streets, but none work. Electrical connections for home use became available in 1984, but only one family (the headman's) has the money to pay for installation. The only government-provided service of long-standing use is the pavement along the main road. Villagers use it as a surface on which to dry fish.

This was the picture of Jalaripet as it looked until the night of December 26, 1984, when a fire swept through the village and destroyed most of it. The municipal government immediately announced that the land on which the village stood would be "reclaimed" for development purposes and the villagers relocated where they could be "rehabilitated." People were given 150 rupees each and told to make other arrangements, until new slab houses could be built for them. Ten years later, the village looks a very different place. The Jalaris kept most of their land and received individual titles to it. The government provided low-interest loans for the construction of concrete houses, installed electric lines, and built a couple of new roads. Meanwhile, the housing developments surrounding the village expanded, and now come to within a few yards of the village boundary. The Jalaris know what their own land is worth, and since they now have title to individual allotments (village land had been held in common previously), they can sell it off to the highest bidder. The result is that although in 1994 the village is still mostly Jalari, the trend to outside ownership and infiltration by other caste groups is well established and increasing rapidly.

The day is soon approaching when "Jalaripet," as such, will cease to exist, having been replaced by a multi-caste urban community of transient and semi-transient families from all over Andhra Pradesh.

APPLICATION

Starting from Kakar (1981, 1989) and others (Erikson 1966; Obeyesekere 1984, 1990; Roland 1988; Samanta 1994; Trawick 1990), I shall claim that the desire for fusion, or coalescence, is the goal toward which knowledge systems, such as myth and divination, are directed in the Telugu fishing caste (Jalari) community that is the subject of my analysis. This goal foregrounds the state of "unity" where otherwise there might be separation, and emphasizes shared dependency over achieved states of independence. Reasons why this is so are a matter of debate, but as Trawick notes, "the manifestations of these feelings in Indian superstructure and behavior are too massive to ignore" (1990:171). Knowledge systems rationalized with respect to this goal function to preserve unity where it exists and to restore it in circumstances where it has been lost, either directly or by displacement to a substitute.

"Fusion" does not imply that Indians never recognize or seek to elaborate purely individual aspects of personality. Some scholars have taken this view and have argued that Indians lack an abstract sense of the individual as an integrated whole (Marriott 1976, 1989). I agree with Mines (1994) that Indians do recognize individuality as an essential feature of ordinary life and, indeed, display a keen awareness of the unique aspects of personality. This awareness, however, is distinct in several respects from Western notions of the individual and of personality.

In the first place, the desire for fusion is not unproblematic, since the means available for its fulfillment are contradictory. Kakar (1981:34) notes that "the essential psychological theme of Hindu culture is the polarity of fusion and separation . . . a dynamic counterpoint between two opposite needs, to merge into and to be differentiated from the 'Other,' where the 'Other' is all which is not the self." But that is only part of the problem, since the means for achieving fusion conflict not only internally but with each other. In the South Indian culture that is the subject of this analysis, the problem locates itself in sibling relations, in the choices brothers and sisters are forced to make between different forms of sibling unity and separation. It is in the domain of sibling relations that the work of achieving fusion is supposed to be done, but it cannot be done given the paradoxes embedded in the sibling relationship.

The reason why the goal cannot be reached has to do with the role of sibling relations in South India. According to one set of norms, brothers should remain together as members of the same agnatic group, living in the same house and sharing its resources. But this is impossible. Fraternal interests diverge as brothers establish their own families, and eventually they split up, each to found his own agnatic group. This is the paradox. As brothers fulfill their chief obligation as members of the same patrilineal group, by creating constituent families, they must eventually destroy the group, once their constituent families become established.

According to the other set of norms, brothers and sisters should cooperate with each other as givers and takers of each other's children in cross-cousin marriage. It is a neatly symmetrical system, at least in theory, but the symmetry is disturbed by the exigencies of each family's circumstances. Either there are not enough marriage partners to go around, or the cross-cousins who should marry don't like each other; or there is competition among brothers and sisters for each other's children. One way or another, something is bound to go wrong, imperiling the ideal of cross-sex sibling harmony. This is the other paradox. Although brothers and sisters want to remain tightly linked, they are prevented from doing so by the very nature of the bond that relates them.

The norms I have spoken of conflict not only internally but with each other. The accompanying chart represents these multiple dialectics diagramatically (see Figure 1). The fact that South Indians cannot simultaneously and satisfactorily fulfill all normative obligations in their roles as brothers and sisters is the source of very deep cultural ambivalences, finding expression in a variety of cultural forms, including myth and divination.

Divination recognizes that *all* problems have their origin in the paradoxes of the sibling relationship. Divinatory explanation consists of identifying the problem and devising a strategy for setting it right—that is, for restoring the unity of these particular relationships, since "unity" is the

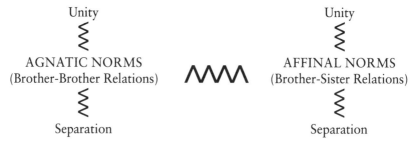

Figure 1. The dialectics of paradox in jalari kinship

paramount directive goal. Jalaris recognize two sources of social dispute as prototypic precipitants of spiritual attack: 1) the agnatic group, composed of male patriline members (prototypically, brothers); and 2) the affinal group, composed of married brothers and sisters whose lineages maintain cross-cousin alliance relationships with each other. I use the word *prototypic* to refer to what seem to be core Jalari understandings: While *agnatic* and *affinal* in fact include additional categories, for the Jalaris they tend to focus on siblings. Disputes are outcomes of situations which arise predictably and inevitably within and between relations of these two groups.

In agnatic groups, disputes occur when brothers marry and again when their children approach marriageable age. Because each of these two crisis moments intensifies, in different ways, each brother's desire to create his own, independent patrilineal group, disputes arise at precisely those points when joint actions are essential, e.g., in offering to the household spirits (*ammavallu*) which represent group solidarity. Between affinal groups, united by cross-cousin marriage, similar crises develop when joint responsibilities arise, as in the exchange of money and in the making of cross-cousin marriage alliances.

Patrilineality and alliance are extensions from fraternal and cross-sex sibling relations and constitute the dialectics of South Indian kinship, as well as the determining nexus of the social disputes which culminate in divinatory explanation. Not surprisingly, there are two typical explanatory scenarios ("scripts" or "models") which must be evaluated in every divinatory session. One is the agnatic and the other is the affinal scenario. They describe the prototypic ways (fraternal) agnatic and (cross-sibling) affinal relations go awry, leading to attacks by the household goddesses and subsequent distress (usually in the form of illness). There are *only* two scenarios, and a choice must be made between them in divination. Inevitably, one or the other is found to be the cause. The directive goal is to put the relationship back together, to restore sibling relations in fulfillment of the ideal of fusion or unity. Solutions are always temporary, however, because the contradictions informing the process remain unaltered. That is why crises are bound to recur, ensuring that the social dialectic they constitute continues as long as the unreachable goal of fusion remains culturally salient.

FROM INDIA TO NEW GUINEA AND BACK AGAIN

Before continuing the analysis of a South Indian culture, the next chapter will digress by way of New Guinea to demonstrate that the approach just described has antecedents in the work of another anthropologist, Gregory

Bateson. In part the purpose of this digression is strategic. I want to show that I am not alone in thinking that dialectical theory is relevant to the integration of cognition and affect in a combined theory of motivated knowledge. Bateson came very close to developing such a theory. By pushing his ideas a bit further, and using Weber and Freud to pull them together, the nature of this incipient theory can be revealed, and then reapplied to the analysis of the ethnographic material Bateson himself presents in his classic work *Naven*.

It is also important for my purposes to show that the theory of motivated knowledge can be applied cross-culturally, and that in at least two places — New Guinea and South India — it can produce fresh insights. Elsewhere (Nuckolls 1995) I take it even farther afield, to the Pacific atoll of Ifaluk, to show how it can be used to achieve a partial integration of Lutz's ethnopsychology and Spiro's psychoanalytic approach. I also apply it to the study of American psychiatric categories and practices, to show that the internal dialectic of core American cultural values — independence and dependence — creates and sustains the peculiar organization of nosological terms and their distribution across gender (Nuckolls 1993b, forthcoming). Here, however, I shall limit the discussion only to New Guinea, and to Bateson.

To most of those who read him, Bateson is a prescient and sensitive thinker. For a person who contributed so much to communication science, systems theory, and psychotherapy, as well as to anthropology, this is no small achievement. His legacy within psychological anthropology is not great, however, and that is surprising, given the topics he addressed and the integrations he proposed. The next chapter can be read as an attempt to recover the legacy of Bateson's theory of motivated knowledge, and to set the stage for its wider application.

Chapter Three

Twisted Thinking and a Dash of Hegelian Dialectic: The Misplaced Legacy of Gregory Bateson

What makes you great is that you cannot end,
And never to begin you are predestined
Your song revolves as does the starry dome,
Beginning, end for ever more the same:
And what the middle brings will prove to be
What last remains and was initially.
    (Goethe, "Unbounded"*)*

The dualism constituted by the opposition of cultural cognition and deep desire is all the more intractable given the failure on the part of those who seek a synthesis (e.g., Holland 1992; Hutchins 1987) to consider the history of past attempts. This is all the more striking in the case of attempts which might have been considered extremely promising, especially in light of current interests (Horowitz 1988, 1991; Westen 1991, 1992, 1994). Of particular importance in this regard is the early work of Gregory Bateson, whose writing on the dialectics of "ethos" and "eidos" offer a possible solution, although not one Bateson himself fully formulated.

According to Bateson, *ethos* includes among its many possible meanings reference to a constellation of concepts that infuses "culture" with affective tone or emotional identity. It refers to the standardization of a culture's affective and emotional aspects, in contrast to what he called *eidos,* the standardization of a culture's informational and cognitive aspects, its logical structures and systems of inference. "The sum," wrote Bateson, "of ethos and eidos, plus such general characteristics of a culture as may be due to other types of standardization, together make up the configuration" (1958:33). By *configuration,* of course, Bateson had in mind the concept formulated by Benedict in *Patterns of Culture,* which Bateson read in manuscript while he was still camping on the Sepik River.

Bateson took the concept of ethos, however, not from Benedict but from Radcliffe-Brown, who never used it himself but suggested it to Bateson at a time when the latter was struggling to develop a new approach to the study of culture. Bateson was bored, he later wrote, with the conventional study of "formal details" and more interested in studying the "feel" of culture (1972:81). While still in New Guinea, he read Doughty's *Travels in Arabia Deserta,* a classic two-volume work of cultural description, and was struck by the author's success in capturing the affective tone of the people. But Doughty had achieved only a literary or artistic representation of the "feel" of the culture. "I was more interested," wrote Bateson, "in a scientific analysis of it" (1972:82). So he appropriated the term *ethos* to refer to standardized emotional configurations, in contrast to *eidos,* the standardization of cognitive configurations. Culture, the combination of both, was best captured through analogy: "The river molds the banks and the banks guide the river. Similarly, the ethos models the cultural structure and is guided by it" (1972:83).

The meanings of ethos and eidos depend on the term *standardization,* which in Bateson's work generally refers to the recurrent patterns which organize and represent feelings and thoughts. Standardized emotions are deep and strongly motivating emotional orientations. They constitute a cultural ethos. Standardized thoughts are habitually associated ideas, located in memory and available to recall, which organize and direct thinking. They constitute a cultural eidos. Standardized emotions and standardized thoughts are general, hence, common to everyone, and impose a conformitory pressure, such that differences tend to be assimilated to a central exemplar or, as Bateson put it, preferred type. The hypothesis is circular, like the system it describes: "It is supposed that the pervading characteristics of the culture not only express, but also promote the standardization of the individuals" (1972:83).

ETHOS: THE STANDARDIZATION OF EMOTIONAL ASPECTS

Taken together, standardized emotions constitute an ethos, but what are such emotions in themselves? If they are no different from the terms which represent them, then, by "standardization," Bateson must have meant the organization of emotion terms in cultural scenarios. But that would be a "cognitive" interpretation, and since the whole point of introducing ethos was to distinguish it from eidos, its cognitive counterpart, the conflation of emotion with emotion terms must be ruled out. The other possibility is that the emotions which make up an ethos are deeply embedded motivational orientations, which people share by virtue of their common socialization and early childhood experiences. In this interpretation, the emphasis is decidedly develomental, and there are Freudian resonances. Did Bateson intend that?

In the epilogue to the second edition of the book, Bateson boldly asserted that "*Naven* was written almost without benefit of Freud" (1958: 282). There is no reason to doubt this, but his remark on what would have followed if *Naven* had been written with benefit of Freud is surely exaggerated: "I would have indulged in an orgy of interpreting symbols, and this would have distracted me from the more important problems of interpersonal and intergroup process" (1958:282). One suspects that Bateson wished to put his readers at ease, many of whom would have had only the greatest distaste for Freud. Official psychoanalysis was synonymous (then and now) with the sexual decipherment of symbols and with the psychological dynamics of "needs" and "wants." This was a narrow and necessarily reductionist enterprise and one that anthropologists early on decided to oppose.[1] We are left with a puzzle, and perhaps a little doubt, as to what Bateson meant by "*almost* without benefit of Freud." How much is "almost"?

We shall return to this question later. For the present let us consider the analysis Bateson presents in *Naven*, since it is here where the dialectical theory of cultural cognition and deep motivation is developed. Several conceptual problems arise immediately, beginning with "ethos." Shortly after introducing the observation that ethos is not one, but two, and differs between Iatmul men and women, Bateson introduces this explanation in a footnote:

> In my description of ethos, I have not hesitated to invoke the concepts
> of emotion and to use terms which strictly should only be used by
> observers about their own introspections. I have been driven to this
> loose phrasing through lack of any proper technique for recording and
> of any language for describing human gesture and behavior. But I wish it
> to be understood that statements of this kind are an attempt—crude and

1. The fact that Bateson distinguishes the psychoanalytic enterprise from the "more important" problems of interpersonal and intergroup processes suggests that he was not aware, or not prepared to acknowledge, that Freud rejected such reductionism very early on, in the early chapters of *The Interpretation of Dreams*. One finds a similar problem in recent works (e.g., D'Andrade 1992; White 1991), which repeat the caricature of psychoanalysis as a reduction of meaning and social complexity to a calculus of invariant needs and wants.

unscientific perhaps—to convey to the reader some impression of the
behavior of Iatmul natives. (1958:124).

Bateson clearly wished to avoid attributing emotions to people when in
fact the only attribution he could make was to himself, to his own impression of their behavior. The emotions he describes, therefore, are his and
not theirs; they refer to Iatmul emotions, but they do not actually represent
them. In the epilogue to the 1958 edition of the book, Bateson tried (once
again) to convey what he meant: "When I stated that the 'tone' of the men's
behavior in the initiation ceremonies was expressive of harshness and irre-
sponsibility rather than asceticism, I meant that the actions performed by
them, the washing of the novice, etc., were *accompanied* by other details of
behavior so that the whole picture was one of harshness" (1958:276). In
other words, the emotions Bateson describes correspond to the observer's
own, experienced in the presence of Iatmul behavior, thus indexing Iatmul
emotions without representing them. If this is what Bateson meant, the
method behind it does not receive systematic development as a theory of
description. For that, it would have been necessary for Bateson to describe
his own emotion categories and to explain how observation of Iatmul behavior triggered them. (An interesting project, to be sure, but not the one
he undertook.) How then does Bateson justify the translation of emotion
experiences and the comprehension of ethos?

We know that Bateson read Benedict's *Patterns of Culture* in manuscript
form while he was still in the field. Its imprint is clearly evident. Benedict
had developed the notion of a universal "arc" of cultural variations, which
all people share, but which particular cultures chose among to elaborate
particular variations. According to Benedict, human beings are born with
the potential to be Zuni or Pueblo or anything else. But once we are social-
ized, and thus equipped to experience only a segment of the arc as real,
we find it difficult to understand people of another culture for whom a different part of the arc has been elaborated. Bateson, presumably, believed
that he was studying that segment of the universal emotional continuum
which Iatmul culture had selected for special elaboration. When Bateson
discussed Iatmul pride, "an attribute of human nature" (1958:116), he believed he had special access to it by virtue of the human nature which both
he and the Iatmul shared. Pride among the Iatmul was elaborated differently, of course, and had different social implications, but it was still in
some sense "pride" as Bateson, as well as every other human being, knows
it, or can know it given appropriate exposure, conditioning, and accultura-
tion.

I have tried to extract a definition of "emotion" from Bateson because I think that one is implicit in his early work, and also because so few anthropologists who write on the subject (then or now) provide one of their own. One can comb the pages of *Unnatural Emotions,* for example, and find nothing more definitive than the comment that emotions are "intensely meaningful" (Lutz 1988:5). One would think that this might make emotion difficult to talk about. To his credit, Bateson devoted a considerable space to the definition of terms in *Naven.* In the end, however, it is the explanatory approach he developed which is important to the argument I shall make in this book. It is to that approach that we now turn.

Bateson developed an interpersonal theory of emotion that might seem to anticipate the work of several later anthropologists, especially ethnopsychologists like Lutz, since the emphasis is on the social construction of emotion categories. Looking back on his Iatmul work, more than thirty years later, Bateson himself confirmed that such a theory was his goal:

> The New Guinea material and much that has come later, taught me that I will get nowhere by explaining prideful behavior, for example, by referring to an individual's "pride." Nor can you explain aggression by referring to instinctive (or even learned) "aggressiveness." Such an explanation, which shifts attention from the interpersonal field to a factitious inner tendency, principle instinct, or whatnot, is, I suggest, very great nonsense which only hides the real questions. (1958:147)

Although this statement, with its implicit disavowal of drive psychology, might seem to constitute an excellent charter for ethnopsychology and the constructivist project, there is more to it than that. In fact, as I shall show, the interpersonal world Bateson constructs looks a lot like the intrapsychic world of psychoanalytic theory, with the same reliance on dialectical conflict and its dynamic principles.

The Dynamics of Ethos: Toward a Dialectical View

Iatmul ethos is a binary relationship in which the emotional orientations of men and women are opposed as well as complementary to each other. It is closely associated with place. The male ethos is best exemplified by male behavior in and around the ceremonial house, a place of ritual and debate from which women are excluded. There Iatmul men vie with each other in displays of harsh vituperation and buffoonery. There is a constant emphasis on making oneself the center of attention, and thus in lessening or eliminating, through insult or mockery, the posturings of other men. The term Bateson repeatedly uses to characterize this ethos is *pride*: pride in oneself as a master orator and the pride in one's clan. "The totemic system has an obvious affective function—a very important one in this culture—of providing the members of every clan with matter for self-congratulation" (1958:127). One might almost take Bateson to mean that the totemic system exists for the purpose of providing satisfactory expression to the pride Iatmul men feel in such overwhelming abundance. This was not Bateson's intent, but it does hint at something more complex: a way of seeing knowledge and motivation as necessarily related and conjoint.

The female ethos of the Iatmul, centered on the domestic sphere and concerned with daily occupation, contrasts with its male counterpart. Where the male is spectacular, the female is unostentatious; where the male is ceremonial, the female is domestic; where the male is individualistic, the female is cooperative. There are exceptions. When women are by themselves they manifest some of the same intemperate boisterousness as the men. But for the most part the female ethos is consistent in its emphasis on "quiet and cooperative attitudes" (1958:148).

Bateson's approach to cultural ethos posits the existence of emotional orientations which the observer observes, then names, using the terms he takes to be their nearest equivalents in English. This was the approach favored by others, such as Benedict and Mead. Where Bateson differed was in his description of an ethos as a binary emotive phenomenon, both parts mutually configuring and neither intelligible by itself. This is central to the synthesis of cognition and emotion implicit in his work. Moreover, Bateson asserted, ethos is not a static phenomenon. It has direction and force. Each aspect defines itself in opposition to the other, and in their conflict, each side compels the other to accentuate the emotional values which define it. The process is necessarily dialectical and progressive, a mutually reinforcing system of opposites in which each moment represents movement toward greater differentiation of values. This is *schizmogenesis.*

Schizmogenesis is either complementary or symmetrical. The first case arises whenever opposites accentuate their different values and thereby increase mutual differentiation. The second differs only in that the values which are accentuated are the same and not opposed (1958:176). Does complementary schizmogenesis provide an adequate conceptual framework for understanding the workings of the Iatmul ethos? Bateson had to consider the fact that the schizmogenic process is progressive and unending. What happens to prevent the schizmogenic entity (a person or a group) from destroying itself through excessive differentiation? A kind of "distortion" or "discomfort" might develop that would render normal psychological or social functioning increasingly difficult. Something must exist, in short, to arrest the progression before it reaches this state.

Bateson's earlier answer to the question was that the two forms of schizmogenesis—complementary and symmetrical—constrain each other and thus preserve the balance of the system. Here is how it works: Actors in a complementary relationship experience increasing mutual hostility, inability to understand the emotional reactions of the other, and mutual jealousy (1958:188–89). One of Bateson's favorite examples was feudalism. The serf is submissive, the lord aggressive, and each responds to the behavior of the other with exaggeration of their assigned role attributes. But if this continued, it would not be long before the relationship deteriorated in mutual hostility. Consequently, something must take place to retard or reverse the schizmogenic spiral.

There are four possibilities. First, symmetrical schizmogenic moments may temporarily interrupt complementarity: "The Squire is in a predominantly complementary and not always comfortable relationship with his villagers, but if he participates in village cricket (symmetrical rivalry) but once a year, this may have a curiously disproportionate effect in easing the schizmogenic strain in the relationship" (1958:193). Second, the meaning of the complementary opposition may change, becoming no less complementary but possessing a different symbolic significance that may make it more endurable. Here Bateson resorted to his other favorite example, marriage: ". . . in a marriage in which there is a complementary schizmogenesis based upon assertion-submission, illness or accident may shift the contrast to one based on fostering and feebleness" (1958:194). Third, an individual's consciousness of strain may prompt him to adopt behavior deliberately at odds with the behavior which sustains the schizmogenic relationship. Iatmul men, for example, suddenly shift from harshness to buffoonery—apparently, as we would say, to provide "comic relief" and thus defuse tension. Finally, persons or groups opposed to each other in a progressive complementary relationship may overcome their opposition by uniting in combined opposition to a third party or group. Bateson speculated that headhunting warfare in Iatmul culture constituted just such a mechanism, uniting the parties usually opposed to each other, and thus controlling the schizmogenesis between the sexes and the initiatory moieties.

Solutions to the problem of schizmogenesis were not united within a theory of psychosocial function that could explain the self-correcting processes just described. Bateson was aware of the problem, but in 1936 he had nothing to offer. Twenty years later, in the second edition of *Naven,* he did have something to offer: "cybernetic" or "systems" theory. Cybernetics has not achieved the status of a master paradigm as Bateson, writing in the 1950s, hoped or expected that it would. The reason might be that "function," which cybernetic theory was intended to rescue, did not survive the advent of new problematics, at least not as the primary architectonic of anthropological discourse. It has become a term of opprobrium. The problem with most forms of functionalism was the implicit teleology—that the end or purpose of a process could be invoked as an explanation of the process itself. This made functional accounts weak and vulnerable to logical critique. Bateson considered cybernetic theory a solution to the teleological dilemma and thus the savior of functionalism, because it substitutes the notion of self-correction for the idea of purpose. The schizmogenic system could now be seen as a circuit-like system consisting of multiple feedback loops.

To merely state, as Bateson had done in 1936, that various countervailing forces might exist to arrest the progression of a schizmogenic process is not sufficient. Cybernetically, one must be able to specify and relate the specific pathways through which self-correcting messages are transmitted. In reviewing the Iatmul materials in 1958, Bateson discovered what he thought must be the primary pathway. It was the *naven* ceremonial itself.

> The *naven* ceremonial, which is an exaggerated caricature of a complementary sexual relationship between *wau* and *laua*, is in fact set off by overweening symmetrical behavior. When *laua* boasts in the presence of *wau*, the latter has recourse to *naven* behavior. Perhaps in the initial description of the contexts for *naven* it would have been better to describe this as the primary context, and to see *lauas*'s achievements in headhunting, fishing, etc., as particular examples of an achieved ambition or vertical mobility in *laua* which place him in some sort of symmetrical relationship with *wau*. (1958:290).

This is an ingenious solution to the problem, but it does not constitute proof, since it lacks a demonstration that symmetrical or complementary behavior does in fact call forth its opposite at certain moments to restore balance and harmony. As Bateson himself remarked: "The questions at issue are whether excessive symmetrical rivalry between clans will in fact increase the frequency with which *lauas* act symmetrically vis-à-vis their *waus*, and whether the resulting increase in frequency of *naven* will tend to stabilize the society" (1958:290). Bateson calls for "statistical study" and "appropriate measurement," to test this hypothesis, but he does not present them.

The importance of Bateson's ethological method is that it attributes to the emotions a motivational force not present exclusively in the emotions themselves, as we are accustomed to think of them, but *in the dynamic* in which they participate. Pride is motivating, in that it prompts Iatmul men to ceremonial display, but pride itself is nothing. It receives motivational strength from the complementary relationship it participates in: Men are prideful and women are cooperative, and as they conflict, they both construct each other and the emotions they are expected to display. Pride is therefore impossible without its structural obverse. It is so with all the emotions which differently make up the ethoses of Iatmul men and women. Emotions do not stand alone, but instead participate in a *relationship* of contrast and mutual self-definition, much as signs within a semiotic system.

Complementarity is the principle of semiological contrast Bateson considered primary. Symmetry, the other principle, is also important, but since it refers to the one-upmanship among men or among women, it does not possess the generative power of a dynamic conflict. That is because symmetry measures the intensity of expression between like sign values. But the meaning of such values depends on their differentiation from others with which they are paired in complementary opposition. The third semiological principle is reversal, as when Iatmul men suddenly shift from prideful display to comic buffoonery, or when women, who are otherwise quiet and cooperative, suddenly become loud and demonstrative. These three principles—complementarity, symmetry, and reversal—are the principles which govern the working of an ethos.

Freud and Bateson: The Psychoanalytic Resonances of Ethos

If schizmogenic ethology were merely a semiological theory, it would not possess the power to motivate behavior. What is the source, for example, of the "balance" which the system tries to achieve? Why do responses to "tension" take the forms they do? This takes us back to the issue of psychoanalysis and its influence on Bateson. We have already considered Bateson's response: The influence of psychoanalysis on the development of his approach was thought by the author himself to have been minimal. The similarities go much deeper than that, however, and they are all the more interesting if, as Bateson maintained, his dependence on the Freudian theory of development was nearly nonexistent.

The schizmogenic theory of the emotions does not depend on an understanding of infant behavior or child socialization. Bateson did not study these phenomena, at least not among the Iatmul, so there can be no question that he based his theory on a developmental psychology. A psychogenic theory of the emotions, such as Freud's, which might have traced schizmogenic processes to early experiences of separation and loss, or pleasure and pain, is not introduced. Nor is there any indication that Bateson thought that sexual development might be involved, despite the fact that progressive sexual differentiation is fundamental to ethological contrast and thus to the construction of Iatmul emotions. Perhaps the concept of "progression" itself, so vital to schizmogenesis as a theory of change, might provide the link to psychological development. But there is no indication that Bateson ever considered progression in this sense. It cannot constitute a dimension of comparability between Freud and Bateson. But the similarity of their approaches to the emotions is too strong to overlook.

What they most clearly have in common is an emphasis on homeostatic balance. Bateson shared with most functionalists the view that society was an organism-like entity which seeks balance as its natural state. Where he differed was in trying to escape the teleology inherent in most functionalist explanations. That is why he turned to systems theory and cybernetics. The other major difference which set Bateson apart from most of his functionalist colleagues, and which made him comparable to Freud, was his emphasis on the emotions and the ethos they constitute as the principal locus for expressing and determining homeostatic balance. He wanted to come up with a cybernetic theory of emotional dynamics as a mechanism for explaining social integration and progress through time.

This is the most obvious link to Freud. In one of his earliest statements on the emotions, *The Neuropsychoses of Defense*, Freud stated that "in mental functions something is to be distinguished—a quota of affect or sum of excitation—which possesses all the characteristics of a quantity . . . which is capable of increase, diminution, displacement and discharge, and which is spread over the memory-traces of ideas somewhat as an electric charge is spread over the surface of the body" (1961b:60). Thus, even at this early point, Freud believed that the "mental apparatus" functioned as a complex reflex arc. Stimuli impinged on one end, either from within the organism or from the environment, and this accumulated excitation was discarded at the other end as motor activity or affect. This is a systems theory, of a sort. But the importance of psychoanalytic theory was in attempting to specify what happened within this system.

Freud retained the notion of the mind as a complex reflex arc in his later work but enhanced the importance of the apparatus which protects it from excessive unbound stimulation, or anxiety. Powered by the twin drives of libido and aggression, the forces of the id motivate the organism to gratify instinctual wishes. The ego cannot hold such wishes in abeyance and is overwhelmed by an influx of stimuli. Psychic energy, unable to achieve its purpose but incapable of restraint by the ego, courses through the system and is experienced by the ego as the affect of anxiety. The experience of emotion is dependent on the ego, for it is within the ego that energy is converted into affect. To make it possible for the organism to avoid anxiety, and satisfy its drives even in the absence of a direct outlet, the ego uses various defensive mechanisms.

In his account of self-correcting functions, Bateson described the loss and recovery of systemic balance in similar terms — terms which seem more like Freud's, not less so, with the accretion of cybernetic terminology in the second edition of *Naven*. Freud, of course, located the circuit in the mind and the functions of self-correction in the unconscious part of the ego. Bateson located the circuit in cultural ethos and the functions of self-correction in ceremonial social interaction. The inner workings of each, however, are astonishingly alike. The "mind" of psychoanalysis and the "ethos" of Batesonian anthropology are both dynamic systems in constant internal conflict.

Let us consider the psychoanalytic account. The mind is divided between its acquisitive and appetitive functions, located in the id, and its own ideal of itself, located in the superego. The needs of the id demand satisfaction, but since reality and social convention prevent this, the ego, as the entity which mediates internal wants and external constraints, represses needs and provides alternative, or compromise, satisfactions. Solutions thus arrived at both represent the conflict which is internal to their generation and partially resolve it, in providing sublimated satisfaction. But because the conflict is permanent, and its compromise solutions never more than partial, a continuous effort or expenditure of energy must be made to keep the system intact and functioning. Over time, and under conditions of acute stress, the system may weaken, with the result that the old compromises must be reinvigorated or new ones devised.

Certain conflicts are basic to the system and cannot be eliminated, since the system itself, and the repertoire of compromises it generates, depends on their continued dynamic existence. They do not cease even in the enlightened age Freud imagines at the end of *Future of an Illusion*. Unconscious wishes, deep in the id, cannot achieve satisfaction through direct expression since they cannot comprehend or control the environment. They must find acceptable direction and form. The superego, as the vehicle of moral constraints, demands compliance, but it cannot provide satisfaction for unconscious wishes. Its demands must be reworked through appropriate compromises. Only the ego, as the mediator of these two, can do both.

It is formed in the clash of opposites, taking form according to the pressures imposed by both, and providing partial solutions to the competing demands that help to constitute it.

Culture, like the ego, is the result of a similar process in social, instead of intrapsychic, terms. Wishes and prohibitions conflict with each other, as they do in the primal scene imagined by Freud in *Totem and Taboo,* and once the need arises, people invent social structures and symbol systems to represent and resolve the conflict. Freud thought that rituals, like the infamous "totem meal" following the primal crime, are particularly effective means to this end. In consuming the animal which represents their father, the primal brothers reexperienced fulfillment of their wish to supplant him, but in conforming to the rules which govern the ritual, they subject themselves to the authority which once their father, but now culture as whole, represents. The ritual is repeated at regular intervals, thus insuring that the functions it performs will continue.

The nature of the agencies Freud proposed, as well as the ontogenesis of the processes which connect them, is less important than the fact that their relationship is a dynamic one, built on conflict and compromise. This is what I suggested in chapter 2, in tracing the debt Freud owes to Kant. Now compare Freud's theory to the Iatmul society Bateson described. Male and female are structural opposites. They define themselves in relation to each other, and for both there is a different emotional orientation: Men are prideful and women are cooperative. As men display their pride, they stimulate women to greater cooperativeness, and the men, seeing this, are prompted to even greater prideful display. Is this not like the relationship between the id and the superego? As one pushes "up," demanding satisfaction, the other pushes "down," repressing these demands—demands which only grow stronger and thus require even greater acts of repression on behalf of the repressing agency. This is complementary schizmogenesis, and it would continue indefinitely, or until the system destroyed itself, without the existence of a control mechanism.

Freud formulated the ego as the agency of compromise, through which the competing demands of id and superego must be negotiated. There had to be such an agency, just as for Bateson a process that would temporarily arrest the schizmogenic progression was necessary, given the dynamic conflict of opposing ethoses among the Iatmul. His answer, ultimately, was *identical* to one that Freud proposed: regular ceremonial enactment. Like the compromise formation erected by the ego to represent and resolve inner conflict, ritual displaces repressed needs and fulfills them through substitution. The Iatmul ritual of *naven* is a case in point, and here, as we shall see, the similarity between Bateson and Freud deepens even further.

The *naven* is a complex ritual, enacted to celebrate the acts and achievements of the *laua,* or sister's child. "Whenever a *laua*—boy or girl, man or woman—performs some standard cultural act, and especially when the child performs this act for the first time in its life, the occasion may be celebrated by its *wau* [mother's brother]" (1958:6). The most important of these achievements is homicide, the first time a boy kills an enemy or a foreigner. Next in importance is assistance offered in the completion of a successful homicide. Lower in the hierarchy are animal kills: killing a crocodile, killing a wild pig, spearing a giant eel, and so forth. Last come more ordinary acts, notable only on the first occasion of their doing: felling a sago palm, using a spear-thrower, sharpening a fish spear, cutting a paddle, beating a hand drum, buying an areca nut, etc. *Naven* ceremonies occur more frequently, and are more elaborate, in the case of male celebrants.

The most outstanding feature in the *naven* ceremony, at least to an outsider, is the transvestitism of the men and women who participate. The *wau,* or mother's brother, dresses himself in filthy widow's reeds, and when so attired is addressed as "mother." Of the women who participate, several, including the sisters, father's sisters, and elder brother's wives, dress as men and wear the very best feather headdresses and ornaments borrowed from men. They are addressed as "sister-man" (in the case of the sister), "father" (father's sister), or "elder brother" (elder brother's wife). Dressed as elderly and decrepit women, the *wau*s exaggerate their frailty and demean themselves through behavior the very opposite of what is normal for them. They hobble through the village, looking for their *laua*s, and often fall down, to demonstrate their femaleness "by assuming on the ground grotesque attitudes with their legs widespread" (1958:12). The women dressed as men meanwhile strut and preen in a great show of pride and pleasure: "Their faces were painted white with sulfur, as is the privilege of homicides, and in their hands they carried the decorated lime boxes used by men and serrated lime stick with pendant tassels whose number is a tally of men killed by the owner" (1958:15).

The self-demeaning behavior of the mother's brother is continued when he locates the intended recipient of his attention, the *laua,* and rubs the cleft of his buttocks down the length of his *laua*'s leg. It is an act called "grooving the anus."

> This was when a *wau* dashed into the midst of a dance and performed
> the gesture on his *laua* who was celebrating the *wau*'s ancestors. The *wau*
> ran into the crowd, turned his back on the *laua* and rapidly lowered
> himself—almost fell—into a squatting position in such a way that as his
> legs bent under him his buttocks rubbed down the length of the *laua*'s
> leg. (1958:13).

The *laua* is supposed to react to this performance with embarrassment and to try to prevent it from happening again by giving the *wau* certain valuables (typically shells) according to the number of times that the *wau* has repeated the gesture—one shell for each rubbing of the buttocks.

Another segment of the ritual, apparently performed only on grand occasions, such as the celebration of a successful homicide, involves both the mother's brother and his wife, the *mbora*. The *wau* is dressed as a woman, as before, and the *mbora* is dressed as a man. The *wau* sticks an orange-colored fruit in his anus and goes up the ladder of a house, displaying this as he climbs. At the top, he assumes the position of his wife, and she that of her husband, and they imitate copulation. The orange fruit, according to Bateson, represents an anal clitoris, "an anatomical feature frequently imagined by the Iatmul and appropriate to the *wau*'s assumption of grotesque femininity" (1958:20). Afterward, the other women who participate in the ritual dressed as men all repeat this act. The *laua* is much ashamed at this spectacle—whether more by this than by the more typical buttock-rubbing, we are not told.

Does *naven* represent and resolve the structural oppositions which configure the Iatmul ethos? The main opposition is that between men and women and the different emotional orientations they represent. Bateson speculated that since these orientations construct each other, each act of self-definition by one side must compel one by the other, and always with some added emphasis or exaggeration, so that the result is an unending behavioral spiral. Something must happen to stop it. *Naven* accomplishes this by reversing gender roles and defusing the tension created by their dynamic conflict. Women who dress as men, and behave during the ceremony with proud male effrontery, temporarily transform the relationship between themselves and men from one of complementarity to symmetry, that is, from opposition to competition. Commented Bateson: "It looks as though these women are stating a symmetrical rivalry vis-à-vis the men, compensating for their normally complementary role" (1958:291). The evidence for this is in the obvious enjoyment the women experience in temporarily dropping their quiet cooperativeness and acting the part of proud men. But can it be said that men who adopt female clothes and behavior do so for the same reason?

It is not easy to argue this point, for while women might wish to experience the power and potency of the male role, there is nothing very obviously attractive for men in the usual female role. This is clear from the choice men make of the feminine role attributes they choose to enact: age, decrepitude, shamelessness. Their purpose, if anything, is to caricature just those aspects of feminine behavior they most despise. The only other alternative would be that the men secretly envy, and must forcefully repress, the attributes of Iatmul femininity. The virtue of the performance is that in it they are able to do both: becoming women, they satisfy their secret envy but preserve their male superiority by simultaneously denigrating feminine attributes.

Bateson toys with this explanation, coming dangerously close to proposing the existence of a mechanism not unlike the one Freud called projective identification:

> Outwardly, at least, they despise the womanly ethos, but it is not impossible that they have some unacknowledged envy of it. Their own ethos would not, in any case, permit them to acknowledge that there was anything to be said for the attitudes of the women and any envy they may have they might well express in scorn of women — dressing in women's clothes for the purpose. (1958:189).

But he dismisses this immediately because it would force him to accept the existence of something which is the opposite of the phenomenon actually observed. He renders this opinion in a footnote: "I hesitate to launch into phrasing which would render my 'behaviouristic' references to emotion ambiguous by implying that the behavior may be the reverse of that primarily appropriate to the emotion" (1958:188 n. 1). So, even though the "symmetrical" explanation of female ritual transvestitism is allowed to stand, because motive and outcome are congruent with each other, Bateson decided to seek elsewhere for an explanation of the male counterpart behavior.

He found what he was looking for in the relationship, not between men and women, but between mother's brother (*wau*) and sister's son (*laua*). The ceremony of *naven* recognizes the accomplishments of the *laua,* and because in this matrilineal society these are more important to matrilineal relations, it is the mother's brother who celebrates them. But this puts the mother's brother in an awkward position. As a man, he is entitled to show pride in his own achievements, as well as anger and disappointment in the behavior of others. Vicarious pleasure in another's success, however, is more problematic, since the male ethos does not make that kind of emotional response easy. There is another serious problem, too. Since the *wau* and *laua* are now in a socially competitive relationship, competing with other in words and deeds, a symmetrical schizmogenesis develops. Something must act to reverse it from time to time in order to keep the relationship intact and functional.

The solution to both these problems is male transvestitism. The *wau* acts like a woman and, as a woman, can express admiration through subservience and self-abnegation toward the *laua*. He also interrupts the competitiveness that is implicit in their relationship by adopting female behavior and thus replacing symmetrical with complementary schizmogenesis (Bateson 1958:289–90). It is a tidy solution to a complex problem.

The Nature and Importance of Ethos

For Bateson, emotions are self-implicating motivational phenomena with direction and force, organized in relationships of opposition, and constitutive of a dialectic. This is the definition implicit, I think, in the Iatmul ethnography. Each of its terms requires separate consideration:

Emotion

All human beings are born with the same repertoire of basic emotions. Cultures choose among the constituents of this repertoire, selectively elaborating or diminishing the salience of its members. Bateson borrowed the concept of qualified affective universalism from Benedict, although it was current in the work of many others, such as Werner in developmental psychology and Fearing in linguistic anthropology. Qualified universalism permits psychic unity and thus allows for mutual understanding, even among those who have elaborated different parts of the spectrum. It also acknowledges, and even anticipates, cultural diversity, since it cannot be known in advance which part of the emotional continuum will have been endowed with special importance. Iatmul "pride," for example, is still pride as we know it, but to understand it is to take into account the unique ways in which it has been elaborated by Iatmul culture.

Ethos

The dynamic relationship between emotions, their distribution and development in a particular culture, constitutes an ethos. Like the dynamic unconscious, it is a system which operates according to certain principles whose function is to maintain homeostatic balance between opposing values. Schizmogenic processes are the working principles of this dynamism. Complementary and symmetrical schizmogenesis, for example, both construct the opposition between values and control the escalation of the conflict by occasionally reversing position. The interplay of forces takes place in and through the agencies to whom opposing value have been allocated. In Iatmul culture, the opposing values of pride and cooperativeness, which together constitute the axis of Iatmul ethos, have been allocated to men and women, respectively. The dynamic relationship between these values is enacted in the relationship between men and women.

Self-implication

Emotions are associated with identities and involve constructions of the self. Social identities are made up, in large part, of the emotional orientations that have been allocated to them and which they are expected to represent in their behavior. An Iatmul man, for example, represents himself through regular display of pride, one of the emotional characteristics assigned to him. Failure to represent oneself in this way compromises social identity and leads to the loss of self.

Motivation

Emotional orientations express themselves as goals in the behavior of those who bear them. Proud Iatmul men, for example, look for opportunities to display their pride in themselves, their clans, and their ancestors. This is the individual level of motivation. Imbalances within the system are experienced as stress or tension. Self-corrective mechanisms within the system seek to restore homeostasis and therefore motivate individuals to act differently, perhaps by reversing their usual behavior. This is the systemic level of motivation.

Direction and Force

Emotional goals provide direction and possess compulsive force. Directions are established by social convention. An Iatmul man, for example, knows that in order to manifest pride, he must seek out and attempt to exploit opportunities for display. The most important of these are formal debate in the ceremonial house and headhunting. The force which compels him is the positive compulsion to act in congruence with his social identity, but it is also the need to resolve the tension to which such action must eventually lead. The "push and pull" of the schizmogenic process, as Bateson called it, alternately advances and retards the dynamic conflict out of which the ethos is constructed and personal identity is formed.

Bateson officially eschewed psychoanalytic theory, but this was no more than window dressing. In developing the theory of schizmogenesis he employed concepts that were not unlike those of psychoanalysis. "Ethos" and "affect" are almost identical in their reference to a motivational system powered by inner conflict, constrained by the need to resolve anxiety, and organized by dynamic processes. Freud attributed ontological primacy to the workings of the unconscious and the primary processes. Out of these develop the secondary processes, intellection and calculation, and the social formations which function as a kind of theater for the displacement and projection of unconscious wishes. In this Bateson differed, since he had no ontology; in fact, he rejected origins altogether in favor of circular processes and closed cybernetic circuits. But he attributed great importance to ethos, occasionally coming close to giving it causal primacy, as in his account of the extraordinary elaborateness of the Iatmul totemic system: "So the whole culture is molded by the continual emphasis upon the spectacular, and by the pride of the male ethos" (1958:129). Ontological primacy is not important, since what Bateson wished to emphasize is that ethological and sociological accounts are necessary to each other because emotional systems and social structures inform each other.

Bateson introduced emotions into social anthropology in a new and striking way, quite unlike Benedict and Mead, who were more directly influenced by psychoanalysis. That makes his contribution all the more interesting. It also makes it different, since Bateson considered himself a structural-functionalist at heart and says so, repeatedly, throughout the pages of *Naven*. When he turned to the emotions, therefore, he did so because he thought that the functionalist account was incomplete without them. His effort to devise something that was compatible with functionalism, but still sensitive to emotional motivation, may help us to understand something important and little recognized about structural functionalism. This is best done, briefly, by considering the author whose work most influenced the development of British social anthropology—Durkheim.

A Conjectural History of the Debt to Durkheim

When Bateson was seeking a concept to help him transcend the weary formalism of the traditional approach, he turned to Radcliffe-Brown, the leader of functionalism and the last person in the world, one would think, to be sympathetic to Bateson's project.[2] But it was Radcliffe-Brown, as I

---

2. It is true that in one of his earliest and most famous articles, "The Mother's Brother in South Africa," Radcliffe-Brown develops the hypothesis of "extension" to explain how sentiments attached to one kin category (e.g., "mother") may be extended to another that is more distant ("mother's brother") (Radcliffe-Brown 1924). This is not unlike Bateson's discussion of the mother's brother (*wau*) in Iatmul society. But for Bateson the emotional consequences of this process are central: A theory of psychosocial functioning ("schizmo-genesis") must be developed to explain how such consequences are managed, all with a view to interpreting the emotional tone of the society. Radcliffe-Brown did not develop a theory of psychosocial functioning, nor was he interested in the description of feeling

pointed out, who suggested the term *ethos*. Where did Radcliffe-Brown get this idea? What I offer is speculation, based on an alternative reading of Durkheim, and according to which the relevance of emotion and motivation to "structural-functionalism" was strongly implicit, at least at the beginning.

Durkheim advanced a theory of metaphorical parallelism, whereby social structures and religious structures were understood to correspond to each other. In "primitive" societies, the correspondence between the two is one to one, so that, for example, the division of a tribe into moieties is the basis for a dualistic cosmology. Ritual was the means by which the integrity of the correspondence system was periodically reinvigorated. Motivation was needed, but there is no systematically developed theory of motivation in *The Elementary Forms of the Religious Life*. Durkheim eschewed psychological argument, since the purpose of sociology, he claimed, was to establish an independent level of analysis that did not rely on alleged properties of mind. But Durkheim was driven to assume such properties at several points, and nowhere more clearly than in his analysis of religious ritual, the periodic performance that creates the "collective effervescence" necessary for restoring social solidarity.

Durkheim compared the feeling of collective effervescence to a jolt of electricity or a state of inebriation. Human beings possess the capacity to experience such states not only in one situation but potentially in many, from the taking of drugs to participating in group rituals. It is only natural that we should attempt to repeat them. It is the capacity to generate these feelings and to do so at will, in different circumstances, that is most basic to social function. Ritual provides repetition, and while the sociological function of ritual is to reaffirm social bonds, the motivation for its enactment is decidedly emotional. The sociological account Durkheim offered rests squarely on this assumption, even though Durkheim never elaborated it. The boundaries between the disciplines would be far better constructed if Durkheim had pursued his brief, but necessary, concession to psychological argument.

Durkheim clearly anticipated Bateson in his discussion of category structure, a structure based on (but not always a direct reflection of) the morphology of social relations. Bateson called it "eidos." The assumption that emotions must be organized the same way was a logical next step. But

---

states. But given the fact that Bateson refers to Radcliffe-Brown's 1924 article approvingly, it is not unlikely that he saw this as a natural extension, which he himself tries to make in the Iatmul ethnography.

here, I think, Bateson drew on the argument Durkheim suppressed. Freed from the orthodoxy he imposed on himself, in his ideological commitment to the independent status of social facts, could Durkheim have devised the concept of ethos?

To speculate: Perhaps it was the lingering influence of just this possibility that led Radcliffe-Brown to propose the term to Bateson. Radcliffe-Brown had no use for it, of course, except as a deus ex machina: Some kind of motivation must exist for the son's extension of filial emotions to his mother's brother, but Radcliffe-Brown, in his famous article on the mother's brother, never tells how it works (Radcliffe-Brown 1924). No doubt that is because he was even more committed to the irrelevance of psychology than his adopted mentor. But he knew it was important, and therefore, perhaps, he bestowed it on someone whose eclecticism and antipathy to disciplinary boundaries could give it a place to develop.

THE DYNAMICS OF EIDOS: A DIALECTICAL VIEW

A mutually defining and self-reinforcing system of complementary and symmetrical emotional orientations, "ethos," is basic to the motivation for actions undertaken in conformity to social norms. Rote behavior in simple adherence with social norms, the only "motivation" Radcliffe-Brown posited, is not enough. Emotions are necessary to the functioning of the social system, but what is the relationship between what people feel and what people think? As Bateson saw it, cultural premises are realized in affective terms and function according to a sociopsychological economy which seeks balance by alternately increasing and reducing oppositions within the system. This is the dialectic of ethos. Why couldn't the same be true of cultural cognition, in which case "ideas" instead of "emotions" would be the relational units? The realization of such ideas, and their organization in some kind of pattern, is what Bateson called *eidos*.

Bateson developed the notion of eidos at an interesting time in the history of social psychology and cognitive anthropology. Cambridge, where he wrote *Naven,* was the site of the Cambridge Psychological Laboratory. Bartlett was there and had just published his famous book *Remembering: Experiments in Social Psychology* (1932), in which the importance of social context to the organization of memory was first proposed. Bartlett is important for many reasons, as we shall see, and Bateson was strongly influenced by him (1958:222 n. 1). But before we examine this influence, let us consider Bateson's objectives in the chapter of *Naven* he devotes to the description of what he called the "cognitive aspects of mental process."

Bateson was struck by the complexity of the Iatmul totemic system, a system that demands of those who know it a prodigious skill in memorization and recall. This skill is apparent in debate, in which a name or a series of names is claimed by one or more conflicting clans. The right to a name can be demonstrated only by revealing certain aspects of its significance in the esoteric mythology in which it plays a role. The trick, as it were, is to reveal enough of these to make it clear that one knows the myth, but not so much that the entire myth is given away, since the integrity of knowledge depends partly on its secrecy. Now, there are thousands of such names; the details relevant to their placement in various myths are even more numerous. How do Iatmul men keep track of all this?

Bateson rejected the possibility that they simply memorize details by rote. If that were the case, then one would expect the order in which terms are recalled to remain the same. But it does not, and in fact there is very little emphasis on order. Another possibility is that the men remember totemic names by representing them in chronological sequences, in what cognitive theorists now call "scripts" (Casson 1983). Bateson rejected this, saying that the Iatmul never engage in such "cognitive rigmarole." He never heard an informant "go back, like a European child, to the beginning and repeat the series of names already given, in the hope that the 'impetus' of rote repetition would produce a few more names" (1958:223). None of these assertions constitute evidence either for or against any hypothesis concerning the organization of memory. Bateson was aware of this problem and conceded that "it is not possible to say which of the higher processes is chiefly involved" (1958:224). But he did make one tantalizing suggestion with reference to the manipulation of physical objecs, which figures prominently in Iatmul debate.

Some objects are displayed in order to substantiate the link between those objects and those who present them. Once, when the subject was totemic ownership of a river, a shell necklace was hung in the center of the ceremonial house to represent the river. One side claimed that the elephant grass which grows on the riverbank belonged to them and, therefore, so must the river itself. To prove it, they produced a spear decorated with leaves of the grass and pointed to it as their own. In another debate about the sun, Bateson reports, a number of the debaters dressed themselves up to represent characters in a myth about the sun (1958:224–25). In all such debates, objects are displayed, or manipulated, by each debater in the act of speaking. The debater uses these objects as tangible emblems to mark points or identify arguments. A speaker will say, "This leaf is so-and-so, I am not claiming that name," and "This leaf is so-and-so's opinion," and he will toss the leaf to the side to indicate his contempt. In a similar fashion, according to Bateson, a small packet of leaves is used to represent a secret, of which the speaker challenges the opposing side to show some knowledge.

The constant manipulation and display of objects that is characteristic of Iatmul debate, in which thousands of totemic names are rehearsed, led Bateson to speculate that cultural knowledge is organized in memory in visual or kinesthetic images. Form and movement, in other words, provide mnemonic gestalts which encode information, including the thousands of names Iatmul men know. Bateson does not elaborate on this hypothesis, but as intriguing as the hypothesis itself is the interest Bateson shows in cognitive representation—something not typical among social anthropologists, then or now. Bateson had come to the startling conclusion that the manner in which cultural knowledge is organized, cognitively, has a direct effect on its social character, so that just any account of structure of knowledge would not do. It had to be consistent with what was known about memory. No other anthropologist in the 1930s said that; few would say it today.

Bateson showed remarkable prescience in anticipating later concern with the forms that memory representations could take. What he called a "chronological" format is today called "episodic," the issue now one of contrast between this and "semantic" memory: How much of memory is organized in the form of episodic sequences, or scripts, and how much is organized semantically, as networks of interconnected symbols? Apparently, human beings have the capacity to organize memories both ways, but the proportion of each, and the way in which they encode and instantiate information, is still unclear (Tulving and Schacter 1990). Bateson had read Bartlett, and Bartlett was the scholar who began this line of inquiry back in the late 1920s.

But more remarkable is the propsal concerning the relevance of visual form and kinesthetic movement to the organization of memory. It is too sketchy to be called a formal hypothesis, let alone a theory, but what Bateson seems to have had in mind was the possibility that perceptual processes mediate memory. This contrasts with the neo-Humboldtian views of Sapir (1921), Whorf (1956), and Lee (1959), who identified the totality of mediating devices with the verbal code. Bateson suggests that there are media for the organization of memory which are below the level of verbal codification and which, because they are close to activity in the world, may rely on perceptual and kinesthetic processes in perception.

At the time Bateson was writing the best-known spokesman for this point of view was the psychologist Heinz Werner, whose work on memory, symbolic mediation, and the organization of thought has been compared to Lévy-Bruhl's. Like Lévy-Bruhl, Werner was then (and, unfortunately, still is) considered unacceptable by most anthropologists because he spoke of "primitive mentality." Far worse, he threatened the principle of semiotic arbitrariness (and therefore cultural relativity) by claiming that universal developmental processes underwrite symbol formation. According to Werner, symbols are given meaning through inner dynamic schematizing activity which intertwines the sensory, postural, affective, and imaginal components of the "organismic state," as Werner termed it (Werner 1978). Some of this is arbitrary, and therefore culturally determined, and some is not.

Like Werner, Bateson believed that the mix was not preordained and that some cultures might endow one component (such as sound or sight or kinesthesia) with particular salience as a mode of representation for the memory of cultural knowledge. Unlike Werner, however, he did present this as an evolutionary hypothesis, according to which societies advance from denotation to connotation, or from symbols bound by physiognomic perception to those more and more free of it. Bateson thus combined variability of form with universality of generative mechanism, asserting that anthropology was to be identified with its capacity to detect and understand both.

The organization and representation of cultural knowledge, "eidos," is not an outcome but a mindful process, with both universal and variable components. It is shaped by cultural premises and assumptions, but it also shapes them, by determining the manner in which knowledge is represented and retrieved. To cast this in modern language: Eidos is a repertoire of cultural models, or knowledge structures, which are variable and multiple, subject to extension or repression, and differently distributed among the members of a group. Today anthropologists tend to favor such a view because it makes culture less monolithic (something people can only "receive" from above) and more supple and manipulable (something people are able to "negotiate" or "transact" among themselves). All of this, I would say, is implicit in the notion of eidos. But there is also an important difference, which takes us back to the issue of oppositional dynamics and dialectics.

Eidos cannot be considered a heuristic construct, like today's "cultural model," which lacks the forms or principles that would make it serviceable as a model of cognition. Anything and everything can be called a cultural model, as long as it possesses generative capacity within a single domain.

But what is a model? Surely it is not the proposition itself, because if it were, we would have to assume that there are millions of such models in the mind. That would be astonishingly inefficient, not to mention inconsistent with what we know about human information-processing. But if it is not the proposition, then what is it?

This is one of the biggest problems with cultural cognition and the theory of cultural models, as a few scholars have begun to point out (e.g., Holland 1992). Nothing is said about the mnemonic forms or cognitive principles which underlie the models and which, presumably, all people share. The problem with cultural models is that they are unconstrained by forms and principles which are testable as hypotheses about cognition. Only recently, in work inspired largely by Lakoff (1987) and Johnson (1987), have there been signs of a change. Bateson, however, clearly wished to make the concept of eidos sensitive to the results of experimental psychology.

For one thing, Bateson acknowledged the importance of recent experimental work in the study of human memory and cognition. That is clear from the several references to Bartlett. He even looked forward to the day when his own conclusions concerning the structures of Iatmul thought would be subjected to experimental verification (1958:229). He did not, it is true, actually pursue this, but the fact that he was aware of the findings and willing to consider them is remarkable enough. Second, Bateson did not think that a cognitive theory necessarily excluded the physical, perceptual, and kinesthetic dimensions of knowledge formation and use. This was a tricky proposition, given how accustomed we are to thinking of knowledge as verbal and of memory as propositional. It would not be too fanciful to suggest that Bateson anticipated the theory of experiential realism being developed by Lakoff (1987). Third, Bateson endowed eidos with organizational principles that were abstract and capable of generalization, much as he had done for ethos. This is what makes the theory of eidos a theory in the true sense, since it is applicable in multiple situations and, ideally at least, susceptible to counterevidence.

The Paradoxical Dialectics of Desire and Knowledge

Cognition organizes itself out of cultural premises, but by "premises" Bateson did not mean principles with organized propositional formats. Premises in that sense are like "cultural models." It is not that they lack generative capacity, but that they fail to ground this capacity in an inner logic which constantly pushes itself forward in pursuit of some goal. What Bateson had in mind, it seems, were premises which possessed the power to generate propositions. *Dynamic power of this kind, in his view, comes out of some kind of conflict.* Here Bateson was true to his intention, described in the preface to the book, to write something with a "dash" of Hegelian dialectic. It was the conflict or, more precisely, the contradiction between opposing premises which generated and governed cultural knowledge. Bateson described this kind of thinking as "twisted" (1958:233). It pervades everything, "so that culture as a whole appears as a complex fabric in which the various conflicting eidological motifs are twisted and woven together" (1958:235).

In looking for generative dialectics, or "twisted" thinking, Bateson was able to reduce the Iatmul eidos to a set of core conflicts out of which everything else is produced:

1. Pluralism vs. Monism: Everything is multiple and everything is one.
2. Expression vs. Concealment: Knowledge must be expressed, in order to make claims of ownership, but knowledge must be concealed, so that its ownership is uncompromised.
3. Diagonal Dualism vs. Symmetrical Dualism: Everything has a sibling and everything has a symmetrical counterpart.

Let us examine these dialectics one by one. The first is this: While it is important to know thousands of totemic names and, by revealing this knowledge, to possess them, it is also important to know that all such names refer to the same thing. Iatmul debate insists simultaneously on the diversity and unity of its subject. The second dialectic is this: Ownership of clan myths can be demonstrated only through revelation of secret details; however, details must be kept secret in order to preserve ownership of the myth. The obliqueness and verbal ellipsis characteristic of Iatmul debate can be understood as an outcome of this inherent conflict. The third dialectic: Things are relatd to each other in pairs, but the link may be between like terms (direct relationship) or between opposed terms (diagonal relationship). Both types of relationship are always present, so the conflict develops when one tries to assign values to them or decide which is more important. The problem may be conceived of thus: Which is more important—the direct relationship between siblings of the same sex or the symmetrical relationship between affines of the opposite sex? As Bateson saw it, this problem is at the heart of the *naven:* It is this which the ceremony both represents and attempts to resolve in a moment of integration, or "supersession" (as Hegel called it), in which oppositions are temporarily brought together.

The similarity between this and the theory of schizmogenesis is apparent, but oddly enough, Bateson himself failed to make the connection until late in the writing of *Naven* (1958:241 n. 1). The logical link between the two, ethos and eidos, is the sharing of the same internal dynamic based on conflict—a dialectical mechanism capable of generating synthetic cultural forms as resolutions, or "supersessions." Dialectic is not peculiar to the inhabitants of New Guinea. Bateson considered it applicable elsewhere, even in his own culture, where "we have the dualism between Mind and Matter and others based on contrast between different levels of personality" (1958:240). Where emotions are involved, as in ethos, the conflict is between desires that mutually construct and oppose each other, and which seek a steady state within a closed and homeostatic system. Rituals like *naven* permit expression of opposing desires and balance them out through cultural formations which temporarily transmute oppositions (through reversal, etc.). The system of such formations constitutes an ethos. Where cognitive constructs are involved, as in eidos, the conflict is between assumptions whose premises logically contradict each other. Systems of thought result. One of their functions is to represent and resolve cognitive conflict. That they do so only partially and temporarily is one of the reasons knowledge systems change.

THE GOAL AND DIRECTION OF CULTURAL DIALECTICS: WEBER AND BATESON

In essence, what Bateson proposes is nothing less than a theory of paradox, which, as I explained in chapter 2, is at the heart of any dialectically developed knowledge system. Bateson himself does not quite say this, but given his fondness for Whitehead and Russell, he probably agreed with them that paradox is powerful because it impels and directs knowledge, giving it shape. Iatmul debate exemplifies this process. Paradoxes inherent in Iatmul conceptions generate the dialectics out of which Iatmul social structures, emotional orientations, and cognitive organization take shape. They are fundamental, just as in Western philosophy, the unresolvable and paradoxical dualism of mind and matter is fundamental to the development of philosophical systems all the way from Plato to Descartes.

If ediological conflict gives shape to cultural knowledge, it is less clear how it provides knowledge with direction. Now, Bateson repeatedly stressed that he had written only a synchronic account of Iatmul culture (1958:256). He did not present, nor did he claim to know, how the structures he described came to be or changed through time. But there are indications not only that Bateson considered time but that a theory of change is basic to his perspective on the dynamics of conflict, both ethological and eidological.

Naven evolved as Bateson wrote it, and in the early sections on social structure there are hints of an implicit processual approach:

> We must therefore conclude that while the structural position lays down possible lines along which the culture *may* develop, the existence of such lines does not explain why the culture should select them for emphasis. We have demonstrated the existence of the lines but we have still to demonstrate the "motive force" which has caused the culture to run along them. (1958:82)

By "lines" Bateson referred to the attribution of maternal qualities to the *wau*, or mother's brother, which are especially evident in the *naven* ceremonies. Such qualities seem overly exaggerated; pushed to an extreme by desires or forces that must be specified. The same is true of the totemic system, with its thousands of names and multiple connections to a labyrinthine mythology. Why has it been taken so far? The same question is relevant to the emotional orientations assigned to men and women. Men are supposed to be full of pride, and they are, to the extent that they seek out every opportunity for exaggerated display. But what is the force behind such a compulsion?

Bateson claimed to discover the answer in the contrasting emotional orientations of the two sexes: "It has provided the little push which has led the culture to follow its structural premises to the extreme which I have described" (1958:202). So we are left with nothing other than the motivational dynamic that was described earlier, in our discussion of ethos, with its implicit reliance on a theory of mental conflict similar to the psychoanalytic version. *"Force" is nothing other than the pressure to achieve satisfaction in a dialectically moving series of incomplete and escalating compromises among opposing values.* This is true, as far as it goes, but it is not sufficient, because it neglects the meanings assigned to these values.

Bateson came to grips with this problem in the chapter on eidos, in his encompassing characterization of Iatmul culture. The Iatmul, quite simply, enjoy the intellectualization of paradox. Such enjoyment is not confined to the ritual elite but common to all. "Among the Iatmul the dialecticians and theologians are not a class apart but are, as we have seen, the chief contributors to the culture" (1958:232). In short, the goal toward which they strive is not orderly completeness or resolution in unity, as in Western science, or "fusion," as in Jalari culture, but the preservation and development of paradox itself.

Now, the notion of a goal that endows cultural forms (both knowledge and emotion) with direction or force is an interesting one, as we saw in chapter 2, because it departs so radically from the Durkheimian view. According to the view we usually attribute to Durkheim, society is a system, the operations of which should be considered analogous to those of a biological organism or machine. *Purpose* refers to the working of the system in balance with itself and its environment. Bateson obviously found this perspective wanting and, through his relationship with Margaret Mead, discovered the different approach offered by the Boasians.

Of greatest importance was the sudden arrival in Bateson's Sepik River camp of the draft version of Ruth Benedict's *Patterns of Culture.* The impact of this book was twofold. First, it gave him an approach to society that did not take for granted that integration should exist but accepted it as a problem to be examined. This was crucial to introducing the notion of conflict so basic to the cultural dynamics Bateson ultimately decided to focus on. Second, Benedict's concept of purpose was nonteleological. In fact, she preferred the word *goal* and used it to refer to an ideal value or state to which a society directs itself and which thereby informs its structure. "Within each culture," she wrote in *Patterns of Culture,* "there come into being characteristic purposes not necessarily shared by other types of society. . . . Taken up by a well integrated culture, the most ill-assorted acts become characteristic of particular goals. . . . The form that these acts take, we can understand by understanding first the emotional and intellectual mainsprings of that society" (1934:46).

Ethos and eidos were therefore necessary but insufficient to a cultural account *unless* it could specify the characteristic goal or purpose to which action is directed. So utterly different is this from the traditional British view that we should pause for a moment and reflect on where Bateson, Bendict, and the Boasians got it. Not surprisingly, the origin the tradition, descended from Kant and Hegel on one side and Goethe on the other, which attempted to link the cognitive and affective in something Dilthey called *geist,* or spirit. The most important realization of this tradition in social science is Max Weber. The theory that Bateson put forward in *Naven* is closer in design to the work of Weber than it is to that of any British anthropologist of the time.

In the idea of cultural goal, providing cultural forms with direction, Bateson reinvented a central Weberian concept: *Wertsteigerung,* or "value intensification." Recall from chapter 2 Weber's argument that as value standpoints become increasingly explicit and their implications for action are developed and made more rational, they also become more distinct as the objectives toward which progress in a particular domain (e.g., religion, music, explanation) is directed. The logic which governs this process is always of a certain kind, one Weber called *Eigengesetizichkeit,* or "law of its own." (Weber 1968:341). From a Weberian cultural-historical perspective, cultures consist partly of rationalized conceptual domains, like religion or music or any other, and must be understood in terms of the socially determined value (*Wertsteigerung*) and developmental logic (*Eigengesetzlichkeit*) they attempt to fulfill and conform to.

The high value that the Iatmul place on paradox and dialectic is a case in point. It is a goal inherent in the system, a system which generates instances to display and intensify this value. Bateson never described it more precisely than that, and to us the statement that a whole culture could be dedicated to the maximization of this value—paradox—must seem difficult to grasp. It could be imagined this way. The "value" of a monistic and unitary conception of the universe has always been important in the West, at no time more so than when it is challenged, as it is at present by what is called postmodernism. Christian cosmology insists on the unique beginning of the world, in the act of a single and omnipotent creator, and on its unique termination. Science seeks unitary laws that possess sufficient generality and abstraction to make them applicable everywhere, independent of local construction or construal. Even the law, in most cases, asserts that only one intention can be real and only one position true. Examples could be multiplied, but the point should be clear: If there is "a" goal toward which Western culture tends (an overgeneralization), at least in terms of its construction of knowledge systems, then it is the value placed on truth as a conception of unity in multiplicity, the one in the many, *e pluribus unum.*

A unitary conception of truth as a cultural ideal or goal has had important implications for Western ethos. We feel, or expect ourselves to feel, good when we are consistent and bad when we are not, when consistency is defined as adherence to a single idea, principle, or behavior. Inconsistency is supposed to cause cognitive dissonance, a powerful motivating force which compels us to revise our preferences or modify our plans in order to make them tally with each other.

This is not true everywhere. The unitary worldview has also had a major role in shaping eidos, the ways in which we organize and retrieve knowledge. The most obvious example is category organization, which, since Aristotle, people in the West have tried to make hierarchical, so that all members are ultimately subordinate to a single superordinate term or being. "Fuzzy set" and "prototype" theories are controversial precisely because they challenge this view. Similarly, argument by deduction, another Western favorite, is a preferred logical process because it starts from universal and unitary precepts. For this reason, other processes, such as context-dependent inference and analogical reasoning, do not have the same standing and are therefore judged instances of "pre-logical" or "magical" thinking.

To imagine the Iatmul worldview one must accept an ambiguous multiplicity in place of the Western ideal and acknowledge that the Iatmul prefer the play of contradiction to the pursuit of a single truth. It then becomes a question of method, for we must have a means for investigating this worldview. It follows from Bateson that the method must be twofold. First, we must locate the set of emotional forces or inner compulsions which drives and shapes the system. This is simply to say we must describe the cultural ethos, which Bateson understands as a conflict-ridden set of opposing emotional orientations, which seeks balance and settles for compromise through dynamic mechanisms (schizmogenesis). In Iatmul culture it consists of the different emotional orientations assigned to men and women. Compromise is reached in the ritual of *naven*. But compromise is always temporary, since it is based on reversal (e.g., transvestitism) and not reduction to unity. The system does not seek unity, so the compromises it reaches and resolutions it constructs are free to emphasize multiplicity and contradictoriness, the very goals which the system applauds. The second obligation under Bateson's methodology is to describe the set of knowledge structures and intellectual operations, which Bateson called eidos. In their elaboration of dialectical oppositions, these structures are like ethos. They develop the same cultural logic and thus seek to maximize the value of multiplicity.

Ethos and eidos must be understood as twin configurative processes, both simultaneously providing motivational force and cognitive form. This recalls the metaphor in which ethos and eidos are compared to a river and its banks: "The river molds the banks and the banks guide the river. Similarly, the ethos molds the cultural structure and is guided by it" (Bateson 1972:83). It should be altered, perhaps, to include "goal" as the river's destination. The point is not that ends determine means, or that form follows function, but that there is a necessary relationship between the emotional and the cognitive, and a subordination of both to cultural goals. This is the necessary unity to which Bateson contributed not a paradigm but the possibility of an integrative approach, one whose possible application we shall consider further in the next chapter.

Chapter Four

The Rationalization of Directive Goals in Explanatory Desires

Human reason has this peculiar fate that in one species of its knowledge it is burdened by questions which, as prescribed by the very nature of reason itself, it is not able to ignore, but which, as transcending all its powers, it is also not able to answer. (Kant, *Preface*, Critique of Pure Reason [1st ed.])

The theoretical integration Bateson proposed was suppressed, not deliberately but accidentally, by an age which did not favor new systems. People admire Bateson because he was a humanist, not a theory builder, and it is the poetry of his work and not the science of it which appeals to many. It is also true that Bateson himself never presented a well-formulated theory that successfully united his interest in knowledge systems and systems of deep desire, or cognition and motivation. The terms he introduced, *ethos* and *eidos,* suggest the possibility of a synthesis—Bateson even said that they were the same thing—but they remain unconnected by any overall conception. If there is such a conception, then it might be the one I proposed, framed in terms of paradoxical-dialectical rationalization.

It is time to examine this conception in more detail, and apply it to a wider range of cultural phenomena. Desire in paradoxical-dialectical systems is twofold, made up of the *goals* toward which knowledge is directed (eidos) and the *ambivalence* which arises as oppositions conflict with each other (ethos). Knowledge structures seek to realize desires of both kinds through repeated revision and reformulation. The last chapter examined the reasons why directive goals can never be reached, thus sustaining the dialectical movement. This chapter will consider culturally defined goals in more detail, in order to find out how they act to shape and constrain the knowledge systems associated with them.

I shall focus directly on the experiences of greatest interest to this analysis: cognitive conflict, confusion, and doubt—the very things which usually prompt recourse to systems of explanation. The source of these experiences is the directive goals whose nature we seek to interpret. We will look for cultural goals in the experience of confusion. If such experiences are different cross-culturally, then it stands to reason that explanation itself must be a cultural artifact. The phenomenon known as "cognitive dissonance" provides a useful vocabulary for discussing this explanatory confusion or doubt, and gives us an access point to the goals which direct different explanatory phenomena cross-culturally.

FROM DISSONANCE TO DIRECTIVE GOALS

Leon Festinger, who invented the term, found that "cognitive dissonance" and the discomfort it creates leads to changes in ideas, attitudes, and behavior: "Just as hunger impels a person to eat, so does dissonance impel a person to change his opinions or his beliefs" (1962:93.) Having made the choice between two attractive alternatives, for example, we exaggerate the good qualities of the chosen alternative and the bad qualities of the rejected, to avoid feeling that we may have made the wrong choice. Cognitive dissonance is thus a motivational state, created in the desire for explanatory consistency, and exists whenever a person possesses cognitive elements that imply the opposite of each other (Wicklund and Brehm 1976:10).

The basic theory has received extensive confirmation from social psychologists working mainly, if not exclusively, in the United States and Britain (e.g., Fazio and Cooper 1983; Gaes, Melburg, and Tedeschi 1986; Zanna and Cooper 1976). But is cognitive dissonance a phenomenon that is generalizable cross-culturally because the goal of explanatory consistency is universal? I will show that "consistency" is not a universal, but a culturally specific goal, and that there are other goals, which produce very different kinds of dissonance. Following Bateson (and also Benedict), I shall argue that directive "goals" are culturally specific and that the circumstances which create dissonance, defining its recognition and delimiting its scope, are culturally constructed. These circumstances are not simple derivatives of formal logic (exclusion, transitivity, etc.) but complex and culture-bound criteria that are closely bound up with local constructions of explanatory goals.

Second, the cognitive work that is done to relieve dissonance varies in nature and extent with the explanatory objectives of the people who perform it. It cannot be limited to the formally rational strategies Festinger and his associates consider prototypic, i.e., seeking consistent information not already present ("selective exposure"), looking at consistent information once it is there ("selective attention"), or translating ambiguous information to be consistent ("selective interpretation"). Third, dissonance is not limited to justification and explanation but may arise in other domains, including the irrational and the affective. It all depends on the nature of the desired ends, the directive goals of knowledge in explanation.

Explanatory consistency is a stock issue in what has become known as "the rationality debate" (Hollis and Lukes 1982; Wilson 1970), and foregrounds one of the central questions in anthropological theory: Does the existence of mutually inconsistent and therefore apparently irrational beliefs force us to accept relativism in its strong form? There are three responses to this question. The first is that apparently irrational beliefs are truly irrational, based on fallacious assumptions (e.g., Hollis 1982) or on compulsive unconscious wishes which cannot be controlled or argued against (e.g., Spiro 1984). The second states that apparently irrational beliefs are not really irrational, but nonrational, and ultimately make sense when enough of their cultural and social context has been described (Horton 1982; Lukes 1982; Shweder 1984, 1986). The third states that they are not really beliefs in the first place, but semipropositional structures which call for different kinds of rational appraisal (Sperber 1985).

The problem with these (and other) responses is that they fail to treat "consistency" itself as a problem. Consistency as a desire, as a goal to which the development of knowledge is directed, must be interpreted before its value as a measurement of rational thought can be evaluated. I do not propose that we abandon the criterion of consistency, since to do so merely runs the risk of overstating cultural differences. It need not be the case that we are prone to value consistency and that others are not, or that dissonance is something we experience but others never do. But even if incommensurability must be taken seriously as a possible outcome, it is still wrong to posit it as a first-order hypothesis.

My finding is that consistency as a value is domain-specific; that in Western cultures (arguably) the goal of consistency in the domain of formal explanation is high, but that in other cultures different domains may have been endowed with dissonance-generating properties, perhaps creating a different kind of dissonance from the kind we know.

To problematize the issue of explanatory consistency is to ask why we should ever desire to maximize it as a goal. That we *should* desire it seems so natural that even to pose the question is perverse. Yet explanation is not the same everywhere. Its meaning and its value both vary with culturally determined epistemological assumptions, and so we must inquire the cultural history of explanation and link it, as we typically do for other symbols, to important cultural assumptions. Among the most important of these assumptions, I will argue, is ontology: a theory of the way the world comes into being.

Cultural epistemologies and ontologies should be studied as mutually configuring systems sharing important underlying assumptions. For example, if we want to understand South Asian explanation, so often described as "context-dependent" (Shweder and Bourne 1984), it makes sense, I will argue, to examine it against the background of Hindu theories of creation. In the same way, if we want to understand Western scientific explanation, often described as "context-independent," it must be interpreted against the background of Western beliefs concerning the way the world comes into being. Different ways of world-making (to take a line from Nelson Goodman) prefigure different ways of explaining the world, making ontology and epistemology necessarily linked.

In what follows I seek to interpret consistency by problematizing it, first for "us" and then for "the other." When I compare Western scientific and South Indian divinatory explanation, I shall show that a concern for consistency is domain-specific and related to different assumptions about the origin and development of knowledge. Origin myths within both cultures reveal these assumptions by presenting the origin of the world and the origin of knowledge as related processes. The myths contain what Bradd Shore has called an epistemogenesis (Shore, 1996), a description of the creation of a knowable world in which ontology and epistemology are coeval. I conclude that a theory of cognitive consistency is possible only within the knowable world each culture constructs.

The Directive Goals of Formal Explanations: Some Examples

Once again we are back to directive goals, but here we shall examine them from a new angle. Two illustrations, one from the United States and the other from South India, will help to define the problem. In both cases, the goal of consistency is foregrounded, but for one it comes up naturally, because it is a cultural goal, while for the other it is imposed by the outside observer. The danger is that we conclude too readily that this makes them incommensurable. It will be shown later that before we can conclude anything, we must consider their different ontological assumptions, and from these their directive goals.

The Trial of John W. Hinckley, Jr., and Its Aftermath

In 1981, John W. Hinckley, Jr., shot Ronald Reagan. At Hinckley's trial, the prosecution and the defense both agreed that he was mentally ill. The prosecution, however, claimed that Hinckley's illness did not impair his judgment. The defense argued that Hinckley's mental state in effect constituted an external agency, "madness," which interfered with his normal ability to act volitionally and think rationally. The jury decided in favor of the defense and acquitted Hinckley "by reason of insanity."

Following the Hinckley trial, many Americans were angry and outraged.[1] Some, of course, felt that an important liberal principle had been vindicated. Individuals under duress, even when that duress is psychological, should not be held as accountable as those who act with complete awareness and conscious volition. Others felt that individuals must be held accountable for their acts no matter what. Despite unanimity in the verdict, even the jurors were conflicted. "I felt I was on the brink of insanity myself going through this," one juror confessed (Caplan 1984:102). The debate intensified as the legal establishment, committees of the House and Senate, and the majority of state legislatures began a long inquiry into revising the "insanity defense." No less than twenty-six bills were introduced in Congress to limit the defense. Even the attorney general, William French Smith, lobbied hard for its complete abolition. Why were these actions taken?

Many people seemed to feel that the issue should be settled, "once and for all," in favor of one perspective or the other, to ensure that similar confusions would not arise in the future. Either a person should be found guilty because he committed the crime or innocent because he did not. The existence of a middle ground, which the insanity defense created, was extremely problematic and had been so, in fact, ever since the famous M'Naghten decision over a century ago. Of course it required a nationally prominent case, such as the Hinckley trial, to bring the issue out into the open. But the terms of the debate, and the dilemma they created, remained the same.

Caplan (1984) suggests that the president's anti-crime stance, in addition to the public's perception of a national crime wave, provided the impetus for attempting to resolve the dilemma at long last. The result was that by the late 1980s a compromise solution was largely in place. A majority of the states had adopted a new category of defense—"guilty but mentally ill," or GBMI—which no longer made it necessary to decide between one or the other. The finding implies that someone who satisfies the standard of

---

1. A *Time* magazine poll indicated that 60% of those contacted in a random sample felt that something was wrong with a criminal justice system that failed to convict a self-confessed murderer. See C. David Mortensen, *Violence and Communication: Public Reactions to an Attempted Presidential Assassination* (Lanham, Md.: University Press of America, 1987); and Lincoln Caplan, *The Insanity Defense and the Trial of John W. Hinckley, Jr.* (Boston: Godine, 1984).

mental illness and insanity can nonetheless be found guilty and thus blame-worthy.[2] Although the controversy still continues, resolution of the matter in favor of a compromise solution won considerable support, in part because it no longer made it necessary to decide between an internal and an external locus of control.

A Case of Marital Infidelity in South India

In 1977, in a small South Indian fishing village, a man found his wife sleeping with another man. The village elders brought the woman to trial and condemned her, but agreed not to punish her if she begged her husband's forgiveness. She did. Asked later (by me) why she didn't protest or at least blame the man she had been caught with, she said that it was all simply her fate—to sin, to be caught, to be blamed. Other villagers felt sorry for her because of her cruel fate (*karma*), but insisted that she must be punished anyway. They said she could have avoided committing adultery if she had really tried.

Following the woman's trial for adultery and the decision to hold her accountable, villagers stopped thinking about the incident. They didn't worry about having to choose between two perspectives which seemed, to an outsider, mutually inconsistent. They never suggested that either perspective—deterministic or nondeterministic—should be rejected or revised. People simply went about their business, with both perspectives intact, functional, and available for use in future explanations. And yet, in terms of public awareness, her trial had been of a magnitude equal to that of the Hinckley case. The fact that this issue had been decided in one way (in favor of a non-karmic explanation) did not preclude the possibility that on another occasion it could turn out differently (with an acceptable explanation framed in karmic, that is, deterministic, terms.)

There are important similarities and differences between the American and Indian cases. In both, explanatory perspectives that allocate responsibility to factors within and outside the individual conflicted. Americans and Indians both had to decide between a locus of control either external or internal to the culturally constructed boundaries of the person. But there is also a critical difference. When American jurors decided in favor of an external locus and acquitted Hinckley, many Americans who had followed the trial experienced a kind of "dissonance" which the confrontation of two favored perspectives created. Something in the nature of this dissonance made it necessary to take action, to do the "cognitive work"

2. See Caplan, *The Insanity Defense and the Trial of John W. Hinckley, Jr.*

necessary to make sure that similar confrontations did not occur again. The solution was to revise the legal code in such a way that the two alternatives no longer presented themselves as equivalent options. But when South Indian village elders decided in favor of an internal locus and condemned the adulteress, the villagers were unfazed. There was no dissonance and no dissonance-relieving "work" to redress the conflict in causal perspectives or to make sure that it never occurred again. The options they had to choose among remained exactly as they had been before.

Examples like these reveal that dissonance is not a natural or inevitable outcome in explanatory situations that might seem similar. Choices between mutually attractive options *may or may not* produce the cognitive discomfort that leads to changes in thoughts and attitudes. That is not to say that dissonance itself is a culture-bound phenomenon, found only in some places (like the United States) and not in others. Intuitively, at least, that seems very unlikely. It is much more likely that: 1) different cultures selectively endow some areas, but not others, with properties which generate dissonance; 2) the culturally defined goals which inform explanation differ; and 3) the definition of dissonance itself must be broadened to encompass these instances.

For Americans, an important dissonance-generating domain appears to be abstract and formal explanation, but for South Indians, another domain has been selected. The central problem with dissonance theory is that it is too narrow, limited, for the most part, to cognitive aspects of explanation, justification, and decision-making which the West has endowed with special cultural importance. What we need is a theory of "ethno-dissonance" within a broadened theory of explanation, sensitive to differences in cultural values, that will help us understand how cultures invoke and respond to dissonance in terms of their own directive goals.

Below I examine a few of the circumstances which create dissonance among one of the cultural communities I know best: cultural anthropologists. I use Weber's concept of rationalization to show that dissonance can be described in terms of a cultural logic which is intimately bound up with ontological premises. For Americans, this logic has an interesting cultural correlate in the logic of biblical cosmology. Similar principles govern both the logic of explanation and the way the world comes into being in the most well-known creation myth, in Genesis. This, I shall show, is not surprising, since the Biblical account makes the creation process dependent on the development of formal explanatory abilities in God and human beings. Finally, I turn to a consideration of South Asian explanation, to show that it is based on different ontological assumptions, different explanatory desires, and is thus productive of a different kind of dissonance—a kind less like dissonance, in fact, and more like what psychoanalytic theorists call ambivalence.

EXPLANATORY DISSONANCE AND DOING ANTHROPOLOGY

Anthropologists like to tell stories about themselves and their experiences in the field. In telling them, they reveal not only what they do, but more importantly, why they do it. Examining such stories, especially the better-known ones, is therefore particularly useful for revealing the dynamics of dissonance and explanation in Western social theory. Three anecdotes are illustrative. The first two are canonical in the lore of the discipline, and references to them abound in many theoretical reviews (e.g., Wilson 1970; Triandis and Heron 1980). The third is from my own fieldwork and significant simply because it emphasized to me how important dissonance—or rather, its suppression—is to anthropological thought.

The Case of the Incomplete Syllogism
Vygotsky's student and colleague, A. R. Luria, submitted incomplete syllogisms to unschooled Central Asian peasants:

> "In the far North, where there is snow, all bears are white. Novaya Zemyla is in the far North and there is always snow there. What color are the bears there?"
> "We always speak only of what we see; we don't talk about what we haven't seen."
> (Ethnographer): But what do my words imply? (The syllogism is repeated.)
> "Well, it's like this: our tsar isn't like yours, and yours isn't like ours. Your words can be answered only by someone who was there, and if a person wasn't there he can't say anything on the basis of your words."
> (Ethnographer): . . . But on the basis of my words—in the North, where there is always snow, the bears are white, can you gather what kind of bears there are in Novaya Zemyla?
> "If a man was sixty or eighty and had seen a white bear and had told about it, he could be believed, but I've never seen one and hence I can't say. That's my last word. Those who saw can tell, and those who didn't see can't say anything!" (Luria 1971:108–9)

The Case of the Witchcraft Substance
Evans-Pritchard asked Zande herdsman how to test definitively for witchcraft. They told him that an autopsy would reveal a "witchcraft substance"

in the body of a real witch. They also told him that this substance was in-
herited. Did that mean that all those people related to a diagnosed witch
were necessarily witches also?

> One would imagine that if witchcraft is hereditary, then a man must
> surely have a good idea whether he is a witch or not from the records of
> his father, his paternal uncles, and his grandfather. But, whilst a man
> will certainly bring up cases in which the corpses of his kinsmen were
> examined for witchcraft and found to contain none in order to boast his
> own immunity, the fact that a man's forebears were witches is not
> stressed. It is generally not even known, for it has no significance either
> to their sons or to other people since no one is interested in the question
> whether a man is a witch or not. To a Zande this appears an entirely
> theoretical question and one about which he has not informed himself.
> (Evans-Pritchard 1937:63)

The Case of the Unaccepted Suggestion

South Indian shamans told me that "false" ancestor spirits, pretending to
be true ones, would sometimes interfere in the divinatory process. I suggested a method of verification: Ask the spirit that possesses the medium
if it remembers an incident only the true ancestor spirit could know about,
e.g., "Do you remember the time we found a baby cobra in your turban?" If
the spirit does not remember the event or remembers an event which never
took place, then its identity, true or false, would be known. The shamans
rejected this test.

The Significance of Dissonance in Anthropological Theory

Fieldwork is rife with experiences like these. As subsequently recalled anecdotes, they serve to illustrate the natives' power to baffle and the anthropologists' power to explain. But why is there a desire to explain? What are
the goals of explanation? How do culturally defined goals influence explanation?

Anthropologists assert formal equality among the cultures they study.
Anecdotes like these three are especially useful because they help to belie the claim that cross-cultural differences depend on good or bad brains
or good or bad upbringing. For example, Luria's peasants are not stupid
because they failed to complete the syllogism. Those who attend school
complete the syllogism test perfectly. The difference between them and
their unschooled counterparts is cultural and comes down to the importance of western-style abstraction (very great in formal education, very
little in everyday peasant life). The cultural-cognitive account pays close at-

tention to the social context of individual experience in the interpretation of thinking (see Cole 1981; Rogoff 1980; Scribner and Cole 1981; Sharp et al. 1979).

Second, the anecdotes focus discussion on the social construction of knowledge and seem to confirm that cultural systems are determinative of category formation and explanatory thinking. For example, the Azande practice sophisticated truth-testing methods which they nevertheles do not develop as a body of theoretical knowledge. That is because such methods are embedded in a "social logic" geared to the maintenance of kinship ties and not to the production of empirically verified information (see Horton 1982; Taylor 1982).

Third, fieldwork anecdotes ground theoretical discussions in the terms (symbolic) and in the language (hermeneutic) that cultural anthropology defines as valid, or at least used to. As Sperber (1975) points out, anthropologists know they are in the presence of a "symbol": An utterance is irrational and fails to conform to the truth conditions we accept. For example: South Indian shamans map everyday occurrences of distress onto divinatory scenarios, explaining commonplace events by translating them into a spiritual idiom. Divinatory accounts try to achieve a "fit" between the phenomenal and the supernatural, between individual experience and the action of spirits. The hermeneutic account interprets this kind of thinking symbolically, devoting noticeably more attention to the symbolic constructs than to the psychological processes which instantiate them (Agar 1986; Sperber 1985).

Because these are crucial precepts—definitive, really, of what many would say cultural anthropology is all about—their anecdotalization as fieldwork experiences appear with regularity. My empirically unverified assumption is that few introductory courses, in which the lore of the discipline is transmitted, get by without them. But is their power to demonstrate important culturalogical precepts *really* what makes them so compelling? Or is it that, in their telling, such stories help to relieve an otherwise disagreeable sensation of dissonance which anthropologists often experience in the presence of thinking they find difficult to explain?

Perhaps because they have not been trained to conceal it, students are especially good at revealing the dissonance they experience in their first attempt to explain "inconsistency" in native thought. After accepting, at least in principle, the basic premises and conclusions of the relativistic culture theory, many still want to know why Luria's informants cannot be led to reason syllogistically on demand. They also find it hard to understand the Azandes' seeming failure to pursue their witchcraft beliefs to their logical conclusion. And they still wonder why—even though they know "why" in an abstract sense—the Indian shamans I talked to refused to consider the hypothetical implications of their spirit beliefs. These illustrations (and no doubt many more) share the important capacity to provoke curiosity and debate, and not only among students: Witness the fact that virtually *every* major contribution to the rationality debate incorporates an almos catechistic retelling of Luria's experience among the Central Asians or of Evans-Pritchard's among the Azande (e.g., Boyer 1990; Gellner 1970; Jarvie and Agassi 1970; Hollis and Lukes 1982; Winch 1970).

Whatever fosters our curiosity in these accounts, whatever forces us (almost perniciously) to keep asking "why," whatever makes us eager to decide the problems they present definitively and once and for all—*that* is the source both of our explanatory desire and of our ethno-dissonance. *This "something" is the goal toward which the rationalization of explanation is directed.* It helps to constitute the desire to know, and thus shapes the anthropological quest for knowledge.

This is the key. The irony is that instead of making this directive force an object of study, we have excluded attention to it through the ways we define our discipline. Just how this happens is worth considering before we move on.

The Neglect of Dissonance in Anthropological Theory

Anthropological dissonance has not been subjected to systematic inquiry for many reasons, not the least of which is the naturally anxiety-provoking nature of self-scrutiny. But there are other reasons. The most important is the epistemology of the social sciences and its relation to cognitive processes, such as explanation and dissonance, and their representation. Anthropology vacillates between two positions on this issue. The first (sometimes called "positivism") variously asserts that knowledge is represented in cognitively, developmentally, or experientially derived structures. The second (sometimes called "interpretivism") variously asserts that knowledge is represented in culturally constituted systems of symbols. Both positions systematically exclude attention to the phenomena under discussion here.

The paradigmatic positivist approach starts from the position that thought processes are best exemplified by mathematical logic, statistical theory, and formal inference (induction and deduction). Everyday thinking conforms rather badly to these models and so gives rise to the several positive sciences dedicated to observing, testing, and describing the shortcomings which humans exhibit in their thought processes. For instance, it has been observed that people behave in ways they cannot explain or are not aware of. This observation leads in one direction to the Freudian interest in the unconscious processes which block insight. It leads in another direction to the postulation of developmental stages and to the Piagetian hypothesis that, under different circumstances, humans may develop or fail to develop fully realized abstract thought. In still another direction, the discovery of "bounded rationality" (Simon 1982) leads to the abandonment of rationality in any strict sense and to the search for various approximating mechanisms or "heuristics," including the various strategies and recipes which, though fallible, usually get the job done for most people, most of the time (Tversky and Kahneman 1981).

Positivist perspectives adhere to the ideal of "perfect rationality"; to the method of describing rationalities through comparison to an imagined (and usually unstated) ideal; and to the discovery of universal cognitive properties. It is on the basis of these (often misunderstood) adherences that cultural anthropologists level at positivists their most damning epithet: "reductionist."

The paradigmatic interpretivist approach starts from different assumptions. Perfect rationality is not the standard of comparison. There is, instead, something called a "system"—a discrete, integrated, and internally consistent whole—which is present in forms generally described as "social," "ideological," or "cultural." The interpretivist account locates explanation within its overall rendering of the system. If the system is coherent, i.e., if it is integrated "in its own terms," then everything else should eventually make sense (Gellner 1970). Cultural phenomena are interesting to the extent that they exhibit characteristics and properties of the cultural system. Uninteresting phenomena are those that cannot be understood as manifestations of the described system.

Differences among the different schools of cultural anthropology—or of interpretivism generally—are not as significant as their mutual fascination with and capacity to generate hypercoherent models of cultural systems. The result is not only a failure to develop what Shweder has called a "science of the subjective" (Shweder 1986:177) but also the exclusion from detailed study of explanation, desire, and dissonance. Only recently has the picture begun to change (e.g., Barth 1987; Dougherty 1985; Holland and Quinn 1987; Lutz 1988; Nuckolls 1991; Shore 1991; Shweder 1991; Stigler, Shweder, and Herdt 1990).

Positivism and interpretivism are recognizably discrete orientations, but they share similar implications for the study of thinking, including dissonance and explanatory desire. These implications are discussed below. Needless to say they do not apply to every instance of (positivist or interpretivist) social science.

Thinking Is Absolute
Positivist and interpretivist approaches insist on the reasonableness of action. However, they recognize neither discrimination among alternative actions nor the possibility that actions may be based on principles inconsistent with the presumed logic—whether that logic is symbolic, cognitive, or anything else.

Thinking Is Relevant
Implicit is the requirement that action be taken in terms of "reasonable" preferences; that action be willful; that action be consistent. Thinking and explaining are relevant to the consistent preferences and willful actions undertaken to fulfill those preferences.

Thinking Is Consistent
Most accounts do not allow for mutually inconsistent choices unless analysis identifies them as resolvable at some other "level."

Thinking Is Precise
Most accounts avoid ambiguity in modes of thoughtful behavior.

Thinking Is Non-reflexive
Most accounts assume that an explanation will not be altered by the outcome it produces, i.e., there is no feedback.

The systematic exclusion from anthropological discourse of the phenomena that are associated with dissonance—confusion, ambiguity, doubt —is nothing new (Gellner 1970; Nuckolls 1993a). As long as explanation and the desire for it are assumed, no other consequence is possible. Of course, many share the awareness that something must be done to correct the anthropologist's imposition of excessive reasonableness (e.g., Boyer 1990). Several recent ethnographies, in fact, go a long way to achieving this correction (e.g., Trawick 1990), but without recognizing the root of the problem. A better approach is to focus the critique directly on the production of knowledge in explanation: What, precisely, are the mechanisms which tell us what kind of knowledge to look for and how to describe it?

SCIENTIFIC OBJECTIVISM AND THE ARCHITECTONIC
OF PURE REASON

Fundamental to the problem of dissonance in anthropological inquiry is
the logic of scientific discovery, a logic synonymous with the quest for what
Bacon called *una scientia universalis,* and made up of universality, comprehensive laws, inclusive theories, and exhaustive categorizations. Kant
called it the "architectonic" and attributed its force to natural reason:
"Reason is impelled by a tendency of its nature to go out beyond the field of
its empirical employment, and to venture in a pure employment, by means
of ideas alone, to the utmost of all knowledge, and not be satisfied save
through a completion of its course in a self-subsistent whole" (1965:630).
According to this view, natural reason and rational principle do not de-
rive from experience; they are innate. The kind of knowledge which they
produce is distinct from the knowledge acquired by experience in context
over time. Kant called the latter "historical knowledge." It is *cognitio ex
datis,* knowledge out of existential fact, whereas rational knowledge, in
accordance with "reason's legislative prescriptions," represents *cognitio ex
principiis,* knowledge from principles (Kant 1965:633, 655). The Kantian
conception of knowledge is the precursor to "scientific objectivism."

Scientific objectivism makes several assumptions possible, beginning
with the assumption that the impetus to scientific explanation develops in
the nature of the ideas themselves. "Reason" has an existence independent
of the human mind, and "it" generates scientific progress. The idea of a
heliocentric solar system, for example, is understood to be correct because
it refers to entities and processes of the objective world. An unimpaired
capacity to reason existing anywhere in the universe must eventually discover this idea as well as the principles which underlie it. Basing its theory
of communication on just this view, NASA equipped its first interstellar
probe (Viking I) with a symbol of the hydrogen atom. The designers assumed that communication between humans and other beings would have
to begin by establishing common ground in the recognition of the simplest
objective entity. The natural ability to reason would do the rest.

Second, scientific objectivism prefers explanatory accounts which are
self-subsistent (consistent and noncontradictory) and whole (encompassing
and generalizable). Mathematics developed as the language of description
because of its ability to conform to these constraints. Newtonian equations
were the archetype. Relativity and the existence of other phenomena (e.g.,
the nuclear "strong" and "weak" forces) which could not be described
using the same language altered this view, but only temporarily, since the

development of a fully subsistent and encompassing theory (the so-called general theory) is still assumed to be inevitable.

Finally, scientific objectivism assumes that categories and the cognitive process which discovers them are "natural." They are assumed to be discoverable in the world through empirical observation and impartial reflection. Early anthropologists certainly took this for granted. The inventor of kinship analysis, Lewis Henry Morgan, believed that "descriptive" systems which categorize kin on the basis of blood and marriage (as in the American system) must develop everywhere as people discover the "natural" basis of their relationships (Morgan 1871). A series of what he called "reformatory movements" in history made classification according to natural principles increasingly more accurate, with the result that the descriptive correctness of kinship systems had improved. Of course, material circumstances here and there had helped or hindered the reformatory process, hence the differential evolution of kinship systems around the world. The underlying logic at work, however, was assumed to be the same everywhere.

If we now see the pursuit of scientific knowledge as a cultural construction, how do we understand its workings? Weber's concept of rationalization is ideally suited, because its descriptive terminology can encompass objectivist logic not just as a set of traits and features, as above, but also as a dynamic process which shapes and directs inquiry. It is the *rationalization* of the objectivist account which makes scientific descriptions capable of generating both the circumstances which create anthropological dissonance as well as the intellectual devices we use to alleviate it.

The Theory of Rationalization and the Rationalization of Explanation

Weber defined rationalization in different ways, using it in his early work to refer to the maximization of the effectiveness of action in the pursuit of predetermined goals. In his later work, he strongly emphasized the fact that different activities could be rationalized in different directions, depending on worldview.[3] "The previous view," as Wolfgang Mommsen remarks, "that implicitly held that there was one kind of rationalization absolutely dominant—namely, that which took material shape in Western civilization—was repudiated" (1985:43). Anglo-American commentators have generally misunderstood the notion of rationalization, limiting it to three types: purposive, formal, and discursive. In its narrowest sense, it is true that rationality for Weber meant *Zweckrationalität*, purposive rationality,

3. This is especially so in the revised version of *Economy and Society*, written in 1920, shortly before Weber died.

i.e., the type of rationality exhibited in the selection of the best means for achieving some well-defined goal. Rationalization is therefore tied up with the increase of economic or bureaucratic efficiency.

But rationality also signifies the imposition of a coherent and orderly system upon some chaotic set of ideas and practices not clearly united by anything. In this sense rationalization is synonymous with the formalization of religious beliefs in the great religions or the systematization of the law in the West. With respect to modes of action, rationalization signifies a transition from "communal" to "associative" forms of social action. While communal action is directed to traditional norms and personal ends, associative social action is oriented to impersonal norms and dominated by strategic considerations. In this sense rationalization takes the form of "practical" rationality. Finally, rationality is related by Weber to the authenticity of an attitude free from illusions and self-deceptions; it is a "disenchantment" brought on by the desacralization of the world.

I am not so much interested in these interpretations as in the theme which unites them all. This is the notion of "direction." Parsons explained (with unusual clarity) what Weber seems to have had in mind: "The most important differences between systems of ideas are not so much those in the degree of rationalization as in the *direction* which the process of rationalization in each case has taken" (Parsons 1947:123, italics mine). *Direction* is the key term. It refers to the pursuit of any goal which a cultural system defines as valid. Rationalization takes different forms which proceed in different directions and toward different goals, depending on the ideal basis that is their starting point.[4] This does not mean that *rationalization* in the other senses mentioned above is irrelevant, only that is incomplete, and that for our purposes the sense elicited by Parsons is the most important.

Although Weber also wrote a very substantial work on rationalization in different musical traditions (Weber 1958), the type which concerned him most was religious rationalization in the ontology of suffering. He identified three primary types. These were dualism, the predestination decree of the *deus abscondidus,* and the doctrine of karma, associated with Zoroastrianism, Protestantism, and Hinduism, respectively. "These solutions," he wrote, "are rationally closed; in pure form, they are found only as exceptions" (1946:275). It is possible, Weber thought, to examine beliefs and

4. Weber's use of "rationalization" in this sense is best expressed in two places, as we saw in chapter 1. The first is the author's introduction to *The Protestant Ethic and the Spirit of Capitalism:* "rationalizations have occurred in the various departments of life in a great variety of ways in all cultural areas" (1958:26). The second is *Rationalization and the Social History of Music.*

practices within different religious systems for the degree to which they fulfill their own internal logics. As Tambiah points out, one can "use the yardsticks of coherence, consistency and so on to test each religion's systematicity in relation to the horizon it has chosen" (1990:154).

Two aspects of the process of rationalization are pertinent to the study of cultural knowledge systems. The first is *Wertsteigerung,* or "value intensification." As value standpoints become increasingly explicit and their implications for action are developed and made more rational, they also become more distinct as the objectives toward which progress in a particular domain (e.g., religion, music, explanation) is directed. The logic which governs this process is always of a certain kind, one Weber called Eigengesetzlichkeit or "inner logic," which he used as an explanatory device in his attack on historical materialism and other monocausal social theories: "We shall see time and again that the structural forms of social actions have an *Eigengesetizichkeit.* In a given case, they can always be codetermined by other than economic causes" (1968:341).

Let us apply the Weberian theory to Western explanatory science. Objectivist explanation is a rationalized conceptual domain, like religion or music or any other, to be understood in terms of the socially determined value or directive goal (*Wertsteigerung*) and developmental logic (*Eigengesetizichkeit*) which it attempts to fulfill and conform to. Dissonance within this domain must be understood accordingly, as an outcome of or response to the copresence of elements that come into conflict in their pursuit of a culturally defined goal. Could certain forms of confusion—say, the confusion of American jurors, legal theorists, and legislators experienced in trying to decide the Hinckley case—be understood in these terms?

In trying to decide the Hinckley case, Americans were trying to decide between two highly valued explanatory perspectives. The result was not unlike the confusion which arises much more mundanely whenever opposing perspectives collide—as in the countless everyday debates over the significance of "nature" or "nurture" in explaining intelligence, criminality, health, and so on (Nisbett and Ross 1980). Dissonance is evident in the conscious dread of inconsistency in decision making. One can even see the process at work in child rearing, when parents are urged to be consistent in enforcing various household rules: "Inconsistency" is thought to do the child irreparable harm (Mahler et al. 1975), despite the abundant evidence to the contrary available from other cultures (e.g., Trawick 1990). Is there a reason one struggles but never quite gets to the bottom of issues like these?

The problem is not so much in choosing between mutually attractive perspectives *but in having to choose at all.* Why do we do that? Something in the way Americans decide such issues forces them to want to decide definitively, "once and for all," either for or against the perspectives available to them. That is not to say that Americans decide all issues this way. Clearly the force of this directive goal exerts itself only in circumstances of great magnitude (like the assassination attempt) which tend to foreground the issue of decision making, making the application of a fully rationalized explanatory logic more noticeable and more difficult. The force that is felt is the force of the culturally and historically determined rationalization of explanation in Western objectivist discourse.

Deciding the Hinckley case did not settle the more important underlying issue: How should we compare, and how should we decide between, internally and externally oriented explanations when both are present as equivalent options? For South Indians, once the decision to punish the adulteress had been made, no further discussion or debate seemed necessary. The villagers did not divide into opposing camps, some supporting karmic explanations and others not. Nor was there any sense that such issues should not be left "hanging." No equivalent of the American legal establishment began a searching inquiry into the "karma defense," to prevent its future confrontation with volitional explanations. Americans, in contrast, demanded and received a compromise solution which, in the domain of formal law, resulted in nothing less than a radically revised plea system.

American explanatory rationalization—*the directive goal of explanation* —demands explanations which maximize the principles of the architectonic of pure reason: abstraction, generalizability, consistency, and noncontradictoriness. Explanations rationalized according to these features appeal to a positive reality outside themselves, to "nature" or to the world "as it is." Since there is only one such reality, according to this view, there can be only one ultimately true explanation. Kant insisted that the architectonic principles are necessary to thought; all thinking beings must conform to them. Yet from the Weberian perspective these must all be considered culturally constituted, united by ideas of what constitutes the proper place of explanation in the process of reasoning. Dissonance ensues when explanation confutes this link—that is, when explanation fails to conform to the rationalizing architectonic of reason and its directive goals.

Below I examine more closely a few of the more obvious characteristics of the architectonic, and afterward I suggest that their combination as a form of explanatory rationalization in Western objectivist discourse resembles rationalization in another cultural system, biblical ontology.

RATIONALIZED EXPLANATORY KNOWLEDGE IN THE WEST

Cultural Goals in Explanation: Abstractness and Generalizability

Rationalized explanations in the culturally valued discourse of scientific objectivism maximize the goals of abstractness and generalizability. Suppose, for instance, that a child misbehaves at school. One explanation is that the child is "cutting up" because children have "high spirits" and "do that sort of thing." Another explanation is that the child is chronically hyperactive due to poor early training in impulse control. Both accounts tend to remove the child from his immediate context and place him, for explanatory purposes, in an abstract category type with generalized role expectations. It is not sufficient to say, as Indian parents might, that the child's behavior must be understood in terms of his particular background and present circumstances (see Shweder and Bourne 1984). Why is this so?

The reason is that explanations which achieve abstractness and generalizability are judged more adequate than explanations which link behavior to a unique background of specific personality factors. It is significant, too, that the two alternative explanations given above do *not* differ in their power to maximize these features, despite the fact that one is "everyday" (the child is a "cutup") and the other one is "scientific" (the child suffers poor impulse control). In their capacity to qualify as rationalized explanations, everyday and scientific explanations do not greatly differ.

Cultural Goals in Explanation: Consistency and Noncontradictoriness

Ideally, rationalized explanations are generalizable and consistent across similar contexts. The same explanatory account should apply with equal force to all instances of a category type. If it does not, then specific contextual features may be needed to explain why a particular case constitutes an "exception." Hinckley's lawyers, for example, argued that Hinckley was "psychotic" when he shot Reagan. Psychiatrists testified on behalf of the defense that Hinckley's traits were consistent with the psychotic category type. The prosecuting lawyers, with their own panel of psychiatrists, argued against this claim by attempting to reassign Hinckley's personality traits to another category ("narcissistic personality type") a category of personality disorders (not the psychoses) much less able to sustain the plea of insanity. Successful explanations depend on establishing as much consistency as possible between individual cases and category types. Arguments against such explanations succeed when it is shown that individual cases contain unmatched traits or traits inconsistent with the category type.

Noncontradictoriness foregrounds several issues crucial to successfully rationalized explanations. First, contradictory explanations are difficult to accept as adequate. To make them acceptable, one must show that they apply at different "levels" or that they are part of a process that will eventually lead to one's acceptance over the other. Fully contradictory explanations, not resolvable in one of these three ways, cannot exist without causing dissonance. Second, in cases of persistent contradiction, the problem may be redefined to make explanation itself unnecessary. Finally, contradictions unresolvable through forced choice, elimination, or redefinition may be upheld as exemplars of paradox, and attest to the workings of a strange cosmos, or may be used to justify a belief system whose mystery precludes "rational" explanation (*credo quia absurdum est*).

THE RATIONALIZATION OF COSMOLOGY AND THE ONTOLOGY OF DISSONANCE

Explanatory rationalization in the West is bound up with understandings of the way the world first comes into being, making of epistemology and ontology something Shore calls "epistemogenesis" (Shore, in press). To understand this relationship between ontology and explanation, the approach taken by Weber—of relating conceptual systems in disparate domains—is especially useful, as I suggested in chapter 2 and demonstrated with reference to Bateson's Iatmul ethnography. In *The Protestant Ethic and the Spirit of Capitalism,* Weber describes the development of Western capitalism through the fortuitous convergence of different phenomena. The Calvinistic quest for salvational certainty, focused on activity in the world, gave rise by a process of unintended consequences to a culture that stressed reason, coherence, and world mastery. Weber is often misunderstood to have thought that a set of religious beliefs independently caused Western-style capitalism to develop. Actually, he argued against oversimplified and monocausal explanation, repeatedly stressing that there was a relationship of synergy, not causality, between religion and economy.

A similar relationship of synergy exists between the domains of biblical cosmology and explanatory rationalization. Now, the reason I bring this up is that there seems to be a relationship, generally, between explanatory knowledge systems and important myths. That is hardly surprising, since myth is often identical with explanatory knowledge. In the case of Western explanatory logic and biblical myth, this is apparent in their shared emphasis on order as a natural and uncreated process; in their disdain for inconsistency and intolerance for ambiguity; and in their definition of the actor/agent as one distinct from the object he attempts to explain or create. A comparison of explanatory rationalization and the biblical creation process reveals these similarities. The purpose of this comparison is not to suggest that one caused the other but to show that the two conform to the same cultural logic. It is also to prepare the way for the argument to follow in the next chapter, in which we examine Jalari myth as a prelude to considering the Jalari divinatory system.

Where Do Directive Goals Come From? Ontology and Epistemology in the West

From the very beginning there is an emphasis in the Bible on the logical order of natural sequentiality in creation. It is the principle which governs this order that is significant here. Genesis divides the early creation process into two parts. The first part, consisting of the first three days, describes the creation of three regions (light, firmament, and land) and their bifurcation into separate environments (light/dark, heaven/waters, earth/seas).

And God said, "Let there be . . ."

LIGHT	FIRMAMENT	LAND
(separation)	(separation)	(separation)
light/dark	heaven/waters	earth/seas

Genesis then decribes the creation of the objects and organisms appropriate to these environments.

1. light/darkness	2. heaven/waters	3. earth/seas
4. sun/moon	5. birds/fish	6. animals/man

What should be apparent is that the second order replicates the first. Objects and beings are created serially, not all at once, and in the same order exactly as their respective environments.

The early chapters of Genesis reveal the inner logic of creation. First, the universe has a unique beginning. Second, the creator is detached and emotionless—a disembodied spirit with no interior sensations. Third, objects are created in a certain order, according to their "natural," i.e., noncreated, properties and interrelationships. A fish needs water, and so the oceans are created before fish; terrestrial animals need land to walk, so the earth is separated from the waters before the animals are created; and so on. Objects and beings thus have preexisting "natural" properties which determine their order of creation even before they come into being. There is no suggestion that God had any choice in the matter.

Now, consider how alike are the logics of biblical creation and formal scientific explanation. Both appeal to a nature or reality that is a priori the supreme arbiter of choice: God can create, but only in a certain order, e.g., water before fish, land before animals, etc. Reality—or what is immanent in reality—constrains him. "Reality" also constrains explanatory rationalization, demanding that explanations ground themselves in the "really real"— hence the never-ending debates concerning "objective" bases on which to build them. A central issue in Western science, for example, centers on whether or not objective foundations should be rationally or empirically constructed. Rationalists, such as Descartes and Leibniz, considered sensual reality inherently problematic and insisted that all forms of reasoning ground themselves in nonfalsifiable cognitive principles. Empiricists, such as Hume, claimed that all that could really be known must be consistent with human sensory experience. Which is more "real"? Major paradigms in Western philosophical discourse can be understood as attempts to answer this question by finding and describing the conditions for an ultimate reality—uncontaminated by human action or perception—and that reality's governing principles.

The second feature both biblical ontology and scientific objectivist epistemology share is the emphasis on order as a natural sequence of bringing things into being. In Genesis, this is clear from the first three chapters, but it continues much further, through the creation of humans and their faculties. God and man, for example, make several "covenants," which require each party to understand and carry out contracted obligations. The first covenant is constructed after the Flood (in chapter 9) when God promises not to inundate the world again and man promises to obey certain dietary and behavioral strictures. But the covenant cannot be agreed on until man has developed several crucial abilities, including the capacity to speak in the future tense and to consider conditional consequences. These abilities develop only slowly and sequentially, one by one, in the preceding chapters—an anticipation, in a sense, of Piaget. By the time of the last covenant, between God and Abraham, man has developed even more abilities—including the ability to anticipate negative outcomes and negotiate terms. The evolution of human cognitive abilities in Genesis—including, most importantly, the ability to make and understand explanations—is a continuing process throughout. In biblical creation, orderly development is everything.

Similarly, in objectivist rationalization, creating explanations with clear logical order is essential for making them convincing. The best explanations, after all, are called formal or scientific because they are constructed according to an order sometimes called "hypothesis-testing" or the "scientific method." Every step should be specified, every relation logically demonstrated. Moreover, these steps should be recoverable and repeatable, as the regime of record-keeping in medicine, research, and law reveals. A doctor who prescribes the wrong medication can exonerate himself if the written record of his decision making reveals that he considered all the facts available at the time. Research results are considered legitimate only if the methodology has been painstakingly described, ensuring step-by-step repeatability. Finally, criminal cases are often dismissed unless the proper arrest procedure ("due process") has been followed. The emphasis on order in explanation is ubiquitous.

Third, the logics of creation and explanatory rationalization define their agents similarly. In both, the agent is separate from the object: God from the universe and the explainer from what he explains. God is the perfect creator in part because of his utter detachment from the thing he creates. His detachment means that he can evaluate creation objectively, and when parts of it fail, he can either correct the failure (as he does after Adam and Eve disobey him) or start all over from scratch (as he does after the Flood). The perfect explainer is very much the same: detached and objective. That is why justice is "blind" and why jurors, as socially designated explainers, are selected on the basis of their disinterest in the case. Admonishments to be objective and consider the facts make sense against this background—a background that assumes that the best decisions are those in which explainer and that which is explained are separate, distinct, and uninfluenced by each other.

The "Beginning" of Explanation and Dissonance

In Genesis, explanation and the existence of something worth explaining both come into being in the same encounter with a physical object—the apple. They first appear in the conversation between God, Adam, and Eve (Gen. 3:9–19). It is simultaneously the *first* conversation, the *first* explanation, the *first* inference, and the *first* explicit decision in the created universe.

In the first part (3:9–12), God assumes the role of interrogator and asks the Bible's first nonrhetorical question, "Where art thou?" The implications of this question are profound. A question about physical location is, after all, a rather mundane inquiry. It signals a lack of the total omniscience that was associated with the creator God in the early chapters of Genesis.

Adam's response—"I heard thy voice in the garden: and I was afraid, because I was naked; and I hid myself"—represents a quantum leap forward for human ability, from lack of any interior sensation and only one mental skill (the ability to name) to the experience of deep inner feelings and the capacity to account for one's own actions. While God has lost many features which distinguished him early in the creation process, man, in the gradual evolution of his cognitive abilities, has acquired many of the features which make him human.

In the second part (3:13), God interrogates Eve, to whom he has traced the chain of events leading up to Adam's hiding. He asks her what she has done, and she answers "the serpent beguiled me." Her answer is terse. She does not bother to repeat the revelations of Adam's testimony. But her answer is also different, in that it goes beyond a direct report of what has happened to an interpretation of its meaning: She *infers* that the serpent deceived her. Inference—the capacity to go beyond the information given—is a vital explanatory skill. It is significant here because Eve's inference suggests that explanation can end in one of two places, either in what beings do (as in Adam's account) or what beings intend (as in Eve's). There is now a choice—the first ever in the created universe—for God as decision maker to make. Should Adam and Eve be blamed for what they did (eating the fruit) or excused for what they did not intend (disobeying God)?

Here is where the great debate between "internal" and "external" locus of control begins—not in twentieth-century social psychology, but in the Bible. There is a choice between conflicting attributional perspectives which both represent reasonable and attractive alternatives. Even though God is apparently unperplexed by the decision he faces (experiencing none of the tell-tale signs of dissonance), there is still a tension immanent in our reading which is essential to the moral lesson this episode attempts to convey. Couldn't God overlook the transgression? Moral decision making permits no extenuating circumstances in the Genesis version of the world's creation. The issue is resolved and dissonance avoided by recourse to the strategy of forced choice. God compels *himself* to act against Adam and Eve by creating the world's first syllogism: Transgression must be punished; Adam and Eve transgressed; therefore Adam and Eve must be punished. It is all perfectly straightforward, absolutistic, and precise: just as good objectivist explanations should be.

In the third part of the passage (3:14–19), God delivers his judgment, recalling the events that have taken place, and distributing punishment among the wrongdoers. The manner in which he does this is significant for four reasons. First, in order to punish, God must specify the violations. Crime and punishment are clearly and explicitly related in a single line of cause and effect; no ambiguity should arise, and certainly no dissonance. In objectively rationalized explanation, the same logic should apply. Second, God links the distribution of punishments to a sequence of connected events, beginning with the serpent's deception and ending with Adam's concealment. Multiple explanatory frameworks are excluded. There is only one legitimate causal account, thus ensuring that the dissonance which could arise from the copresence of competing frameworks is ruled out. Objectively rationalized explanations should achieve the same result. Third, God's judgment endeavors to decide matters "once and for all," even when, as here, alternative perspectives might exist. There is no consideration of extenuating circumstances, no possibility of subsequent appeal. Explanations constructed according to the standards of objectivist rationalization and its directive goals should eventually achieve the same result, through decision-making processes that have been designed for that purpose. Fourth, there is a similarity in the ways biblical explanation and biblical creation take place. The biblical universe has a unique beginning; it develops through a process whose details can be described; and it ends, in a momentous apocalypse, not to be repeated. It is process with a definitive beginning, middle, and end. The contents and processes of this universe follow suit, reproducing in their structures the distinctive flow and developmental logic of the entire process. God's decisions and pronouncements are good examples: They take place in a certain order, beginning and ending in an argument whose premises are first stated, then acted on, as if the whole process of explaining and deciding were as natural and inevitable as the creation process itself.

Explanation is rationalized in the West according to directive goals that thus bear a striking resemblance to the logic which informs the creation of the biblical universe. The same goals and principles are shared, making it easier to understand why both appeal to a reality that is "natural" and, at the same time, "outside" themselves. In the case of the mythical creation, the whole of reality still depends on God, an external agency, to initiate it. God starts the process, but once it is set in motion, it is the process itself—and the natural principles that govern it—which controls and directs all things. There is no need for further intervention. In rationalized explanation, the need to explain and the existence of something worth explaining both depend on the presence of the explainer, whose interests and intentions determine both. But once the process of explaining has been set in motion, it is believed to follow the "natural" principles of logical development in a single direction to its ultimate conclusion, if uninterfered

with. Conventional metaphor even bears this out: We speak of ideas that
"run away with us" and that "speak for themselves" (see D'Andrade 1987:
112–48).

EXPLANATORY DISSONANCE AND DIRECTIVE GOALS: TOWARD HINDU INDIA

The argument for a broadened conception of consistency that will do more
than simply recapitulate Western explanatory rationalization will be more
convincing if we compare Western-style explanation to something else. For
material, one could turn to a number of different sources: to the Azande
and their "social logic" (Evans-Pritchard 1937), to the Ifaluk and their concepts of nurturance and danger (Lutz 1988), or to the Balinese and their
striving after balanced "feeling-thought" (Wikan 1990). All of these offer
examples of explanatory systems which seek something other than the universalizing, the abstract, and the generalizable. But as the rest of this book
is about India, I shall return to it for a comparative account.

Formal explanations in South Asia are directed to different culturally
defined goals and thus differ from their counterparts in the West. This
makes our understanding of South Asian explanatory systems, like divination, different from our understanding of Western explanatory systems,
like American psychiatry. Whereas in the West there is a predisposition
to universalizing explanation, because that is one of its directive goals, in
South Asia the reverse is the case. The best explanations are those which
particularize the most. Since the goals of particularism run counter to the
ends of abstract generalization, it matters less that explanations be consistent with each other than that they recognize the particular attributes and
characteristics of their subjects. Dissonance is the result of a failure to pay
attention to differences in particularity.

An engaging account of Hindu particularism is provided by Ramanujan
in a story about his father:

> I looked for consistency in him, a consistency he didn't seem to care
> about, or even think about. When I asked him what the discovery of
> Pluto and Neptune did to his archaic seven-planet astrology, he said,
> "You make the necessary corrections, that's all." Or in answer to how he
> could read the *Gita* religiously after bathing and painting on his fore-
> head the red and white feet of Visnu, and talk appreciatively about
> Bertrand Russell and even Ingersoll—he said, "The *Gita* is part of one's
> hygiene. Besides, don't you know, the brain has two lobes?"
> (Ramanujan 1980)

Ramanujan reveals the dismay characteristic of non-Indians when confronted by the apparent inconsistencies of South Asian beliefs. Explanations seem too thoroughly grounded in the immediate and the concrete. Ramanujan's father, clearly aware of and enjoying the dilemma this creates, responds with humor.

This is not to arrive at the counterintuitive conclusion that encompassing generalizations are never possible or preferred. South Asians are no less capable than Americans of extrapolating from repeated instances to some kind of covering rule. The rule which states that objects dropped from a height must fall is an example of a logical proposition to which both South Asians and Westerners would readily assent. But in the West this proposition is linked to a universal "law," whereas in South Asia the observation remains just that—an observation of a regularity. It is not productive of "scientific" explanation, because formal explanation is directed to different cultural goals—to the understanding of particularities seeking fusion or coalescence, which Hindu social thought regards as no less significant than abstract universals.

Inconsistency in formal explanation is not productive of the dissonance or the dissonance-relieving work which we assume to be natural under such circumstances. That is why anthropologists of South Asia have gone to such lengths to explain its absence, labeling the Indian mind "compartmentalized" (Singer 1972) or "context-dependent" (Shweder and Bourne 1984) to explain why mutually inconsistent alternatives do not provoke discomfort and prompt resolution. However, it is not the case that there is no dissonance and no dissonance-relieving work. Following Weber, we must assume that some domain other than formal explanation has been rationalized and thus endowed with dissonance-generating properties.

This domain is the domain of the relational and the affective, not that of the abstract and the rational. Within it the highly elaborated logic of particularism is focused on the affective dynamics of social relationships. In India, dissonance is not so much a failure of things to come together abstractly, in the realm of logic, so much as the failure of things to come together relationally, in the realm of the affectively charged.

It has been said that Americans will tell you what is true about someone, whereas South Asians will tell you what someone has done (Shweder and Bourne 1984). While this supports the view that South Asians are relatively more "context-dependent," the preference for particularism does not in itself constitute motivation. We know *that* South Asians are context-dependent, but we do not yet know *why*. What is the value that is being maximized? One answer that is often given is that South Asians subscribe to a sociocentric world-premise, one that "directs their attention and passions to particular systems, relationally conceived and contextually appraised" (Shweder and Bourne 1984:189). To attribute the difference solely to a "world-premise," however, is to return the issue to the domain of the abstract and propositional where Western-style explanatory rationalization can make sense of it. This is misleading, since what is rationalized in South Asia may be of a different nature. I refer to the fact that the language of objectivist explanation—of "premises" and "appraisals"—is the language of conscious rationality, and to the possibility that, for Hindu South Asia, a different language may be required: the language of the desire for affective fusin and coalescence.

One can find this desire in a variety of places, detected by scholars who are not necessarily predisposed to psychoanalytic interpretation. Take for example Samanta's analysis of Bengali sacrifice, which is less a sacrifice than a kind of communion. In the ritual, sacrificer and the animal sacrificed become more and more closely identified, until finally, in coalescence, they become transformed into something divine. Whereas in the Western tradition God and man are perceived as two separate beings, the distinction between sacrificer and deity is ambiguous. The ritual of sacrifice accentuates this ambiguity by drawing the two together through the connecting being of the sacrificed animal. According to Samanta, there is "a homology between the 'self' (*jiva*) of the sacrificer and the sacrificial animal (*pasu*), and the 'consumption' of the 'self-animal' by the goddess over many lifetimes until it achieves union with divinity and liberation (*moksa*)" (Samanta 1994:782). This makes sense only if it is understood that union or coalescence is the goal and that the ritual is a means of achieving it.

In his biography of Gandhi, Erikson points out that it is important to see the "baseline" of explanatory truthfulness in India, and to recognize that "principles" such as *dharma, artha, kama,* and *moksha* cannot be compared with Western principles in the sense that they provide categorical prohibitions and permissions. "Rather," Erikson writes, "they are forms of *immersion* in different *orders* of *self-abandonment*" (1969:42; italics in original). Another way to put is that the state of fusion, not differentiatin, is a developmental goal. Fusion is the state of intimate absorption that is characteristic of mother-infant relationship. In the West, development quickly replaces this state with more and more refined states of differentiation, to ensure that the child's ego is functionally autonomous as soon as possible (Mahler et al. 1975).

In South Asia, as Kakar explains, the opposite is true: "The child's differentiation of himself from his mother (and consequently of the ego from the id) is structurally weaker and comes chronologically later than in the West with this outcome: The mental processes characteristic of the symbiosis of infancy play a relatively greater role in the personality of the adult Indian" (1981:104). The mental processes referred to are called "primary." A consequence is that secondary-process thinking, as Freud called it, with its emphasis on consistency and control, is not as salient in South Asian explanation as primary-process thinking, with its emphasis on desire and dependency.

There is growing evidence, both clinical and ethnographic, that the culturally sanctioned persistence of primary-process thinking and perception is a real phenomenon in South Asia (Erikson 1969; Kakar 1981, 1982, 1989, 1990; Kurtz 1992; Lindholm 1982; Nuckolls 1991a,b, 1993; Obeyesekere 1981, 1984, 1990; Roland 1988; Samanta 1994; Trawick 1990). This makes sense, especially if we accept Noy's view that the primary process is related to the integrations and expressions of the self (Noy 1979). "In a culture that so emphasizes harmony within complex hierarchical relationships, with a highly cultivated subjectivity involved in mythology, ritual, and aesthetics, primary process thinking is highly adaptive" (Roland 1988: 274). One of the problems with the use of the term *primary processes,* however, is that Freud thought that such processes do not develop, and consequently any indication of their presence suggests regression to more primitive mental states. Psychoanalysts today dispute this (Noy 1969; Tyson and Tyson 1990).

Rather than "persistence," therefore, I would prefer to call it "rationalization," to suggest that in South Asia primary-process thinking is elaborated as a vehicle for the expression and fulfillment of the desire for fusion.[5] This may seem like an odd use of the term *primary process,* since Freud did not explore the primary process as a mode of cognition. The defining feature Freud attributed to primary-process thinking, its "free cathexis," ignores or obscures the cognitive side. There is no reason for us to accept so restricted a view. Admittedly, this may seem like a peculiar use of the term

5. Kakar provides several examples to demonstrate that certain elements of the Hindu world image are consistent with this desire: "The widespread (conscious and pre-conscious) conviction that knowledge gained through ordering, categorizing, logical reasoning, is *avidya,* the not-knowledge, and real knowledge is only attainable through direct, primary-process thinking and perception; the imperative that . . . to reach their avowed goals they must enlarge the inner world rather than act on the outer one; the injunction inherent in the karma doctrine to accept and use outer reality for inner development rather than to strive to alter worldly realties; the indifferent respect given to eminent scientists and professionals, compared with . . . the innumerable shamanic gurus . . . : These are a few of the indicators of the emphasis in Hindu culture on the primary processes of mental life" (Kakar 1981:107).

rationalization, but it follows Weber's insight that the irrational, just like the rational, is capable of order and development. It is the social value of this desire for fusion which, in Weber's sense, sets the direction and establishes the course, "rationalizing" the primary processes in this direction and thus giving them a cultural significance they generally lack in the West.

The rationalization of the primary process in India is reinforced, not just by psychodynamic factors, but by socioeconomic ones as well. What Marcuse (1955) calls the performance principle dominates in the capitalist West, putting a low premium on leisure and causing the barriers between ego, id, and superego to be comparatively strong. While all infants are born "polymorphously perverse," as Freud said, the performance principle directs these impulses into genital sexuality and monogamous marriage. An extremely punitive superego generates abundant guilt and ensures that the principle is obeyed. In South Asia, on the other hand, a very different reality orientation exists. As Obeyesekere notes, there is a much greater premium on leisure and a lesser one on the performance principle. "Concomitant with this there is a greater tolerance of fantasy and of the primary process in general"(Obeyesekere 1990:63–64).

From the elaboration and development of the desire for fusion several consequences follow:

1. Secondary processes constitute the domain of abstract logic and thus highlight the importance of logical contradiction and inconsistency;
2. Primary processes constitute the domain of desire, especially of the desire for connectedness, and thus highlight the importance of certain affective states, such as attachment and separation;
3. Dissonance in the former is therefore most often associated with inconsistency, whereas in the latter dissonance is associated with object loss.

It is the latter type of dissonance that is characteristic of South Asian social thought and explanation, including the complex divinatory system to be described in part 3. However, to call it dissonance is probably misleading, since dissonance is from the vocabulary of the cognitive, and what we require is a term more specific to the primary processes.

The term *ambivalence* will do much better, if we use it as Robert Merton (1976) does, to refer to a state or condition which ensues when the desire for attachment is unachievable because of competing role expectations and contradictory social obligations. Notice that ambivalence in this sense is a cultural phenomenon, not a psychological one, although it may (under certain circumstances) be manifested that way. This is what makes it comparable to cognitive dissonance both in the classical sense, since a competition between attractive alternatives still takes place, and in the sense I mean it, as a cultural phenomenon with a long social history behind it.

What I wish to suggest is that the various particularities of Hindu thought, especially as they relate to social relations, are refractions of the primary attachment of the infant-mother bond. This is not a new idea. "The deep nostalgia for fusion is reborn," as Erikson notes, "from generation to generation out of the diffusion of the mother in the joint family" (1969:42). Ambivalence arises when the norms governing particular relationships conflict, making it impossible for any one to realize the sought-after state of attachment. Through transformation and displacement (forms of primary-process thinking) the ambivalence-generating paradox is recast in another idiom, where it can be resolved (at least temporarily). Such idioms include the mythical and magico-religious, as I demonstrate in the next chapter, but also the formal explanatory, as I attempt to show later.

Kakar's thesis is that the mother-infant bond is so close and long-lasting in Hindu India that it generates a compelling adult desire for a return to a state of primitive maternal fusion, realized in religious terms as *moksa*. This view has been challenged by Kurtz (1992), who argues that none of the available evidence on Hindu child rearing—and this, by the way, is scant—proves that mothers and infants are as close as they are in Western societies, where a constant emphasis on the mother-infant dyad is to be felt. On the contrary, he says, they are less so; mothering in India is almost always "multiple," involving many female caretakers and not just one, so it is impossible for the infant to grow up feeling that he has an exclusive bond with only one mother. His love is diffused among many. There is therefore no primitive state of intense maternal fusion for him to want to return to.

Kurtz does not deny that the religious goal of fusion with the whole, *brahman,* exists or that something in childhood experience predisposes Hindus to seek this end (Kurtz 1992:162). He challenges the source of this predisposition, and having rejected the regressive desire for maternal fusion, he replaces it with what he calls the "ego of the whole." This kind of ego develops when a child voluntarily relinquishes primary attachment to a single individual in return for membership in the group: "Having made this renunciation, the child's ego is consolidated through a sense of having incorporated and having been incorporated by the group" (103). This is what the Hindu seeks to recover and reinforce in the contemplation of *moksha* (162). Kurtz claims that psychoanalytic authors have been misled by their unconscious commitment to Western individualism and therefore ignore the overwhelming importance of the group in the formation of the Hindu ego.

Although I will argue later against Kurtz's interpretation, for the purposes of this discussion it does not matter whether through regression to maternal fusion or through extension of the "ego of the whole" a Hindu comes to seek a coalescence of the self with collective Being. Kakar and Kurtz may differ on where the predisposition comes from, but they agree that it exists. That is what is important here, since what we are interested in is the fact that emotional coalescence, fusion with the whole, or submergence in the collective—whatever its psychological roots—can serve as a goal toward which explanation, like any other cultural domain, might be rationalized.

A Hindu Creation Myth

For Western-style explanatory rationalization, the Genesis myth functions as a charter, linking the creation of knowledge to the creation of a knowable world, and both to the directive goals of objectivist rationalization. South Asian creation myths function similarly, but the emphasis is on the creation of desire for unity and the management of attachment as the goals of rationalization. We will be examining specifically Jalari creation myths later. Here I want to consider one of the better-known pan-Indian creation myths, known both in the North and the South, and in the Telugu fishing village where I did fieldwork. It is the story of the primeval man, Purusa:

> He was afraid; therefore the one who is all alone is afraid. He reflected, "Since there is nothing other than me, of what am I afraid?" He did not rejoice; therefore one who is all alone does not rejoice. He caused himself to fall into two pieces, and from him a husband and wife were born. He united with her, and from this mankind was born. She reflected, "How can he unite with me after engendering me from himself? For shame! I will conceal myself." She became a cow; he became a bull and united with her, and from this all the cattle were born. She became a mare; he became a stallion. She became a female ass; he became a male ass and united with her, and from this all whole-hooved animals were born. She became a she-goat; he became a billy-goat and she became a ewe; he became a ram and united with her, and from this goats and sheep were born. Thus he created all pairs, even down to the ants. (O'Flaherty 1975:34–35)

If we compare this to the Genesis account, several interesting differences immediately stand out.

First, the emotional state of an embodied creator is described. He is lonely, and the purpose of his creation is to overcome this feeling, since "one who is all alone does not rejoice." The God of Genesis, of course, is utterly detached and disembodied, and his motivation for creating, if it exists, is never revealed. Second, Purusa is an androgynous being who creates through a process of sexual subdivision and transformation, mating incestuously with his other half to create successively all the beings of creation. All beings are thus his children and share equally of his bodily substance. God, however, creates and remains separate from everything. One can imagine God as Blake did, as the great geometrician setting the laws of nature in motion and then withdrawing, but to think of Purusa that way would be impossible since the world and the primeval man are one and the same, and both are suffused with desire. Third, each act of creation on the part of Purusa is an attempt to reunite with his other half; following separation, all actions are attempted reversals, and in the process creation itself is realized. This is quite unlike the Genesis account, in which there is no nostalgia for the state prior to God's first creative act.

The theme of fusion and separation is as basic to the Hindu creation myth as the theme of differentiation and autonomy is to its Western counterpart. *Both represent culturally defined goals, the ends toward which knowledge systems, such as mythology and divination, are rationalized.* In Hindu myth, the value to be maximized is emotional fulfillment or completion in the return to a unified state. Rationalized on the basis of this value (*Wertsteigerung*), and for the purpose of achieving this end Eigengesetzlichkeit explanation is to achieve emotional synthesis and integration. The theme of the Western myth carries a very different goal-value. Since the order it creates is assumed to be "natural" and "absolute"—outside of all desire—explanation is rationalized as the attempt to reproduce that order, through separation of the explainer from that which is explained.

Western explanation is given to making distinctions, based on the ever more refined ability to tell things apart. It is a cold and cognitive ideal (Weber 1958:183). In Hindu culture, the opposite is true. Explanation is directed to reassembling primary unities, to achieving emotional coalescence or fusion. Truth has no independent status as a natural absolute but is always at the service of the processes whose chief aim is to fulfill the desire for attachment. It is with respect to *this* directive goal that explanation has been rationalized. It has no independent status outside or beyond its ability to contribute to the goal. There is even some suspicion that reason, given too free a rein, can seriously disrupt progress to any worthy end—hence the many warnings in Hindu philosophy that the knowledge gained through ordering, categorizing, and discriminating is *avidya*, the not-knowledge.

Western-style explanatory rationalization calls for explanations which maximize the culturally defined goal of consistency, completeness, generalizability, and noncontradictoriness. These values are closely bound up with concepts of objective reality and natural order, revealing an underlying symmetry between epistemology and the ontology referenced in myth.

There is an underlying congruence between ontology and explanatory rationalization, revealing that the values associated with both are of long-standing cultural-historical significance. But to say that explanation may be rationalized on quite different grounds, affectively and in terms of primary-process thinking, would seem to deny the possibility of universal rational foundations, e.g., identity, transitivity, conditionality, etc. Is this not to put ourselves on the brink of a relativistic void?

It is not. The relativity of rationalization does not do away with "a strong core of human cognitive rationality common to the cultures of all places on earth and all times since the dawn of properly human social history" (Horton 1982:256). Without comparable rules of inference there can be no method for the crossing from one language to another. "In so far as thoroughgoing Relativism denies such an area of comparability," Robin Horton remarks, "it precludes the possibility of translation and is therefore, literally, a non-starter" (1982:259).

Horton asserts that basic rationality exists everywhere, but in so-called theoretical cultures, such as our own, rational forms have been highly elaborated and systematized. He accounts for this by claiming that differences among Western society's various constituent groups—ethnic, religious, philosophical—force people to compete with each other and develop a common explanatory language, so that they can more effectively argue. Horton's account is overly mechanical, and counterexamples, such as India, are too easily adduced. What is important is that the rationalization of explanation, though always culturally constructed, does not create logical relations. It only endows them with scope and significance, establishes their direction and course, and provides instructions on their use.

This chapter began with the observation that when we encounter "inconsistent" explanations in different cultures—explanations which, to us, do not make sense—we experience dissonance. There is an incongruity between statements about the world as we make them and as others do. I argued that dissonance is the result of contact, not just between different concepts, but between knowledge systems directed to different *goals*. What we need are new means of acquiring insight into goals, both generally and in their multiplicity, so that we can understand the development of the knowledge systems these goals inform.

In the next chapter, we consider the Hindu goal of fusion from a different angle, to examine the primary relationships between parents and children, and the secondary relationships between brothers and the sisters. These are the "places" where the paramount goal of fusion is represented, and pursued through means that are essentially contradictory to each other. The norms of South Indian kinship oppose each other, thus creating a dialectic whose oppositional dynamic finds temporary resolution in the knowledge structures of myth and divination. We will examine the mythology first as a charter for the second, and the cultural ambivalence it both represents and resolves, before proceeding to the divinatory system.

Part 2

Rationalization and Ambivalence

Chapter Five

Cultural Ambivalence and the Paradoxes of Desire in Kinship

> *You are aware of only one unrest;*
> *Oh, never learn to know the other!*
> *Two souls, alas, are dwelling in my*
> *breast,*
> *And one is striving to forsake its*
> *brother.*
>
> *(Goethe,* Faust, *part 1)*

The most important characteristic of cultural goals is that they cannot be reached, because the values they represent are contradictory to each other. Contradictory values in pursuit of a goal that cannot be reached generate dialectics, and such dialectics become the framework of knowledge systems. Why are we motivated to seek solutions to problems that can never be solved? Partly because the goals themselves supply motivation. They "pull" knowledge, as it were, giving it direction and scope. But knowledge is not only a matter of goals. Something else "pushes" it as well. The push is provided by the desire to resolve the underlying ambivalences. What we need, therefore, in addition to a theory of goals, is a theory of cultural ambivalence.

The idea that social structures generate what Merton (1976) called sociological ambivalence has been around for decades (see Coser 1976; Durkheim 1965; Freud 1964; Grathoff 1970; Langer 1942, 1953; Lynd 1939). Ambivalence of this kind exists among people in conflicting institutions and complex interrelationships such that no single commitment dominates one's life. Related to ambivalence of the psychological type, sociological ambivalence focuses on the ways in which ambivalence comes to be built into the structure of social statuses and roles. "It directs us to examine the processes in social structure that affect the probability of ambivalence turning up in particular kinds of role-relations [and] . . . it directs us to the social consequences of ambivalence for the workings of social structures" (Merton 1976:5).

Some scholars view ambivalence of this kind as socially functional. Merton considers it a device "for helping people in designated statuses to cope with the contingencies they face in trying to fulfill their functions" (1976:18). Others focus on the psychological consequences of ambivalence, finding that it generates anxiety, dysphoria, or other pathological states (Coser 1976; Wexler 1983). They observe that cultures typically provide patterns of representation and interpretation that predefine resolutions to felt contradictions. Some of these patterns include joking and humor (Coser 1976), narcissism (Slater and Slater 1965), religion (Weigert 1988), and membership in countercultural groups (Yinger 1982).

Merton's ideas are especially relevant. Instead of looking at social roles as a set of dominant attributes (such as functional specificity), he asserts, we must see them as dynamic organizations of norms and counternorms (Merton 1976:17; cf. Parsons 1951:61). Within each role, opposing normative tendencies call for potentially contradictory attitudes and behaviors on the part of those who occupy the defined role. Conflicting norms are built into the social definition of roles that provide for acceptable alternations of action as the state of a social relation changes. Role behavior is alternately directed to dominant norms and counternorms, generating conflicts and producing ambivalence, which various social structures function to cope with.

One of Merton's examples, "the physcian," illustrates the dynamic of contradictory role tendencies. For each norm governing the role there tends to be at least one coordinate norm which is at least sufficiently different to make it difficult for the person to fulfill both. Second, norms are defined in terms of how they are put into effect. They come to be defined as a requirement of the role, even though fulfilling the requirement is virtually impossible. The following list of values in the practice of medicine illustrates how this works, specifically with respect to the norms governing the physician-patient relationship:

1. Physicians must be emotionally detached in their attitudes toward patients, keeping "emotions on ice" and not becoming "overly identified" with patients.
   But: They must avoid becoming callous through excessive detachment, and should have compassionate concern for the patient.
2. Physicians must not prefer one type of patient over another, and

must curb hostilities toward patients (even those who prove to be uncooperative or who do not respond to therapeutic efforts).
But: The most rewarding experience for the physician is the effective solution of a patient's health problems.
3. Physicians must gain and maintain the confidence of patients.
But: They must avoid the mere bedside manner that can quickly deteriorate into expedient and self-interested salesmanship.
4. Physicians have a right to expect a "reasonable fee," depending upon the care given and the economic circumstances of the patient.
But: They must not "soak the rich" in order to "provide for the poor." (Merton 1976:68)

Roles are made up of competing tendencies which must somehow be organized into a pattern of behavior. No matter how well organized, a completely stable pattern cannot develop, because competing norms remain in tension with each other. Ambivalence results. Consequently, various structures must be developed to resolve the opposition—if not permanently, then at least temporarily, so that the person may function in the designated role. Merton acknowledges this, but he does not describe such structures or analyze the knowledge systems they support, nor does he ever turn his attention to kinship roles.

Merton was concerned most with occupational roles in complex societies. If he had developed a theory of kinship, it might have resembled the theory of dominant themes and dyads developed by Hsu (see Hsu 1971). Each culture, according to Hsu, selectively emphasizes one dyad over others—preferring, for example, to stress the relationship between father and son or husband and wife. In societies that stress father-son relationships, concern will focus on matters of succession and inheritance, with greater attention to authority and control. In societies that stress husband-wife relationships, there will be more attention to the formation of independent families, with concomitant weakening of extended kinship. The selective emphasizing of one dyad systematically affects the nature of all the others. What if more than one dyad is emphasized, and they conflict with each other?

Hsu was correct to hypothesize that in some societies different kinship relationships are emphasized and that this emphasis affects the kinship system as whole. But he did not explore the issue of conflict among relational dyads, or the consequences of conflict for cultural institutions. If he had, the theory of sociological ambivalence developed by Merton would have been extremely useful. Quite simply, it tells us that something has to happen in order to prevent the ambivalence from becoming psychologically and socially disabling. More than that, it suggests that ambivalence can lead to creative compromise formations, and by extension, to the development of new knowledge systems. Just how this might be so and a synthesis of the Hsu and Merton theories achieved, is best considered by returning to South India, and to the fishing-caste group that will be the focus of the analysis.

THE ELEMENTARY STRUCTURES OF AMBIVALENCE
IN JALARI KINSHIP

The Jalaris are a South Indian fishing-caste group resident in villages which dot the eastern coast of India, from Orissa to Tamil Nadu. Their great concentration is in the state of Andhra Pradesh, where Telugu (a Dravidian language) is spoken. Jalaris conform to the South Indian pattern in kinship relations: They are patrilineal and practice bilateral cross-cousin marriage, with a preference for the mother's brother's daughter. The village I worked in, Jalaripet, is near the port city of Visakhapatnam, one of India's largest. The population of the village is around 6,000 and consists almost exclusively of Jalaris. Traditionally, the men go fishing in the Bay of Bengal, and when they return, they sell their catch to their sisters, who take it to market. For a more complete description of the village and its environs, see Nuckolls (1987, 1991a, b, 1993c).

In Jalari culture, cultural ambivalence refers to a set of emotional orientations which are opposed because the kinship norms they represent are contradictory to each other. The paradox this creates realizes itself in a series of conflicts and attempts to resolve them, all directed to the culturally defined goal of fusion or coalescence. The goal of fusion is realized in Jalari culture in kinship terms—not philosophically or religiously—in experiences classical Hinduism calls *moksha* or *nirvana*. The Jalaris have never heard of these experiences and do not use the terms. Nevertheless, fusion is present—not as a philosophically articulated objective, but as a life-goal which the kinship system attempts to realize. It cannot be realized, due to the nature of the system within which it participates, giving rise to the cultural paradox that is simultaneously cause and outcome. The Jalari kinship system is paradoxical, directed to a goal that cannot be reached, and productive of a cultural ambivalence which seeks (but cannot find) permanent resolution. To the Jalaris this is not merely an abstraction. It is as real as their relationships to each other, and as strong as their desire to see these relationships fulfilled according to the norms that define them.

Clearing the net

I shall apply the concept of cultural ambivalence to the interpretation of South Indian kinship, to show: 1) that kinship roles are contradictory, both internally and with each other; 2) that the system promises the fulfillment of contradictory norms in the achievement of unity; and 3) that such fulfillment is forever unattainable, in constant tension with separation.

Jalari kinship presents an ideal of harmonious unity in which something given up is replaced by something given in return. Men give up their mothers and sisters, women their fathers and brothers, but through cross-cousin marriage a return of the relinquished is promised, if not directly, then through substitution. The woman given in marriage in one generation is returned in the next. A brother and sister divided by their marriages to different spouses are reunited in the marriage of their children. But the exigencies of real life prevent this ideal from being achieved, creating unfulfillable desires. Cross-cousin marriage, as Trawick notes (1990), is sustained not simply because it is "there," the only system available, but because it holds out for people the possibility of redemption. They are moved by it, not realizing that the promise is illusory, the quest for fulfillment permanently fleeting.

Jalari kinship is not a system of rules but a dynamic of conflicting

Preparing boat for departure

obligations which people are motivated to fulfill. Seven relational dyads stand out.

Primary Relationships	Secondary Relationships
Father and son	Brother and brother
Mother and son	Brother and sister
Father and daughter	Sister and sister
Mother and daughter	

In agreement with Hsu (1971), and against the argument advanced by Kurtz (1992), I believe that the four primary relationships are critically important, both in themselves and as sources of transference. The last three relationships—between same-sex and cross-sex siblings—are secondary, and in some sense derivative. They represent a transformation of the parental relationships which becomes, through patrilineal cross-cousin marriage, the nexus through which competing desires are represented and partially resolved.

All seven of the relational dyads share this: They represent pathways for the fulfillment of the goal fusion, realized in relational terms as continued

Women taking catch to market

unity in the face of multiple contingencies which push toward separation. In all societies, perhaps, the opposition of unity and separation arises
(Fiske 1991). But only in some does the opposition assume the status of a
cultural paradox and become the basis of cultural dialectics. In Jalari culture, the opposition becomes paradoxical in relation to the goal of fusion,
which tends to foreground the issue and endow it with a certain weight or
prominence. The reason the goal cannot be reached is that the pathways
are contradictory, both internally and with respect to each other. That does
not mean that the goal ceases to be motivating. On the contrary, as we shall
see, the system endures at least partly because of the ambivalences which
arise in direct consequence of opposed, and therefore unfulfillable, pathways toward the goal.

The Paradox of Unity and Separation in Same-Sex Primary Relationships

Father and Son

The father-son relationship is problematic because a son inherits property,
perpetuates the patriline, and officiates at his father's funeral, thus assuring
the safe passage of the father's spirit to the world beyond. But the son may

not cooperate. He may quarrel with his father, or with his own brothers, and in one way or another fail to fulfill the obligation to his father because his own wishes and desires run counter. "Men have good reason to be anxious," writes Trawick, "first, lest they have no sons, and second, lest their sons abandon them, unshoulder the burden of their land, their lineage, and their sins" (1990:163). Jalari men refer to the pleasure they take in their sons and the disappointment felt when their sons rebel. When they are reminded that they also rebelled as young men against their own fathers, they do not recognize the contradiction, but recall the pain of separation.

Mother and Daughter

The mother-daughter relationship is parallel to the father-son and is problematic for similar reasons. Fears of discontinuity and interruption incite tension and prevent the unity which both mothers and daughters say they want. These fears are most acute at the time of the daughter's marriage, according to Trawick, when the daughter is "cut off not only from the mother but from the entire natal home and family" (1990:167). But this is not the case in Jalari society, to the north of the region Trawick studies. Jalari daughters leave the parental home to join their husbands in households that may be no more than a stone's throw away from the place they grew up. There is no question of a distant separation. Moreover, daughters trade fish in small cooperatives organized by their mothers, and this continues long after their marriages.

It is not the daughters' marriages which cause such groups to break up, but the marriages of their children. They compete with each other for their brothers' daughters. This usually happens after their mother has died or relinquished control to an elder daughter. The issue is thus more one of sibling rivalry. Of the two same-sex parental relationships, the mother-daughter relationship is the least problematic, since it is not an official building block of patrilineal society. It is not a primary relational dyad, to use Hsu's terminology. But this may actually conceal the true emotional significance of the sororal relationship and its relevance as an origin of cultural ambivalence.

The Paradox of Unity and Separation in Cross-Sex Primary Relationships

Mother and Son

According to Kakar, a son identifies with the mother and defends himself against the threat of castration by his father by voluntarily renouncing sexual maturity as a man. This outcome (which Freud called "negative") results in slippery gender boundaries and the development of the "maternal

Women lighting cigars

feminine" as ego ideal (Kakar 1989, 1990). Psychoanalytic writers describe the relationship between mother and son in India as intensely close and prolonged. When it is finally superseded by the relationship to the father, the loss is experienced as overwhelmingly painful and traumatic. Kurtz (1992) disagrees and insists that the maternal relationship is not as close as it would seem. From very early on, he claims, the male child is led to renounce exclusive attachment to the mother in favor of a more mature immersion in the group. What of the mother's erotic attachment to the son, which Kakar asserts is one of the sources of the terror of mature female sexuality? Kurtz also dismisses this with the claim that in the few instances in which it occurs it is due to the failure of normal upbringing.

The conventional psychoanalytic theory is that an intense but suddenly interrupted period of maternal fusion predisposes Hindus to develop split maternal images and a whole host of descendent psychocultural forms, in cluding benign and malign goddess images and regressive yearnings that realize themselves in the concept of *moksha*. Kurtz asserts that psychoanalysts have missed the glaringly important fact that mothering is not single, as it is the West, but multiple, and therefore all the theories that base their conclusions on the nature of the mother-infant bond alone are badly

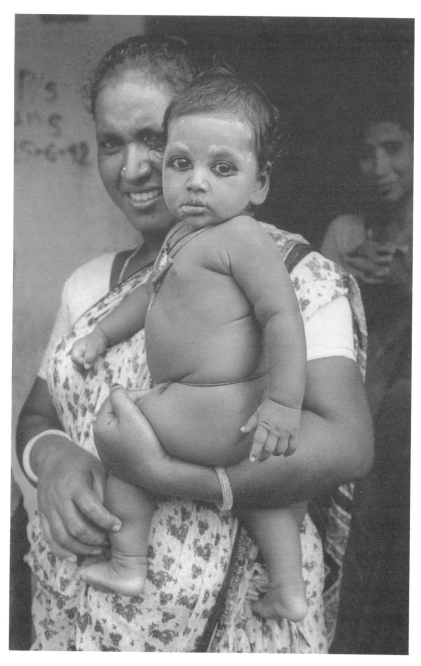

Mother and son

126

skewed, predisposing us to view Hindu development as a pathological variant of the Western norm.

Kurtz calls attention to what he calls the *ek hi* phase, the developmental movement away from the natural mother and toward mature immersion in a larger and more fundamentally benevolent group of mothers, a group in which all the mothers are one (hence the name *ek hi,* which in Hindi means "just one"). The result of this movement is not formation of an individuated ego, helped along by oedipally induced threats of castration, but a voluntary renunciation of pleasure in return for membership in the group. Kurtz calls this process the construction of an "ego of the whole," followed during the male child's sexual awakening by the construction of a "phallus of the whole."

Is it true that there is little or no "mirroring" of the infant by his mother, and thus little basis for the intense fusion other psychoanalytic writers have described? This is not so, at least not in the Jalari caste villages where I have been doing fieldwork for the last twenty years. In Telugu there are many expressions for the kind of play that involves what we would call mirroring, including one (interestingly enough) that includes the expression "to mirror" (*addalu pettu*). The second presumption is the more serious of the two: that when splitting does occur, it is not because of an original split between good and bad mother but because of the difference between the good mother and the bad (in-law) mothers. That only makes sense when the mother and her husband's family members are not related by any other tie. But in South India, *where cross-cousin marriages are preferred*, they are related and known to one another since early childhood. The same dynamic tension cannot possibly arise so easily and certainly not as it would in the North. If there are many mothers, as Kurtz maintains, then there are at least several major cultural variants within Hindu developmental practices, and to conflate them all as "Hindu India," as Kurtz does, is a mistake.

Kurtz presents a less problematic account of early childhood experience in India—one not so dark or so threatening, since the troubling suggestions of incestuous fantasies, both maternal and filial, do not arise. This is too simple. Kurtz is right to say that a Hindu child is led toward the group, but "group" is by no means an unproblematic thing, especially when agnatic and affinal groups vie with each other for attention and support. The cross-sex sibling relation, the symbolic core of Jalari society, is made up of conflicts and ambivalences which themselves have their origin in early childhood, in the relations between mother and son and father and daughter.

Kurtz asserts that the relationship between mother and son must lose its exclusive attachment as a boy accepts inclusion by a group of mothers

Mother and children

consisting of in-law women. Mothers simply encourage it. Perhaps this is true in joint family situations in which "all the mothers" live together and share responsibilities for raising each other's children. The problem with this view is that it applies only to an ideal type and not to the reality of family life. There is no such thing as *the* joint family in the overarching and highly generalized sense that Kurtz uses the term. Rather, there are dozens of regional variations, and it is dangerous to assimilate them to a standard type. It is essential that we know what kind of "joint family" is being discussed before we access its consequences for the maternal relationship.

The relationship between mother and child in Jalari culture is close, and no amount of quantified data on the number of people who handle the child or the amount of time spent with him, can alter the fact that this is how mother and son *say* they feel about each other. The bond is not dependent on "objective" factors. It is the *idea* of attachment, not the quantifiable measurement of it, that must be considered. If the idea is strong, intermittent contact between mother and child might actually make feelings of dependency more intense, not less so. Do we not make the same assumption when we say that absence makes the heart grow fonder?

But other evidence is available if we consider the relationship between mother and son a form of attachment, after Bowlby (1969). Attachment manifests itself as the tendency of a child to seek proximity to and contact with a specific figure and to do so in certain situations, especially when he is frightened, ill, or tired. In almost all cases this figure is the natural mother, a fact so congruent with primate evolution that it should be taken for granted unless demonstrated otherwise. Bowlby found that attachment behavior among children is universal, although it varies in intensity and the speed of its development. The results contradict Kurtz on two points: (1) that attachment is not directed primarily at the mother, and (2) that attachment can be diffused among a set of mothering figures.

Kurtz does not discuss the attachment behavior of young North Indian children, and so we do not know what children do when they become frightened, tired, or ill. The Bowlby hypothesis would suggest that they seek the attention of their primary caretakers, their uterine mothers. But if Kurtz is right, then they would seek the attention of any of the "mothers" who happen to be available at the moment. The material Kurtz relies on does not address this question, and therefore it is not possible to test Kurtz's hypothesis. However, I can cite observations from my fieldwork in Jalaripet that tend to support the Bowlby hypothesis in its application to Indian child rearing.

A Jalari mother and her children live together as a distinguishable unit, in a *gadillu* ("room house") or a *peddillu* ("big house"), depending on whether the husband is united with his brothers in one lineage group or separated. In either case the family (*kutumbum*) is always a nuclear family. Of course, children are in close contact with the wives of their father's brothers, whom they address as "small mother" (*cinnamma*) or "big mother" (*peddamma*), depending on age. However, from a very early age Jalari children can distinguish between these "mothers" and their "own mother" (*sonta amma*). No doubt the physical separation of Jalari households contributes to this discrimination, but so does the child's tendency to seek out his own mother for support and nurturance even when other "mothers" are present and available.

The first observation is that Jalari children nurse from their mothers until four or five years of age. Children seek the breast when they are hungry, but since they rely very little on breast milk for nutrition after the first year, most seeking behavior is for comfort. It is especially common when children are weary or frightened. Mothers terminate breast-feeding on demand rather abruptly, when children are about four years old, thus lending support to Kakar's claim that a radical rupture in maternal nurturance takes place at this age. In the early years, however, breast-feeding

Mother and child

is intense and prolonged. This can only add to the propensity for maternal attachment, which the Bowlby thesis predicts. One would expect *more* attachment between mother and child in India, not less, to judge by the evidence on breast-feeding alone.

The second observation is that children seek the proximity of their birth mothers when there is any kind of threat or danger. A child runs to his own (*sonta*) mother even when his other "mothers," the wives of his father's brothers, are equally near. Probably the most frequently encountered danger, at least from the child's point of view, was me. When I visited a family for the first time, or after a long absence, the young children of the household invariably showed hesitation in my presence. What could be more natural? In all instances (and this is no small number) the frightened children sought the protection of their own mothers even when other "mothers" were present and available. They would run to her and envelop themselves in the folds of her sari, and if young enough, they would pull at her sari blouse and try to suckle.

The third observation concerns feeding. Extended families in Jalari society have as many hearths (*poyis*) as there are married men. Usually these hearths are located in or near the separate "room houses" which adult men occupy with their wives and children. Wives do the cooking, or, if they are busy, elder daughters take over. Children up to the age of four or five are invariably fed by their mothers three times a day, in meals consisting of the two Jalari staples, rice and fish. The mother feeds the child by hand, rolling the food into little balls and popping them into the child's mouth. If the child tries to perform this task himself—a feat most American parents would reward with increased freedom to self-feed—the Jalari mother objects, and continues to feed the child herself. I have seen this go on for years, intermittently, up to the point when a child is eight to ten years old and already feeding himself. On these occasions the child might be very tired, ill, or in some way needy, and the mother responded by feeding him balls of food, just as she did when he was an infant. In one instance, I observed a mother feed her thirty-year-old son by hand when his wife was away visiting relatives in another village.

The fourth observation is that children are not expected to relieve themselves independent of adult supervision until they are four or five. The mother is almost always the one who takes charge. She cleans up after the child when he is younger and takes him outside when he is old enough to indicate that he needs to go. In such instances the child seeks his own mother when other closely related women are present. Even when children are old enough to undertake this task themselves, they still run to their mothers afterward and invite them to come to the site and inspect the results. Mothers always oblige and praise the children if they have particularly fine bowel movements and cleaned themselves adequately.

There are many reasons for believing that maternal attachment is not attenuated in Jalari society, in contrast to what Kurtz claims is the South Asian norm. There is simply not enough evidence available regionally to justify such a sweeping conclusion, and in its absence, ignoring what we *do* know about differences in family life between North and South India would be foolish. The rules of residence and cross-cousin marriage are especially important, and this will be even more evident when we consider the details of Jalari family development. Despite the fact that Kakar does not consider these rules or understand their relevance to attachment either, his theory of the mother-son relationship is applicable, because it (unlike Kurtz's) acknowledges the relationship's central importance to the development of cultural ambivalence.

Ambivalence in the mother-son relationship has two sources, the first in the inevitable conflict between erotic desire and repression, and the second in the crisis which develops in the sudden separation when the son is around five years old. Following Freud, Kakar states that erotic desire in the mother-son relationship is universal and must undergo repression. But in India this desire is especially intense, given the closeness of the relationship and the fact that the mother may feel inclined to fulfill her frustrated erotic desire for the husband through the son, a desire she may communicate to the son in a manner that makes him fearful of adult female sexuality (Kakar 1981). The argument applies with special force to the North, where women are segregated and separate from their husbands and sons are the principal means through which women validate their family status. In Jalari society, however, a different logic is at work.

Jalari women want sons to satisfy the society-wide demand that the family produce a male heir to transmit lineage identity to the next generation. They do not differ in this respect from women elsewhere in India. But Jalari women also want sons so that they can present them to their brothers, as marriage partners for their brothers' daughters. Jalari women see this as a necessary return to their own (i.e., natal) family of the gift their family made at the time of their own marriages. This is not just implicit. Jalari women state the matter in exactly these terms. It is a matter of family honor (*mariyada*), they say, and the maintenance of the alliance relationship between marrying lineage groups (*varasu unna vallu*, lit. "between those to whom there is line") depends on it. Although it would be difficult to measure, this would seem to give Jalari women, and southern women generally, a greater stake in the birth and development of sons than women in the North.

All this merely adds to but does not constitute the attachment which, as Kakar points out, carries an erotic component for both mother and son which must be repressed or redirected. Ambivalence is the result of the strong desire to maintain the attachment but also to render its conflicting demands inert. Jalari mythology is full of solutions which temporarily resolve ambivalence by doing away with their source: the mother. Matricide is a common theme, and usually involves the killing of the erotically demanding mother and her replacement by a mother whose troublesome desires have been shifted to the women whom men may marry. In "real life," different problems and outcomes arise, emerging most clearly in the case histories of men and women who become possession-mediums.

Such people are not aberrant or strange but simply represent in extreme form values and attitudes that are widely distributed in Jalari society. Near the Jalari village, there are four possession-mediums (*pati*s) who practice on behalf of Jalari clients (Nuckolls 1991b). Two are widows who support themselves through their occupation as mediums. Both live alone in huts. The other two are unmarried men and, like the women, support themselves through their professional practice.

There are three interesting differences among them. The first is that the men first experienced anticipations of their future role in childhood. Transformation was gradual and was accompanied by friction among family members. The two women, in contrast, fulfilled perfectly normal roles as Jalari wives and mother. Transformation in their case was sudden and unaccompanied by any family disharmony. The second difference is that the men who work as possession-mediums claim to have been chosen by spirits who are the principal goddesses of the area. Their selection signified devotion to the deity and attainment of perfect *bhakti* (devotion). The female practitioners, in contrast, are possessed by their own dead sons. Selection began as an experience of loss, not gain, and was completed through the transformation of the possession spirit itself, from son into "hero" (*irababu*). The "hero" remains as the Jalari practitioner's chief possessing agent and guide, but in no sense does the possession-medium consider herself to be her deceased child's *bhakta,* or devotee. Finally, the male practitioners signify the relationship with the possessing deity by identifying with the goddess through habits of dress, speech, and behavior. The female practitioners do not attempt to identify with their possessing spirits. They do not dress or behave like "heroes," either in everyday life or in the possession state. While the male practitioners make every effort to identify with (and to be identified as) their deities and to signify identification in word and deed, the female practitioners do not.

The relationship between mothers and sons is central to the process of becoming a possession-medium. An important feature of this relationship is ambivalence. On the one hand, a boy is drawn by memories of his mother's intense nurturing to idealize the feminine. On the other hand, fear that the mother may reject him or, worse, exploit him for the fulfillment of her own sexual needs, compels him to constrain the feminine, to keep its power to envelop him under control. Ambivalence in the maternal relationship resolves itself among particular men in the experience of becoming a possession-medium, a role which normatively allows certain men to immerse themselves in a nurturing feminine role identity and at the same time control that identity through the practice of possession-mediumship. For the two male possession-mediums of this study, this is what seems to have happened.

Consider now the position of the mother. Wanting sons is natural in a culture where fulfillment of a woman's role is contingent on the production of male offspring. This is not unique to India. But in having sons, an Indian mother must eventually acknowledge their loss to a wife who will supplant her and (in Jalari culture) to a set of affines who become competitors with her for her son's attention and support. Under some circumstances, ambivalence in the maternal role—between wanting mature sons and knowing that their maturity means some degree of disaffection from her—is intensified and then resolved in the experience of transformation into a possession-medium. As a medium, the mother regains total control over her son, whom she incorporates as her permanent tutelary spirit. The son never grows up; he can never leave; and he can never be alienated. For the two female possession-mediums of this study, this is what seems to have happened (Nuckolls 1991b, 1993b).

Resolution of ambivalence in the relationship of sons and mothers is possible in different ways. The first way is through symbolic transformation of the son to make him less problematic for the mother. The second way is through symbolic transformation of the mother to make her less problematic for the son. Both patterns of resolution are present in the cases under study. The male possession-mediums resolve the ambivalence in favor of the son. The son recovers the mother through his own symbolic transformation and then complete immersion in a female persona which becomes (for him) a controlled object of devotion. The female possession-mediums, by contrast, resolve the ambivalence in favor of the mother, who then recovers the son through a process of reabsorption into herself. In both cases, the significant other is returned and simultaneously relieved of its ambivalence-causing nature through symbolic transformation into an inalienable possession as well as a source of divinatory power.

Cases of possession-mediumship are not like the cases seen in a psychiatrist's office in Delhi, which Kakar cites as supporting data. Kurtz (1992) dismisses clinical cases as too unusual or aberrant to be considered representative. But possession-mediums are members of society and their role as mediums is normative. They are not aberrant. Moreover, everyone in Jalari culture undergoes possession at some point in his life, often by goddesses (in the case of men) or deceased sons (in the case of women). Mediums have experienced the development of these desires more intensely than most, but that does not make their experience too unusual to be considered representative.

Ambivalence in the mother-son relationship also arises when a son leaves the world of his mother and is thrust into the world of men. Kakar (1981) finds that the son experiences the separation as a sudden withdrawal of maternal affection. He cannot reconcile the image of his mother *now,* at the moment of withdrawal, with his mother *then,* during the long years of close support and constant attention. He therefore splits the two images. The split-off "bad" mother becomes the basis for the evil goddesses who are violent and unpredictable, like Durga. The split-off "good" mother becomes the basis of the benign and passive goddesses, like Sarasvati and Padmavati. The same goddess can represent both, alternating at different moments between good and bad. Most Jalari goddesses are of this type. But Jalari goddesses always begin as sisters, not mothers, *and this is a crucial difference.* The difference lies in the conversion of attachment and ambivalence between mother and son into attachment and ambivalence between brother and sister.

Father and Daughter

The relationship between father and daughter is parallel to the one between mother and son, but according to the conventional view, the father is too distant for the relationship to excite problematic desires or tensions. Once again the failure to acknowledge regional differences is crucial, since what is true for the North is not for the South. Kakar does not consider the relationship between Hindu father and daughter but assumes, if I read him correctly, that the father's distance renders him insignificant as an object choice. Perhaps this is true in North India, where female segregation is more stringently enforced. But it does not characterize the relationship between fathers and daughters in Jalari society.

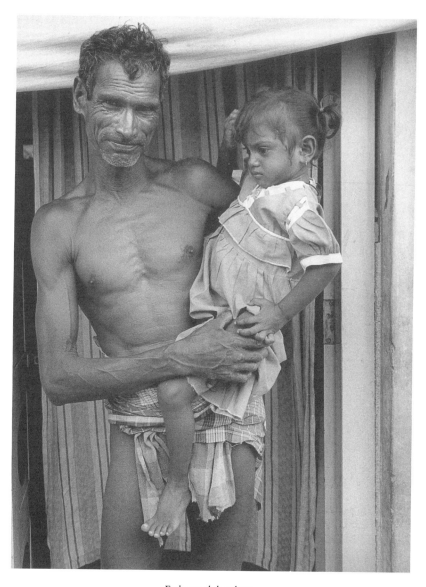

Father and daughter

Daughters are greatly valued, and fathers lavish affection on them from almost the moment they are born. Daughters can be seen in the company of their fathers much of the time. Older girls, of course, are with their mothers most of the day, but when they are old enough to assume household duties, they often feed and care for their fathers. There is a paradox in the relationship of father and daughter, between the ideals of unity and separation, and it is analogous to the problem that arises between mothers and sons. It is probably true, as Rank pointed out, that the incestuous potential of the father-daughter relationship is greater than that between mother and son, especially in patriarchal societies: "[T]he father has an authoritative influence over his daughter, a *patriae potestas,* lending more force to whatever impulses and wishes he may have than is possible in the son's subordinate relationship with his mother" (Rank 1992:301). But a father knows that he must give up his daughters in marriage to his sisters' sons, and looks forward to it with ambivalent feelings.

This is quite explicit. It is not just that he loses a valuable source of household labor, to be replaced by the arrival of daughters-in-law. In Jalari society, the daughter possesses something the father wishes to retain, and this may be fundamentally sexual in nature. It takes the form of *sakti,* a sexualized power which a daughter possesses and uses to benefit her father until she is married. In the myth of Shiva and his daughters, for example, the father is weakened by the departure of his daughters, who leave to visit their mother's brother. He loses a battle and almost dies. Shiva's two wives, Parvati and Ganga, do nothing to help him. Only his unmarried daughters can save him from certain death at the hands of the evil *raksasas* (demons), because only they possess the right kind of power (*sakti*). It is a power Shiva knows he must eventually give up when his daughters leave to get married. As we shall see, this is the source of a deep ambivalence, as Shiva alternately advances and impedes the progress of his daughters' departure for the home of their mother's brother and potentially marriageable cross-cousins. The daughters are no less ambivalent. They alternately afflict their father with terrible diseases and cure him. Then they force Shiva to accept their leaving, but once they have left, they think of him and pray to him constantly for assistance.

The Paradox of Unity and Separation in Secondary Same-Sex Relationships

Brother and Brother

What is true of the father-son relationship is true of the relationship between brothers, but with several added complications. Sons usually accept the authority of their father, however much grumbling they do. But once he dies, leadership of the family falls to the eldest brother, and younger brothers do not accept his authority as willingly. Fraternal solidarity is a vitally important ideal, but it becomes progressively weaker as a reality until one or several brothers separate and create their own lineage groups. Even then, brothers express great longing for the fraternal group and lament the circumstances that caused them to divide. This is the source of the ambivalence between brothers, and a theme of great prominence in both Jalari mythology and divination.

Sister and Sister

Unity and separation also mark the relationship among sisters, but because sororal solidarity is not marked, its importance as a source of ambivalence might seem to be less. Mothers and daughters form groups which endure for years, well beyond the marriages of the daughters. Just as groups of brothers go to sea together, sisters buy and sell fish and cooperate in making loans and getting credit. Even when the mother dies, the group may continue to operate for a long time. There is no pressure to divide and to form new groups, as there is for men.

But such groups do not last forever. Inevitably, competition between sisters for their children's marriage partners causes sororal aggregates to disintegrate. In a clear signal of ambivalence, adult sisters alternately condemn each other's selfishness and praise the erstwhile solidarity of the group. This ambivalence finds its way into the goddess myths, which can be read as fantasies on the theme of sororal solidarity when it remains uncompromised through marriage and the development of competing interests. Many of the stories I refer to below were collected from women who, as sisters, were near the point of breaking up as members of the same cooperative group.

But matrilineality and sororal solidarity do not crop up in the knowledge structures of Jalari divination. Divinatory knowledge is organized around two scenarios only, one dealing with relationships within households (prototypically between brothers) and the other with relationships between households (prototypically between brothers and sisters). There is no divinatory script specific to the relationship between sisters, and this, I think, is related to the fact that Jalari social structure is officially patrilineal. Whatever the social origin of a dispute within or between households—and no matter how much it may be due to relations among sisters—it is assimilated to one of the two standard scenarios. These scenarios function as filters, selectively adapting a multitude of possible social precipitants to conform to models that reduce social disputes to problems

Sisters collecting fish on the beach

between brothers as members of a patrilineal group (the agnatic script) or to problems between brothers and sisters as members of patrilineal groups in affinal relation to each other (the affinal script). It is quite possible that sororal relations do inform divinatory knowledge—in fact it would be surprising if they did not—but only indirectly and after translation into the explanatory structures of patrilineality.

The Paradox of Unity and Separation in Secondary Cross-Sex Relationships

Brother and Sister

The relationship between brother and sister represents a displacement or extension of the attachment between a parent and child of the opposite sex. Psychoanalytic writers typically consider the sibling relationship a "second edition." Rank went so far as to state that "it is only through the primary parent complex that the significance of the sibling complex can correctly be appreciated and understood" (Rank 1992:363). In India, the attachment may be stronger and thus the displacement to siblings even more profound. However, none of the psychoanalytic writers on Indian social relations has considered this in any detail.

Trawick is an exception. She suggests that strong erotic feelings for the

Sister and brother

Sister and brother

Brothers and sisters clearing net

mother exist, but because they cannot be fulfilled (at least not directly), such feelings are directed to an opposite-sexed sibling (1990:171). Trawick argues that erotic love for the mother is converted into attachment between brother and sister, but because it can never be acted on or realized, it becomes the focus of longing and tension. The evidence from Jalari society supports Trawick's conclusion.

Like their father, Jalari brothers have mixed feelings about their sisters' marriages. The alliances maintained by such marriages are important, and brothers usually take the lead in arranging them. But the sisters' departure is experienced as a loss, which helps explain the lengths Jalari brothers go to in emphasizing continued affection for their sisters. Asked several times (by me) whose plea they would respond to most readily, a sister's or a wife's, Jalari men always replied, "the sister's." Yet the utmost anxiety attends the possibility that a sister might not marry or might remain too long at home.

Husband and Wife

Even though marriage is basic to Jalari social structure, the relationship between husband and wife is not. That might seem odd, but it reflects the fact

Jalari woman

that the relationship between husband and wife in South India is peculiar because of its vagueness and potential for rivalry. In Jalari society marriage does not depend for its formation on attachment between husband and wife, yet both usually come to their union with expectations of this kind. While the expectations are real, they remain vague and difficult to fulfill, inasmuch as the marriage relationship itself does not depend on them.

Rivalry arises because the wife is equal to her husband in earning power. Most women work outside the household and for money, and there are plenty of indications that the old taboos and prohibitions, such as purdah, are fading (Minturn 1993; Trawick 1990). Jalari women do not accept submission to their husbands easily. Consequently, the relationship between husband and wife is often disputatious; they can act independently of each other, and their different priorities can conflict.

However, the relationship between husband and wife is not considered a building block of society. It is never the focus of divinatory inquiry, when people consider the social disputes that cause goddesses to attack and make trouble. It comes in myth only by omission. In one sense, of course, the relationship is vitally important, since marriage is what sets in motion all of the problems and paradoxes which characterize the relationship between siblings. But in itself, it is not symbolically prominent; psychosocially, one might even go so far as to say it is hypocognized. That is why I did not mention it among the primary or secondary relationships.

THE DYNAMICS OF PARADOX IN KINSHIP

Trawick discusses the ambivalence of key relationships but limits these to only four: Father and son, mother and daughter, brother and sister, and husband and wife. She tries to show how the logic of cross-cousin marriage affects these relationships, but there are problems with this approach. First, there are more than just four relationships to be considered, as I have shown. Second, cross-cousin marriage does much more than merely affect these relationships. It plays a determining role in constituting them. The problem is that Trawick does not take seriously enough the importance of regional differences. In her Tamil ethnography, evidence from North India is presented whenever possible, and without critical comment, to supplement her observations on the South. The purpose of her four primitive relational dyads, consequently, is to constitute a set of primordial relational archetypes that are general to South Asia and which the dynamics of cross-cousin marriage merely play upon and elaborate in culturally distinctive ways.

So the question comes down to this: What, exactly, *is* the effect of cross-cousin marriage on the relationship between fathers and sons, mothers and daughters, brothers and sisters, and husbands and wives that might give to the South a different twist on common Indian themes? The fundamental dynamic of Dravidian kinship is realized in the relationship between siblings as individuals and as groups whose desires *must* and *do* diverge. The divergence is central to the kinship system, which necessarily opposes the desires of those related agnatically and affinally. As soon as brothers marry and bring their wives, vast structural changes begin to occur within the patriline they constitute as prototypic members. New wives are notoriously jealous and (in a scenario familiar from throughout South Asia) quarrel among themselves over the distribution of family resources. At the same time that wives come, sisters leave by marrying out. Married sisters are their brothers' primary trading partners, buying their fish and selling it in the market downtown. They expect favorable trading terms which their brothers, either individually or collectively, find difficult to meet or agree on. Both groups, wives and sisters, compete for the brothers' assistance and support, making the effort to balance their competing needs increasingly difficult.

Because of their sudden juxtaposition as competing expectations, I refer to the copresence of intense affinal obligations at this point as the first "crisis moment." It may take months or years to develop, as all the brothers and sisters marry and begin their own families. It comes to an end when brothers can no longer agree on the distribution of resources, including money, food, and fishing equipment, to their dependent affines. Factions develop. Several brothers (usually the younger ones) push for greater individual control and other brothers (usually the older ones) advocate continued collectivization and control of resources by an elder. The result is always the same: dissolution of the patriline as a residential and coparcenary unit.

Following division of the patriline's property, the brothers leave their joint residence and live apart, in physically separate *gadillu*s ("room houses"). But the patriline remains "joint" under the authority of the senior male, usually an elder brother, since by this point the father has died. To be sure, that authority no longer means control over or access to collective property or earnings. It pertains to the group's ritual identity—that is, to its members' identification with one "big house" (*peddillu*), where the senior male lives; one "goddess shrine" (*sadaru*), where patriline members worship patriline spirits; and one "goddess money" (*ammavari dabbu*), to which members contribute a portion of their income for the support of rituals. Patriline members remain, both in their own and in the community's eyes, "birds of a single nest" (*oka guduki paccilu*).

Agnatic unity, represented prototypically in the solidarity between brothers, defines the patrilineal ideology that constitutes the ideal of Jalari social life. By "ideology" I refer to what Chasseguet-Smirgel and Grunberger call "the system of thought which claims to be total, [a] historical and political interpretation whose (unconscious) aim is the actualization of an illusion, of illusion *par excellence,* that the ego and its ideal can be reunited by a short-cut, via the pleasure principle" (1986:25–26). This illusion, with its powerful directive force, is challenged by the fissiparous tendencies of brothers, which become particularly intense when they marry and start their own families. Eventually these give way and brothers divide their residences. The paradox is that this is not what Jalari men want, or are supposed to want, given the directive goals their culture creates for them. They would prefer to remain united, in multigeneration families, because such families can become powerful in the village both economically and in terms of social prestige. Ironically, the very effort to achieve this ideal results in it receding further, until it becomes irretrievably lost.

After the first crisis moment, the deaths of senior males weaken the soli-

Father and grandson

darity of the patriline, leading to changes which now begin primarily on the agnatic axis, in the relationship between brothers. Family problems have shifted from the women who marry into and out of the patriline—the cause of the first crisis moment—to the men whom they marry. The shift reflects a change in structural focus, from concern with the incorporation and exodus of members through marriage to a concern with the continuation of the patriline through the bearing and raising of children. The more serious disputes now begin and end among men, and concern the allocation of ritual identity, not living expenses.

The reason is that Jalari men become increasingly familocentric as their children grow up, devoting more of their resources to their children's (especially their sons') care and training. Men are increasingly disinclined to contribute any of their heavily committed funds to the "goddess money," the last collective resource patriline members possess. Serious quarrels between patriline members eventually focus on this money—on how much each member is or is not contributing and on how the collected money should be spent. Since the "goddess money" represents the ritual identity of the patriline, disputes of this kind are really disputes about agnatic unity.

As pressures mount within the patriline for its dissolution, they necessarily affect relations between the patriline and its affinally linked households, especially the households of married sisters. For one thing, brothers and sisters typically find trading with each other less profitable than trading with others. Then, too, brothers may not respond to their sisters' demands for help or, if they do, may respond in ways their sisters don't like. Finally, either a brother or a sister may abrogate an alliance relationship, deciding to marry their children to other related households or (in a growing trend) to households not related at all. Such problems eventually develop, no matter what.

Between brothers and sisters, normal obligations for support and assistance add considerably to brothers' extrapatrilineal obligations and thus diminish the resources they can devote to the maintenance of the patrilineal group. To support affinal relations to the extent normative obligations require means reducing the amount of support allocable to the patriline. And because obligations to the patriline are most intense at this "moment," when brothers are older, that becomes extremely difficult. The opposite is true also. Fulfilling patrilineal obligations means abrogating some or all of the obligations owed to affines. The patriline is caught in the middle, increasingly unable to hold its own ground against the fissiparous pressures exerted by cross-sibling bonds.

Kinship tensions between affinally related patrilines, like tensions within them, cause arguments among patriline members centering on contributions to the goddess money. Because of competing affinal obligations, brothers stop contributing altogether or demand the return of certain sums to meet personal expenses. Jalaris recognize these acts as symptoms of underlying tension and the result of competing role expectations. They invariably signal members' growing disaffection from the group.

The centrality of the goddess money attests to the importance of spirit-human relations as one of the influences codetermining the family's passage through crisis moments in its development. Household spirits require periodic offerings which family members pay for from the goddess money. When family relations are unsettled, members cannot join together to make offerings. As a result, the spirits become angry and attack, usually by inflicting illness or by causing a sudden drop in the fish catch. Family members then reexamine their sibling relations, to address the social problem which caused them to neglect the offering in the first place.

Early in the group's development, disaffected members may reunite and resume regular contributions to the goddess money. But later, when the brothers are older and their contributions to the patrilineal groups more difficult to maintain, brothers will claim that dividing the patriline, rather than keeping it together, is the best way to avoid future attacks. The result is a complete breakdown of the group. Brothers enter the "big house" and split off chunks of the goddess shrine (*sadaru*). Each brother takes a chunk to his own house where he consecrates it as a new *sadaru*, thus making his house into a big house, the symbolic nucleus of a new patriline. The second crisis moment is now over and fission of the old patriline is complete.

Symbolic Consequences

The paradox is that although brothers must someday separate, the ideology of fraternal solidarity cuts against this, making brothers ambivalent about their role in the group and their efforts to divide it. When brothers say, "We are birds of a single nest," they represent to themselves the intense bonds which constitute the patrilineal ideology and bind them together as members of the same patriline. Considerable emotive force is bound up in this expression. A Jalari man expresses his love for, and complete dependence on, the patriline by referring to himself as a bird and to it, the patriline, as his nest or branch. Most men cannot discuss this subject without being visibly moved. Some are brought to tears.

Brothers want to remain together but cannot, and in fact do everything they can to bring about their dissolution as a group. This they then regret. Similarly, brothers and sisters want to remain united but find this increasingly difficult given their competition with each other and their growing inability to meet each other's needs. Eventually they go their separate ways, signifying their break in a ritual of chicken sacrifice made at the door of the sibling. But they always regret it and think that somehow the split might have been prevented. The paradox of sibling relations gives rise to cultural ambivalence, which finds temporary resolution in mythology and divination.

In myth, contradictions are overcome and ambivalences relieved by transforming the agents who carry paradox into different kinds of beings for whom the paradox no longer arises. In divination, contradictions are temporarily resolved by transforming them into individual or family interests and then adjudicating the conflict between these interests in a forum presided over by judges. In both cases, however, nothing is done (because nothing can be done) to relieve the underlying causes of ambivalence. This is what makes myth and divination so necessary and compelling, year after year.

Brother and sister haggling

Jalari myths about goddesses represent the conversion into sibling relations of ambivalences originally experienced in the relationship between parent and child. Such a conversion is not surprising given the psychoanalytic finding that feelings for a parent can be transferred to a sibling of the opposite sex. In South India the process of conversion is made especially complex by the exigencies of patrilineality and cross-cousin marriage. The sibling relationship carries not only the weight of parental transference but also the special obligations imposed on it by the marriage system. It has more structural weight, as it were, and that is why it is the primary subject of Jalari divination.

By parental transference, I refer not only to the relationship between mother and son, which psychoanalytic writers always highlight (either to emphasize or deny it) but also to the relationship between father and daughter. There are layers to Jalari mythology, and in what I would claim is one of the lowest, we find the expression of the originating parent-child ambivalence before it undergoes conversion into the sibling relationship and reconfiguration under the impact of the cross-cousin marriage system. Sibling myths are also important, especially since Jalari goddesses come into being mainly through the transformation of sisters.

Kinship and Dynamic Structures

I have suggested that we should view kinship as more than the mechanical implementation of structural rules. In this I agree with LiPuma (1983) and others (e.g., Bourdieu 1977) that rule-like statements about kinship do not in themselves structure kinship relations and that to confuse one with the other seriously distorts the ethnography and produces poor analytic treatment. My analysis is based on the notion of conflict and dynamic tension and suggests that what actually motivates kinship behavior is not blind adherence to norms but dynamic conflict and the repeated attempts to resolve it, even if permanent resolution is impossible. This is a view very different from the revisionist kinship theories of LiPuma and Bourdieu, which tend to view marriage rules as socially disseminated "lies," whose purpose is to correct the symbolic effects of strategies forced on them by economic and political necessities (see Bourdieu 1977:43).

Following Trawick (1990) and her superb analysis of Tamil culture, I find it useful to consider Jalari kinship as an ideal never realized in practice and thus fundamentally "incomplete" in its own terms. It promises a unity which it cannot deliver and thus creates conflicted longings that cannot be fulfilled. The reasons are found in the exigencies that arise socially and economically; thus they conflict with the ideal of harmony and structural reduplication embedded in the kinship system. As Trawick puts it: "It is possible to see kinship not as a static form upheld by regnant or shared principles, but as a web maintained by unrelieved tensions, an architecture of conflicting desires, its symmetry of imbalance, its cyclicity that of a hunter following his own tracks" (1990:152). The desire created by the gap between ideal and practice is not merely a by-product of the system, but crucial to it.

In the next chapter, we shall examine the consequences of structurally induced ambivalence for one of the knowledge systems that is of interest to us: myth. In the worlds myth creates, kinship-based paradoxes can be resolved by transforming those who represent ambivalent wishes into different kinds of agencies. This is not to argue that myths "function" only to relieve ambivalences, although this is one of their functions. Myths develop from the creative potential locked in ambivalence, by transforming ambivalence into a source of creative energy. In this sense, they become progressive, as Obeyesekere (1990) uses the term, and develop according to their own cultural logics.

Chapter Six

Myth and the Dynamics of Desire in Kinship

There has always existed in the world, and there will always continue to exist, some kind of metaphysics, and with it the dialectic that is natural to pure reason. (Kant, Critique of Pure Reason*)*

It has long been recognized that myths may provide a *reconciliato oppositorum,* representing and reconciling contradictions within social systems. Contradictions and their attendant ambivalences may even be at the heart of the religious experience (Eliade 1962; Otto 1923; Thom 1983; Leeuw 1933). It is not my purpose to make or support these claims, however. Instead, I wish to focus on the Jalari kinship system and its systematically induced ambivalence, to show that the mythology of Jalari goddesses represents the ambivalence and attempts to resolve it within a system of knowledge.

In the world myth creates, contradictory opposites can be eliminated by being transformed. Jalari myth is full of transformation, all of it motivated by conflictual themes in the primary and secondary relationships. How can brothers remain united after their marriages? How can mothers and sons continue their intimacy, despite the erotically troubling nature of their relationship? How can fathers and daughters achieve a satisfying relationship, despite the exigencies of marriage? How can brothers and sisters remain close, despite the workings of the marriage system? Myth renders the conflicting desires implicit in these questions inactive; more precisely, it changes them into something else, so that they become sources of spiritual power.

Myths are multifunctional, by which I mean not only that different myths have different functions but also that a particular myth typically includes several functions, among which the most important are these:

1) Myths allow the expression of unconscious, usually repressed, ideas in culturally sanctioned form; 2) myths use the emotional energy attached to these ideas to energize the nonemotional function of myth; and 3) myths provide cultural responses to psychological conflicts, both universal and culture-specific, that are shared by the people who make up the society. If we wish to interpret the psychology of myth, to know its motivational content and its consequences for knowledge structures, the only appropriate theoretical tool available to us is psychoanalysis.

Anyone who has read this far must be at least interested in the possibility of psychoanalytic interpretation. At this point in the book, it should be the results that matter most. In the next four sections I focus on the myths which transform and resolve the problematic attachment between mothers and sons, fathers and daughters, and siblings (same-sex and cross-sex).

THE STORY OF ADI SAKTI

Resolving the Paradoxical Desire of the Mother for the Son

The Jalaris tell a variety of stories about the beginning of the world and the birth of human beings. One of the best-known is the story of Adi Sakti, mother of the universe. "Sakti" means "energy" or "power" and can refer to either the power itself or the feminine form that contains it, as in a goddess. "Adi" means "first" or "primary"; thus the story below is about the primary energy of the universe, a female force out of which everything else is created. The story was related to me by Laksmanayya, a thirty-five-year-old fisherman.

The three principal gods (*trimurti*) of classical Hinduism appear in this story as brothers, the children of Adi Sakti. In order of seniority, they are Visnu, Shiva, and Brahma. It is unusual for the *trimurti* to be given a kinship relationship, but the Jalaris usually configure relationships this way. If there is no kinship tie to begin with, one is imposed. Otherwise it would be impossible to understand the interaction between the agents. Jalari thought does not simply fill in the gaps, however, inventing kin relationships where none usually exist. There is no father in this story, for example, nor does the paternity of the three brother gods seem to be an issue. The myth is content to leave this out, because its purpose is to tell us something about the relationships between mothers and sons, between brothers, and, to some extent, between husbands and wives.

Adi Sakti herself is an elemental force, driven by hunger and intense erotic desire. She has no other motivation. Like most Jalari goddesses, she bears little resemblance to the refined goddesses of classical Hinduism, such as Laksmi, the goddess of wealth, or Sarasvati, the goddess of learning. She is like Purusa, the creator deity of the Vedic period, who creates the world out of a feeling of loneliness and a desire for unity, a state he can achieve only by dividing himself in two and copulating incestuously with his female half. The Jalari creator is female and acts in order to restore a lost unity, but instead of dividing herself into parts, she lays eggs.

The role of eggs in Hindu stories of creation is manifold. Purusa is a cosmic egg before he splits apart into male and female halves; Rudra (Shiva) emerged androgyne from Hinanyabarbha, the golden egg (Kramrisch 1975). In the Jalari case, the reason for this is twofold and has to do with the logic of Jalari cosmology and Jalari kinship as well as the connection between the two which the symbol of the egg mediates.

The egg is totally self-created and self-sufficient, the only thing in the universe of this type, say the Jalaris. It comes out of a chicken, but then it requires nothing beyond itself. It is a perfect whole. For the Jalaris, to imagine a process of purely unitary creation prior to any differentiation is to imagine a chicken and an egg. It might be for a reason similar to this that when we contemplate original causes we use the same analogy, albeit in the form of a nursery-school tautology: "Which came first, the chicken or the egg?" The ability of the egg to represent uncreated beginnings might also explain why it is used at death, when the Jalaris place a raw chicken egg on the right shoulder of the body when it is buried. Unlike other Hindus, the Jalaris do not believe in reincarnation, but they do believe that time is cyclical and that nothing is every really lost. The egg buried with the body seems to represent this, as well as reunion with the creative energy of the earth itself, since Adi Sakti and the earth are thought to be one and the same.

The second reason the egg is present is because it represents an analogy between its own physiology and the cross-generational dynamics of Jalari kinship. The relationship between a chicken and the chick which comes out of the egg is not an immediate one, the Jalaris say. The chicken gives birth to the egg, but the egg itself gives birth to the chick, making three generations out of what we would consider two. The same thing is true of a grandmother and grandson. To follow the Jalari analogy: Sexual relations between two chickens, the one born from the egg of the other, is possible because they are not related as mother and child. Therefore no incest actually exists. The same is true between a human grandmother and grandchild. As alternate instead of adjacent generations, they are not so closely related as to prohibit sexual relations. But are such relations morally correct?

They are not, the Jalaris insist. But the degree of separation does permit the growth of sexual desire. Therefore something must be done to prevent it. That is why a boy is never left alone with his grandmother (either maternal or fraternal) in the Jalari village. If caught unaccompanied in her presence, he will be subjected to a humiliating round of joking: e.g., "Did she fondle your penis nicely?" or "Did you massage her breasts to her satisfaction?" A Jalari friend was scandalized when I once remarked that my son had been left with his grandmother for a few hours. The Jalaris go to great lengths to eliminate or reduce sexual desire between grandmother and grandson, justifying such measures on the analogy of the chicken and the egg. They use various means to discourage the desire between grandmother and grandson should the circumstances for its expression arise.

This, I think, is indicative of the ambivalence they feel in the presence of something both attractive and repellent. There is more to this dynamic than meets the eye, however. Is it really the relationship between grandmother and grandson, or is it something else, which displacement onto alternate generations only partly conceals? The story of Adi Sakti provides a possible answer. Adi Sakti, the primal mother, tries to use the "chicken and egg" argument herself when she tries to persuade her sons to have sex with her. Threatened by her overpowering desire, and, indeed, by their own desire for her, the sons have no other choice but to destroy their lustful mother and transfer her sexual energy to their own newly created wives. Here is the story, as related to me by Laksmanayya:

> Adi Sakti took thought to herself that she would like to have sex if only she had a man. As a result of her lust, she laid three eggs. Adi Sakti covered the eggs with her right eyelid, making it into a nest, and used her left eyelid as a cover.
> Adi Sakti was hungry and ate one of the eggs. Accidentally she kicked the second egg and broke it. She sat on the third egg for six months. At the end of that time, the egg broke open. The upper part of the shell became the sky. The lower part became the earth. Various small fragments became the stars. Some other pieces became mountains. And the central portions became the sun and moon. The water within the shell turned into the seas. Out of the egg Visnu, Shiva, and Brahma were born.
> Then she was alone. She was lusty from her strong diet and she had no control over her desire. So she went to Brahma. She came to the earth and Brahma saw that his mother was coming, and asked her what she came for. She told him that she wanted to have sex with him. Then Brahma refused. She said, "Look, there is no other man here, so you

have to satisfy my desire." When Brahma told her that it would be wrong, she said that it wouldn't be, because the egg was like her daughter, and therefore the children born out of the egg are like her grandchildren. There is nothing wrong, she said, in sexual relations between a grandmother and grandson. But Brahma still refused. She became angry and chanted the *mantras*. Brahma was turned into a stone.

Then Adi Sakti went to Shiva. She went to Shiva and told him to make love to her. He replied, "Mother, Adi Sakti, I will not make love with my own mother." She insisted, however, repeating the argument she first used with Brahma. But she still calls him son, saying, "Son, have sex with me." Finally he said, "If you want to kill me, go ahead, but I won't have sex with my own mother." Then she chanted the *mantras* and Shiva was turned into a small mountain.

Then she went to Visnu in his milk ocean. Visnu knew that she was coming full of anger and lust. She demanded that he have sex with her. He smiled and then laughed, saying "Mother, we are not like those who have sex with their own mothers." She told him that she would slit his throat if he refused to accept her. Then he said, "OK, mother, I will have sex with you. But give those *mantras* to me."

She was senseless from lust and agreed to give him her *mantras*. Visnu said, "Mother, I will have sex with you. But women have menstrual pollution. First take a bath in the ocean and come back clean, then I will have sex with you." So she left to take a bath quickly. Visnu chanted a *mantra* and all the water dried up.

Adi Sakti became furious and opened her mouth, one jaw to the sky and one jaw to the earth. Visnu saw that she was coming and realized that she would swallow him. Visnu is very intelligent. He chanted a *mantra* and a huge ocean formed in between them. Then Adi Sakti made herself normal again and took a bath. She then took off her wet clothes and put on dry ones. She came to him.

Visnu chanted another *mantra* and turned Adi Sakti into a stone. Then he went to Brahma and with a *mantra* brought him back to life. Both then went to Shiva and restored him. They all three talked about their mother. The younger brothers left it to their elder brother to decide what to do.

Then Visnu restored his mother with a *mantra*. The brother said, "We don't have any women other than our mother." Brahma said, "We have to kill our mother and burn her to ashes, then divide the ash into four portions." So they went to fetch some sandalwood with which to burn her. They brought the wood and burned her on a pyre. They made the ash into four portions, and kept three of them separately. Then Visnu chanted a *mantra,* and turned the three portions into the goddesses Sarasvati, Parvati, and Laksmi. Brahma took Sarasvati as his wife; Shiva

took Parvati; and Visnu took Laksmi. The fourth remaining portion
became their mother again. The mother said, "Son, give me a handful of
rice." She asked Visnu to give her a handful of rice every day.

The theme of maternal desire is so strongly expressed that it hardly requires exegesis to elicit it. The mother desires her sons, and when they
refuse to satisfy her, she becomes a devouring demoness who threatens not
only them but the whole created universe with annihilation. She must be
transformed into something else, to relieve her of her sexuality and to allocate the desire she feels for her sons to their wives, in whom it may properly
express itself. The mother will no longer be threatening but content to receive from her sons the only thing that is properly her due: a daily handful
of rice.

On closer inspection, the story reveals many of the themes noted by
others in their discussion of the sexually threatening mother in Hindu
South Asia (e.g., Kakar 1981; Obeyesekere 1984, 1990; Roland 1988). Adi
Sakti gives birth to three eggs and becomes hungry—so hungry, in fact,
that she seems to be on the verge of devouring her own eggs. She does eat
the first one, demonstrating her power to reengulf the being she created. In
her frenzy she accidentally breaks the second egg. This "accident" implies
a threat, as if to warn that in the exercise of her desire the mother may destroy the very things she creates. She nurtures the third egg until it breaks
apart, the top becoming the sky and the bottom the earth, and out of the
middle the three gods, Brahma, Shiva, and Visnu, are born. The whole universe is created out of an act of frustrated erotic desire, hunger, and lust.
Adi Sakti is still hungry, but now her desire has a focus: sexual union with
her sons.

In trying to seduce her sons she uses the analogy of the egg to justify the impropriety of her desire. But her sons are not persuaded. Brahma
and Shiva both refuse outright, and she turns them into stones by chant-
ing magical spells (*mantras*). Only Visnu remains. Instead of refusing his
mother, he devises a ruse. Let her bathe first, he says, washing away the
smell of menstrual pollution, and then he will copulate with her. The reference to menstruation reinforces the attribution of active sexuality to Adi
Sakti. At the same time, the fact that she is "polluted" signifies that her
sexuality is doubly dangerous, since a menstruating woman can destroy
virility. But Visnu removes all the water from the world, so she cannot fulfill
her side of the bargain. In a fit of anger, she opens up her mouth, "one jaw
to heaven and the other to earth," and prepares to swallow Visnu whole.

Oral engulfment is a frequently encountered theme in the mythology of all Jalari goddesses. Temple images depict goddesses (*ammavallu*, lit. "mothers") as huge and menacing, their mouths open and full of teeth, with red tongues protruding. Jalaris believe that the goddesses are always hungry and need to be fed. Unserviced, they become angry and afflict people with illness or loss of livelihood. This is the primary impetus to divinatory recourse. In the story of Adi Sakti, the link between sexuality and hunger—between erotic desire and oral aggression—is explicit, and stems from the erotic feelings of mother for son. Could the same be true of religious devotion, the offerings of food made to the goddess to be understood as a means of keeping at bay the dangerous sexuality of a mother figure?

It is the tension created by this threat that becomes the source of all creation. In the story, only because the incestuous desire of the mother first exists can it be refashioned to become the desire between husband and wife, on which the world depends for its own reproduction. The same is true for religious devotion. Maternal eroticism is transformed into hunger, through which it can be satisfied in the food given by devotees as offerings. This is also a creative process, since the *puja* ensures that the ritual order governing the working of the universe is continually reproduced in the transactive language of worship. Both kinds of creation depend on the transformation of one form of desire, forbidden and powerful, into a form of desire that is normative and necessary.

My conversation with the storyteller Laksmanayya reveals that such themes are accessible to conscious appraisal, and suggests that Obeyesekere is right when he suggests that the contents of the Indian unconscious are more accessible because they are less repressed (Obeyesekere 1990). In any case, the storyteller came to the point quickly enough when I asked him to tell me what the story was all about:

> Laksmanayya: The sons burned their mother and satisfied her lust. Her lust came out with the wives. They did all this because it is not right that they should have sex with their mother.
> Charles: *So the mother's lust was transferred to the wives. If they have sex with their wives, is it the same thing as having sex with their mother?*
> L: Yes. The wife became the equivalent of the mother. The wives assumed a different form (*rupamu*). Now the sons give a handful of rice to the mother. Sexual desire is satisfied in that form, not in this [the maternal] form. We might also be tempted to have sex with our mothers if it were otherwise. That is why elder sister's daughter is marriageable. My elder sister was born along with me. I am marrying the child born to her.

C: *Now, you are talking about marrying elder sister's daughter. Does this kind of marriage have anything to do with satisfying the mother?*
L: What is happiness to a mother? They did not satisfy their mother's lust in that form but satisfied it in another and made their mother happy. Food and clothes are happiness to a mother. Adi Sakti is like a grandmother to them. They were born out of an egg. When a hen lays eggs and chicks come out, the same chicks will eventually mate with their own mother. The mother hen is like a grandmother to the chicks. There might be sexual relations between grandmother and grandson. Visnu killed the grandmother and made a mother out of her. Grandmother had asked for sex but the mother did not. Instead the mother asked only for food.
C: *What, then, are the wives to the three brothers?*
L: We cannot have sex with a grandmother as it is. They had sex with her only after changing her form. Why should we marry our elder sister's daughter? She is of our own blood. Some people in Kerala marry their brother's daughters. What's the reason? The brother's daughter is equal to our daughter in Andhra. If that is that way, this is this way. That is why our sister's daughter had our blood. She has our sister's blood, our blood, our mother's blood. But how can we marry her? We call it *menirikam*. We take her as our brother-in-law's daughter.
C: *If Adi Sakti had known that her sons would refuse, she would not have asked them. But what if they had agreed?*
L: But how can that happen? If it did, then people would have sex with their own mothers. There would be no chance of marrying outside girls. We give birth to children and they marry others. Visnu knew that it was a sin to have sex with someone of the same blood. Adi Sakti did not know. She is stupid.
C: *But she is their mother!*
L: My own mother is there, isn't she, Charles? Suppose I studied up to B.Com. and returned from America. How will I look on my mother?
C: *You mean Visnu is wise and his mother is stupid. OK. They made four portions out of Adi Sakti's ash and out of three of them made their wives. What did they do then with the part they made into their mother?*
L: Now she is not in the form of Adi Sakti. She is in the form of a mother. She has no lust in that form. She burned in the ash. All the lust was transferred to the three wives. The mother now wants only food and clothing. What do we give to our mothers? They cannot remarry! Adi Sakti in the form of mother does not have lust. She needs only food and clothing.

Laksmanayya does not beat around the bush. He says that the story is about the creation of the world from maternal eroticism, transformed into marital desire before it can become incestuous. The transformation is not complete, he also says, since the desire repeats itself in the relationship between brother and sister. This confirms the hypothesis that desires emergent in the relationship between parents and children are converted into the desires between siblings, where it assumes special prominence given the exigencies of patrilineal descent and cross-cousin marriage.

Laksmanayya calls attention to two marriage practices. The Kerala people he refers to are the matrilineal Nayars, who permit marriage between the children of brothers, a marriage that would be considered a form of sibling incest anywhere else in India. This form of marriage should be forbidden, Laksmanayya says, because people of the same "blood" (*raktam*) should not marry. Yet the Jalaris do the same, he says, when they sanction cross-cousin marriage and the marriage of a man to his elder sister's daughter. Laksmanayya does not offer an explanation of the Nayar practice but suggests that the Jalari practice is sustained through displacement of incestuous erotic desire, first for the mother and then, by secondary displacement, for the sister. He implies that there is a link between maternal incest and cross-cousin marriage, such that the desire born in the first is partially satisfied through conversion in the marriage between the children of brothers and sisters. This is not merely something I postulate, to make a point congruent with psychoanalytic theory; it is recognized and articulated by the Jalaris themselves.

Like other Jalari men, Laksmanayya views cross-cousin marriage (MBD) and marriage to the elder sister's daughter (eZD) as problematic, in part because the demands made by near relatives contradict each other but cannot be ignored. The problem goes a lot deeper than that, however. Intermarrying cross-cousins cannot easily dissolve the alliance, since their parents are brother and sister to each other and the relationship between them is considered one of the strongest there is. This is good, the Jalaris say, since it makes society more stable and marriage alliances more permanent. But it is also bad, since it is really the power of the cross-sex sibling bond and not the strength of the marital relationship between husband and wife which holds society together.

The issue of elder sister's daughter (eZD) marriage is especially difficult, for in addition to the problems just mentioned, there is an added side effect, which Jalari men mention only with hesitation: impotence. Wives who are also the daughters of elder sisters remind Jalari men of their elder sisters too directly. "Every time I made love with her," one Jalari man told me, "I saw my sister in her face." When we recall that elder sisters often stand in for mothers, taking care of their younger brothers as if they were their mothers, we can see how this might be the case. The sexual impotence that results makes marriages of this kind extremely difficult to sustain, as Jalari men and women point out. Many end in divorce.

If Trawick is right and cross-cousin marriage receives emotional valence from the transferred desires of brothers and sister, then it works as well as it does because the transference is strong—but not too strong. This is not the case with marriage to an elder sister's daughter. So, just how strong does the transference have to be in order to work? This is one of the questions Jalari mythology itself tries to answer in the story of Adi Sakti. The mother goddess makes a tenuous case for appropriate displacement in her reference to the chicken and the egg. She is not really a mother to her sons, she says, but a grandmother, and so the desire she feels for them is appropriate. The sons reject this argument, but not necessarily because the logic is flawed. What the myth says is that maternal desire *is* allowable after it has been displaced to the women who becomes the sons' wives. The problem with Adi Sakti's argument is that the transference it advocates is not good enough. The myth tells us what the solution must be: marriage to women who can serve appropriately (without incest anxiety) as receptacles for the mother's erotic desires. Presumably, although the myth does not say so, these women are cross-cousins, preferably the mother's brother's daughters.

Adi Sakti is the embodiment of maternal desire, an overwhelming and dangerous force that must be transformed and redirected. Why does Adi Sakti not realize this herself? Laksmanayya answered that Adi Sakti is "stupid." This does not mean that she lacks intelligence (she is clever enough to debate her sons) but that she lacks the capacity to control or regulate her desires. This is one of the functions of *manasu,* which can be translated as "intentional consciousness" or "directed judgment." Jalaris say that women naturally possess less of this than do men. It is up to men to use this capacity to control the dangerous potential of women (see also Wadley 1980).

This potential is the energy referred to as *sakti.* It is the motive force and primal urge behind all being, and women possess it in abundance. The creator mother is Adi Sakti, the "first" or "primal" (*adi*) energy in the universe, but because she lacks the governance of a male *manasu,* she is dangerous. Her sons provide governance by transforming the creative energy of their mother into the controlled reproductive capacity of their wives.

The Jalari story of creation is an account of desire and its transformation from the uncontrolled eroticism of mothers into the normative sexual energy of wives. Marriage accomplishes this transformation, but in a system of cross-cousin marriage, this has important implications that are no less paradoxical. First, the primary target for the displacement of Oedipal desire is the brother-sister relationship. Where cross-cousin marriage is banned and contact between adult cross-siblings infrequent, as in North India, this may leave behind no more than a vague longing, to be ritually commemorated in the yearly ceremony of *raksabandh,* when sisters return home and tie bracelets on their brothers' wrists (Bennett 1983). But in South India, where cross-siblings remain in extremely close contact, the transference of desire to the relationship between brother and sister has a different outcome.

Cross-cousin marriage represents a kind of resolution of the desire of brothers and sisters for each other, not directly, but indirectly, through the marriage of their children. Marriage to the mother's brother's daughter (MBD) or father's sister's daughter (FZD) is efficacious to this end because the transference is sufficiently close, but not too close. Desires are given expression but do not become sources of incest anxiety. This is not the case with elder sister's daughter (eZD) marriage. Here the emotional distance is not as great. Incest anxieties return, to be expressed in male impotence and the higher divorce rate that prevails for this form of marriage.

THE RITUAL SONGS OF UPPADA NARSIGODU

Resolving the Paradoxical Desire of the Son for the Mother
The story of Adi Sakti focuses on the desire of the mother for the son, and on the transformation of maternal desire into the conjugal relationship. What is true for the mother is also true for the son, since filial desire is no less powerful or full of paradox. It must also be transformed, to preserve its dynamic force but remake it into something normative. This new form is the ritual language of goddess worship, in which an intensely erotic relationship between goddess and devotee is developed.

South Indian devotional poetry is well known for its erotic conceptualization of the goddess-devotee relationship, but usually eros is a metaphor for devotion. In the Tamil tradition, for instance, *bhakti*-oriented love lyrics cast the devotee in the role of lovesick woman who pines after her "dark lord," the gods Krishna or Shiva. There is no explicit description of their erotic encounters, nor does sexual enjoyment figure very prominently, if at all. The *bhakti* songs and poems in Telugu, by contrast, display a deep fascination for the erotic, not simply as a metaphor for devotion, but as an experience which in its own right deserves religious celebration. As Ramanujan, Rao, and Shulman remark: "The Tamil devotee worships his deity in a sensually accessible form and through the active exploration of his emotions; he sees, hears, tastes, smells, and perhaps above all, touches the god. But for the Telugu *padam* poets, the relation becomes fully eroticized, in a manner quite devoid of any facile dualistic division between body and metaphysical or psychological substratum" (1994:19). These authors are referring to Telugu poems that are several hundred years old; of the present, they say that the erotic sensibility of the poems "has largely died away in contemporary South India" (1994:36). Nothing could be further from the truth, for if the Telugu tendency in devotional forms has been to revel in the erotic play of deity and devotee, this tendency finds full and living expression in the Jalari songs of the goddess Polamma.

All village goddesses receive ceremonial worship, but only one, Polamma, receives a festival that attracts different caste communities from all over coastal Andhra Pradesh. On the last night, *anupu,* the Jalaris march from their village to the temple in a procession of groups lead by village priests. One of these groups sings devotional songs, to invoke the goddess so that she possesses the priest. The goddess must possess the priest in order for the festival to be a success. The songs are important because of the language they employ, a form of sexual banter in which the goddess is portrayed as a lustful woman and her male devotees as ardent lovers. The words used are extremely graphic. That is the point, say the Jalaris. Without explicit sexual references the goddess will not be roused sufficiently to make her appearance.

For the most part the songs concern the exploits of two characters. One is the heroic Jalari *dasudu,* or shaman, Uppada Narsigodu, whose feats of strength, resistance to outside authority, and sexual prowess are the subjects of many ballads and stories. He is the model Jalari man. The second character is Maddi Papamma, Narsigodu's wife or mistress. She is not a Jalari, but a member of the Reddi caste which lives in a village next to the Jalari community. The Reddis are one of the two agricultural caste groups which live in a village near the Jalaris. Their relationship to the Jalaris is significant for a number of reasons, not least because of their assumption (some Jalaris would say usurpation) of originally Jalari religious functions in the great Polamma festival.

The fact that Maddi Papamma is Reddi is important, because her relationship with the Jalari hero, Uppada Narsigodu, symbolizes the relationship between the Reddis and the Jalaris. The meaning of the symbol varies with context. Sometimes it is taken to mean that the Jalari man is so overwhelmingly virile that no woman, regardless of caste, can resist him. To other Jalaris the relationship proves that the Jalaris and the Reddis are closely related. Lately, however, in the atmosphere of intercaste tension just described, the relationship between Papamma and Narsigodu has taken on a new meaning—one of defiance. The Jalaris assert their resistance to the Reddis by claiming to have seduced one of their women. As we shall see, the identity of this woman—Papamma—is complex, for not only is she a Reddi caste woman, she is also the goddess Polamma.

The Songs

i

You are the most intelligent under the sun, our mother;
You lived in a multi-colored mansion, Royal Polamma.

ii

Full of desire I went to screw in the burial ground;
Although I am alone, I do not have fear and do not want, mother (*amma*).

iii

That cunt is like a pumpkin, so crisp, and like a cucumber;
Against that cunt, legs spread open, comes the cock.

iv

Cinnola Papamma arranged a prayer meeting;
She put her cunt on a leaf and made us lick it.

v

That whore with the unbrushed teeth arranged the prayer meeting;
The elder sister showed us her ass and asked us to screw her.

vi

Such *kambams* have fallen into the fire;
Where is she, that whore, where is she?

These verses are ambiguous, using words with multiple meanings and confusing subject and object. They also stimulated the most interest. This was most apparent in the discussion which followed, in which Tata, the priest who sings the songs, and I talked about the "screwing" in the burial ground and the experience of fear. The verse does not specify the link between the two, so in our discussion, we focused on this question. To set the scene, I shall describe my relationship with Tata and the circumstances in which we had our discussions.

Tata is in his mid-fifties and in failing health, possibly as the result of years of heavy drinking. He still enjoys a drink, and during his visits to my house, and mine to his, we usually enjoyed a couple of beers. No doubt this served as a disinhibitor, on his part as well as my own. Tata is married and has two adult sons, now married and with nuclear families of their own. The extended family lives jointly. Tata used to go fishing but stopped several years ago because of his physical condition. He continues to perform his duties as a ritual priest at the annual celebrations for the goddess Polamma. However, he concedes it is time to pass this function to a younger man. He worries that neither of his sons is interested.

I have known Tata for several years—not as a friend, really, but as an "informant" who could always be relied on to provide good information. Recently, I have gotten to know him much better, and the reason probably has a lot to do with my own changing status. At first, twenty years ago, I was categorized as an unmarried youth. Now I am an "elder" (*pedda vadu*), married and with a son, and entitled to converse with other elder men without fear of embarrassment. Even so, as you will see, our conversation about sexuality was not quick and easy. It took both of us a long time to make sure of each other; to make sure that the revelations we would discuss would not provoke fear or resentment or shock. The Jalaris engage in sexual joking all the time. But in nonjoking contexts, sexually related topics are avoided with an almost puritanical zeal. I found this entirely congruent with my own cultural expectations, having been raised as an Oklahoma Methodist in the middle of the rough-and-ready oil business. Tata and I felt our way slowly at first, but then, it seemed to me, with increasing enjoyment that our new-found intimacy with each other could be mutually rewarding, and fun.

So, to return to the verse: Why does this "screwing" take place in the burial ground, and why does the speaker say that he is not afraid? Tata contradicts himself repeatedly, saying that sex in a burial ground is good because it protects the identity of the lovers, but that in this instance no sexual encounter took place because the man is not afraid. It is the very contradictoriness of his response which provides the clue to a deeper meaning.

> Tata: If we do whatever in that burial ground no one will say anything, because there will be no one there. Whatever we want to do, we can do. No one will say anything. To that he said "no." In other words, whether or not we do anything here, people will suspect that we have. So he rejected her proposal.
> *Charles: Whom did he say that to?*
> T: To *amma* ("goddess" or "mother"). We don't know who *amma* is. She is a woman.
> C: *What does it mean when you say "fear that I am alone"?*
> T: It means that I am alone and you are alone. We do not have any fear. That is why I don't want to do it.
> C: *Is he saying that he isn't interested in having sex with her?*

> T: Fear of being alone means that we do not have anyone. "No one observed us. If we indulge in sex or not, they will think that we did. We don't want that," he says. That is how he is sending her away.

Tata seems to indicate in his manner and by repeating the verse that he recognizes the peculiar nature of what he has said up to this point. What would be the point of going to the burial ground in the first place if the purpose was not to make love? What is the source of the fear and why is it important for the man, whoever he is, to demonstrate that he is fearless? We returned to this point.

> C: *Sending her away means that someone came there, to the burial ground?*
> T: Only the one woman came. "I don't want to do it, *amma*," he said to her.
> C: *(repeats question)*
> T: *Vallakadu* means burial ground. Fear of being alone means there is no one. "If I do anything, no one can object. I don't want to. Go away," Narsigodu said to her.
> C: *That must mean she came to the burial ground in the first place?*
> T: Yes, he called her. "I screwed all through the burial ground," he said, "no one can do anything to me now." Like that he saw her and sang this verse. "I called you into the burial ground. When you came, I thought someone might observe. But there is no one, *amma*, my salutations to you, now go," Narsigodu said.
> C: *That means he called her there for someone to observe?*
> T: No! He called her there to have sex. There was no one else there. She appeared like a mother. That is why he is sending her away.
> C: *Narsigodu called her to the burial ground to screw her. Did she appear to him as mother when there was no one around?*
> T: She appeared like a mother (*amma*) who gives you birth.
> C: *How? Why did she appear like that?*
> T: Why does a man ever call a woman? To screw (*dengu*) her.

Tata repeats that the man called the woman to the burial ground for sex, but felt no fear, and then sent the woman away. When asked to consider the reason for the man's rejection, Tata asserts that it is because the woman was like a mother. He cannot make love to a mother, so he sends her back to the village. Is it not significant, however, that he called her there in the first place?

> C: *Suppose I ask a woman to come to burial ground for sex and she comes. Does it make sense for me to say, "Mother, please go away"?*
> T: You tell me.
> C: *I don't know.*

T: He said that there is no one around, I am alone . . .
C: *Yes, it will be more convenient if he is alone.*
T: Yes. He asked her to go. I do not want that, *amma.*
C: *Why did he ask her to go?*
T: He said that he did not want it. You tell me the meaning. "I don't have any connection with this," he said. "There is no one around; I have no fear; so please go."
C: *I don't understand.*
T: The meaning is that he doesn't have any fear of being alone. He is alone but he is not afraid. "You go, *amma,* I had sex with you," he said.
C: *You mean he finished screwing her?*
T: Yes. He did it. He said earlier that he screwed her. So he did it and now he is telling her to go, saying that he has no fear of being alone.

Tata now claims that Uppada Narsigodu did make love to the woman. His fearlessness is significant in light of this act, but what could he have been afraid of? Just before, Tata said that the man was reluctant and wanted to send the woman away because she reminded him of a mother. His fear or lack of it could be related to the sexual act and what it signifies, either joyous union or incest. Which is it? There is no way to answer. In fact, the power of the verse may actually depend on it *not* being answered, since it is the tension between the two meanings that makes the verse meaningful in the context of the goddess festival.

C: *Suppose we call a woman and screw her in the burial ground. We do not have any fear because we are men. But she may be afraid to go back alone. So we accompany her. But here, he is telling her to go on alone.*
T: He is saying, "I am alone but I am not afraid. You go, *amma.*"
C: *Even if he wants to stay in the burial ground, he can still accompany her to her place.*
T: He did not tell it like that.
C: *Why did he remain in the burial ground?*
T: He did not say that he would stay there. He said that he is alone and told her to go. He will leave after her. What will he do there? If both go back together, people may suspect that they are involved in something. That is why he asked her to go.
C: *Who is the woman?*
T: Some woman . . .
C: *Is she Papamma?*
T: She is Papamma. Either Cinnola Papamma or Maddi Papamma. He had sex with Cinnola Papamma, Maddi Papamma, Polamma. He sings to these women.
C: *Polamma? He had sex with the goddess Polamma, too?*

> T: (Tata slaps his cheeks, usually a sign of embarrassment.) He sings to
> the goddess (*ammavaru*). He sings, and abuses her as a whore. He refers
> to *ammavaru*, saying "Whore, where is that whore daughter?" It means
> that Narsigodu is asking her to show her truth (*nizam*).

The heroic Uppada Narsigodu, whose notorious disregard of propriety
other songs celebrate, conceals his love tryst and makes sure that his
coming and going from the burial ground remain undetected. He is "un-
afraid," but this begins to look like whistling in the dark when we consider
reasons for his anxiety.

There are other reasons for his fear, connected with the woman's identity, which Tata now reveals. "She is Cinnola Papamma, Maddi Papamma,
Polamma," he says. The first two are Reddi caste women who figure in all
the Uppada Narsigodu songs. There is no difference between them, and
their names are used interchangeably. Fear could result from the awareness that in making love to this woman he has violated caste boundaries.
But I doubt it. The third name, Polamma, refers to the goddess herself in
whose honor the festival is being celebrated. Tata mentions it in passing,
but when I call his attention to the reference, he is embarrassed. He even
slaps his cheeks in the way Telugu people do when they have said or done
something shameful. Very possibly it just slipped out, a significant event
because it suggests awareness of the theme which becomes more and more
prominent with each verse. Papamma and the goddess are the same, and
what is done to one is also done to the other.

The third verse, "That cunt is like a pumpkin, so crisp, and like a cucumber; against that cunt, legs spread open, comes the cock," continues the
theme with the food-based sexual metaphors—a favorite of Jalari poetics.
The man is Uppada Narsigodu and the woman is Papamma. From the way
Papamma is described we learn more about the characteristics which make
her exciting. The fact that her "cunt" (*puku*) is like a pumpkin or a cucumber signifies that she is young. She is moist, "like a cucumber," having just
attained puberty, and therefore not a mature woman whose organs are old
and worn out ("like a piece of okra," Tata said). The shape of the pumpkin is important. When it is cut, Jalari men say, the pattern of its internal
divisions resembles the female genitals. The pumpkin is also important in
the festival. From its flowers two garlands are prepared, one for the priest
who plays the role of Uppada Narsigodu and one for Polamma. The priest
wears his in the procession as he sings the songs, and when he reaches the
house of the Reddi priest (the one who administers the Polamma temple)
he puts the second garland around the image of the goddess, which will be
returned to the temple at the end of the festival.

In their benign aspect village goddesses are thought of as young girls on the verge of maturity. Kakar (1981) speculates that Hindu men fear adult female sexuality because of its threat to their masculinity and therefore prefer young women, if not as sexual partners, then as objects of fantasy. Behind this presence stands the looming image of the mother. Her desire overwhelms the son and he responds either by denying his own sexuality (thus the various myths about self-castration) or by retreating from mature women in preference for younger ones whose eroticism appears less threatening. The goddess Polamma preserves her sexuality and partially rids it of its threat, since she is simultaneously a mother (*amma*) and a maiden, ripe for sexual experience. Of course, this is not expressed directly. The sexual part is split off and allocated to Maddi Papamma, who enjoys the fulfillment of erotic desire with Uppada Narsigodu, a man more powerful than ordinary men and therefore "not afraid." The song itself accomplishes this, reconciling opposed images of the goddess and permitting fulfillment of desires which otherwise should oppose each other: filial devotion and erotic desire.

Such meanings are near the surface and not difficult to elicit. After Tata identifies the woman in the verses as both Papamma, the Reddi woman, and the goddess Polamma, I ask him directly: "Polamma? He had sex with Polamma?" This is what I thought we had been leading up to, first in the denial and the subsequent admission that there was a tryst in the burial ground, and now in the conflation of Papamma and Polamma. The gesture Tata makes in response—slapping the cheeks—is one Telugu people use to indicate embarrassment in the face of a shameful admission. It takes the place of the words one does not wish to utter.

The fourth verse, "Cinnola Papamma arranged a prayer meeting; she put her cunt on a leaf and made us lick it," refers to Cinnola Papamma, another Reddi stand-in for the goddess Polamma. Papamma invites the singer of the song and his chorus to her house, ostensibly to conduct a prayer meeting in honor of the goddess. In fact the meeting is an opportunity for sexual joking, because instead of serving them the food appropriate at such a meeting, she serves herself as a sexual object. The rapid shift between contexts of devotion and desire, food and sex, is a consistent feature of these verses, as if to achieve one it is necessary to fulfill the other.

The fifth verse, "That whore with the unbrushed teeth arranged the prayer meeting; the elder sister showed us her ass and asked us to screw her," repeats the reference both to the prayer meeting and to the sexual encounter it represents. Why does the singer describe Papamma's teeth as unbrushed? Tata said that the event takes place early in the morning, after a full night of festival activity. Neither Papamma nor the members of the chorus have had a chance to bathe and brush their teeth. They are still in a state of uncleanness which the Jalaris compare to being "animal-like" (*jantavalulaga*). This makes them more apt to behave like animals, he said, and thus ignore the strictures imposed on human behavior.

But there is another reason. When Papamma invited the men to come for prayer and eat, they accepted her invitation, assuming (so Tata claimed) that it was a legitimate one. Then they discovered that she really wanted them sexually. They oblige her, Tata says, but resent the deception. That is one of the reasons why they call her a whore. The other reason is that "anger" (*kopam*) is a sexual emotion, according to the Jalaris, and it must be triggered before any sexual enjoyment can take place. Papamma makes the men angry by deceiving them, promising them one thing and giving them another, while the men reciprocate by calling her a whore. The anger they feel for each other is not contrary to the experience of sexual desire, but essential to it.

The "elder sister" of the second line could not be identified, since Papamma has no elder sister. Tata could not offer a conjecture. But given the economy of expression in these songs, it is unlikely that the reference is there for no reason. The referent is probably the goddess Polamma herself, who is considered the "elder sister" of all the goddesses of the region. She is often referred to as "elder sister," with no other qualification. We already know that Tata conflates Papamma and Polamma, so the fact that he may be doing so here is not surprising. Once again there is a rapid shift between religious devotion and erotic desire. But here, unlike in the previous verse, "anger" is present as both a stimulant to desire and a marker of disappointment. The men are promised food but given sex, and although anger is to sexual desire what sexual desire is to religious devotion, the fact that it all begins in disappointment over food should not escape us.[1]

The songs' power to invoke strong but conflicting emotions results from ambivalence, stemming from desire for the mother goddess and fear that the goddess's own desire will engulf the devotee. "Anger" represents the desire as well as the fear, because both have their origin in the same experience: the mother-son relationship.

Kakar has shown that the Indian son seeks maternal affection but feels threatened when it becomes a vehicle for maternal desire. But how exactly

1. Food can be a token for parental affection, as Spiro demonstrated long ago in his study of the Ifaluk (Spiro 1950, 1952, 1953). Where parental affection is also erotically charged, food can also represent the erotic relationship between child and parent, so that in this myth, the quick transitions between eating the food provided by, and having sex with, a woman who stands in for a maternal goddess become especially significant.

does maternal affection communicate itself, especially early in life? Certainly not directly. It is mainly through oral gratification, first in milk and then in food, which the mother gives (Mahler et al. 1975). The song reflects this, since the men have come to the mother for food, but it also reflects their disappointment when instead of food they are offered sexual access. In real life there is no solution to the dilemma, but in the mythic song cycle there is: The mother becomes "Papamma," a woman whose distance from the men is further emphasized by making her into a member of different caste. In that form, both can enjoy each other, free of the ambivalence which otherwise accompanies the relationship, but not so far removed from it that it ceases to be stimulating.

The last verse, "Such *kambams* have fallen into the fire; Where is she, that whore, where is she?" concludes the song cycle by insulting the goddess and insisting that she reveal herself by possessing the priest. *Kambam* is the group itself, the priests and chorus, and when they finish singing they are exhausted but exhilarated. They have expended all the energy that it is in their power to give. It is like they have fallen into a fire, Tata said, and this is probably significant. Being burned in a fire is closely linked with sexual satisfaction, as we saw in the Adi Sakti story. Now it is time for the goddess to finish the process and burn them up completely in the act of possession.

I asked Tata about the possession experience, and since we had been discussing the relationship between religion and sex, I was specific: "Do you experience an orgasm when the goddess possesses you at this moment?"[2] He caught hold of my arm, as if to tell me that I had grasped an important point, and rapidly nodded his head in agreement. Then I asked him: "Is this tantamount to saying that you have had sex with the goddess?" There were several Jalaris present when I asked this question, and they encouraged Tata to be blunt.

> Charles: *If he has sex with the goddess, is that the same as worshiping her?*
> Tata: Screwing her is the same as worshiping her. Everything in these songs refers to the goddess only.

2. Literally, what I said was this: "When you start the *kambams,* you start very slowly and gradually increase the speed. Then, as soon as the goddess comes, you do it swiftly and then fall down. Do you know what it reminded me of? It was like sex: starting slowly at first and then speeding up, and then becoming tired." (miru kabalu pettinappudu nemmidiga modalupetti koncem spidu petti ammoru ragane dham dham cesi padipoyaru. naku etla ani pencindo telusa? baga baga dengi alisi poyi padipoyinotlu vundi.) Tata's response: "It is just like that. When we sing, we get angry, and as we get angry, we sweat, and as we sweat, and we fall down, just like in an 'engagement.'" (alaga vundi. kopam vaste baga cemata vaste, appudu padipotanu . . . engagementlo alaga vundi.) Tata uses the English word "engagement" as a euphemism similar to "intercourse" to refer to the sex act.

C: *You mean to say that if Narsigodu screws Papamma it is the same thing as screwing the goddess, and thus worshiping her? If so, why does she have to entice him?*
Laksmanayya: The goddess is testing his strength.
T: Why will he be interested?
C: *But Narsigodu is always acting as if he doesn't have sex in mind, as if Papamma or the goddess is driving him to it. Why is that?*
T: The goddess is saying, in essence, "if you have the strength come to me." She is teasing him, in order to make him mad. He will not agree immediately.
C: *So what everything is driving to is that Narsigodu must screw Polamma?*
T: He must screw Polamma. He is abusing Polamma. What is Polamma doing? She has the name of Papamma. Even today there is a woman in the Reddi village by that name, who dances with me on the night of the festival, when I play the role of Narsigodu.
C: *So are you supposed to have sex with her?*
T: She's too old.
C: *But you used to?*
T: Oh yes!
C: *Is that the same as having sex with the goddess?*
T: Yes, it is. Sex (*dengadam*) and worship (*pujincadam*) are the same.

Earlier in our conversation Tata admitted the sexuality of Polamma, but only reluctantly and indirectly. We have now arrived at the point where he freely acknowledges it, and even says that it is essential to the practice of worship. Why this change? Tata has learned to guard his words. He knows that in the current effort to sanitize the worship of local goddesses many old traditions, like animal sacrifice and erotic songs, are no longer tolerated. Earlier he suppressed the sexual content and only allowed it back in when he realized that I would not censure him.

Fear of censure was only part of the reason, however. The verses reflect ambivalence in the relationship between devotee and goddess, and since we now know that sexuality is central to this relationship, it is fair to conclude that the ambivalence is sexual in nature and derivative of the mixed emotions son and mother feel for each other. The devotee is like a son and desires the mother, but fears that she may engulf him. The conflict between wanting and fearing is the dynamic tension on which the Uppada Narsigodu songs build.

Resolution of this tension occurs in two ways. First, the mother goddess allocates her erotic desire to Papamma, her stand-in, thus safely distancing herself. Then the devotee becomes Narsigodu, a powerful and heroic man who can meet and match Papamma. An ordinary devotee and the goddess cannot achieve union directly, but only indirectly, through their human counterparts, Papamma and Narsigodu. This is not the final solution, however. The ultimate goal is fusion, accomplished at the very end when Tata in his role of Narsigodu undergoes spirit possession, has an orgasm, and falls unconscious, immersed in the female persona that envelops him.

THE STORY OF THE GODDESSES' VOYAGE

Resolving the Paradoxical Desire of Fathers and Daughters

The father-daughter relationship is notably absent in studies which relate family structures and goddess mythologies in South Asia (e.g., Carstairs 1967; Kakar 1981; Kurtz 1992; Nuckolls 1991a, b, c; Obeyesekere 1981, 1990; Roland 1988; Trawick 1990). Is that because the relationship is unimportant compared to relationships centered on the son, to which so much attention has been given? It could be argued that because daughters leave the household in order to marry, their continuing role in patrilineal solidarity and succession is minimal after that point. Myths in which daughters figure prominently are few, according to this view, because women as daughters do not figure prominently in patrilineal ideology. On the other hand, in South India, the dynamics of cross-cousin marriage foreground the exchange of daughters between allied clans, and the role of daughters in maintaining patrilineal succession and solidarity is vitally important and recognized as such. In this setting, isn't there a reason we might expect a commensurately greater role for daughters in South Indian mythologies?

There are many reasons why this question should interest us. First, myths about village goddesses who begin as wives or sisters, or unmarried maidens, have been the focus of almost all the studies which have been done to date, as we have already seen (Kakar 1981; Obeyesekere 1984; Shulman 1980). The impression exists that such myths are representative, constituting the great bulk of religious narratives about goddesses. This impression may be due for a correction, since in the myth to be considered here (and in many like it) the role of goddesses as daughters is clearly foregrounded.

Second, various interpretations have been offered to explain the charac teristics of Hindu village goddesses, from the fact that they are typically dualistic (with benign and malign aspects) to the fact that they are orally voracious and somewhat capricious. For the most part, as we have seen, these interpretations explain such characteristics with reference to the dynamics of the mother-son relationship in Hindu South Asia (Kakar 1981,

Fathers and their daughters

1982, 1989; Obeyesekere 1984, 1990; Roland 1988). The goddess is a maternal imago, refracted through the culturally shaped vicissitudes of the Oedipus complex and projected onto the landscape of religion. This view privileges male developmental experience and relegates the relationships of the daughter to a secondary status at best.

There is a third reason, too, which is straightforwardly ethnographic. Studies of goddess mythology in South India are not abundant. For the most part, they are secondary and derivative, and depart very little from the earliest work of Elmore (1925), Thurston (1909), and Whitehead (1921). Of course there are exceptions (Beck 1981; Erndl 1993; Hiltebeitel 1989; Obeyesekere 1984; Richman 1995; Shulman 1976, 1980; Trawick 1982). But it is still true overall, and especially so of Andhra Pradesh and the Telugu-speaking area. We need more material.

In Jalari society, the daughter possesses something the father wishes to retain: *sakti,* a sexualized power which a daughter possesses and uses to benefit her father until she is married.[3] In the myth of Shiva and his daughters, to be considered in more detail below, the father is weakened by the departure of his daughters, who leave to visit their mother's brother. Shiva loses a battle and almost dies. His two wives, Parvati and Ganga, do nothing to help him. Only his unmarried daughters can save him from certain death at the hands of the *raksasas* (demons), because only they possess the right kind of power (*sakti*). It is a power Shiva knows he must eventually give up when his daughters leave to get married. As we shall see, this is the source of a deep ambivalence, as Shiva alternately advances and impedes the progress of his daughters' departure for the home of their mother's brother and potentially marriageable cross-cousins. The daughters are no less ambivalent. They alternately afflict their father with terrible diseases and cure him. Then they force Shiva to accept their leaving, but once they have left, they think of him and pray to him constantly for assistance.

In twenty years of fieldwork among the Jalaris, I have yet to record a complete version of the "voyage myth," perhaps because, like the *Mahabharata,* it has many plots that can be told in almost any order. The core of the story, however, is the voyage itself, which begins when Shiva's daughters tell him that they want to visit their mother's brother, Nagaraju, on the island kingdom of Nagarajupatnam. In conventional Jalari discourse, going to the mother's brother is synonymous with marriage, since the daughter who marries her patrilateral cross-cousin takes up residence in the house of the husband's father, i.e., her mother's brother. There are two ways this could be understood. Patrilateral cross-cousin marriage (from the point of view of the male ego) is not the most common form of cross-cousin marriage in Jalari society, coming a close second (by my informal reckoning) to the matrilateral form. Why does the myth prefer it? There is no obvious answer, and "officially," according to the storyteller, it made no difference. But it is interesting that the storyteller sometimes slipped back and forth between male and female pronouns when referring to the seven sisters, as if to suggest that there was a certain ambiguity in their role as daughters. After all, as the myth reveals, Shiva's daughters frequently take on the behavior more appropriate to sons. And if they were sons, then, of course, marriage to the mother's brother's daughters would be preferred. To accentuate the ambiguity in their role as daughters, and increase the tension

---

3. Several of the contributions to *The Power of Tamil Women* (ed. Susan Wadley) have noted the same phenomenon among the Tamil speakers just to the south of Andhra Pradesh and the Jalari areas.

which the myth seeks to resolve, the story presents the journey as if it were being undertaken by sons, not daughters—hence the seeming reversal of the marriage preference.

A second possibility is that the story is just what it purports to be: a journey undertaken by daughters who seek marriage with their mother's younger brother. This is the kind of marriage usually (from the male's point of view) referred to as "elder sister's daughter" (eZD) marriage, and it is found throughout South India and among the Jalaris, although it is not common. Indeed, Jalari men are circumspect when discussing it. Marriage to one's elder sister's daughter is a by-word for marital conflict. The reason: male sexual impotence. Jalari men say that the daughter of a sister is too much like the sister herself—"we can see our sister in her face"— and in these circumstances normal sexual desire is impossible. Such marriages are almost always childless and end in divorce. Why should the myth invoke this theme, if it does? Again, the explanation could be in the tension it arouses, not only for the daughters but for Shiva himself. It also foregrounds the theme of forbidden desire, which elsewhere in the myth focuses on the father-daughter relationship. How can such desires be resolved? This is the question the myth seeks repeatedly to answer, and therefore we should not be surprised to see the eZD marriage option invoked, even implicitly, since it only serves to deepen the tension of desire in kinship.

In the myth, Shiva tries to prevent the voyage, first by persuasion and then with supernatural intervention, but in the end he relents. The sisters reach Nagarajupatnam and meet their mother's brother. They play dice with him and agree that if they lose they will remain as his slaves but if they win he must give his wealth and kingdom to them. Eventually, after several close calls, they win. But the sisters do not take their winnings. Instead they board the ship and resume the voyage, traveling down the eastern coast of India and stopping at fishing villages along the way to inflict the inhabitants with epidemic diseases. That is how they became the village goddesses worshiped in coastal Andhra today.

The story of the goddesses' voyage is made up of elements drawn from several popular and well-known sources, including the story of Shiva's war against the demons (asuras) in the Mahabharata and the story of goddesses in the Devi Mahatmya, part of the Markandeya Purana. In the first, Shiva is called upon to destroy the demons in their triple city, because the demons had become overbearing and threatened the world. The gods appealed to Shiva, and he agreed to slay the demons by shooting a great arrow through their triple city (Kramrisch 1988). As we shall see, the story of the demon war begins the story of the goddesses' voyage, but there are important differences between the Jalari and puranic versions.

First, in the Jalari version, Shiva cannot defeat the demons by himself. He must call upon his daughters, the seven sisters, for help. Second, the goddesses themselves cannot defeat the demons because of their capacity for unlimited reproduction: Each drop of their blood that is spilled creates a thousand more demons. The seven sisters must invoke the assistance of another goddess, whose ability to drink up the drops before they fall to the ground prevents the demonic proliferation. This episode, of course, comes directly out of the *Devi Mahatmya,* from the part concerning the creation of the goddess Kali (Coburn 1991). But here, too, there is an important difference. The seven sisters do not create the blood-drinking goddesses, as Devi creates Kali. Instead, they create a brother, Potanna, whom they agree to give in marriage to the goddess Adi Sakti, in return for her help in destroying the demons. In the Jalari version, the defeat of the demons is contingent on the relationship between sisters, first and foremost, and between sisters-in-law.[4]

The Jalari myth presented here is one of the shorter renditions, told by a young and aspiring Jalari storyteller who shortened it in order to fit it into the new festival calendar, which only allows one day for recitation. Normally it would take a week. Compression is not unusual but is characteristic of most ritual functions, from goddess festivals to marriage ceremonies. The Jalaris do not have the time and cannot afford the money necessary for the longer enactments, so they have devised shortened versions of almost everything. It is a mixed blessing, for while we lament the passing of older forms, the newer compressed versions have one virtue: They distill narrative elements into a concentrated amalgam that enhances the most salient features. This is of particular importance here, since what stands out most clearly is the relationship between a father and his daughters.

Translation

Once upon a time, Shiva was defeated in the Rastulapatnam ("demon-city") battle and was wandering from place to place. He was weak, as if crushed beneath a black stone. He said, "I have daughters, but I could conquer many cities if I had sons." Shiva was very sad and cried.

The seven sisters were collecting flowers. They sensed Shiva's tears on

---

4. The goddess with whom the seven sisters make this arrangement is Adi Sakti, creator of the universe, whose orally voracious temperament threatens creation almost as soon as it exists.

their feet. They wondered why their legs were becoming wet. Then, with her divine vision, Nukalamma said that their father had been defeated in battle: "Sisters, we seven shall avenge the defeat of our father. Let's go to battle!" Sridevi Nukamma (Nukalamma) said. They purified themselves by bathing, combed their hair, put on eye makeup, plaited their hair, and went to their father. The seven sisters started for Rastulapatnam.

At last they reached Rastulapatnam and saw their father. Angrily, they asked him why he had come here without telling them. If he had, they could have joined him in the war. "You are an old man," they said, "and should not fight." Then they made him ill with little fevers, big fevers, headache, eye ache, body pains. These were all inflicted by Nukalamma. Then she inflicted him with smallpox. Shiva was rolling on the ground in pain. He was in agony and cried. Nukalamma saw that her father was crying and said, "We are able to see the sun through the holes in your body. Even the moon is visible." Then Nukalamma made everything peaceful and went to fight.

All seven sisters went to fight *rastulu* (demons). They fought and blood dripped on the ground, and from the blood, millions of demons were born. The seven sisters were sweating, and feeling very bad. They tried to think of ways to defeat the *rastulu.*

Nukalamma took *vibhuti* (sacred ash) from her nail and tried to find ways to kill them. She called Peddammavaru and said to her: "You are the eldest one. When *rastulu* die, and blood falls on the earth, millions of demons are born. There is a way to kill all the demons. Take out some *vibhuti* from your nail, chant a "bronze" *mantra,* and sprinkle *vibhuti* on the ground. You will give birth to your brother Potanna (Potu Raju)." Then she did it.

Potanna immediately became twelve years old (the age of maturity). They called him younger brother (*tammudu*). Nukalamma said to him, "We cannot fight with the *rastulu.* If you bring Adi Sakti, these *rastulu* will go." But he didn't know where Adi Sakti lives. "You will find her in the seven hills, in between them. But don't go near her. She will eat you," Nukalamma said. He asked her what to do. Nukalamma said, "You call her 'Adi Sakti' from a distance, so she thinks about who is calling her. Again you call her 'Adi Sakti.' Then she comes out. Immediately run off when she sees you. Don't stand there. You will die if you stand there." [5]

He listened to all this. She took out *vibhuti* from her nail and sprinkled cowdung water with a bronze vessel. She gave it to her younger brother, Potanna. He flew off. After some time, he crossed all the hills and called

5. Adi Sakti, literally "first" (*adi*) "power" (*sakti*), the mother of the universe.

out for Adi Sakti. There was no response. Again he called. "Who is it?" asked Adi Sakti. "It is I." "Oh, you human! I've been starving here for a long time. I want to eat you," she said, coming out. Potanna ran. It was Adi Sakti, *mayadari maradalu* (deceitful younger brother's wife).[6] The younger brother's wife is *maradalu,* no? Potanna's wife is sister-in-law to Nuka-lamma.

Adi Sakti opened her mouth, one jaw to the earth and the other to the sky. She was ready to swallow Potanna. Nukalamma carried him on her back to safety. Then she took *vibhuti* from her nail and sprinkled cowdung water with a bronze vessel. Then she (Adi Sakti) became a twelve-year-old girl, a sister-in-law, and bowed to Nukalamma. Nukalamma told her that they needed her help to defeat the *rastulu.* She offered her something in re-turn: marriage to Potanna. Adi Sakti agreed. Nukalamma told her to put one jaw to heaven, the other to earth. "When I kill the demons, the blood should not hit the ground. You should drink it all. Then all the *rastulu* will die. Father wins the battle." Adi Sakti agreed. Then this sister-in-law, Adi Sakti, took *vibhuti* from her nail and manifested herself as Adi Sakti. She opened her mouth and went with Nukalamma to the battle.

The seven sisters all went to fight, and they killed most of the demons. "If I ignore them, they will again give birth to demons," Adi Sakti said to herself. So the sister-in-law caught them and held them by their hair, and brought them. She tore open their bellies. She tore their spines, and brought out the *veda*s (sacred books) and the *yuga*s (cosmic ages).[7] She re-viewed the demons' stars of birth and said, "This one stole the *veda*s from his father and swallowed them." She tore open his belly and rescued the *veda*s. Then the sister-in-law went to Shiva.

His illness vanished. The sisters said, "Father, you humiliated us at Ras-tulapatnam. When you had daughters, you claimed that you would prefer sons. You said that if you had sons, you would conquer the cities. You are not an idiot. You are smart and clever. Why did you insult us? We felt bad." Then Shiva admitted his mistake and offered a boon. "Oh, father, how can I ask for a boon, because we were in trouble, let us go to our native place." So they went home. All seven sisters settled in their room. Shiva went to Parvati and slept there.

Nukalamma remembered her father's promise of a boon. She took a

6. *Maya* ("illusion," "deceit"), an epithet often applied to goddesses in general, to refer to their power of illusion (see Coburn 1991:128), and also, among the Jalaris, to the god-dess's tendency to trick and deceive her human devotees.
7. This part of the text refers to the well-known story of the demons who steal (and some-times eat) the *veda*s.

bath and put on new clothes. All the other sisters were in the house. Nuka-lamma went alone to Shiva. He saw her coming from the seven-storied building. "My daughter is coming," he said. He called to Parvati and told her that the younger daughter is coming. Parvati saw her. How beautiful she was! What an adornment! The sun might have a scar, but not this daughter! She felt proud of her daughter, proud of giving her birth.

Shiva came down and asked why she came. Nukalamma told him that she came for a reason. She came inside and sat down on a chair. "Oh, father, when you went to Rastulapatnam for battle, and you were defeated, and we won. We married Potanna to our sister-in-law. You promised us a boon. So give it to us."

He asked her why she didn't bring the other sisters. She said they were in their place and that they told her to ask on their behalf. So he gave her permission to speak. "I have money and grain, and I have visited several countries. But I haven't been to Nagarajupatnam," said Nukalamma. "So what do you want?" asked Shiva. "Nothing. If you give us a ship, we will go to Nagarajupatnam for a visit." "Please don't ask this boon," he said, "only those who have a mustache and hair on his chest can visit there. Girls do not have a cord on their waist (*molatadu*).[8] They cannot go."

Why? Because it is *ganga*, the sea. Shiva told them that, in the first place, they do not know the sea, and second, they are women. But Nukalamma insisted, and told him to prepare the ship. "Please don't go," he said, "if you want money or buildings or anything else, like sheep and goats, I will give. But don't ask about Nagarajupatnam." "But father, you are not sticking to your promise. You promised to give us whatever we want. You must do it." Shiva called on Parvati, saying, "Your youngest daughter wants to go to elder brother's place. How will they go? They are women and they will pollute the sea. There will be spirits in the sea. If these spirits sense pollution, our daughters will die. You tell them not to go," he said.

Parvati told Nukalamma not to go, and to ask for something else. "Mother, we are not bothered about losing anything, or even dying. We were promised long back, and now we are asking. Please give it to us. Why should you bother about our deaths," she argued with her mother. If a king goes back on a promise, that is a sin!

At last Shiva agreed. He asked all the daughters to come. Then Sridevi

---

8. It is not clear why Shiva says this, since girls do normally wear waist-cords (*molatadu*). This is not the sacred thread (*janjamu*) worn by members of twice-born castes but a rope or cord placed around the waist at the time of birth and removed only at death, signifying caste membership.

Cinnari (Nukalamma) got angry. Her eyes were mad. Her blue eyes filled with anger, and that anger is unmeasurable. She tightened her eyeball and reddened her eye. "Father, there is no need to lie. I asked all the seven sisters and came here."

She got mad and went to her sisters. She said to them that her asking was, of course, the same thing as all of them asking, but the father is abusing her. "He asked me to bring all the sisters. Do you want me to ask or else should I ask him?" "Oh, younger sister, you ask him and we will be with you." So she went to him again. "See, father Shiva, all seven sisters are coming. You promised that you would give." "Oh, daughter, I will give. I will make the ship, but I need three months."

Then Shiva sold gold and silver, bronze and copper, to the blacksmith, because he needed money. He got seven bags of money. Mailapilli Maimudu sells wood. Shiva went to him. "If I want a ship to give to my daughters, I need wood from you." Mailapilli asked him which kind of wood he wanted—timber, gourd, or whatever. He agreed to give those. He was a rich man. He took the money, went into the forest, and felled the trees belonging to seven species. He sent that wood in a cart to Shiva's place.

So, who will build the ship? He needed an overseer. He called the seven daughters and said, "So, the wood came, and all we need is a man to build the ship." Nukalamma said that he should call younger brother Potanna to build it. Potanna said he didn't know how. So she called Polappa (Polamma). The elder sister didn't know how. Everyone said the same thing. Finally Mailapilli was called. Nukalamma called a *dasudu*.[9] Peddammavaru (Polamma) put a dot on Nukalamma's forehead. She did that for everyone. They did *puja*. Then Nukalamma perceived with her divine vision how to build a ship. She built it, with Potanna and Mailapilli.

After the ship is built, it needs to kept in the sea. It was built in the dock. So they slipped it into the water. There were no cranes to lift the boat and put it in the water. The ship did not move. Peddammavaru (Polamma) was angry because she had not been offered a goat in sacrifice. Then Nukalamma went to her and said, "If you are angry, how can we go to Nagarajupatnam? So don't be mad, I will give you a goat and a rooster, and offer blood as well." Then she performed the sacrifice and the ship moved into the sea.[10]

---

9. *Dasudu*s are shamans or curers, and also function as priests at major goddess festivals.
10. It is always necessary to pay homage to the goddess Polamma before setting out to sea. This is as true for the goddesses themselves as it is for human beings, according to the Jalaris.

All the necessary things were in the boat, including food, bread, onions, chili, dal, oil. But three items were not there. Nukalamma knew that they could not leave without those items, so she went to her *pinni talli* ("mother's younger sister"), Ganga, and consulted her. It was Ganga, in fact, who told Nukalamma that the three items were missing. Ganga told them to ask their father.

So Nukalamma went to her father and asked. He said he didn't know, so she went back to Ganga. "My father asked me what were those items, and we don't know." Ganga told her: *avalu* (mustard seeds), *mentulu* (fenugreek seeds), and *mariyalu* (black pepper). If, she said, you have those three items with you, you will be able to make the voyage. "How clever father is! He knew that without those items we would be forced to come back." Then she went to Shiva and demanded those three items. "What items?" he asked. She told him. He wanted to know how she knew about all that. She said, "We will become impure, and bad smell will issue forth. We will be cursed and die. So you must give us those items." She told him that if he didn't provide what they need, then they won't go. If he wants them to live, then he must give them what they need. If he wishes them to die, then he need not give it. He should not show any disparity between a son and a daughter.[11] So he gave it to them. He gave them a packet with jaggery, coriander, and other spices. He told her to throw the packet into the sea when the *sapta devatas* come.[12]

Nukalamma told Peddammavaru to board the ship. "How can I get in," she asked, "I am old and my legs don't work. So I won't go. You go instead." "If you don't go, I won't go," said Nukalamma. So Nukalamma helped Polamma board the ship. Then all the seven sisters got on board, and prayed to Narada and the *ghandarvas*.

The ship started sailing. Shiva thought, "If women go on the sea, and fish, what will men do in the ages to come." He caused a wind to come up. The ship started rocking. Nukalamma came up and saw this. Gales and rain. Younger brother Potanna is at the rudder.[13] She asked him to take care. He said, "Older sister, as long as I am here, don't worry." Nukalamma was afraid.

Nukalamma asked Shiva, "Father, you have built this ship for us and

---

11. One of several places in which the myth explicitly emphasizes the theme of equivalence between sons and daughters.
12. Usually, the *sapta devata*s ("seven goddesses") refers to the seven sisters, but here the term applies to the ghosts and demons which threaten to attack the seven sisters if they go upon the sea unprotected by the substances Shiva at first omits, then agrees to supply.
13. Also known as Potu Raju.

loaded it with supplies for one year. Do you want us to die or to come back safely? Where are you, father?" she cried. Those tears fell on her father's head. They are pious women, that is why the tears fall on his head. He saw their situation with his divine vision.[14] Like binoculars. When he saw his youngest daughter drenched in the rain—she was crying and needed help—he felt that he brought them up, after all, and he should not let them die now.

Shiva called the kings of all four directions and asked them, what is this? They said that it was being done according to his instructions. They said: "You told us that women should not go on the sea. As you ordered, we sent a storm. Now you're scolding us." Shiva said, "What can I do, they are my daughters." Nukalamma is crying. Then the four kings agreed to stop the storm. Suddenly the wind and rain stopped.

They hoisted the sails, but there was no wind. The ship was not moving. Nukalamma asked her father, "It has been three days and still there is no wind. How can we reach Nagarajupatnam?" Again Shiva summoned the four kings and asked them to give a little wind. The east wind came up, a cool breeze. The ship started moving, with its sixty-six sails and thirty-three oars. The ship traversed the seven seas.

A Jalari man was sailing alone. Nukalamma went to Peddammavaru (also called Polamma) and told her that they should ask about the way to Nagarajupatnam. "Let's ask this Jalari about the route." "OK, let's go," Peddammavaru said. They went near and anchored, and called to him, "Elder brother, elder brother!" His name was Oligunta Rudrayya. He was afraid as their ship came near. Nukalamma said, "Elder brother, give us some help." He told them that he does not have money or lands or buildings. "But if I can help, I certainly will," he said. Nukalamma said that they didn't need anything like that, only directions to Nagarajupatnam. He replied that many great men, great kings, even Visnu could not go there. Men with mustaches could not go there. "How can you go?" he asked. They told him to show them the way. "We may die, or kill them or marry them. You just show us the way. We will give you whatever you want." He said, "OK, I will show you the way. But you must give me what I want." Nukalamma promised to do so on their return. Then he told them to go east, across the salt seas, the yellow sea, the white sea—a total of fourteen seas, all different colors. After that, the sun will rise. "You go on toward the rising sun. That's the way," and he asked for his reward. They promised to give it to him on the way back. The ship started out.

14. *drsti.*

Oligunta Rudrayya is an expert fisherman. He used to catch fish the size of elephants. When he takes his fish home, his wife throws it away. Such a strong woman. She used to drag a fish weighing a thousand pounds just by its tail.[15]

Nukalamma crossed fourteen oceans. She saw the rising sun, and turned the sails in its direction. After going a long way she reached the city of Nagaraju. It was brighter than the sun. She wanted to see the city. The nearer she approached, the brighter it was. It was bright red, like Nukalamma herself.

Nalamaramma, the daughter of Nagaraju, saw the ship and was surprised. The ship was more beautiful than the moon. She fainted at seeing such a sight. Regaining her senses, she was determined to prevail on her father and see the ship. Whoever goes to Nagaraju must gamble with him with dice. Whoever meets him must play dice with him. Nalamaramma went to her father and told him about the beautiful ship that had come. She must see it at any cost. "Make me its owner." Nagaraju said he would, by playing dice with the owners and winning.

They came to the port and saw the ship anchored. Nukalamma and the others were napping for awhile after eating. Then they got down from the ship and went to see the city. Polamma said that she was too old. She would remain in the ship and guard it. Meanwhile, Nagaraju went to the ship and inquired who was there. The old woman came out.

Polamma was not really old. She was pretending, so as to find out what her younger sister was up to.[16] She came out and said that she was there in the ship. Nagaraju asked why they had come. She replied that they came to play dice with Nagaraju. "Can you play?" asked the king. "That's why we're here," she said. She got down. Nagaraju had twelve dice. Among them were magic dice. He asked for the wager. She wagered money as a bet. They went on playing. He cast the magic dice and won. She took out all the gold, worth ten crores. He sent Nalamaramma home and got all their gold. The dicing started. She lost again, and again challenged him. He asked her what she bet. She said silver. Again she lost and again.

He won everything. Peddammavaru started worrying. Nukalamma sensed it. She called her sisters, saying, "Nagaraju is taking away the ship, and our sister is in danger. She is left only with her saris." Nukalamma then challenged him to play. Nagaraju agreed. She asked for the dice. Naga-

15. Oligunta Rudrayya, one of several Jalari heroes known for their strength and sexual prowess.
16. Polamma's reference to Nalamaramma as "sister" would seem to anticipate the relationship she and her sisters will soon develop with the daughter of Nagaraju.

raju gave her the twelve shells, thinking that she didn't know much. She was left with only small articles and drums to bet. She started playing and won. She continued playing and she won. She thought that if she does lose, it is only at the hands of her mother's brother. Whose mother's brother? Nukalamma's. Nagaraju's younger sister is Parvati Devi. Her daughter is Nukalamma.

Nukalamma continued playing and won back all that had been lost before. The gold, the money, and the ship as well. She again challenged Nagaraju. He agreed and bet all his wealth, and lost, and became like a pauper. Nukalamma got everything and owned the village. She wanted to name the village after herself and Peddammavaru. She declared that the kingdom belongs to the seven sisters. Nagaraju and Nalamaramma were ashamed. Nukalamma told him that he should not have felt so proud. "Self-assertion hampers your duty. Enmity will destroy the family. Greed breeds grief," she told him.

Then she embarked on the return journey, visiting other cities. She stopped her ship at a port. There was a goddess called Poleramma. They got down to see the city. Poleramma, who was young, came to ship in the guise of an old beggar in rags. She came to the ship and asked them to allow her into the ship. She said she could then die, since God had promised her a place in Vaikunta if she boards the ship. They told her to board and wait until they had come back. She said yes.

They went to see the city. The old woman turned into a sixteen-year-old maiden immediately after boarding the ship. "I have never seen such a wonderful ship. I've toured fourteen countries and never seen such a wonderful ship. I shall take it," she thought to herself. The ship began to move. Nukalamma could see this. How would they now go to their father, Shiva? Nukalamma got angry. She had obtained from Visnu the ability to know things through divine vision. Only Nukalamma had that boon. "You are Poleramma? I can reduce you to ashes by casting a glance on you. Go!"

The sisters waited on the land. They were eating on the road like orphans. They lived like that for two weeks. No water, no milk, no clothes to wear. They were furious. They decided to loot the town, so they distributed seven portions of the town between them. People began to die from vomiting and diarrhea. The elders of the town were running to *kaniki*s and *pati*s.[17] One *janam* (soothsayer) was passing through the town.[18] He said

---

17. *Kaniki*s and *pati*s are practitioners of different forms of divination, who are used, for among other things, identifying the goddesses who arrive from time to time, causing epidemic diseases.

18. *Janam*s are sometimes associated with the *golla* (shepherd) caste of Andhra Pradesh.

that he could cure them. The elders sought his help to save the people from dying. He agreed to show the way out, but demanded 500 rupees. They said they would pay it.

Analysis

Locked in conflicting inclinations, Shiva and his daughters struggle against a need for each other but find themselves united at critical moments, their mutual desire too strong to overcome. The myth of the voyage offers no solution to this oscillating movement, only a series of partial integrations. Such integrations become creative acts, however, when they are linked to the origins of goddess worship.

The myth has two parts, the demon war and the voyage to Nagarajupatnam, which can be presented in either order. The storyteller began with the voyage, since he was prompted to the recitation by my question concerning why women should not go to sea. The story of the voyage provides the explanation. Usually, the story is presented in the order of its chronology, beginning with Shiva's war against the demons. I shall begin there as well.

The story of the demon war is famous throughout India (Kinsley 1988), in each village told with a slightly different emphasis. In the Jalari version, the emphasis is on the relationship between Shiva and his daughters. Daughters in Jalari culture are very important, since as the Jalaris quickly point out, without them the system of cross-cousin marriage alliance would break down. Shiva has seven daughters, and when he goes to the city of the demons (*Rastulapatnam*) to destroy it, he fails to ask their help. He suffers a terrible defeat. His tears fall on their feet even though they are miles away, and they are moved by pity to help him, but not before punishing him with diseases so severe that the moon is visible through his ravaged body. The seven sisters kill all the demons and ask their father for a boon. This boon is permission to visit their mother's brother, Nagaraju, on his island kingdom of Nagarajupatnam.

The story has a cautionary tone, as if to warn men against forgetting their daughters, who act as protectors and defenders of the family. This is not unlike the "forgetting" Jalari men refer to when they try to explain why their family goddesses sometimes afflict them with fevers. "We forgot to pay homage to them," they say, "and so the goddesses attacked us, to make us remember them." Forgetting of this kind is simply too routine to be considered merely negligence. It has to have other roots, motivated, perhaps, by ambivalence toward a "mother" who is simultaneously the source of nurturance and the threat of engulfment. Forgetting daughters could be similarly motivated, helping men pretend to themselves that the ideal of patrilineality and male self-sufficiency can be realized. In other words, daughters are desired by their fathers but must be relinquished to other men in marriage in order to sustain the cross-cousin alliance system. One way to avoid the ambivalence this creates is to accept just what the patrilineal ideology of Jalari culture says: Women are merely means to an end since the patriline is made up of men and men are the basis of patrilineal unity. What is "forgotten" is not only the importance of women as daughters but the whole cross-cousin marriage system which women help to sustain.

When Shiva goes to fight the demons, leaving his daughters behind, he acts in congruence with the patrilineal ideology. Jalari men applaud this, because from the standpoint of this ideology men are more important than women. But the feeling that this is not really so lies very near the surface, and when Jalari men are reminded that it was a woman (Adi Sakti) who created the universe and women (the household goddesses) who sustain it, they are quick to concede the point: "Oh yes, you're right, women are much more important and more powerful than men." Then, to prove it, they recall that the earth itself (*dharani*) is female. Could the opening segment of the story seek to reinforce this message?

The oscillation between unity and separation that characterizes the ambivalent relationship between Shiva and his daughters comes up more than once. The daughters receive the boon of travel to the residence of their mother's brother, the reward for helping Shiva win the battle against the demons. Shiva does not want them to go, but relents. He even builds them a boat. When they discover that the boat has not been completely outfitted and lacks several key provisions, they ask again for help. At first he rejects their plea, but again relents. Interestingly, the missing items were spices whose smell the sisters must use to ward off attacks by sea-dwelling ghosts and demons, offended by the sisters' menstruation. This tends to emphasize the association between female sexuality and power, and the need for a man to control and direct it (Wadley 1980). Will this man be Shiva, the father, or other men—perhaps the husbands of the goddesses, should they marry when they arrive at the place of their mother's brother? These two possibilities are in tension with each other. But unlike in everyday life, the myth is free to resolve it not through marriage, and the allocation of female power to husbands, but through the transformation of the sisters themselves.

Shiva's daughters set out on their voyage but find their progress impeded by mighty gales and raging seas. Shiva is responsible, of course, and his daughters know this, so they beseech him to lift the storm or they will die. Again Shiva gives way. Alternately helping and hindering signifies an ambivalent attitude, as if Shiva desired both to prevent his daughters' departure and to facilitate it. When we consider the timing and destination of the voyage, the reason for the alternation becomes apparent. Shiva's daughters are unmarried, and their budding sexuality is repeatedly emphasized in references to menstruation and the danger it poses to their safety. They are on their way to their mother's brother, to see the place where he lives. What will they do when they get there? "We may kill them or we may marry them," says Nukalamma, addressing the Jalari fisherman who gives them directions. In other words, the goddesses are on their way to marry or consider marrying. This makes sense when we recall that visiting the mother's brother signifies betrothal for ordinary Jalari women. Marriage to a mother's brother's son is a preferred form of alliance.

The violent alternative Nukalamma mentions ("we may kill them") reflects the interfamilial rancor that accompanies the failure of a planned cross-cousin marriage. Families sometimes renege on such deals, either because the intended marriage partners do not like each other or because one family has decided to marry its son or daughter into another family (also related as cross-cousins). Disputes between families that either were or might have been allied through marriage constitute one of the foremost reasons for goddess attacks. This is what I earlier referred to as the affinal paradox. Nukalamma sums up the typical Jalari view of the cross-cousin marriage: an inevitable process, and a highly ambivalent one, accompanied by many risks and leading to making allies or enemies.

Indirect references to the daughters' sexuality cast the father's ambivalence in a particular light, suggesting that its source is a problematic attachment. The father wants his daughters but must relinquish them in marriage to cross-cousins. There are other reasons, too. As I said before, women are viewed as repositories of a power (*sakti*) that men can only seek to manage or direct. Shiva himself is sometimes considered the husband of the goddess Sakti, the embodiment of power, and from her he obtains the capacity to act. A family considers itself more powerful the more women it has. Brothers pride themselves on their sisters, since sisters are their primary trading partners in fish as well as the source of their own children's future marriage partners. Women also have power over the goddesses of their natal families, with the ability to control them and direct them at will. This power continues even after the daughters leave to join their husbands, making any married woman within the family she marries into doubly dangerous. Not only does she retain influence over her natal family's goddesses, she also assumes control over her husband's family's goddesses as well.

The fact that the father-daughter relationship is no less ambivalent for the daughter is apparent when we consider how Shiva's daughters treat him, alternately risking death to save him and inflicting him with terrible diseases. When he is about to lose the war with the demons, only his daughters (*not* his wives, Parvati and Ganga) have the power to rescue him and win the battle. Then they turn around and almost kill him with an illness that causes his body to wither, full of gaping holes. When they announce their intention leave him, to begin the voyage to Nagarajupatnam, they must force him to build them a boat and provision it. But at sea and beset by various troubles, they call upon him (and no one else) repeatedly for divine assistance, which he provides. When one fails to recognize their mutual dependency, the other responds (typically aggressively) to make sure that the importance of the bond is emphasized.

In a sense this is bound to happen. The daughter-goddesses must leave and face temporary loss of male attachment, to regain it only when they marry and develop attachment to other men. This much is typical of father-daughter relationships. But Jalari culture gives it a special twist and, with this myth, a special solution within the sibling relationship.

Jalari brothers carry the same load of ambivalence fathers do, but for a much longer time and in a different way, since brothers are the source for their sisters' children marriage partners. Notice the difference between this and the pattern elsewhere, in cultures where brothers and sisters do not remain so close. In the United States, where sibling interaction diminishes through the life course (Dunn 1988; Weisner 1993; Zukow 1989), the strength of fraternal transference and its ability to generate ambivalent feelings probably decreases. In Jalari culture the opposite is true. Brothers and sisters remain close, and their relationship becomes especially intense when their children reach marriageable age. Whatever ambivalence the brother represents for a sister can only increase, given the nature of their relationship in Jalari society.

Shiva's daughters do not have any brothers, except for Potanna, the "younger brother," whom they create out of sacred ash. More will be said about Potanna in a moment. The myth of the voyage focuses exclusively on the relationship to the father, emphasizing that it is so full of mixed feelings that it causes the father and the daughters to act inconsistently, as if they are not sure what they want to do with each other. Why should the myth preserve this emphasis while others, such as the Ramanamma narrative (below), relocate the ambivalence to brothers? The reason could be that although the problem—ambivalence in the relationship between fathers and daughters—remains the same, the myths present different solutions, each the basis for a different kind of explanation. The voyage myth is an explanation of the arrival of goddesses on the Andhra coast, and significant because it relates this crucial event to the history of ambivalent feelings that arise in relation to the father. These feelings are never resolved, and the myth makes sure of that, by causing the seven sisters to leave Nagarajupatnam unmarried even after they have visited their mother's brother. When they arrive, they become goddesses activated by emotions which are decidedly mixed.

For the Jalaris this explains a great deal. It explains why the goddesses can be both nurturant and protective, why they are fickle, and why they must be worshiped in ceremonies in which they are alternately addressed as "whore" and "mother." Ambivalence toward the father is not the only explanation available for this, since other myths focus just as strongly on the vicissitudes of the brother-sister bond. The father complex is important as one explanation among many, and also, possibly, because it is the root of all of them. In her relationship to her father the Jalari woman experiences for the first time the ambivalence that will characterize her relationship to other men, especially her brothers.

Who then is Potanna, the younger brother of the seven goddesses? In South Indian villages, Potanna is represented as a stick or pile of stones that is placed outside, in front of the main sanctuary of a goddess temple (Elmore 1925; Whitehead 1921). In the battle the goddesses cannot kill all the demons since they propagate so quickly. When one is killed a thousand more spring up from its blood. To stop them a way must be found to prevent the spilled blood from falling on the ground. The elder sister, Polamma, tells the youngest sister, Nukalamma, to create a younger brother, Potanna, from sacred ash. She does so and Potanna, a fully mature man (at twelve years of age) springs to life. But Potanna does not do much on his own. (He is certainly no Uppada Narsigodu). His mission is to visit the orally voracious goddess Arini, also known as Adi Sakti or Dana Sakti, and invite her to join the battle. She will drink the blood of the demons before it hits the ground. Thus the goddesses can finally win the war. In return, Potanna will be given to her as a husband. Potanna is therefore a male whom the sisters create in order to obtain a powerful sister-in-law.

"Potu Raju" means "male buffalo king," and elsewhere in South India villagers assert that he is the buffalo-headed husband of the goddess who must be killed and given in sacrifice to her. When buffaloes are sacrificed to the goddess at her yearly festival, they may be referred to as "Potu Rajus." "Potanna" is a variation whom the Jalaris identify as the goddesses' younger brother. His job is to beat a drum at the time of the festival. Men who dance at the goddess festival and flagellate themselves with twisted pieces of rope, to incite the goddess, are called "Potannas." However, there is no Potanna temple, priest, or festival day. No one considers Potanna a household deity, and no offerings are made to him. His role, to put it simply, is to guide a goddess who is always much more powerful than he is, but who may lack a sense of direction.

In Jalari culture, Potu Raju is thus different from the "Potraj" referred to by Elmore and Whitehead, and more recently Hiltebeitel (1980), in their studies of South Indian religion. In these accounts, Potraj is usually the brother of a powerful goddess, but unlike the Jalari figure, he is powerful, and performs the function which the Jalaris assign to his wife, the goddess Arini. According to the version Elmore cites, the goddess Renuka cannot protect her father's kingdom from the demons, because every time a drop of their blood touches the ground a thousand more demons spring up. Consequently,

> Renuka now thought of her brother Potu Raju, who immediately stood before her. "My brother," she said, "if you will help me in this trouble I will see to it that you receive a sheep as tall as the sky and a pile of rice as high as a palm tree." (Potu Raju agreed). Renuka directed him to spread his tongue over the ground as far as the kingdom of the Raksasas extended, and not let one drop of their blood fall to the ground. Thus the propagation of the Raksasas was stopped and the battle was won. This is the explanation of the offering of a sheep and a pile of rice to Potu Raju whenever the village deity is worshipped. (Elmore 1925:85–86)

The Jalaris attribute this power to Arini, and to Potu Raju merely the power to attract Arini to the sisters' cause. He becomes Arini's husband, and the villages goddesses win by enlisting the support of another powerful female. The Jalaris believe that the power to attract and arouse the goddess is a primary male function, a function which must be performed any time a goddess's help is being solicited. But beyond this, the idea that Potu Raju has any power on his own, or should be placated with offerings, strikes them as unnecessary and absurd.

Whitehead does cite one Telugu myth according to which Potu Raju is the husband of the goddess, but his role is very different from his role in the Jalari myth. Here Potu Raju is a liar, and his sin justifies murder by his goddess-wife.

> A Paraiyan passed himself off as a Brahmin in a foreign village and was given the daughter of a blind karnam (accountant) as his wife. The Brahmin wife discovered by chance that her husband was an Outcaste,

so she burned herself alive by setting fire to her house. After her death she appeared as a goddess to the villagers and instructed them to behead her husband, put one of his legs in his mouth, and fat of his stomach on his head, and a lighted lamp on top. After being sacrificed in this manner, the husband was reborn as a buffalo, and therefore a buffalo is sacrificed to the village goddess at ceremonies in which the descendants of the couple play a part. (Whitehead 1921:117–19)

The Jalaris do not attribute any moral significance to Potu Raju's acts, which are merely instrumental. But there is an underlying similarity, if we view Potu Raju's crime as an act which transforms his wife into a goddess and creates the sacrifice that sustains the relationship between her and her devotees. The Jalari Potu Raju is also a facilitator, as we have seen.

There are several points in the story at which male characters, like Potanna, perform minor facilitative functions. When the goddesses need a boat but find that they cannot build it themselves, Shiva arranges for a man, Mailapilli, to do it. When the goddesses need help getting to Nagarajupatnam, a Jalari man, Rudrayya, helps them on their way. When the battle is about to be lost, the goddesses create Potanna—not to fight, of course, since like all men he has limited power, but to invite another goddess, Adi Sakti, to come and join the fray. He performs this simple function and disappears utterly from the story. Potanna thus fits a certain pattern which highlights the power of women and the need for men to direct this power so that it may properly exercise itself. The Potanna episode also strengthens the theme of father-daughter ambivalence, stressing that the power of women is something desirable and necessary for men.

Potanna is not Shiva's son, even though he is the younger brother of Shiva's seven daughters. This is surely significant. The goddesses could have enlisted the help of another man to help them win the help of Adi Sakti in the battle against the demons. They certainly do so in other contexts, depending on Mailapilli to build the boat and on Rudrayya to direct them to Nagaraju's city. The creation of Potanna is a special act with a meaning that must be related to his status as the child of a daughter who uses him to save her father.

A daughter whose attachment to her father cannot be fulfilled may fantasize about giving him a child (Freud 1991). The gift is all the greater in the present instance because, according to the myth, Shiva has no sons. His youngest daughter, Nukalamma, gives birth to Potanna thus affirming her attachment to Shiva by giving him a son who helps to save him from defeat. The fact that it is the youngest daughter should not be overlooked. Jalaris believe that the attachment between fathers and daughters is very strong, doubly so in the case of the youngest daughter, who may end up looking after her father as he grows old.

Adi Sakti, usually called Arini, is the goddess who drinks the demons' blood and marries Potanna. She is a complex figure. The name itself hearkens back to the creatrix, the devouring and erotically demanding mother-goddess who begins the world. This Adi Sakti is probably a transformation. The other goddesses refer to her as *mayadari maradalu* ("deceitful sister-in-law") to emphasize her kinship role, but this is more important than it might seem.[19] Unmarried daughters resent the arrival of brothers' wives, who supplant them. Usually they try to subvert this process, either by challenging the sisters-in-law for influence or by trying to control the sister-in-law and use her as a source of domestic labor. Arini is a danger to the sisters. They wish to use Arini's power while at the same time protecting themselves against it. They do this in several ways. First, they are in no danger of losing their brother, Potanna, since they created him. Arini is deprived of her terrible power by a magical spell, but only temporarily, since the sisters intend to use this power to defeat the demons. With another spell the power is restored and Arini is sent to battle, "one jaw to heaven and the other one to earth," to consume all the blood of the demons before it can fall to the ground.

This is important because it represents the sole instance of affinality in a myth otherwise focused on relationships within the patrilineal household. As we would expect, given the nature of these relationships, marriage is viewed as problematic. Ambivalences in the relationship between mothers and sons, fathers and daughters, and brothers and sisters become especially acute when old members leave or new ones enter, as they must when marriages take place. That is because outsiders are viewed as dangerous, especially when they are women, since incoming wives are accompanied by the dangerous goddesses of their natal households. Other myths present the problem from the point of view of men. The voyage myth, however, looks at it from the perspective of the daughters of the household and presents a solution: Let the dangerous sister-in-law put her power at the service of her husband's sisters, thus preserving and enhancing the status of the household's daughters.

The next important episode takes place when the seven sisters arrive in Nagarajupatnam, the kingdom of their maternal uncle. The fact that Naga-

19. All goddesses can be referred to as *mayadari*, "deceitful," to indicate that they have dual characteristics, at once both nurturant and punishing. Here the *mayadari* referred to is Adi Sakti, the orally voracious goddess who represents a return of the same Adi Sakti who creates the universe, then tries and fails to seduce her three sons.

rajupatnam is an island may be significant, because of what it may represent. To a girl given in marriage to her mother's brother's son, the residence
of the mother's brother can seem like an island, an isolated and remote
place from which there is no rescue. This is true even in the Jalari cross-
cousin marriage system where the degree of physical separation may be
quite small. A married daughter is supposed to remain with her husband's
family, except at long intervals, when she may return home with the permission of her mother-in-law. If she remains there too long, it is grounds
for divorce. The anxiety of the seven sisters increases when they discover
that Nagaraju's own daughter, Nalamaramma, wants their boat even if
this means stranding the seven sisters. In a way, of course, this is what is
supposed to happen. Sisters marry and depart, and married sisters-in-law
arrive and remain. The myth emphasizes that these changes are anxiety-
provoking.

Once again, we are reminded of the tension that characterizes the relationship between sisters-in-law. In this case, it is Nalamaramma who
is concerned about the arrival of the women who could marry into her
family. Nalamaramma is not married and lives with her father, at least up
to this point, paralleling the career of Shiva's seven daughters. No mother
is mentioned, or even any brothers, once again emphasizing yet again that
the father-daughter relationship is the story's main concern. Depriving the
seven sisters of the means to leave would therefore ensure that they remain under Nalamaramma's control, at least until Nalamaramma marries.
Much of the story from this point concerns the measures which the sisters
take to ensure another outcome. The dice game is the crucial event.

Nagaraju challenges the seven sisters to a game of dice. Polamma plays
first and loses everything. Then the youngest sister, Nukalamma, takes
over and wins back all that they have lost, plus Nagaraju's own posses-
sions. Instead of taking them, however, Nukalamma simply admonishes
her maternal uncle: "Self-assertion (*paurusam*) hampers your duty. Enmity
(*virodham*) will destroy the family. Greed (*duruddesam*) breeds grief." Then
the goddesses leave Nagarajupatnam and resume their voyage. This would
seem to be the crucial moment in their transformation, since from this
point onward they no longer act as daughters of Shiva but as goddesses
(*ammavallu*) in their own right.

In a longer version of the myth, the dice game is a complex affair and
ends with an alliance between the seven sisters and Nalamaramma, Nagaraju's daughter. At first the sisters lose everything. Then Nukalamma takes
over and they win everything back, including the items they wanted all
along: drums, tents, and flower garlands, the items that are important because they are used in the festivals for the goddesses. The story of the wager,

therefore, is the story of how these materials were obtained. At first Nagaraju does not wish to give them up and threatens war. Only the helpful intervention of his own daughter stops him, in parallel fashion to the protection offered Shiva by his daughters. Nalamaramma reminds Nagaraju of his *dharma* as a king: He must live up to his obligations or the kingdom he rules will be destroyed. When he relents, the seven sisters take what they came for and offer Nalamaramma a share, which she accepts. Since Nalamaramma is a village goddess, too, the story explains how she obtains the items necessary for her worship.

Not surprisingly, given what we already know, everything in this part of the myth hinges on the relationship between daughters and fathers— between the seven sisters and their father, Shiva, and Nalamaramma and her father, Nagaraju. When Nukalamma starts betting, following the disastrous serious of wagers conducted by Polamma, the sisters have nothing left to bet except themselves. They agree to become the property of Nagaraju if they lose. They have not asked Shiva for help up to this point, but they do so now, since they run the risk of falling under the control and domination of their maternal uncle: "Hey, whore-son, do you have any love for your daughters? We are selling ourselves. We are betting with Nagaraju. He is giving brooms to our hands and making us sweep the dirt."

The sisters are threatened with loss of their status as daughters when they go to the house of their mother's brother in the status of . . . what? Normally such a move would signify marriage, but the myth lacks any direct reference to the goddesses' possible matrimony. The allusions are indirect, as here, where the sisters' duties as servants in another household refer to their new status as daughters-in-law. They pray to Shiva to save them from this.

Shiva responds by casting one of his *mantras,* magically altering the fall of the dice, so that with each throw the sisters win back a little more of what they lost. Finally, they have won back everything and threaten Nagaraju with the loss of his kingdom. As the storyteller related:

> He was sleeping when suddenly he heard the pleas of his daughters. He looked down with his celestial vision. Oh, flames were coming out of his eyes! "Nagaraju," Shiva thought, "you are shaming my girls, troubling them and making them weep. You are causing them to sell themselves away." Shiva looked with his third eye and chanted a mantra. The mantra went into the dice and the result was in his daughters' favor. Nagaraju was defeated.

Jalaris use the vocabulary of buying and selling to describe the marriage transactions between families related by cross-cousin marriage. Shiva wants to stop the sale of his daughters to Nagaraju, so he alters the play of the dice to produce the result most favorable to them. Shiva acts this way because he does not want to give up his daughters, and the daughters, despite their voyage, do not want to give up their father, even though it is clear that they want to transform themselves and their relationship to him. That is what makes this episode so crucial: It is the place where this decision is finally and definitively made.

By settling the wager with the acquisition of festival goods, we get an inkling of what this transformed relationship will be. The daughters will be converted into powerful goddesses, the only status they can occupy which both preserves their status as daughters *and* protects their power from appropriation by other men. The myth presents the marriage situation as a bet, one that women lose when they accept marriage into the house of their mother's brother. The myth reverses this, telling us that if women could win, they would become the powerful beings we know as goddesses. Compare this to the story of the goddess Ramanamma, later in this chapter. She undergoes the same transformation, and for the same reason, except that in her case the ambivalence to be overcome is not parental but sibling-based.

Nagaraju's daughter, Nalamaramma, also changes. When the seven sisters arrive on their golden ship, Nalamaramma wants it so that she can leave. We are not told what her destination might be, or why she wants to leave, but we can guess. She probably wants to visit the place of her father's sister, i.e., the abode of Shiva and his wife, Nagaraju's sister. Her only purpose in going there would be to form a marriage alliance. She wants her father to win the bets so that she can take the ship and go. But when her father loses and threatens to fight the seven sisters, Nalamaramma chastises him and reminds him of his kingly *dharma*. She does not want the ship anymore. The seven sisters respond by offering her some of the festival items they have won, and she accepts. She is on her way to becoming a goddess, too, and just like the seven sisters, she is moved along in this process of transformation by changes in her relationship to her father.

The relationship between father and daughter is crucial to the origin of Jalari goddesses. It begins in mutual desire and attraction, and with the realization that the relationship cannot be sustained anxiety-free. It must be made into something else. Usually, daughters marry and leave home, just as fathers accept their departure and the arrival of their replacements, the daughters-in-law. A powerful desire is thus tamed by being redirected into conventional kinship relations—a favorite Jalari theme. But what would happen if it were left intact? Its power is too great to be contained by the conventional father-daughter relationship. That is why the relationship must be altered to reflect the daughters' growing power and ability to exercise it independent of the father's will. At the same time, father and daughters want to remain closely connected. Only when the daughters are transformed into goddesses can the creative potential of this dynamic tension be fully realized. That is what the myth accomplishes.

Once they leave Nagarajupatnam, the seven sisters take on new powers. They did not act like goddesses before, on their way to the island, but now they do. When they arrive in a new place, they demand worship from the inhabitants, and to demonstrate their power, they inflict the people with deadly diseases. Temples up and down the eastern coast of India are established. The myth refers to this process, simultaneously explaining the arrival of new goddesses; the appearance of new epidemic diseases; and the need for divinatory methods. Since two or three goddesses have "arrived" in the Jalari village in living memory, the myth accounts for a situation the Jalaris know extremely well.

The myth is also a celebration of sororal cooperation and solidarity, a fact that should not surprise us when we recall that Jalari sisters trade together in small cartels that dominate the markets in the vicinity of the fishing village. The only event that stands in the way is marriage. Sisters compete with each other for the children of their brothers, to be given in marriage to the sisters' own children in cross-cousin alliance. The myth of the goddesses considered here excludes brothers, except for the younger brother (Potanna or Potu Raju) whom the sisters themselves create, so the problem of marriage competition cannot arise. Instead, the story explores the relationship between sisters when nothing at all exists to impede it—neither their own marriages nor the marriages of their children—and finds that it is extremely powerful. It is sororal unity that ties together the whole Jalari pantheon of goddesses.

The myth of the voyage is not just a fantasy on the theme of sororal unity, however. It considers how unity can be elaborated by extension to other women related by (real or potential) marriage alliance. The seven sisters seek alliances with other women—Adi Sakti and Nalamaramma—both of whom stand in the category of sister-in-law. The problem in real life is that sisters-in-law can be dangerous, since their interests compete with the sisters' own vis-à-vis the men who are the former's husbands and the latter's brothers. But the myth solves this problem by eliminating marriage and marriageable men from the picture, except for Potanna who does not pose the same problem. Women are free to unite and form groupings that are not divided by the conflicts that characterize sisters and sisters-in-law in ordinary life.

Instead of dealing with ambivalent desire by repressing it, or transferring it onto other agents, the myth uses it as a source of dynamic energy, a power which can create and transform. The Jalaris are not unique in harnessing incestuous desire to make it the engine of creation. The ancient Hindu myth of creation is a case in point. Purusa begins the creation of the world in the process of pursuing and mating with his split-off female half. Jalari myth participates in a universe of meaning already rich in exploration of this theme. What makes the Jalari case special is that it is shaped by the structures of Jalari kinship practices.

THE STORY OF THE GODDESS RAMANAMMA

Resolving the Paradoxical Desire of Brothers and Sisters

Like all Jalari myths, the story of Ramanamma is a prolonged meditation on the paradoxes of Jalari kinship, in this case the paradoxes of siblingship. The Ramanamma myth shows how Jalari goddesses are born out of paradox, and how the goddesses, as paradoxical creatures themselves, reassert the antitheses of competing normative demands at a different level, where they become the causes of human misfortune. Like most Jalari goddesses, Ramanamma "arrived" in Jalaripet as an epidemic disease (in this case, cholera). This version of the story was related to me by the possession-medium who first detected Ramanamma's presence in the village during an outbreak of smallpox.

The Story of Ramanamma

That *amma* ("woman," "mother") had seven brothers. She was the daughter of Cencu Naidu. After the seven brothers were born, Cencu Naidu performed *tapas* (ascetic acts) because he had no daughter. Then that girl was born as a boon.

The child was born already twelve years old. Her brothers built a house of twelve windows and put her in that house. Then they went out on a bird hunt. After that, she took twelve ministers and seven companions to a flower garden. The Koyavadu (lit. "the Koya man") saw her and desired her. She saw him and thought, "He is a magician, he is coming for me!" She climbed a green tree. He remained below, waiting to catch her. After a while, she got down and started walking. He caught her and said, "Little girl, what is your city, which is your village?" She told him where she lived.

He felt excited. He did not go, but thought, "I can have sex with her anytime." Taking twelve Koyas, he went to her house. He dug a tunnel

The goddess Ramanamma

and went through it, to where she stays. She was sleeping. He went in and without touching or contacting her, she became a woman nine months pregnant. In ninc minutes, the Koya formed a nine months' pregnancy.

At midnight, she woke up. She saw that her sari blouse was open, that the edge of her sari had slipped, and that her makeup had been rubbed off. There was no more eyeliner around her eyes. "While my brothers were not here, that man came and spoiled me. When I get up in the morning, all the neighbors will hear of it. When my parents hear, they will not approve," she said and went into the forest.

She went to the seven wells and to one well, the "ilabuddi" well. At the seven wells she took a bath. She went to the big "ilabuddi" well. As she suffered, who heard her suffering? Parvati Devi, Sarasvati Devi, and Laksmi Devi heard it. The three of them came. Sarasvati assisted as midwife in the delivery. Parvati Devi prepared the milk mixed with castor oil. Laksmi Devi prepared the bed. Then they made her into a golden flower ball (bangara pula banti). They made her and the child into a marantha (parijati) flower.

Meanwhile, the brothers were searching for her. Finally they came to sleep under a shade tree.

That amma saw them. "My elder brothers came. They came searching and searching," she said and went into the dream of the youngest elder brother. "Brother, I am here! That Koya man spoiled me. I became the mother of a child. My child and I, together, are in the 'ilabuddi' well. Why are you searching?" she said.

The younger one woke and alerted the eldest brother, "Elder brother, our sister is in the 'ilabuddi' well. Come, we'll go!" When they were coming, she assumed the form of a raksasa ("demon") and stood near a lake. She thought, "They might be afraid of me and run away," and she changed her form. "Brother, it is I," she shouted.

"Ramanamma, let's go! Let's go to our house!" they said. "I won't go just like that to our village," she said. "I will come only for a festival."

"What do you want? What shall we offer?" they asked. She told them: "You must go to the weaver's house, to the potter's house, to the cane worker's house, to the eye-shadow maker's house, to the makeup seller's house. Then you must apply cow-dung water and draw muggulu (designs). Then I shall come." She wanted many things: bangles, beads, eye shadow, boxes, mirrors, and combs. And for those who want meat, meat; to those who want bread, bread; to those who want toddy, toddy; to those who want marijuana, marijuana; to those who want brandy, brandy. Give these to those who want them. "If you perform a nine-day festival, with costumes, flags, and toddy, then—if you do all this—I will come to your village."

Chicken sacrifice to Ramanamma by daughter of village priest

201

Then the brothers went to their father and told him. "What do you say?" they said. "If we give all these sorts of things, she will come. If not, she won't come." Then the sons asked, "Father, take our money and do it," the father said. "You should bring the sister to our house."

She came to Jalaripet. From East Mayagiripatnam (*maya*, "illusion," *giri*, "hill," *patnam*, "town"). So she came to Jalaripet. She came to Bhimlipatnam (another fishing village). After a few years, she ate some number of people. She stayed here. We give flowers to her there, don't we? That night she came here and for three months cholera came. She ate 570 people. After our elders knew, they went to possession-mediums (*patis*) and to diviners (*kanikis*) and found out. Then they built a temple for that *amma*. They built it, and now they perform a festival for her once every three years.

Ramanamma as Sister and Goddess: The Dynamics of Siblingship in Jalari Myth

The integrity of the patriline is threatened from within by fraternal interests, which, for senior brothers, center increasingly on their constituent conjugal units and not the patriline. This is the central paradox of the agnatic group, since brothers both desire and struggle against the solidarity of the group. At the same time, the patriline is threatened from outside by affinally related families and, especially, married sisters, who demand their brothers' support and attention, and who frequently play off brothers against each other in order to get what they want. Yet brothers and sisters want and need each other. This is the central paradox of affinal groups. The conflict within and between these groups constitutes the complex dialectic which informs Jalari mythology.

Brothers reluctantly admit their divisiveness, but point out that it is not they but their wives who are to blame. Wives bicker constantly over alleged inequalities in the distribution of patrilineal resources, their husbands say. Eventually, brothers must separate in order to preserve peace in their own homes. The meaning, at least implicitly, is clear: If there were no wives (an impossibility, given the need to produce sons and preserve patrilineal continuity), then brothers could remain together forever as "birds of a single nest." The Ramanamma myth is partly a speculation on just this theme because it answers the question, "What would the world be like if there were no wives?"

Now consider the affines. The natal family does not readily assent to the loss of its daughter/sister to another household, and the daughter herself is torn emotionally about her new role as a mature woman and wife. She wants marital union, but fears it, and cannot conceive of pleasure outside the boundaries of her natal household, the only environment she knows, and apart from her own brothers, the only male figures she is sure she can trust. But worst of all, married sisters become arch-competitors for patrilineal resources. As their brothers' primary trading partners, they demand special buying terms. And as the source of their brothers' children's marriage partners, they each demand special and possibly conflicting consideration. Not only do sisters as a group create problems for the patriline, but individually, as competitors for their brothers' resources, they frequently conflict. By enlisting brothers individually as allies, they produce fissions in the patriline. The Ramanamma myth offers a fantasy-speculation on the question of what life would be like if sisters were never alienated from their brothers.

Jalaris want daughters, and so the mythical Cencu Naidu gets one by performing *tapas* (ascetic acts) and compelling the gods to give him one. In the next scene, Ramanamma, now twelve years old and fully mature, is placed by her seven brothers in a large house with twelve windows. This is what psychoanalysts call an "obtrusive event," since there is no manifest reason the story should provide this information. The size of the house and the number of its windows attest to the family's wealth and, more importantly, reemphasize the number twelve. Twelve years is considered the age of sexual maturity, and sexual maturity initiates the crisis the myth attempts to resolve.

Notice that it is the brothers who place Ramanamma in the twelve-windowed house. This is another obtrusive event. If the house is the father's (Cencu Naidu's), then surely there would have been no need to place Ramanamma there so deliberately. She would have been there already. But if the house had been constructed for Ramanamma, exclusively, it would suggest that the brothers saw some special need to confine her at this time. It really makes no difference which is true, as long as we note the fact that Ramanamma's brothers put her in a special place (a house) at a certain time (the onset of womanhood).

What are the implications of this? Apparently, the brothers wished to keep Ramanamma in the house, under their control, and sequester her from outside influences, especially from those who might corrupt her at her present age of awakening sexual maturity. It is not the father, Cencu Naidu, who announces or enforces these strictures, but the brothers themselves. This is strange, since preserving the daughter's chastity is chiefly the parents' obligation. But the father plays no role, and the mother, if she exists, does or says nothing.

For the brothers to assume the role of principal protectors suggest that for them Ramanamma's budding sexuality has special significance. We recall with David Shulman the folk motif of the brothers who keep their sister or sisters unmarried in order to retain the power vested in the virgin. Discussing this power in relation to South Indian myths from the Tamil region, Shulman writes:

> This power is rooted in the erotic potential of the woman, in her threatening and enticing sexuality. The incest motif, especially in its appearance in folk myths in connection with the love of brothers and sisters, expresses clearly the idea of a dangerous eroticism, of sexuality gone awry, of the power that lurks in the virgin and that seeks an outlet in violent, potentially destructive and even forbidden behavior. (1980:153–54)

Possibly, Ramanamma's brothers keep her to guard against the loss of a great source of energy. On the other hand, Trawick's interpretation of an Oedipal themes in South Indian family life is equally tenable. The intense erotic love for the mother might be converted into an attachment between older brother and younger sister (1990:16). We have already considered this possibility. Both could explain Ramanamma's brothers' desire to protect and isolate her. But even if this were true, what are they protecting her from?

In this version of the story, the seven brothers leave their sister to go hunting for birds. Ramanamma, accompanied by twelve ministers and seven companions, visits a flower garden. This is interesting for two reasons. First, Ramanamma's departure from the house takes place as soon as the brothers leave, suggesting that if they had still been present Ramanamma might not have been able or willing to leave. Second, her destination is a flower garden, a site with strong associations to romantic love and erotic behavior. In Telugu, Tamil, and probably other South Asian languages, the garden represents a woman's sexuality, which is said to "bloom" at the time she matures. Ramanamma's journey into the garden would appear to be a metaphor for entry into her own sexuality.

Her companions are not mentioned again and appear not to be present beyond the first scene. Ramanamma is alone when the Koya man first sees her. "Koya," like "Cencu," is the name of a largely non-Hindu, non-Dravidian tribal group resident in the hills of far northern Andhra and southern Orissa. It is also the name that Telugu plains folk apply to all tribals generally. As far as the Jalaris are concerned, "Koya" means "tribal," or "from the hills." The Koya man resides in the garden or, according to another version, came there from the "Koya village" to hunt birds. Notice that he and the brothers are described as being on identical quests (this is true in a deeper sense, as we shall see). The Koya sees Ramanamma and feels a strong desire for her ("his eye fell," as they say in Telugu). Ramanamma sees him and fears he may be a "magician" (*mantramuvadu*), one capable of casting spells (*mantras*). In Jalari belief, *mantras* originated among tribals. Jalari skill in the use of *mantras*, for good or for evil, is still thought to be acquired from tribal peoples. Ramanamma is afraid and climbs a tree, where she remains until evening. After climbing down, she is observed again by the Koya man. He approaches and asks her to name her native place. She complies.

The Koya man's intention is clear: "I can have sex with her anytime." The text repeats that Ramanamma told him where she lives. The Koya man follows her directions and goes there, accompanied by twelve companions, who, like Ramanamma's companions earlier, disappear as soon as they are mentioned. The Koya digs a tunnel beneath the wall and the foundation, to the room where Ramanamma stays. He finds her sleeping. The story takes pains to emphasize that he never touches her and that she never wakes up. But "in nine minutes, he formed a nine months' pregnancy in her." He then leaves and no more is said about him.

In the story, Ramanamma symbolically enters her own sexuality when she enters the garden. There she finds a male figure, a tribal, waiting for her and wanting her newly developed sexuality for himself. The Koya, as a being from the "hill country," represents a being from "beyond" the domain Jalaris recognize as "culture." Through magic or some other extraordinary means, he can acquire something that is forbidden to his more culture-bound counterparts. The Koya man thus "stands in" for individuals still "in" culture, satisfying on their behalf desires which they are forbidden to experience. Ramanamma feigns reluctance, but not before letting slip the crucial information about where she lives. The Koya man then digs a hole—a powerful metaphor for the sexual penetration to follow but which, because it is forbidden, must be represented as or displaced to the act of digging. Ramanamma is impregnated without knowing what happened to her.

The impregnation occurs in Ramanamma's own house, where she has been specially placed by her brothers. The act represents not just the failure of the brothers' protection but possibly the fulfillment of the brothers' own unconscious and forbidden desire: to keep their sister to themselves. The Koya man is thus a transformation of the brothers. He acts "for" them, achieving merger with and control over the sister, and thus doing what they cannot acknowledge wanting to do themselves. Ramanamma, asleep during this process, notices that she has been "spoiled" when she wakes and sees her clothing in disarray. She knows that something bad has happened and that her reputation will be destroyed if she does not leave. So she "crosses the *yuga*-s (a very great distance)" and enters the forest. The "forest" (*adivi*) is a land beyond the village and beyond the world of normal humans and their affairs. For the Jalaris, it is the abode of tribals, the locus of esoteric knowledge, and the birthplace of goddesses. It is only fitting that the *human* Ramanamma should enter this region to be transformed into the *goddess* Ramanamma. Once there, she travels to a series of wells (sometimes identified as seven in number) and to one well in particular, the "ilabuddi" (of uncertain etymology). In some versions, she jumps in the first six wells, but finds them too shallow, and so proceeds to the deeper "ilabuddi" well. In this version, she goes directly to the "ilabuddi" well and takes a bath. She prepares to give birth and is assisted in the delivery by three great pan-Hindu goddesses—Parvati, Sarasvati, and Laksmi—who perform different tasks related to the birth. Afterward, the goddesses make Ramanamma into a "golden flower ball" and the child (whose name and sex are never mentioned) into a marantha flower, and throw both into the well.

In another version recited by the same storyteller, Ramanamma approaches the well and reflects on her past:

> O, sinner Koya man! Why did you spoil my chastity (*pati vrata*)? What life will I lead? I am in such misery. I couldn't protect my chastity for even a short while following my maturity. My parents will cry for me. How much they will suffer! I am the last child. This is how I came to be: My parents climbed the hills, and made a vow. But a female child was not born. Then they received a boon. Having gone to Shiva, they received a boon. My father went to Vishnu. Vishnu gave a boon, saying, "You will have one female child. But your daughter will acquire ill-fame (*apakirti*). Through your womb a daughter will be born. She will have trouble because of a Koya man. She will "eat" the kingdom. There's no need for you to fear. That *amma* will be there for you. Although she goes upon the kingdom (i.e., causes epidemic disease), she will be there for you." Thus I was born. After, the sinner Koya man spoiled my chastity.

She prays to Visnu and he, not the three goddesses, assists her in the birth of the child (here unnamed but identified as female.) Afterwards, Ramanamma throws the child into the well, to purify it, and then contemplates going home to her parents. But she realizes they will detect the odor of childbirth on her clothes. So she jumps in the well with her child.

Let us consider what has taken place so far. Ramanamma's first reaction to her deflowering is to leave the house that her brothers built for her and to flee into the forest, the domain of wildness, from which her illicit lover and father of her child first appeared. In the forest, she can act without constraint and outside everyday social strictures. She can call upon the deities to help her, and they respond. Perhaps more than a domain of wildness or "nature," the forest represents a realm of possibilities (a liminal zone), where people are reconstituted in new forms before returning to society. Such a realm is not empty, though. It contains all that is unacknowledged but secretly wished for. Other South Asian societies employ the image of the forest in a similar way. As Desjarlais, writing on Nepali shamanism, comments:

> It is a place . . . where rationality and culture are lacking, and where the beasts and goblins of the dark, and the wild side of human action run rampant. Westerners have another term for this experiential domain, an image equally metaphorical, located less among the shadows or our physical terrain and more within the symbolic matrix of our corporeal selves: we call it "the unconscious." (1989:295)

This is what the forest represents in the first place in the Koya who impregnates her: a part of socially unrestrained "wildness" which breaks through into "culture" in the form of a disguised breach of the sibling incest taboo. Ramanamma is part of that realm (through impregnation by the Koya), and so it is to that realm that she goes in order to be transformed.

She gives birth to a child in a well. The well is a frequently chosen site for committing suicide in India. But perhaps because of its intimate associations with death, the well also represents the possibility of life and life-giving: What "dies" in one form in the well can be reborn in another form. This is what happens in the Ramanamma story. She and her child are made into a "golden flower ball"—the image of goodness and purity—and become, according to the myth, the joint being "Ramanamma."

The seven brothers search for their sister. Obviously they desire her and want her back. Notice that no mention is made at any point of the brothers' wives, if they have any, or of their own families. For them, the sister constitutes the vital core of the family. They sleep for awhile in the shade of a tree, and while they sleep the youngest brother has a dream in which Ramanamma appears to him. She tells him what happened and where to find her. As much as they want her, she wants them, and the stage is set for their reunification.

Reunification, however, is impossible on the basis of their previously existing sibling relation. The *sister* Ramanamma has been impregnated by a tribal, given birth, and then undergone a miraculous transformation. As if to underscore the magnitude of these changes, Ramanamma changes herself into a *raksasa* or "demon." Not only is she no longer a sister, she is the most horrific of female forms, the total reversal of the unmarried sister's role. The demonic form represents Ramanamma's old "self," made up of unfulfilled dependency wishes centered on her brothers. But she knows that if she appears to them in this form, her brothers will fear her and refuse to return her to the village, so she assumes another form more appealing to her brothers. In another version of the story this form is described: "She has a lotus on the sole of her foot; she has a bell in her navel; she has a cestus as bright as the world at her waist. At her back there is a white whisk. On her forehead, there is a crown, as bright as the whole world." This is one of the descriptions of a Jalari goddess, an *ammavaru*. The form she first assumed and then abandoned—her demonic form—remains hidden for now, to be revealed on future occasions, to chastise her "brothers" (now defined as "devotees") for failing to appease with offerings of fruit and light.

Ramanamma, the goddess, reveals to her brothers the conditions under which she will return to the village. These conditions include a festival, the collection and preparation of various festival items, and the distribution of festival gifts (meat, marijuana, brandy, etc.) to those who want them. The brothers relay these demands to their father, who agrees to accept the brothers' contributions. The father tells them "to bring the sister back to the house" and so Ramanamma returns to the village. She is installed as a goddess.

Finally, the myth reveals how Ramanamma came to Jalaripet and, presumably, to all the other villages where she is resident as a goddess. She arrived in what may be described as her alter ego, her demonic *raksasa* form, and inflicted a cholera epidemic, killing several hundred people. At first her identity was unknown. The villagers consulted possession-mediums (*patis*) and diviners (*kanikis*). The medium who related the story also identified Ramanamma and spoke for her, demanding on the goddess's behalf that the festival be performed and a temple built. The villagers obeyed, and Ramanamma has since been one of the two main village goddesses.

To summarize: Ramanamma's brothers wanted to keep their youngest sister to themselves. This makes sense if we recall the discussion of parental attachment and sibling transference, a theme originally explored by Rank in 1912. The male child's intense erotic love for the mother may be converted into an intense attachment to the younger sister. A resolution of the Oedipal crisis is then possible when the mother is given up, but the sister retained, as the locus of earliest emotional attachment. A similar dynamic might be at work for sisters: The female child's longing for her father may be displaced to her brothers. She avoids separation by retaining close affective ties with her brothers. But the problem remains. How can these dependencies be resolved in a way that avoids permanent mutual frustration?

In real life they cannot, at least not permanently, and that is why the resolutions provided by divination (which we examine later) are always temporary. In the myth, however, the sister escapes social constraints on her sexuality by entering the "garden," i.e., by becoming a sexual being. She realizes her sexuality by unconsciously, but deliberately, inviting access by the tribal man and allowing herself (while asleep) to be impregnated by him in her own house. The agent of her downfall and transformation — a tribal — represents both the absence of constraint and the wish fulfillment this absence permits. To be impregnated by him in her own house is the fulfillment of her wish to be merged erotically with her own brothers. Realization of the act, not the act itself, forces her to leave and to seek a new status that accommodates her roles *both* as sexual being *and* as sister, achieving, as it were, "the best of both worlds." In Jalari culture, that new status — and therefore the resolution to the dilemma — is the status of the *ammavaru*, the goddess.

The brothers, on their part, cannot realize their desire for their sister except through confining her and keeping her to themselves. Although they keep her, they cannot remain close to her, lest the forbidden object exert too powerful an attraction. So they leave the house and go hunting, shooting their arrows and killing birds — behavior that could certainly be construed as erotic displacement, especially when we recall from Rajastani miniatures (often used to decorate the pages of the *Kama Sutra*) the figure of a man who is simultaneously making love to his wife and drawing a bow to strike a passing lion with an arrow.

When the sister departs, the brothers desperately seek her to bring her back. But she cannot return with them as their sister, having abrogated that status through an illegitimate impregnation and childbirth. Ramanamma's midwives, who are goddesses themselves, transform her into a new being. In her new form she is neither a sister nor an ordinary human female. She can return to her brothers on the new terms this new form establishes if the brothers accept these terms. Although this makes her return possible, it does not free her and her brothers from the ambivalence which pervaded their earlier relationship. Rather, ambivalence is projected outward into a realm — the realm of goddess worship — where it can be transformed through rules which govern divine-human, and not cross-sibling, relations.

Ramanamma's new form represents her more positive sisterly feelings and conveys her willingness to protect and guard her brothers. But she is unwilling to bestow these on her brothers unless they satisfy her by making offerings and performing festivals. To signify her intention, she assumes her demonic shape. Henceforth she, and not her brothers, will be in control. Her relationship to her brothers will be transactive, based on their giving of offerings and on her bestowal of good fortune. She is freed from them as they are freed from her—but only in terms of a new dependency which replaces with "religious" transaction the old dependency relationship's reliance on the sublimation of unrealizable desires (on the nontransaction of sexuality, so to say) for its maintenance.

The myth reveals how ambivalences generated by the kinship system and its patrilineal ideology work themselves out in a mythic form. Male patriline members inhibit attrition among themselves by excluding (from the patrilineal perspective) a potent source of discord—their wives. Whether Ramanamma's brothers are "really" married or not is of no consequence. They are represented as single in the myth, and this is what counts. They attempt to control and manipulate another source of trouble—their sister. The brothers keep her at home, out of contact with other men, and preserve her power for themselves. Of course, the solution is partial and ultimately fails. Brothers and sisters cannot remain a unit unto themselves without violating norms and creating contradiction (that is, if keeping in the sisters and keeping out the wives solves one problem, it creates another, namely, the problem of producing the next patrilineal generation). The myth solves this in a creative manner. It allows siblings to commit an act of unconscious and displaced incest. But no one survives the normative breach as he or she was before. The mother (with her child) is transformed into a goddess and readmitted to the family as a household deity. The brothers are transformed into her "devotees." And their relationship goes from an ambivalence-laden bond between brother and sister to a bond between deity and devotee which is much easier to "transact" because the roles it defines do not generate ultimately unfulfillable expectations.

The sibling relationship is generative of ambivalence, just like the parent-child relationship is, but it is also more, because of its role in marriage. That is probably why myths about siblings are more numerous than those about fathers and mothers, and why sibling issues figure so prominently as causes of goddess attacks and thus targets of divinatory scrutiny. The several myths we have considered are like an answer to the question: How would the patrilineal ideology be fulfilled in a world in which contradictory obligations and competing allegiances among parents and children, and among brothers and sisters, had been eliminated by being transformed into something else?

As we have seen, contradictory kinship norms induce ambivalence by putting at risk the consciously upheld value of sibling solidarity, the symbolic core of Jalari social structure. Brothers are "birds of a single nest," but fight among themselves over leadership and distribution of resources. Eventually they divide, creating several new patrilines where before there had been only one. To create, therefore, one must destroy; to achieve solidarity, one must reject it. This is the paradox. The dialectic between paradoxical objectives constitutes the movement which in myth results in the creative transcendence of religious transformation. Fraternal solidarity without division becomes possible in myth because the paradox of patrilineality is transcended in the transformation of brothers into devotees, the elimination of wives, and the elevation of the unmarried sister to goddess.

The attachment between brother and sister is both reinforced and undercut by cross-cousin marriage, the paradox of combination and separation becoming increasingly intense as siblings compete for their children's marriage partners. Brothers and sisters struggle against fissiparous tendencies to fulfill strongly felt dependency needs for each other. Myths provide resolutions by acknowledging such needs and satisfying them through culturally legitimate means. It is as if the Ramanamma myth says, "If Jalari brothers and sisters need each other, but Jalari norms forbid their union, then let brothers be transformed into devotees and sisters into goddesses." In that way, strong emotions can be resolved through the transactive language of worship. As a goddess, the sister can be retained and her special power employed to benefit her brothers. The sister never becomes a threat to patrilineal solidarity by marrying out. Finally, wives are not present and, for all practical purposes, do not exist within the structure of the myth, thus eliminating a potent source of friction. As a result, the brothers remain together, as "nest birds," and as co-worshipers of their sister-turned-goddess, without division through competing interests.

To what extent the patterns described here for Jalari myth can be found elsewhere will be seen in the next chapter, in the study of divination. This study suggests that kinship structures which are productive of ambivalence frame all divinatory explanation. These explanations begin in the diagnosis of spirit-human relations but always end in the diagnosis of social relations which, it is believed, precipitate the crises which interfere in the relationship between people and deities. Not coincidentally, the social relations of greatest divinatory concern are those between siblings.

Chapter Seven

The Dialectical Rationalization of Cultural Paradox in a Formal Explanatory System

Unlike myth, divination cannot resolve dialectical oppositions in moments of integrative compromise, because divination is not free to reconstruct the world to allow the expression of conflicted desires. Instead, divination suspends the dialectic by settling the opposition temporarily in favor of one side or another. By "sides" I refer to the ideals of fraternal and cross-sex sibling solidarity and to the impossibility of reconciling them. They conflict not only with each other but internally, in the dialectical opposition of unity and separation. Jalari divination is a knowledge system which pursues the culturally defined goal of interpersonal integration and emotional coalescence in terms defined by the pathways of kinship and marriage. Solutions are temporary, prompting the dialectical cycle to begin again and forcing opposed ideals into conflict with each other, leading once again to divination.

The same goal is sought in different ways throughout Hindu India, and possibly, this is part of what "being Hindu" means. *Mokṣa* is the philosophical expression of an experience which all Indians who undergo the most typical form of Hindu socialization share. Kakar thinks so and believes that it represents the desire to return to a state of egoless fusion in which the boundaries between self and other no longer exist. Its precursor is prolonged infantile dependence on the mother and the meaning given to it (Kakar 1981). The Jalaris do not speak of moksha, the extinction of the ego or the absorption of the self into the cosmos. That does not mean they do not share the same civilizational goal. Instead of making it a consciously expressed ideal, framed in philosophical terms, the Jalaris configure it as the experiential ideal of relatedness through kinship.

Relatedness in Jalari culture is a dualistic order, conjugated through the twin norms of agnation and affinality, and realized (prototypically) in fraternal and cross-sex sibling relations. Sibling solidarity is the goal toward which Jalari knowledge systems are directed. Agnation represents the ideal of fraternal solidarity which would be realized, if it were possible, in the complete and permanent unity of a group of brothers whose interests always coincide. Affinality represents the ideal of solidarity between adult brothers and their married sisters, which would be realized, if it were possible, in complete cooperation and marriages between their cross-cousin children.

The normative obligations of brothers and sisters inevitably diverge. In order for brothers to realize the ideal of fraternal unity, they must marry and produce sons—sons whose own marriages, in turn, must be arranged to continue patrilineal succession. The preferred form of marriage is cross-cousin, which means that married sisters are the principal source for their brothers' sons' wives. Each time a marriage is arranged, therefore, brothers must look outside the agnatic household to their married sisters, acknowledging in the very way they preserve fraternal solidarity and patrilineal succession that affines are necessary. This is not what Jalari men want to believe. The paradox of the agnatic relation is that it cannot be what it pretends to be—a self-sufficient and harmoniously united brotherhood which is not dependent on external and ultimately conflictual alliances.

Compounding the paradox is the fact that patrineal succession cannot preserve agnatic unity for more than a couple of generations before it breaks down, as brothers separate to form the nuclei of independent lineage groups. The logic of succession is to blame. Ideally, each brother has sons and so fulfills the obligation to increase the size of the agnatic group. The sons grow up and compete with each other not only for resources but also for wives. Their fathers preserve the solidarity of the group as long as they can, but eventually their efforts fail and sons separate, dividing the property.

The larger the group of agnatic families, the harder it is for them to sacrifice their independent interests for the well-being of the whole group. No large agnatic group has ever survived more than three generations. Even this is rare. The inevitability of division is not the ideal Jalari men express when they speak of the agnatic household as a "nest" and themselves as "nest birds." The internal paradox of the agnatic relation is that even without the competing interests of affines it cannot escape inherently divisive tendencies.

At the same time, the ideal of affinal solidarity promises restoration of unity among brothers and sisters, but this unity is never more than a dream, since the only way to achieve it is indirectly, through unification of children in cross-cousin marriage. Even this is hardly satisfactory, nor can it be, given the exigencies of cross-cousin marriage. Married sisters compete with each other for their brothers' sons. Brothers compete to obtain the available sisters' daughters in marriage to their sons. As each other's principal trading partners, meanwhile, brothers and sisters contend with each other in matters of business and compete with each other for the most favorable terms.

Divinatory knowledge structures realize the contradiction inherent in opposed but mutually valued social formations. One structure is oriented to the solidarity of the patriline and the relationship between male members, represented (prototypically) by brothers. The other is oriented to affiliation and the relationship between allied patrilines, represented (prototypically) by brothers and sisters. The paradox is that one cannot simultaneously and satisfactorily fulfill the desires created by the norms these social formations impose. Desires conflict, creating ambivalence and motivating the search for a resolution. In Jalari divination, it all comes down to a decision to attribute the cause of misfortune to events that arise either on the agnatic or affinal axis.

BASIC ASSUMPTIONS OF JALARI CAUSALITY

Divination determines the causes of and remedies for instances of suffering. Not all or even the majority of instances result in recourse to diagnosis, however. The Jalaris respond to most forms of suffering by treating them as unremarkable aspects of everyday life. The prevailing attitude is one of confidence rather than despair, of denial rather than exhibition. Despite this, Jalaris are quick to resort to complicated divinatory strategies when conditions warrant. Prototypic conditions include illness and the failure to catch fish.

Three criteria are recognized as relevant for deciding on divinatory recourse: situation, magnitude, and duration. Another variable, the developmental phase of the family considering divination, is not something the Jalaris themselves recognize, and will be discussed later. Situation is the most important of the three criteria the Jalaris consider. It includes the age, sex, and social status of the affected person or persons, i.e., in the event of illness, of the patient, and in the event of poor fishing, of the group of men who fish together. For example, a low-grade fever that persists for several days does not call for divination if the sufferer is old and thus subject to frequent incapacitations or is already in such poor health that additional ailments are expected. However, a low-grade fever that lasts even a few hours in a young man or pregnant woman will cause great alarm and immediate divinatory inquiry. Persons in these two categories are considered especially valuable and therefore vulnerable to spiritual attack.

Illnesses which do not meet the criteria for identification as spirit-related disorders are classified as *jabbu* (illness) and are assumed to be curable by modern medical means. The Jalaris identify illnesses as medically treatable until the patient's social situation strongly suggests that the magnitude or duration of his ailment is spirit-related. A spirit-related disorder is classified as *ammavari jabbu* (goddess illness) and specific diagnostic and curative strategies are initiated.

Causal explanations are constructed following this progression:
The identification of
1. Manifest symptoms (illness or poor fishing) and
2. Efficient causes (spirit attacks) and precipitating causes (social disruptions) leads to recourse to
3. Primary divination (pulse or seeing-stone) and
4. Secondary divination (seeing-stone, *kaniki*).

After provisional definition of an event as spirit-related, a *dasudu* (shaman) is called to perform one of two types of primary divination. The first, *nadi cudadam* (seeing the pulse), diagnoses the manifest symptoms and identifies the efficient causes of physical illness. The second, *cupa rayi cupincadam* (showing the seeing-stone), diagnoses the manifest symptoms and identifies the efficient causes of poor fishing. Manifest symptoms are evident and obvious, such as a high fever or an inordinately low number of fish caught over some period of time. Efficient causes are those which are proximal to (i.e., spatially and temporally contiguous with) the manifest symptoms. Efficient causes are always household spirits, either the victim's or someone else's. Pulse and seeing-stone divinations identify attacking spirits and their proximal reasons for attacking.

Primary Divination and Efficient Causes

Pulse and seeing-stone divinations take place in the house of the client and his family. An important difference between them reflects the unequal status of personal ailments over group loss. Pulse divination is performed in the house in which the patient actually resides, in the *gadillu* (room house). Seeing-stone divination is performed in the *peddillu* (big house), the ritual center of a patrilineal group and residence both of the patrilineal spirits and of the group's current leader (either a father, a widowed mother, or an elder brother). Since personal illness affects only the patient and his immediate family (*kutumbamu*), it is sufficient and preferable that only the patient and his family members are involved in the divination. Poor fishing, on the other hand, affects more than one household, as the senior male members (usually brothers) of a patrilineal group go fishing together. In this case, because the entire group is involved, the search for efficient causes takes place in their common ritual center ánd at a time when all can be present.

Nadi Cudadam (seeing the pulse)

Household members call the *dasudu* to come to their house to examine the ill person. The patient assumes no particular posture and may be involved in activities unrelated to the divination (eating, sleeping, sewing, talking, etc.). The *dasudu* sits near the patient but asks no questions concerning the onset and symptoms of the illness. Family members may volunteer information, from the kinds of medical treatment used to the progress of the illness, but such information is brief and receives no acknowledgment from the *dasudu*. The spirits he communicates with, not the human beings present, are the ones who should reveal the facts of the case.

The *dasudu* holds the patient's left hand by the wrist, pressing his left thumb against it to detect the arterial pulse, then invokes the goddesses and spirits of the dead, asking each to confirm or disconfirm its role as the immediate agent of the patient's condition. Questions are actually complex narratives that link multiple propositions as one interrogatory statement. In pulse divination, a distinctive quickening of the pulse confirms the spirit's activity. Disconfirmation of the household spirits' role forces the *dasudu* to consider the role of outside spirits (*pai ammavallu*) and to look for confirmation from them. In the event that these spirits also deny involvement, the *dasudu* concludes that the illness is a *daktar jabbu* (doctor illness) and advises the patient's family to seek further medical treatment or to do nothing.

Confirmation that a particular spirit has attacked concludes the strictly diagnostic portion of the divination and initiates a segment devoted to prediction. The *dasudu* asks for money, ties it into a cloth bundle and holds it up as he reinvokes the goddesses. He tells the spirits that this money is a *mudupu*, a symbol of the intention to make offerings. The family will make these offerings only after all signs of illness abate within a set period of time. The *mudupu* is buried outside the house at a secret location to prevent someone from taking money that is designated for the spirits. The pulse divination concludes when a family member (usually the senior man or woman) takes the bundle outside and buries it.

Cupa rayi cupincadam (showing the seeing-stone)

Selection of the seeing-stone presupposes a recent decline in the fish catch for a group of fishermen who are related as brothers. The format of the seeing-stone differs from that of pulse divination. First, the constituent families of the patrilineal group attend and pay close attention to the process. Unlike with pulse divination, they participate by advising and instructing the *dasudu* and by discussing their own interpretations. Second, the divination takes place in the spirit room (*ammavari gadi*) near the shrine (*sadaru*) of the big house where patriline spirits are worshiped. This intensifies the association between the event (poor fishing) and the group to which that event is relevant. Third, there is a different emphasis on proof (*rujuvu*). The swinging of the stone in the *dasudu*'s hand indicates the spirits' responses but also validates them by providing visible evidence of what they are. The changed emphasis from seeing (*cudadam*) to showing (*cupincadam*), from observation to demonstration, is important. Patriline members as a whole must accept the outcome of the divination. "Showing" makes consensus possible.

The *dasudu* enters the *ammavari gadi* (goddess room) and sits opposite the shrine, surrounded on the remaining three sides by family members. In his left hand he holds a long string, from which the seeing-stone is suspended. His left wrist rests on his raised left knee, and the stone hangs almost to the floor. The spirits he invokes are believed to travel from their dwelling places to this stone and stand on it. In his right hand he holds a piece of tumeric root (*pasupu kommu*). Spirits are attracted by tumeric, and the root is used to draw them onto the stone. There the spirits indicate their responses to the *dasudu*'s questions by moving the stone back and forth, the degree of movement being understood as an indication of the intensity of the spirits' replies. Swinging signals a positive response; the absence of swinging, a negative one.

The *dasudu*'s questions contain multiple propositions, as in pulse divination. This is in contrast with the *kaniki* form of divination, in which questions can be asked and answered only one by one. When the *dasudu* completes a question and the spirit answers by making the stone swing, the *dasudu* stops the stone by cupping it with the hand holding the tumeric root. He then repeats the process with a new question. There can be

Dasudu and his wife

as many as fifty questions and answers in a typical thirty-minute session. When the *dasudu* completes the diagnostic phase, he uses the same technique to predict future events, conditional on the promise to make offerings if the spirits stop attacking. A few coins are gathered together, tied into a *mudupu*, and buried by a senior family member at a secret location outside the house. The participants expect the results to be evident in the next day's fishing expedition.

The Aftermath of Primary Divination

The outcome of primary divination is the identification of attacking spirits, either the victim's own or someone else's, paralleling, in spiritual terms, the dialectical alternatives (agnatic or affinal) of the cultural system. If the spirits are the victim's own household spirits, people infer that they attacked because family relations are too disrupted to permit offerings to be made. Invariably, all attention focuses on the brothers, whose solidarity (or lack thereof) measures and marks the integrity of the patriline itself. If the spirits are someone else's, people infer that the spirits attacked because relations between the victim's household and the household of the attacking spirits are strained. In the prototypical instance, this means that relations between groups allied through cross-cousin marriages are disturbed, and since these marriages are governed by cross-siblings, attacks by outside goddesses must signify a disruption in the relations between brothers and sisters.

If manifest symptoms subside during the period stipulated by the *dasudu,* the affected individuals conclude that the diagnosis was correct, that the efficient causes (the attacking spirits) were identified, and that the spirits' proximal reasons for attacking have been revealed. But they do not make the promised offerings. First they consider the event's precipitating causes through secondary divination.

The reason they do not consider efficient and precipitating causes all at the same time and by means of one divination is that a successful primary divination is supposed to result in the immediate reduction of symptoms by means that are simple and readily available. This is true in two ways. Pulse and seeing-stone divination are easy to arrange and to conceal. Both are performed on demand, without prior arrangement, and in the privacy of individual houses. Spirits, moreover, are assumed to be tractable. The *dasudu* is supposed to promise them offerings, and the spirits are supposed to accept them and stop attacking. Attention is focused on restoring the sick person to health or the fish catch to its previous levels. Because Jalaris do not have to probe further at the preliminary stage to achieve these results, they do not. Only after the success validates primary diagnosis do they inquire further into precipitating social causes.

Secondary Divination and Precipitating Causes

Precipitating events are understood to stem from disruptions within and between households. Disruptions most often occur when households reach a certain stage in their development. This is especially true when affinal or agnatic relations become strained, because these relations are intrinsically problematic and paradoxical. As a result, the patrilineal group fissions and new groups form, repeating the whole process.

Jalari family relations are cross-cut by two axes which are both internally as well as mutually contradictory. The first is the agnatic axis and refers to relations between male patriline members, prototypically brothers. Within this axis, the desire to maintain unity contradicts the equally powerful desire to separate and create the nuclei of separate patrilineal groups. The second is the affinal axis and refers to relations between groups allied through cross-cousin marriage, represented prototypically in the relations between married brothers and sisters whose children become marriage partners. Within this axis, the desire to maintain particular alliance relations is contradicted by competition between affines. Agnatic and affinal ties are extremely difficult to maintain, a fact all Jalaris quickly point out. The problem is worsened by the fact that agnatic and affinal relations also conflict with each other: Every success in maintaining agnatic relations comes at the expense (so it is believed) of relations among affines, and vice versa. Yet Jalari norms emphasize the importance of success in both. This is the set of paradoxes which is at the heart of Jalari culture.

In a mature family with children at marriageable age, tensions on both axes, agnatic and affinal, are likely to be strong. Disruptions on one axis usually exacerbate those on the other. A powerful negative synergy sets in. Problems escalate to the point that when a misfortune occurs it immediately triggers an explosion of accusations, some directed internally to the fraternal cohort and some directed outside to married siblings and affinal households. This is readily apparent in the divinatory session, as clients switch back and forth between diagnostic scenarios, investigating which one (agnatic or affinal) is responsible for the event in question.

The goal of secondary divination is to identify and address these social factors. It cannot be achieved without the painstaking development of a complex argument structure, because a satisfactory divination is one that generates an argument convincing enough to make people do something. Without a good argument structure, people cannot be persuaded to rethink their social relations and, if necessary, to adjust them to avoid future spirit attacks.

Cupa rayi cupincadam (showing the seeing-stone)
What most distinguishes the seeing-stone is its emphasis on identifying and describing the precipitating social causes, which Jalari causal thinking always attributes to either agnatic or affinal relations. It limits potential causes to situations more or less remediable by the unilateral actions of the client. The client's goal with the seeing-stone divination is not to alter the precipitating social situation but to restore it to the status quo that prevailed before the spirit's attack. Situations are judged suitable for seeing-stone divination according to social distance and social tension.

Distance is defined in terms of near people (*daggara vallu; kavalasina vallu*) and far people (*pai vallu*). Near people are those to whom one is related agnatically, as brothers. Far people are those to whom one is related by actual or potential marriage. Tension refers to the extent to which the social relations are strained. It is marked by the client's choice of divinatory form. Key indicators are *kopam* (anger) and *matladadam* (talking). The presence of anger is signaled by the absence of talking and signifies increased tension.

The greater the social distance, the greater the likelihood that the other form of secondary divination, *kaniki,* will be chosen. The less the social distance, the more likely that the client will choose the seeing-stone. Because relations among near people are supposed to be amicable, every effort is made to settle disputes peacefully and out of public view. Secondary divinations are made by means of the seeing-stone, which maximizes the potential for preserving amicable relations and reducing outside involvement. Relations among far people, on the other hand, are characterized by mutual suspicion. In cases involving affines, divinatory clients want the public proof and verification that only the *kaniki* can provide. An emphasis still exists on preserving relations, but the potential for permanent disruption is recognized.

Tension usually depends on social distance, but high tension among near people (agnatic household kin) may override other considerations and stimulate recourse to *kaniki* instead of the seeing-stone. Such cases usually involve brothers, who inevitably break away from the natal patriline and start their own units. The formation of new units is a public act. Consequently, publicly observed and validated divinatory practices, like *kaniki,* are associated with disputes among agnates.

Kaniki

When the client wants to repair damaged social relations, he picks the seeing-stone, but when his objective is to alter social relations to reflect new interests and aspirations, he chooses *kaniki.* Structurally, *kaniki* is not very different from the seeing-stone divination, but it more rigorously specifies and tests the logical links between actions and events. That is why the arguments constructed in the *kaniki* look like highly technical legal briefs suitable for presentation in a court of law. The client uses the argument he constructs in *kaniki* not to conciliate but to persuade his opponents and the whole community that his position is valid. His goal is to win, to restore damaged social relations on his own terms, or to sever those relations permanently.

The *kaniki* performer is a non-Jalari man or woman who lives outside the Jalari village. The Jalaris go to him or her in groups of three or four, usually including the client, his *dasudu,* various family members, and a member of the village whose honesty and integrity is beyond question. The trustworthy person serves as a witness, to attest to the results of the divinatory inquiry. The diviner sits facing the *dasudu* and his clients with a winnowing basket (*ceta*) in front of her. It contains a brass pot filled with water. The client hands her a bag of rice of about a kilogram, which she empties into the basket; she then pushes the grains into a heap. Then she chants a prayer to her chief tutelary deity to assist her. She takes a coin from the client and drops it into the water-filled vessel as an offering to this deity. At the end of her prayer, she takes three small handfuls of rice and drops them in rapid succession into the water, then remains silent. Her only role is to drop handfuls of rice into the vessel while the Jalari *dasudu* asks from forty to seventy questions addressed to the household spirits of the client or of those the client suspects. Whereas in pulse and seeing-stone divination questions are presented in narrative chunks, here they are asked one by one. This makes it possible for the *dasudu* to be much more precise. As the *dasudu* finishes a question, the client hands the rice back to the performer, who drops it into the vessel. If the rice floats, the spirit has answered no, and if it sinks, the spirit has answered yes.

The *kaniki* achieves validity in several ways. First, it is public and therefore open to observation and scrutiny. The more the observers attesting to its validity, the more the legitimacy of the argument structure is enhanced. This is especially important when the division of a patrilineal group is possible, since the community must acknowledge and approve the creation of new groups. Second, *kaniki* is more precise because the format (a series of yes-or-no questions) requires inquiries that are straightforward and precise. Third, *kaniki* is seen as trustworthy, because the roles of investigator and manipulator are divided between the Jalari *dasudu* and the non-Jalari *kaniki* performer, and because of the presence of outside observers. This adds a degree of objectivity (inherent in the Jalari concept of *rujuvu*, "proof") that is absent and unnecessary in the other three modes of Jalari divination.

Despite its greater precision, completeness, and objectivity, *kaniki* is used only as a last resort. Its ultimate effectiveness rests in its ability to rally community support for the client, but this runs the risk either of not working (the community may reject the argument structure) or of permanently damaging relations with the opponent. Just as the rewards are high, so are the potential dangers. There is some indication that the Jalaris used *kaniki* less frequently in the past than they do now. Modern trends have encouraged greater individualism, as with young men who prematurely try to start their own patrilineal units. The trend encourages greater willingness to risk social solidarity.

Pati

Possession mediumship is common throughout South Asia, but its role in Jalari society differs because of its position at a particular stage in the divinatory process. *Pati* occupies an ancillary position (Nuckolls 1991b, 1991c) intermediate between the primary and secondary forms. It is an advisory forum whose main function is to work out tentative hypotheses before they are submitted for rigorous scrutiny by methods that are productive of visible and verifiable proof, e.g., seeing-stone and *kaniki*.

*Dasudu*s and *kaniki* performers never come into direct contact with the spirits. In pulse divination, for example, spirits signal their presence to the *dasudu* by causing the patient's pulse to quicken. With the seeing-stone, spirits respond by standing on the stone to make it swing. The *kaniki* performer entices the spirits to come and to cause the rice grains to float or sink. Only the *pati* practitioner is possessed by the spirits he/she invokes. They "sit" on his/her head, and in that position the spirits, not the *pati*, answer questions and suggest interpretations. The goal is to satisfy the client's need for assurance that the interpretation he has formulated makes sense, seems valid, and provides resolution of the underlying problem.

The preponderance of women among the *pati*'s clientele can be explained by a sexual division of labor in divinatory matters. Men take already formed hypotheses for divination by methods which are evidentiary. Men's divination (the phrase is mine, not the Jalari's), like the *kaniki*, produces proof through argumentation which Jalari men hope will be persuasive to others. Women, on the other hand, take unformed hypotheses for divination by methods which are exploratory. Women's divination (again, my own phrase) generates assurance, not proof, the purpose of which is not to persuade others, but to convince the client and her family that they are on the right track. The two styles are complementary, since men send their wives to *pati* with tentative hypotheses which, depending on the *pati*'s outcome, they then submit as fully formed arguments in the seeing-stone or the *kaniki*.

Whereas in other forms of divination the practitioner submits questions to the spirits and the spirits confirm or disconfirm, roles are reversed in *pati*. Here the spirits speak and formulate hypotheses, while the client confirms or disconfirms their relevance to the case. In some ways the *pati* resembles a psychotherapy session in which the therapist suggests interpretations for the patient to respond to and consider. *Pati* also appears to have therapeutic effects. In the course of a session a client who entered confused and

Pati

upset grows excited, often cries, and sometimes falls unconscious. Sooner or later, the spirits' interpretations elicit the client's assent. She departs and returns to the village with an explanation of her case that is satisfying to her, laying the groundwork for whatever remedial action she will take.

Pati's take place in the houses of the possession mediums, in an area set aside for the worship of spirits. Spirit idols and ritual paraphernalia are placed on a shrine, the form of which varies among individual mediums. The medium faces the shrine, not her clients, and addresses herself initially to the deities which the shrine contains. These are her tutelary deities, usually goddesses or the spirits of her own recently deceased children. The session begins when the medium occupies a sitting or fully prone position on the floor, her head toward the *sadaru*. In a slow, rhythmical chant the medium invokes her tutelary deities. Soon, one or more of these spirits possess (*digu*, lit. "descend onto") her and speak through her voice to the client seated nearby.

The possessing spirit's first task is to establish the names of the client's household spirits. The spirit does this by trial and error, listing likely names for household goddesses and deceased family members. Clients always indicate through their verbal interjections when the medium correctly identifies them. Once the names are assembled, the medium's tutelary spirit invokes the household spirits of the client, using verbal formulas essentially no different from the *dasudu*'s with pulse, seeing-stone, and *kaniki* divinations. These spirits replace the medium's tutelary deity as the possessing agents. From then on, the client is in direct communication with her own and other family's household spirits.

Pati divination follows a pattern that should now be familiar. First the spirits identify efficient causes. Did the client neglect to make offerings? If not, are another family's goddesses suspected of attacking? The client indicates by her verbal and nonverbal responses what she thinks, even though she may not be able to formulate her suspicions by herself. Then the spirits ask more detailed questions about precipitating causes. Did she neglect the offerings because others in the family would not cooperate? Each time the client answers she supplies additional information. The spirits use it to narrow the range of possibilities until they have constructed a complete causal account, linking precipitating social conditions to efficient spirit-related causes, thus generating a plausible explanation.

Explanations constructed in *pati* are always highly contingent. If, they state, the client will act thus, certain events will follow. *Pati* is an advisory forum; the method is exploratory, not evidentiary. Clients do not seek proof but want specific recommendations on how to act toward others, how to overcome specific social difficulties, and how to avoid, if possible, taking the matter all the way to *kaniki*.

Divination in the Jalari village is frequent. Of the village's 549 households, almost three-quarters had recourse to at least one of the four forms of divination in the previous year. It is not that Jalaris suffer often from forms of distress they define as spirit-related. Divination is the principal means by which people alleviate suffering and organize responses to social change. An incidence of illness or poor fishing is trivial in itself unless it occurs against a certain background, when it then triggers immediate recourse to divination. Once the social precipitant is identified, the result is either a return to the social relationships of status quo ante or the transformation of those relationships. Early in household development, during the first crisis moment, it tends to be the former. Later, during the second crisis moment, it tends to the latter. Relations are severed and new patrilineal groups are constituted. At both moments, tension between competing agnatic and affinal demands exists and helps direct the process of family development. The ontology of suffering and the mechanism of social change are thus closely connected in divination.

KNOWLEDGE STRUCTURES AND DIVINATORY CLASSIFICATION

Knowledge structures in Jalari divination are storylike scenarios and represent the prototypical causes of everyday distress. They are few in number and highly generalized, not unlike the stereotypic scenarios of Ndembu divination which embrace "the whole sorry story of misfortune, loss, and death in Ndembu life and of the mean, selfish and revengeful motives believed to be responsible for these afflictions" (Turner 1975:216). Cases are mapped onto these scenarios, with case-specific details either assimilated directly, because they conform, or selectively distorted in order to achieve a fit. Divinatory scenarios are kinship-based and focus on disruptions in agnatic or affinal relations (precipitating causes) that lead to attacks by inside or outside goddesses (efficient causes). Any particular divinatory session will consist of both, instantiated to some degree of detail in order to find out which one applies to the case at hand.

The goal of primary divination is the discovery of efficient causes, which are always attacks by spirits, either one's own or someone else's. Two knowledge structures, which I term "primary scripts," are available. Scripts are episodic and hierarchical, like stories which can be told at a higher level of generality, the level of "scenes," or at a lower level of generality, the level of "episodes," depending on the level of detail desired. The first primary script is the "inside spirit attack" script (ISA). It represents the series of higher-order scenes and lower-order episodes which culminate in an attack by one's own household spirits—prototypically the spirits of the agnatic group. The second primary script is the "outside spirit attack" script (OSA). It represents the series of scenes and episodes which culminate in an attack by someone else's household spirits—prototypically the spirits of affinally related households.

An initial divination does not require an elaborate argument structure. Its purpose is simply to alleviate symptoms (illness or bad fishing) and not to develop persuasive explanations addressed to precipitating social situations. The *dasudu* therefore instantiates primary scripts, both "inside" and "outside," *only* at the higher level of abstraction, the level of scenes. His goal is simply to establish the identity of the attacking spirits and their proximal reasons for attacking. In secondary divination, where detailed and persuasive arguments are needed, the *dasudu* instantiates the two scripts at their lower, episodic levels. He also employs two new, "secondary" scripts, to determine the social precipitants of the spirits' attack.

The purpose of secondary divination is to build an argument structure convincing enough to motivate resolution of precipitating social disputes, either agnatic or affinal. Of course, such resolutions are always temporary at best. Primary scripts explain only the efficient causes. In secondary divination, the *dasudu* tests and verifies primary scripts by elaborating their constituent episodes and by confirming the links that bind them together in a causal chain. That is important to reconfirming their applicability, but the real focus is on secondary scripts, since these provide the frameworks for understanding precipitating social causes.

Not surprisingly, Jalaris recognize two, and only two, sources of social dispute as prototypic precipitants of spiritual attack: 1) *the agnatic group,* composed of male patriline members, prototypically brothers; and 2) *the affinal group,* composed prototypically of married brothers and sisters whose lineages maintain cross-cousin alliance relationships with each other. Disputes are outcomes of conflictual situations which arise (predictably and inevitably) within and between relations of these two groups. Since the norms governing each necessarily conflict, both internally and mutually, such disputes must arise at various points in family development. The frequency of disputes means that divination is a routine occurrence.

As we have seen, disputes in agnatic groups occur when younger men marry and again when their children approach marriageable age. Because each of these two passages intensifies each agnate's desire to create his own, independent patrilineal group, disputes arise at precisely those points when joint actions are essential, e.g., in offering to household spirits. Among affinally related groups, similar crises develop when joint responsibilities arise, as in the exchange of money and in the making of cross-cousin marriage alliances. The paradoxes of patrilineality and alliance—agnation and affinality—are the axes of Jalari kinship and the determining nexus of the social disputes which culminate in spirit attacks.

There are two secondary scripts (see Nuckolls 1991a for a detailed description). One is the "agnatic script" and the other is the "affinal script." They describe the prototypic ways agnatic and affinal relations go awry. A choice must be made between them in secondary divination, just as in primary divination a choice must be made between "inside spirit attack" and "outside spirit attack" scripts. Where do such scripts come from and what makes them compelling as alternative explanations?

The answer is cultural paradox. Opposing normative values embedded in the kinship system make it inevitable that conflicts will arise and that choices between competing values be made. There are two dialectical axes. One is the axis of agnatic solidarity. As agnates par excellence, brothers value unity but desire to act separately of each other. How can they do both? This is the source of a cultural ambivalence which finds expression in repeated attempts at divinatory resolution. The other is the axis of affinal solidarity. Married brothers and sisters are affines par excellence, and desire unity. But they find it difficult to meet each other's needs as partners trading both in goods (fish) and in people (their own children as cross-cousin marriage partners). Again, how can they do both?

The two axes conflict, internally as well as between each other, and give rise to a series of disputes which the divinatory system attempts to resolve. Divination can do that, certainly, but only temporarily, by deciding a case in favor of one axis or the other (agnatic or affinal) and then in favor of continued unity or separation. It all boils down to a two-step decision process:

—Step one: Agnatic or affinal?

—Step two: Agnatic unity or separation? / Affinal unity or separation?

Whatever decision is made, the solution cannot escape provoking another crisis that eventually will make similar decisions necessary in the future, culminating ultimately in the decision to separate.

The agnatic script is related to the ISA script as an enabling condition and describes the circumstances which must occur to initiate an attack by inside spirits, the spirits of one's own agnatic household. Disruptions between agnates occur in diverse contexts, since fraternal relations are complex and multifaceted. But this complexity converges in one culturally recognized scenario, involving the transgression of agnatic norms. Such transgressions occur when individual patriline members, prototypically brothers, express interests which diverge from the interests of the group. There are two common instances: 1) when male patriline members marry and set up independent dwellings; and 2) when male patriline members have children and the children approach marriageable age. Of course, problems can (and do) come up at any time. The point is that such problems are more likely to receive divinatory attention when they arise during these moments. Then they will be assimilated to the standardized action scenarios, or scripts.

In the first instance, senior agnates divide their residences. The father or, if he is dead, the oldest son remains in the patrilineal "big house" (*peddillu*) where meals are cooked and the patrilineal spirits worshiped. Younger sons move out and set up "room houses" (*gadillu*s), which are either physically part of the "big house" (separated from it by partitions) or satellite structures built nearby. The family remains joint, however, as "birds of a single branch"—the Jalari way of saying that even though they live separately, brothers still together as members of the same patrilineal group (*doddi*), eating, working, and worshiping together.

In the second instance of crisis, a few years later, members divide completely and establish their own patrilines around their own, independent "big houses." Patriline units consisting of more than three living adult generations are virtually unheard of. Fission is natural and bound to occur, but that does not mean brothers actually want it. In a sense, of course, they do, but at the same time they express deep longing for the nurturance of the joint family, and try to preserve it as long as they can.

Before a crisis produces fission, a state of relations exists which I term "breach" but which the Jalaris describe in more interesting language, referring to "birds who have flown away, each to a separate tree." "Birds" are male patriline members and "trees" are their separate houses. The problem is that they find it difficult as brothers to join together in fulfilling their collective duties. Inevitably this state of affairs culminates in the failure to contribute to the goddess money. Members become reluctant to contribute, either on time or in full measure, as their disaffection from the patriline grows. Sufficient money for the offerings cannot be collected, with the result, of course, that a state of offertory neglect ensues. This state triggers the inside spirit attack sequence, culminating in an attack by the inside spirits and the attack's observed effect (poor fishing or illness).

The affinal script exists as an enabling condition to the outside spirit attack script. Disrupted affinal relations occur in a variety of contexts. Prototypically, they all converge in one relation (brother and sister) and in one situation (the transaction of cross-cousin marriage obligations). Adult brothers and sisters have two sets of obligations to each other. The first is the obligation to take and receive material goods from each other. In practice, this becomes the basis for an important business relationship, since a Jalari man's sister is his most significant trading partner. The second obligation between brothers and sisters is the obligation to make and maintain marriage alliances between their children.

In everyday life, obligations (both financial and matrimonial) are transgressed. Jalaris all readily agree that brothers and sisters' business transactions—often involving buying and selling on credit—may undermine the unity of the patriline. It is easy to see how. Brothers tend to invest their funds separately among their sisters and not in their conjugal or joint families. Family members (especially wives) resent this and encourage the men to break them off. Brothers, meanwhile, attempt to satisfy their sisters' and family members' conflicting demands, with the result that no one ends up feeling satisfied.

Other pressures specific to affinality undermine the creation and preservation of alliance relationships. Siblings compete with each other for their children's marriage partners. In this contest, someone will be disappointed.

In recent years, a few individuals have decided not to marry cross-cousins at all. This has led to even greater tension between brothers and sisters, who feel increasingly helpless in their own families and resentful of the situation created by the helplessness of others.

Disappointment, either in the context of material transaction or marital alliance, constitutes the state of breach in relation to the norms governing the prototypic affinal script. This realizes the state of social offense, to which siblings respond with an emotional state analogous to anger (*kopam*). This is already familiar from our discussion of the outside spirit attack script. The spirits of the offended sibling rush to the house of the offender and attack a member of his family, initiating the sequence of events which culminate in (1) divinatory recourse, (2) the construction of an explanatory account, and (3) the (temporary) resolution of the precipitating dispute.

It might seem that Jalari divination is simply a matter of stringing a bunch of scripts together. But divination is not a rote process. The real work of divination is not to instantiate scripts but to build argument structures convincing enough to motivate social change, to achieve temporary resolutions in the conflicts that arise predictably from the paradoxes of Jalari kinship.

THE DIALECTIC OF THE BROTHERS

Of all the normative obligations a Jalari man must try to fulfill, one of the most important is the obligation to protect and preserve the patrilineal group into which he was born. This is not a situation unique to Jalari culture, or to South India. One finds it throughout South Asia and probably everywhere a "patrilineal ideology" (Lévi-Strauss 1985) exists. Jalari men express their adherence to the ideology in repeated references to themselves as "birds of a single nest" and to the group they constitute as their "nest." They enjoy listing the advantages such a group possesses. The greater its size, and the more cohesive it is, the richer its members both in terms of material assets and social prestige. When I asked what would constitute the ideal patrilineal group (*doddi*), in terms of size, no one could think of an upper limit. The bigger the better, they said, and their actions, most of the time, did not belie their words.

Brothers must uphold the value of the group's integrity, and know that by doing so they inevitably lead to the group's destruction through division into subgroups, the nuclei of new patrilineal groupings. The Jalaris are not the only patrilineally organized people to experience the force of this paradox. As Murphy (1971) points out, the problems of patriliny are paradoxes which in many places create and sustain social dialectics. What is interesting is what they have done with it, dialectically, in the building up of cultural institutions such as myth and divination. On this point I agree with Lévi-Strauss in assigning to the structures of kinship a central role in constituting cultural knowledge systems. In fact, I would go further. Kinship structures are sometimes deeply paradoxical, and some cultures have chosen to elaborate these paradoxes dialectically, in the form of knowledge systems such as myth and divination.

In the evolution of a patrilineal group, crises will erupt which at certain times prompt the members of the group to seek resolutions in the form of divinatory explanations. Uniting all such crises is the paradox which is central to the patrilineal ideology itself. The group must remain united, but it cannot, therefore it must divide to form new groups, which repeat the process. Divinations interrupt this process, providing temporary respites, but they do not cause it to stop. To look in any detail at a divination performed during the periodic crises of patrilineality is to see the process at a particular moment in its evolution. In some cases, the group is nearing the point of division but has not reached it. There are still a few more crises to go. The divination arrests the process, providing a sort of breathing space and preserving the family for a while longer. But in such moments the tensions which will cause the same crises to erupt again are evident.

In the following case studies, I shall focus on the *kaniki* form of divination. It provides richer contextual detail because it tends to be very detailed. It has to be detailed to be convincing. Information that is otherwise assumed or highly compressed is given expression in the *kaniki,* which makes it useful to the observer who wants to know how the arguments developed in divination actually work.

The typical *kaniki* consists of diagnostic and predictive sections, in which the *dasudu* considers the causes of events and the effects of proposed remedies. The first section is always predictive. It requires the spirits to confirm that they will correctly identify the attacking agents in the inquiries to follow. The second section is largely retrospective and repeats the initial pulse divination to reconfirm that efficient causes (attacking spirits) were identified and that proposed remedies (offerings to the attacking spirits) were accepted. Then the *dasudu* investigates precipitating causes, to determine which of the opposed axes, agnation or affinality, is the locus of the dispute. In the *kaniki* this is where all the action is. He calls up the two secondary scripts, agnatic and affinal, and tests their applicability to the case at hand. Careful attention is paid to ruling out alternative scenarios. Once that is done, and the social precipitants of the attack are identified, the *dasudu* concludes with a final section devoted to prediction. He asks the spirits to confirm that if certain social adjustments take place, laying to rest the precipitating crisis, the spirits will not attack again. That concludes the divination.

Depending on the kind of case, one or the other of these two sections (diagnosis or prediction) may assume special prominence. In a case where the social precipitants of an event are contested, more time may be spent in diagnosis. On the other hand, if the course of action to be taken is in doubt and various alternatives for corrective action exist, more time may be spent in the predictive section.

Within each section, phases exist in which the *dasudu* and others address specific topics. For example, the *dasudu* might devote special attention to confirming or disconfirming the applicability of the inside spirit attack script. Or the observers, in considering some fine point of logic or protocol, might request that a question be resubmitted, revised, or abandoned altogether. Typically, the phases are marked by the conversations which precede and follow them, in which observers comment on the success or failure of their inferential strategies.

Inferential strategies have to do with the ways a *dasudu* and others ask questions of the spirits. Some questions are simple and direct, as in, "Did you attack him?" Other questions are more complex and may be framed as conditionals ("When he didn't offer, did you attack?") or as counterfactuals ("If he had offered, then you would not have attacked?"). The *dasudu*'s choices are constrained by the kind of divination he performs and by his divinatory goals. In the pulse diagnosis, for example, complex argument structures are not required. The *dasudu* does not wait for the spirit to respond to individual propositions but presents many propositions at the same time, in a "chunk," to which the spirit responds as a group. In the *kaniki,* by contrast, the purpose of the argument structure (to motivate social change) and the constraint of the divinatory format (a series of discrete yes-or-no questions) allow for and require more intricate strategies. Among these are the following:

1. The *dasudu* can run a script forward, from cause to effect, or backwards, from effect to cause.
2. The *dasudu* can test separate propositions ("Did you attack him?") or link multiple propositions to test their relationship to each other ("Did you attack because he did not offer?").
3. The *dasudu* can test multiple propositions by asking relational questions conditionally or counterfactually. For example
   Conditional question: When he failed to offer, did you attack him?

Counterfactual question: If he had not failed to offer, would you have attacked him?
If, for example, the ISA script applies, the spirit should answer "yes" to the first question and "no" to the second. That lends credibility to the argument.
4. The *dasudu* can emphasize particular events by asking the spirit to confirm them either several times or through several different formats. This makes them appear especially prominent in the causal chain.
A *dasudu*'s skill is determined by his ability to manipulate these strategies as he assembles an argument structure favorable to his client's position.

THE CASE OF AGNATIC CONFLICT: TEDDI AMMORI
AND HIS BROTHERS

Teddi Ammori's wife, Papamma, was pregnant and had a fever. Fevers in late pregnancy are almost always signs of spiritual attack, so Ammori called a *dasudu* to perform a pulse diagnosis (*nadi cudadam*) and identify the efficient cause. The diagnosis revealed that Ammori's household goddesses were afflicting his wife. The goddesses were angry because Ammori and his brothers had not performed the annual patrilineal goddess festivals. Since the inside spirit attack (ISA) script applied, the *dasudu* accepted its implications as valid. He promised on the family's behalf to make offerings to the attacking household goddesses when Papamma recovered.

Papamma's condition worsened and Ammori rushed her to a hospital, where she was given antibiotics. Ammori returned to the village and conferred with the *dasudu*. They reviewed the diagnosis and decided that other spirits, probably the spirits of recently dead family members, had blocked the *dasudu*'s homage to the goddesses. The ancestors' interference *in effect* constituted another form of attack on Ammori's family. Ammori inferred that the ancestors were angry for two reasons. First, the family had not performed their final obsequies, including the large funeral feast to which the whole village must be invited. Second, Ammori and the *dasudu* had promised offerings to the household goddesses, but not to the ancestors. The ancestors therefore felt jealous of the goddesses and blocked their receipt of the promisory homages. All spirits are capable of blocking offerings to each other. The *dasudu* agreed with Ammori's assessment and paid homage to the dead, promising to perform the necessary ceremonies as soon as Papamma recovered.

Within a few hours Papamma delivered a healthy son. Ammori began to plan the performance of the ancestors' funerary rituals, to fulfill his side of the bargain. But he was immediately thwarted by Bujayya, his younger brother, who refused to participate. Without Bujayya's participation, the rites could not be performed. At that point Ammori decided to go to the *kaniki*. In fact, he went twice: The first time to prove that offerings to the spirits must be done and the second time to prove that Bujayya must participate in making those offerings.

Background to the Case

Teddi Ammori is a member of the Teddi clan, one of the largest in the village. He is *pedda* or "head" of a large group of five constituent families, including his own. More than three generations ago the ancestor of this patriline had two sons. The two sons lived together for some time and then divided their residences. They remained joint, however, and continued to identify themselves with on *peddillu* (the house where the lineage head lives and where the household spirits are worshiped). Their sons continued the process of residential division, and each built his own *gadillu* (room house). The last surviving member of that generation was Jampayya, Ammori's *pedda nana* (lit. "older father," elder paternal uncle), who preceded Ammori as *pedda*.

There are now five constituent families (*kutumbamus*) under Ammori's lineage headship. The first is Ammori's own family. It is the "senior" family and Ammori, therefore, is head of the patriline even though he is chronologically junior to several other men (including Bujayya). The second is the family of Ammori's father's younger brother's deceased son, Parasanna (also called Parasa), and includes Parasanna's widow and six living children. Parasanna's family is under the care of Bujayya, whose own nuclear family constitutes the third group and includes his wife and three living daughters. Parasanna and Bujayya were sons of the same mother but different fathers. The fourth group is that of Jampayya's deceased older brother and his family. Finally, there is the deceased Jampayya's own family.

Ammori's patrilineal group, his *doddi,* consists of families whose male heads are mature men in their late thirties. They live separately from each other, in independent *gadillu*s. Ammori occupies the *peddillu* with his family. Constituent families are nearing a period of social crisis when fissiparous pressures threaten to divide the patriline and reconstitute it as separate patrilineal units. The case described here illustrates this process, as well as how the internal dialectic of fraternal relations (unity against separation) works itself out, in this case by preserving patrilineal unity.

Let us consider first an episode from the patriline's history: the relationship between the now deceased Jampayya, former head of the group, and

Parasa, also deceased. Many years ago Jampayya and Parasa quarreled. It seems that Parasa, as head of his own constituent family, wanted to separate from the patriline and transform his house from a *gadillu* into a *peddillu*, thus founding his own patriline. Jampayya stopped him, and shortly afterward Parasa died.

In cases like this, when junior patriline members try to divide, seniors do not openly do anything to preserve unity and prevent separation. They wait for an appropriate event, usually illness or poor fishing, to take place. Through diagnosis, they explain the event as the result of offertory neglect (the inside spirit attack script). Such neglect would not have occurred, they argue, if the disaffected junior had fulfilled his obligations as a member of the patriline. And now, as a result of that neglect, the household goddess attacked. In this case, a divination revealed that a household goddess attacked and caused Parasa's brothers to get sick. Parasa was held responsible, and as a result, he abandoned his bid for independence. The group approached separation, but pulled back in the nick of time, restoring unity.

The present case duplicates the Jampayya-Parasa case structurally. In Jampayya's place (as senior) there is Ammori and in Parasa's place (as junior) there is Bujayya, Ammori's brother. Their problem shows how crises on the agnatic axis, centering on the issue of agnatic unity, structurally duplicate each other until they culminate in the destruction of the original unit. It also demonstrates how repeating structural crises persist in modern form, even in the wake of the village's increasing contact with urban South Asian culture.

Many features of Jalari life have changed since Parasa fought Jampayya for his independence. The village itself has gone from an isolated coastal hamlet to a suburb of metropolitan Visakhapatnam (one of the largest port cities in South Asia). Jalaripet's contact with urban Indian culture has had deep consequences for Jalari social life, one of which is (for lack of a better word) "individualism." The Jalaris call it *ahankaram,* from the Sanskrit term for "selfness." The urban environment provides (or is seen to provide) opportunities for people to fulfill themselves outside the village, the family, and the household. On closer inspection, however, the "new" individualism turns out to be nothing very new at all. To be sure, young Jalaris like the sort of men they see in the city: the men who dress in the latest "cinema" style and ride fast motorcycles. But Jalari men do not try to imitate this style when they return to the village. Instead, they express "individualism" in entirely traditional ways, by establishing their own *peddillu*s and creating their own patrilineal groups. At the same time, traditional resistance to segmentation still exists, as do the methods senior agnates use to stop it.

Bujayya praises the memory of his brother. He sees himself as Parasa's successor in temperament and role: both young and both determined to achieve independent patrilines. But unlike Parasa, Bujayya had developed characteristics strongly inclined toward the urban lifestyle. He went downtown, saw Telugu movies, ate in cafés. He acquired cosmopolitan attire: polyester shirt and pants, plastic sandals, and sunglasses. He gave up smoking Jalari-made cigars for the more sophisticated and expensive factory-produced cigarettes. He cut his hair in the latest style and wore a thin mustache, both trademarks of Telugu cinema actors.

Even before Jampayya died, Bujayya had begun to dissociate himself from the patrilineal group. But his experiments in cosmopolitan living cost him more money than he could afford. Like all patriline members, he had been contributing part of his income to the goddess money. Jampayya kept the money in the *peddillu* and under his control. In debt from his urban lifestyle, Bujayya needed extra money and asked Jampayya to loan it to him from the goddess money. Jampayya refused and rebuked him severely, whereupon Bujayya promised never to enter the *peddillu* again. From that time onward he has not participated in any family ceremony conducted in the *peddillu*, but since there have been no ceremonies planned during this period, no one has tried to force the issue.

Various efforts to reintegrate Bujayya and restore fraternal unity failed. Jampayya died and was succeeded by Ammori as *pedda*. Apparently, Bujayya's attitude toward the family was not ameliorated by the succession of his genealogical junior to the position of headship. Bujayya considers himself the head, if not by right, then by reason of greater intelligence. Since he cannot lead his natal patriline, therefore, he seeks to establish his own.

Meanwhile, obligations within the patrilineal group accumulated. As always, there were the annual goddess rituals to perform. But now, too, the final funeral rites for three deceased family members (including Jampayya and Parasa) had to be done. Without Bujayya's participation, they could do nothing short of dissolving the old patriline and permitting Bujayya to create his own (and that would make Ammori, as head of the patriline, look even worse). The problem thus came down to this: Would Ammori maintain control over the patriline, including Bujayya, and thus preserve the unity of the agnatic group? Or would Bujayya break free, forcing the agnates to separate and found the nucleus of a new patrilineal group?

Problems like this, involving the continuity of the patriline and solidarity among brothers, are not recognized or redressed openly or explicitly. People wait for a triggering event, such as illness or poor fishing. The event is explained so that the explanation itself alters social reality. Now, the sort of event that would validate Ammori's position would be an illness among the members of his extended family. Diagnosis would reveal that the event resulted from an inside goddess's attack, motivated by offertory neglect, and precipitated by fraternal disunity and the threat of separation. Since Bujayya is currently the "odd man out," he would be blamed for the spirit's attack on an innocent victim and forced to concede. Success would depend on the plausibility of Ammori's argument structure, to be assembled in the *kaniki* diagnosis.

Bujayya, meanwhile, could pursue another strategy. He could argue that *if* he entered the *peddillu*, rejoining the family, he would break the promise he made not to do so. The "promise goddess," Sati Polamma, would attack him or some member of his family. No one could reasonably expect Bujayya to take such a risk. Bujayya would thus win by default.

Papamma's fever and difficulty in childbirth constituted the relevant triggering "event." Ammori plausibly inferred that family goddesses and dead family members had attacked because family disunity had prevented their celebratory and final funeral rites from being performed. When Papamma's recovery confirmed the likelihood of that inference, Ammori went to the *kaniki* and established that offerings by the entire patriline must be made.

There were two *kaniki* diagnoses. In the first, Ammori demonstrated that offerings to the dead must take place. Apparently, he assumed that Bujayya would return when the *kaniki* verified the importance of making offerings in which the family as a whole must participate. When Ammori realized that Bujayya's refusal was serious and possibly well grounded, he returned to the *kaniki,* to reconfirm the necessity of joint offerings *and* to establish that Bujayya runs no risk of attack by the promise goddess if he participates. The second *kaniki* is the one discussed here.

Summary of the Kaniki

Section One—Phase One

In any *kaniki,* the *kaniki* performer has to anticipate the developing argument structure. This is not hard, since the basic elements are few, but it does take time. She manipulates the rice, dropping it from a height to make it sink, generating "no" responses, and sliding it onto the surface to make it float, generating "yes" responses. At the beginning, however, the performer does not know the intended argument structure and must depend on signals (intonation and commentary) from the participants to correctly generate answers. Sometimes she gets it wrong. Jalari diagnosis possesses a theory of error which enables the *dasudu* and his client to interpret and correct such errors (though only up to a point, as we shall see).

In this *kaniki*, early questions are asked to elicit the inside spirit attack (ISA) script. This is to confirm the results of the initial pulse divination and establish that the patriline's two principal household spirits, Polamma and Nalamaramma, attacked. Later questions are supposed to confirm that homages were made and that the goddesses, in return, would bestow their protection. This is where the "error" comes up. The spirits answered the first set of propositions negatively and the second set positively. This creates the illogical scenario according to which the goddesses did *not* attack but *did* receive homages, which are promised only *after* a spirit's attack has been diagnosed.

The Jalari theory of error assumes that these answers must be correct but that they result from interference caused by outside spirits whose identity must be established. The *dasudu* therefore asks the inside spirits if outside spirits attacked. If they answer affirmatively (it is *not* assumed, by the way, that the goddesses can answer falsely to this question) the *dasudu* has his proof. With inside spirits' help, the *dasudu* identifies the outside spirits by name. With this act of naming, the outside spirits' power to "interfere" with household spirits' answers is stopped. The *dasudu* accomplishes this task in Phase Two.

Section One — Phase Two

Household goddesses attacked Papamma, Ammori's wife, and as a result, Ammori paid homage to them, promising to make the required offerings. But somehow the household goddesses never received the promissory homage. Confirmation of the outside spirit attack script in Phase Two reveals that outside spirits interfered by "blocking" the household goddesses' receipt of homage. The outside spirits were jealous and would not permit offerings to the inside goddesses until they were satisfied. The *dasudu* identifies these spirits as the family's own ancestors (Jampayya and Parasa). This may seem strange — after all, are not the spirits of the dead also inside spirits, just like the household goddesses? The explanation is that when one set of inside spirits (such as dead people) interfere with or "block" another set of inside spirits (such as goddesses), they in effect act like outside spirits even though they are not.

Section One — Phase Three

The *dasudu* wants to establish that the ancestral spirits of Jampayya and Parasa attacked, received homages, and promised to bestow protection.

This protection was contingent on arrangements for making the promised offerings. The remainder of the *kaniki* focuses on these arrangements and what they mean for relations between Ammori and his estranged brother, Bujayya. But first, the *dasudu* establishes that no other outside spirits have attacked. This is important, because Jalari divination recognizes only two prototypic efficient causes: inside spirits and outside spirits, which in essence index the two sides of the Jalari social dialectic. The choice between them plays a determining role in deciding whether the precipitating problem is on the agnatic or the affinal axis, and here, of course, they are working on the hypothesis that the agnatic axis is the relevant one.

But does this question contradict the earlier finding that outside spirits did attack? It does not, because the later question was addressed to a different spirit. The earlier answer confirmed that outside spirits *now* identified as the family's own ancestors attacked. The later answer now confirms that no *other* outside spirits attacked. This is a crucial finding, since it rules out the possibility that affinal relations and problems with married sisters might be involved. It means that the search for efficient causes need go no further and that one side of the social dialectic (the agnatic side) can be given more weight.

Section Three—Phase One

Deciding on offerings to the attacking spirits assumes special prominence because different offertory arrangements have different implications for Ammori and Bujayya, and for the dialectic of fraternal unity. Phase One established that offerings must be made under carefully defined circumstances. The *dasudu* wanted to make the fulfillment of these circumstances contingent on Bujayya's participation, since that is what will ensure Bujayya's continued membership in the patriline. His strategy was to establish that alternative scenarios that might permit Bujayya's exclusion are not acceptable to the goddesses and ancestors. The *dasudu* was acting on behalf of his client, Ammori, who wants to preserve the agnatic group.

If the family does *not* perform the offerings, the *dasudu* asks, will the spirits extend their blessings? The spirits of course answer negatively. Bujayya therefore *cannot* claim that the offerings are simply unnecessary. The next question restates the same proposition, now in terms of a positive conditional premise: If the family *does* perform the offerings, will the spirits extend their blessings? The spirits answered affirmatively, as expected. So far, so good.

Now the *dasudu* turns to another issue: Since offerings are necessary, perhaps offerings to one spirit, Parasa, are not. Recall that Bujayya, Ammori, and Parasa are classificatory brothers (*annadammullu*.) But Bujayya and Parasa are "own brothers" (*sonta annadammullu*) because they have the same mother. Bujayya is therefore Parasa's closest living male relative and *must* officiate in offerings to Parasa if offerings to Parasa are made. Bujayya might claim that offerings to Parasa are not necessary and, therefore, that his participation is not essential. The *dasudu* understands the strength of this argument and anticipates it, confirming (first with Jampayya and then with Parasa himself) that offerings to Parasa must be made. Bujayya thus loses another potential argument against participation.

One of the client's friends anticipates a complication, one that Bujayya himself might anticipate and use to justify his lack of participation. As we know already, a long time ago Parasa had attempted to separate from the patriline and Jampayya stopped him. Ammori's friend suggests that enmity between the two may still exist (even in death) and that offerings to them both at the same time might not be accepted by either. It is a plausible argument, given what we know about spirits and their feelings, and one that Bujayya might advance to justify excluding Parasa and thereby himself from the offerings. The *dasudu* asks the spirit of Jampayya if joint offerings, to himself and to Parasa, will be favorably received. Jampayya answers affirmatively, laying to rest another of Bujayya's possible objections. The issue of offerings to the ancestors is now settled, the *dasudu* having established that the goddesses and ancestors require offerings and that making them requires Bujayya's participation as a member of the united agnatic group.

Section Four

The *kaniki* has confirmed that no arrangements can be made to accommodate Bujayya, either by excluding him as a participant or by excluding one or all of the spirits in the offerings. This was what the *dasudu* and his client, Ammori, wanted to establish. Their goal is to preserve the unity of the patrilineal group and resolve the dialectic in favor of fraternal integrity. The *dasudu* left the most crucial test to last. His goal was to show that concessions to Bujayya were unnecessary in the first place because Bujayya's primary objection, fear that if he enter the *peddillu*, Sati Polamma will attack him, is unfounded.

The *dasudu* asks the ancestor spirits to accept Bujayya's exclusion from rites performed in the *peddillu*. Significantly, the *dasudu* puts this question to Parasa, the one spirit whose funerary rites Bujayya *must* be present for as chief mourner. This is quite deliberate. The spirit of Parasa was expected to say no and thus confirm that Bujayya cannot make his offerings separately. But the spirit of Parasa does not comply, and answers affirmatively.

Nervously, one of the client's friends restates the objective of this line of inquiry: "They will bring the younger brother (Bujayya) to the threshold of the *peddillu* and pay homage." He tells the *dasudu* to ask the next question so that "they [Bujayya's family] don't have a loss."

Things begin to go badly, so the *dasudu* switches tactics. Instead of asking the spirit of Parasa to agree to Bujayya's exclusion (to which Parasa should have responded negatively), the *dasudu* asks him to agree that if Bujayya enters the *peddillu* he will not experience any "loss" (illness or bad fishing). Parasa should respond positively because, like any inside spirit, he is supposed to resist the exclusion of patriline members from joint offerings. But Parasa answers negatively. The *dasudu* repeats the question and receives the same bizarre reply from Polamma, the family goddess. This is very unexpected. The integrity of the argument structure hangs on this point and on the *dasudu*'s ability to put matters straight in the remaining questions.

In the midst of this confusion, the *dasudu* retreats to a position he feels sure the spirit would respond to appropriately, enabling him to confirm the absolute necessity of keeping the patrilineal group intact. Without even mentioning Bujayya, the *dasudu* asks the spirit of Parasa if he would protect Teddi Ammori if he makes offerings along with his brothers. At long last Parasa answers as expected. Now the *dasudu* thinks he has the *kaniki* on the right track again.

Confidently, the *dasudu* turns to the household goddesses and repeats the previous question, asking if Bujayya will incur any loss if he participates. Naturally, he expects the goddess to answer negatively, since it is in her interest (as the embodiment of the group's unity) to keep Bujayya safe and a member of the agnatic group. But the goddess answers affirmatively: Bujayya *will* incur a loss if he so much as sets foot in the family's *peddillu*. This was not what anyone had expected. One observer vents his frustration, saying, "If that's the case, then the goddess will just eat us up." He meant that the spirits were behaving indifferently toward their household members and so the participants might as well give up.

The *dasudu* wants to avoid explicit reference to Bujayya's alleged promise and to the division of shares. Mentioning such issues is too risky, he later said, and in any case, there are simpler and safer methods. Sometimes, simply by altering his intonation or slightly rephrasing the questions, the *dasudu* provokes the desired response. But the spirits' latest responses left the *dasudu* no choice but to mention the terrible issue and hope that the spirits answer appropriately. If they don't, not only will the client have failed to achieve his objective, he will have achieved Bujayya's objective for him by validating his exclusion from the *peddillu* and division of the goddess money.

The household goddess is asked if the promise Bujayya made remains in effect. This puts the issue of Bujayya's excuse squarely on the line. The goddess replies that the promise is still in force. The *dasudu* had expected her to say no, and thus falsify the basis of Bujayya's refusal to enter the big house. Now the *dasudu* recognizes that the time has come for him to adopt a desperate strategy, threatening the goddess with dissolution of the patriline and separation of the brothers by calling on her to approve the division of shares. Naturally, the participants expect her to forbid the division and return of individual shares to the brothers. But the household goddess replies that she condones it. This is not what household goddesses are supposed to say. Having tried a desperate strategy and failed, the *dasudu* gives up in frustration. The *kaniki* is a failure, and everyone goes home.

On the way, Ammori's friends state with deadly clarity that the worst has come true: "Everyone will lead his own life." The patriline will divide and its members live separately, ending the dialectic of agnatic unity and separation in this family system in favor of separation. One suggests that perhaps Bujayya himself "will not let it be done," i.e., that he will back out at the last minute and rejoin the family. After all, he says, "Bujayya's share"—his allegiance—"is there." Another speaker retorts that Bujayya obviously doesn't care about the money (by extension, allegiance to the patriline) and may simply forgo the money and leave. The friend cannot believe that this is possible. Surely, he says, when the funerary ceremonies are performed Bujayya will not willingly exclude himself. The patrilineal ideology may assert itself, even over Bujayya. Reflecting a very strong sentiment in Jalari culture, one of the observers says, "All the people of the family, all should live at the place of the family. When they do, it is good."

Of course family unity is what they all want, at least at this moment, and the fact that it cannot be achieved in any permanent sense is not the point. Ammori is the most optimistic when he says, "It will take nearly a year." To Ammori, I realized later, the *kaniki* had signified only a temporary setback, but only the events of the next few weeks told me why. But why did the *kaniki* fail, or appear to?

The beginning of a *kaniki* is tricky, because the performer doesn't always know or can't always understand what kind of argument the *dasudu* is putting together. The ending is tricky too, for different reasons. In this case, the performer became impatient and (perhaps unconsciously) generated answers she knew would bring the inquiry to a premature conclusion. I cannot prove this. But I knew the performer, Citamma, pretty well by this point, and I knew that she was anxious that day to see her daughter, who was in a hospital for medical treatment. As the *dasudu* kept asking his questions, it was getting late. And so, I believe, the performer sabotaged the final stages of the *kaniki*—in order to catch the afternoon bus for downtown. Clearly, this is not something she does very often.

Aftermath of the Kaniki

At the end of the *kaniki,* agnatic unity and the integrity of the patrilineal group seemed to have been given up in favor of fraternal breakdown. But Ammori's defeat was only apparent. It was he, not Bujayya, who had the support of his other patriline brothers and the rest of the Teddi clan. Bujayya, an acknowledged introvert and a self-made outsider, had almost no family or community support. And Ammori possessed one decisive advantage over Bujayya, having to do with how he and Bujayya had positioned themselves with respect to future causal explanations.

Misfortunes occur with a certain frequency. But in circumstances defined by an already confirmed diagnosis of inside spirit attacks; by the absence of offerings to the goddesses; and by the absence of funerary rites for the dead, events like these were bound to be interpreted as inside spirit attacks. And it is only one step from this to the inference that *if* Bujayya were an active participant in patriline affairs and *if* the patriline had completed its offertory obligations, such events would not occur. Here lies the inherent strength of Ammori's position. Ammori need not *do* anything, but simply let events take their natural course. The appropriate inferences would be drawn. Inevitably, Bujayya would be blamed or blame himself, and return to the patrilineal group.

Bujayya does not have the same advantage, since events could not easily lend credence to his position. The one exception would be abrogation of his promise not to enter the *peddillu.* If misfortunes then occurred (if Bujayya's family were attacked by Sati Polamma, the promise goddess), then Bujayya's position would be validated. But no one expects him to enter the house. Therefore, it is only the *absence* of relevant events that maintains Bujayya's position as tenable. If the inside spirits do not attack anyone—that is, if no patriline members suffer illness or poor fishing—then no offerings need to be made and Bujayya need not rejoin the patriline.

But what really made Bujayya's position weak was his own ambivalence, typical of any brother just on the verge of attempting to break away from his natal patriline group. Cultural ambivalence can become psychological, especially in the case of individuals who experience conflicting expectations more intensely. Bujayya's ambivalence became apparent several weeks after the *kaniki,* when his pregnant wife was nearing the end of her term. Bujayya had no sons. He and his wife hoped this next child would be a boy. Some villagers said the ancestors would attack Bujayya by inflicting suffering on his pregnant wife or newborn child. This possibility could not have escaped Bujayya. If mother and child were safe, the "nonevent" of illness or death would add credibility to his position. If complications developed, Bujayya's position would suffer in due proportion to their seriousness.

A week later Bujayya's wife gave birth to twins, a boy and a girl. Neither seemed very healthy. The girl died within a week. Bujayya, in a state Ammori later described as hysterical (*picci*), entered the *peddillu* and pleaded with his patriline brothers to help him save his son. But there was no time. Within a couple of days, the boy also died. In my presence, Bujayya asked Ammori and his patriline brothers to help him with the burial and funerary rites. It was understood that Bujayya had rejoined the patriline group and would participate in ritual activities within the *peddillu* when called on.

No one openly referred to the children as victims of the household spirits' attack. Ammori and Bujayya themselves denied it, though neither suggested an alternative explanation. No one showed any surprise that Bujayya had entered the *peddillu*. Bujayya himself denied any reason for surprise. Didn't entering the house mean breaking his promise and inviting attack by Sati Polamma, I asked? Bujayya denied that he had ever made a promise or that the risk of an attack by Sati Polamma had ever existed.

What Bujayya felt as his newborn children began to die I cannot say. Here was a man who must have been deeply ambivalent before but hid it beneath a calm exterior as he struggled to achieve independence from his brothers. When his infant daughter died, his defenses collapsed. Bujayya panicked and went to the *peddillu* to seek comfort and guidance. After all, the *peddillu* is the "nest" and Bujayya, for all his bluff, was still a "nest bird." Ammori and the others rallied to him at once, as brothers should. But before anything could be done, the boy died. From that point Bujayya gave up any pretense of separateness from the patriline, and even began to deny that a serious rift had existed in the first place.

How are we to understand these denials: Denial that Bujayya had tried to divide from the patriline; denial that the promise existed; and denial that Bujayya's children had been killed by the patriline spirits? Quite simply, no one had anything to gain by claiming differently. For Ammori and his patriline brothers, the issue was closed. Better to forgive and forget. Even so, how could they deny that Sati Polamma, the promise goddess, posed a threat to Bujayya? Bujayya, of course, now disclaimed the "promise" story. But Ammori and the others could not deny the promise's existence after repeatedly confirming it in the *kaniki*. I asked Ammori this and received (what was to me then) an unexpected reply: The *kaniki* had demonstrated that Bujayya's promise was no longer in effect and that Bujayya therefore did not run the risk of attack by Sati Polamma if he entered the big house. Ammori and the others were not trying to deceive me, or the village community, or even themselves. They believed what they said. They had reconstructed their memory of the *kaniki* to fit the pattern of events which followed and, more significantly, which *would have followed* from the argument structure. Aspects of the *kaniki* that did not agree, like the disastrous final segment, were forgotten.

Teddi Bujayya deserves reconsideration. Over the last few years, he had adopted the mannerisms characteristic of the cosmopolitan Indian elite. He withdrew from participation in patrilineal activities, following the pattern set by his close friend, half-brother, and probable role model, Parasa. His goal, like Parasa's, was to found a new patriline. But there was a crucial difference. Unlike Parasa, Bujayya did not shape his individualism to fit the Jalari pattern, nor did he try to become a community leader and the "rightful" head of a separate sublineage. In any case, Bujayya was much like other Jalari men in his avowed adherence to the norms of fraternal solidarity. He spoke warmly of the integrity of the patriline, of his father and grandfather, and he liked the idea of solidarity among brothers. But he also wished to act independently of his brothers and, ultimately, to set up his own patrilineal group with himself as head. These conflicting orientations existed side by side, and the result is an ambivalence which could be only temporarily resolved in favor of one or the other.

Ammori had tried to bring Bujayya back to the group. He proved that his wife's illness resulted from agnatic disharmony and Bujayya's disaffection. No family member could be safe as long as Bujayya refused to participate in family rituals. Though confirmed and validated in an earlier *kaniki*, this explanation failed to sway Bujayya. Instead, Bujayya exploited the possibility of attack by Sati Polamma to justify his refusal to return. So Ammori conducted a second *kaniki*, not only to justify the necessity of Bujayya's participation but to invalidate Bujayya's excuses. In this, of course, Ammori had seemed to fail.

Bujayya's reaction to the first infant's death revealed his severe emotional stress, probably the result of the ambivalence he had felt all along in his attempted disaffection from the group. He reacted as traditional Jalari values prescribe by retreating to the "nest" and to his fellow "nest birds." Bujayya must have believed, and not merely been resigned to, the fact that he was responsible for his children's deaths through his disaffection from the patriline.

Bujayya's nascent cosmopolitanism may or may not have given him access to urban Hindu causal concepts. Using these concepts, he might have attributed a family calamity to *karma*, headwriting (*talarata*), astrological influences, or any number of things people elsewhere throughout India believe in but which the Jalaris, generally, have not heard of or are not interested in. It would have been easy, given such access, to dismiss Jalari causal thinking as "superstitious" or "tribal"—that, after all, is what non-Jalari Telugus usually say about the Jalaris. Let us assume that Bujayya did possess some kind of access to these ideas. As long as no difficulties arose for him, he never had to put them to the test. Differing Jalari and non-Jalari premises about causality never openly conflicted.

But difficulties occurred in Ammori's family and finally in Bujayya's own. Ammori's argument structure explained these and predicted that more would follow unless the brothers made offerings to the household spirits. When Bujayya's children died, as this structure predicted, it may have overwhelmed Bujayya and his ability to cope with already very ambivalent feelings. Its explanatory power was too great, and the competing structure's power too weak or too poorly assimilated, to offer any feasible alternative. Bujayya therefore abandoned his weakly incorporated urban causal schemata as he underwent the trauma of his first child's death. He had no recourse then except to the only other available explanatory structure, the one constructed by Ammori in the first *kaniki*. Bujayya may have felt that this would save his son. But when the children died, Bujayya could not simply return to his old ways, comfortably maintaining conflicting causal frameworks. The two had conflicted and one, the Jalari framework, had won. Bujayya therefore jettisoned the other.

Brothers, Mothers, and Family Goddesses

When the search for a plausible explanation reaches the *kaniki* method of divination, the outcome can be only one of two explanatory scenarios. Either the precipitating social dispute is a problem between brothers or a problem between brothers and sisters. Whichever the locus, the precipitating dispute must be resolved in favor of continued unity or separation. In families early in their development, when adult siblings are younger, settlements usually favor continued unity. Later, when brothers and sisters are older, disputes typically end in separation. When ideals conflict, they tend to give rise to a motivational dynamic which pushes people to resolve oppositions in favor of an overarching synthetic goal. This goal is a state of fusion or coalescence discussed earlier, detectable in repeated calls for fraternal unity and joint action, and on a return to a common "nest."

Teddi Ammori and his brothers do not speak of the continued unity of their patrilineal group in terms of fusion or coalescence, nor would they have any reason to accept my hypothesis that such goals receive emotional valence from experiences in childhood. So what is the link between the two which justifies the movement back and forth between cultural goals and developmental experiences?

Nothing so completely sums up the unity of a patrilineal group than its goddesses, and of those, the one goddess that is paramount over all others. The goddess is *amma*, "mother." She represents the group as the icon of its united identity. Jalaris identify themselves as members of a particular patrilineal group (*doddi*) by referring first to their apical ancestor and then to the principal household goddess (*inti ammavaru*) whom they worship. Her role as maker and upholder of the group is repeatedly emphasized. When the group is threatened from outside by affinally related goddesses, she rushes to protect it, and when the group is threatened by the divisive tendencies of the brothers, she punishes them to remind them of their subservience to her. She *is* the group; its interests are hers, and she must react to threats against it as a nurturant but aggressively protecting mother. This tends to confirm Kakar's (1981) point that the Hindu group is symbolically female, and the femininity which suffuses this symbol is decidedly maternal. Group membership recaptures the intense dependency of early childhood, a state which Jalari adults try to preserve even though such efforts are doomed to failure.

THE DIALECTIC OF BROTHERS AND SISTERS

The last section considered a case of conflict between brothers, examining the dialectic of unity and separation when agnatic solidarity is the object of divinatory inquiry. Depending on the family's stage of development, a conflict between affines is equally possible—and ultimately inevitable. Affinal conflict is the other major dialectic of Jalari society, and it pits the value of unity against separation. The focus of divinatory inquiry is the relationship between adult brothers and sisters, since cross-siblings, as exchange partners in business as well as in cross-cousin marriage alliance, are affines par excellence.

Lévi-Strauss defines cross-cousin marriage as the first institutionalized form of exchange to follow the dialectical resolution of culture and nature in the incest prohibition (Lévi Strauss 1969). He postulates two patrilineally organized groups coming together, one of them giving a woman, for a net loss, to the other, for a net gain. The imbalance can be redressed only by returning a daughter of this union to the wife-giving group or one of the wife-receiver's sisters to the wife-givers. If the exchange is delayed one generation, the man who gives his sisters may take a daughter of her union for his son, and this too is cross-cousin marriage. The cross-cousin system acquires coherence "only in so far as it incorporated in a certain system of antithetical relationships, the role of which is to establish inclusions by means of exclusions, and vice versa, because this is precisely the one means of establishing reciprocity, which is the reason for the whole undertaking" (Lévi-Strauss 1969:114).

It is not my purpose to make or support claims on behalf of this view but to consider the nature of the antithesis. According to Lévi-Strauss, one gives up a sister who is desired, in the expectation that the loss will be recovered, if not immediately, then in the next generation. The result is a system of reciprocity which unites groups in cross-cousin marriage. I think Lévi-Strauss is right about this. But is the recovery ever complete, and the promise of a return ever completely fulfilled? In practice this is unlikely, since the exigencies of cross-cousin marriage make it impossible for intermarrying groups to achieve the state of perfect harmony and balance that is their terminological ideal. What is the consequence for a society in which repeated frustration is the necessary and inevitable result of the kinship system?

What we call "reciprocity" is hardly sufficient, either as a description of what happens or of its motivation. If it were, then the only consequence of frustration would be the abrogation of the alliance relationship. But alliance is more than a relationship between intermarrying groups. It is also a relationship between individuals, for if we follow the logic of Lévi-Strauss's argument, the alliance relationship is mediated by the *desire* of brother and sister for each other. It is a desire which the cross-cousin marriage system depends on and whose fulfillment the system constantly promises but never actually provides. Surely this is relevant. Brothers and sisters try to realize the unity which is the ideal, using the only means at their disposal: the marriage uniting their children. In this way they realize the paradox at the heart of the system.

THE CASE OF TEDDI PARASAYYA

Three brothers, members of the Teddi clan, were "experiencing difficulties" (*ibbandilu padutunnayi*), a Jalari euphemism meaning they were being attacked by spirits. Teddi Parasayya, the eldest, has a son whose continuing fever has resisted all curative measures. Under most circumstances this would signal the activity of spiritual agencies. But until recently there was no reason to suspect any spirit of attacking. Then the wife of one of the brothers recalled an incident others in the family immediately recognized as relevant.

Kutamma is younger sister to the Teddi brothers. She is married to a Ramulu clan man. The Teddis and the Ramulus are related by marriage and have been for generations. Someone in the Teddi group (it is not clear who) recalled that Ramulu Kutamma had refused to pay the ten rupees she owed them for fish they had sold her several weeks before. When one of the Teddi brother's wives asked for it, Kutamma was insulted. The brothers now suspect that Kutamma "lowered her face" (*mukham dincu*) and caused her goddess, Sati Polamma, to attack the eldest brother's son. A *kaniki* divination was done to find out whether or not Kutamma's goddess had attacked because the Teddi brothers and their wives insulted her by demanding repayment of a loan.

The remembering of an incident involving loss or insult is not unusual prior to a divination. A misfortune occurs; someone in the affected family recalls an incident when someone, probably an affine, argued with a family member. In itself the argument may not have signified much. Jalari men and women are accomplished rhetoricians, who hone their skills in frequent roadside arguments involving the most barbed invective possible in spoken Telugu. For an argument to be remembered, therefore, it has to occur in the context of already disturbed relations, either within the family or between affinally related families. Then, if the right kind of misfortune takes place, the remembered argument or dispute incites family members to consider divination. Instead of addressing the dispute directly—in, say, a village court—Jalaris wait for misfortune to strike, then for the remembrance of some perceived transgression involving either brothers or sisters. Divination is the next step. The case that follows is typical of crises that develop on the affinal axis, as a consequence of competing (and necessarily opposed) normative demands.

Summary of the Kaniki

Section One—Phase One

The *dasudu* directs most of his early questions to Ellamma, the Teddi family's principal household deity, and confirms the ISA script. Ellamma attacked because the Teddi brothers had neglected her worship. But this is not what the *dasudu* had in mind when he began. He wants to *eliminate* the ISA script, not dwell on it, because he is fairly sure that the precipitating conflict is between the brothers and their married sister, Ramulu Kutamma.

The *dasudu* starts all over, to disconfirm the attack script with the testimonies of Gurappa Demudu and Kanaka Durga, the other two household goddesses of the client family (the Teddi brothers). Once again he fails to disconfirm the ISA script. The Teddi household deities say that they attacked because the brothers transgressed. This directs attention to the agnatic script, away from consideration of affinal relations. What went wrong?

It is possible that the *dasudu* failed to properly signal the performer, preventing her from generating the desired answer. By "signal," I refer to the verbal cues the *dasudu* must use to indicate the direction he is going and the answers he expects to follow (Nuckolls 1987, 1991a). Or it could be that the performer mishandled the rice, causing it to sink when it should have floated. Either is possible. The *dasudu* is not completely familiar with the case. The performer is not a Jalari and knows nothing of the participants. Between the two of them, it is possible that mixed signals could have been given and received. But the Jalari answer to the question of what went wrong is this: Inside spirits may answer "yes" when they mean "no" and "no" when they mean "yes," either when they are angry and want to be difficult or when outside spirits are obstructing them. Jalaris attribute "errors" to one or both of these two factors, and in this case, like the agnatic case examined above, the participants favor the latter. There must be an interfering outside goddess.

Section One—Phase Two

From his limited background knowledge, the *dasudu* assumes that outside spirits attacked and therefore infers that the inside goddesses answered affirmatively to ISA questions because they had been "blocked," that is, obstructed in some way by the outside goddesses who are really the attacking spirits. The *dasudu* tests this hypothesis: "You are attempting to lie, Ellamma. Is there a darkness (i.e., another spirit, either a goddess or an ancestor) at your throat?" Ellamma answers affirmatively, confirming the *dasudu*'s inference: outside spirits are "blocking" her, making her answer erroneously. Once the interfering outside spirit has been identified, the blocking should stop and Ellamma should be able to answer "correctly." Instead she reconfirms her attack.

The participants were unhappy, since this was not what they expected. The *kaniki* performer herself intervened to explain: "Because of the darkness (an attacking goddess) she (the household goddess) is going away," she said. What this means is that the goddess's answers are distorted the "further away she goes" to escape the interference of the attacking outside goddess. A particularly hostile outside goddess, such as Sati Polamma, causes the inside goddess to retreat even further, and thus further distort her answers. One of the observers agrees. He tells the *dasudu* to abandon this line of questioning and "tell us just about the darkness."

The failure to disconfirm the ISA script left the *dasudu* with no alternative but to continue the development of the OSA script and hope for the best. The Teddis' own household goddess, Ellamma, responds that an outside spirit is attacking, confirming the OSA script. But this information adds very little. The need to develop the OSA script, to specify and contextualize its internal constituents, is expressed in the *dasudu*'s request to the client for information ("Whom do you suspect?"). But it is offset by the need to eliminate the ISA script as a lingering alternative. Jalari divination is a forum in which attention to such small details as this is necessary, and expected.

One of the observers, Danayya, has seen the difficulty and tries to eliminate it by casting doubt on the idea that Ellamma herself really attacked: Why, he asks, would she do that? It doesn't make sense; and if she did attack, why would she attack one brother more severely than another? The emphasis on logic and correct form should not go unnoticed. He urges the *dasudu* to "catch hold of Ellamma" and ask her, in order to eliminate the ISA primary script once and for all.

Section Two—Phase One

To eliminate the ISA script and enter the domain of precipitating causes, the *dasudu* transforms and reduces the ISA into the prototypic agnatic script. In other words, he takes key scenes of the agnatic script and submits them to the goddess as questions. Recall that the agnatic script is simply an enabling condition for the inside spirit attack script. Eliminating one of the scenes from the agnatic script effectively rules out the script of which it is a part and retroactively eliminates the higher-order ISA script the *dasudu* failed to disconfirm earlier. Ellamma responds that she did not attack and disconfirms the whole proposition. That was what the *dasudu* wanted to establish. No more time needs to be wasted on investigating causes on the agnatic axis. The *dasudu* and his audience return to consideration of the OSA script and its precipitating cause, which they all assume to be the problem with the sister, Ramulu Kutamma.

Section Two—Phase Two

First of all, they have to identify the attacking outside spirits. Danayya suggests that the attacking spirit must be Sati Polamma, a particularly vicious goddess. The client and his brothers oppose this suggestion. Sati Polamma is not an ordinary household goddess like Ellamma. She does not receive offerings at the *sadaru* of the patriline's *peddillu*. She has no festival day. She has no permanent representation, in temple, house, or other location.

Sati Polamma is a despised goddess, loathed as much as feared for her power to attack, and she is "acquired" by individuals in circumstances of moral transgression, usually sexual in nature.

If one Jalari and another argue, each swears by "beating the earth" (*bhumi kottadam*) that he is telling the truth. Usually the circumstances surrounding the making of the promise are sexual, e.g., a man accuses another man of sleeping with his wife. The one who lies is attacked by Sati Polamma, the personification of the abrogated promise (*satya pramanamu*). Sati Polamma is acquired in other ways, too. A younger woman who sleeps near another woman who has Sati Polamma may "catch" the goddess by accident. The risk is greatest if the younger woman is menstruating. Typically, daughters-in-law who sleep near their Sati Polamma-possessing mothers-in-law are affected. An unmarried man who sleeps with a woman possessing Sati Polamma runs the same risk. There are thus several modes of acquisition, one associated with the breach of an explicit promise or implicit sexual taboo, the other associated with the accidental combination of possessor with vulnerable and unsuspecting recipient. Sexual impropriety is involved in both cases, either directly or indirectly, and it is contagious even among the innocent and unsuspecting.

The *dasudu* knows that Kutamma has Sati Polamma, so he begins to ask a question premised on that assumption. The client, Parasayya, stops him, but not before he invokes Sati Polamma. The goddess responds that she did not attack. Danayya and Parasayya argue over shifting attention to Kutamma's ordinary household goddesses or returning to Sati Polamma for additional questions. Their decision has serious implications. First, if Sati Polamma attacked, it would tend to suggest that the relationship between the Teddis and Ramulus is on the verge of being permanently rent. Teddi Parasayya would have to make a blood sacrifice, and blood sacrifices inevitably precede complete dissolution of the social bond between the giver and the receiver, whether agnatically or affinally related. Neither the Teddis nor the Ramulus want the social stigma a dissolution of their alliance relationship would bring. Second, once Parasayya and his family offer to Sati Polamma, they too acquire Sati Polamma and must make yearly offerings to her. Parasayya prefers to ask the household goddesses and, if possible, confirm that they, and not Sati Polamma, attacked.

Parasayya's strategy seems to work. The *dasudu* assents to the change and asks if he should proceed by asking the Ramulu household spirits. But Danayya is an experienced and well-respected *kaniki* observer who does not tolerate lapses in format. If Sati Polamma is not involved, he retorts, how do we explain the extent of the Teddis' losses? Household goddesses do not attack so severely. The effect must be equivalent to the cause. The only reasonable surmise, Danayya insists, is that Sati Polamma must have attacked. We will consider Danayya's support for this hypothesis later.

Parasayya rebuts Danayya's claim with an interesting counterargument: "When our mother and Kutamma quarreled, they shouted that our mother's goddess had attacked them." Parasayya is saying that the Ramulus suspect that his goddesses, the household goddesses of the Teddi household, attacked Kutamma's family. This is the first we have heard of this possibility. The client does not need to prove it, only to suggest that the Teddi goddesses attacked the Ramulus. Then it would make sense that the Ramulu household goddesses attacked the Teddis, in direct reciprocity. There is a balance to this equation—household goddesses mutually attacking each other's households—which the attribution to Sati Polamma ("that stinking goddess," as Parasayya called her) would upset.

Danayya turns to the history of the case and to past instances to demonstrate the logic of his argument. It cannot be denied, he says, that Ramulu Kutamma has Sati Polamma. Everybody knows she does. Furthermore, if it can be shown that Sati Polamma attacked the Teddis in the past, then a precedent exists, and she might have attacked in the present. The fact that Sati Polamma herself denied attacking earlier in the *kaniki* is of no consequence. Everyone knows that goddesses give erroneous replies at first, to increase anxiety. "Goddesses are like that," Danayya said. So Danayya examines the history of the case, to reopen the possibility that Sati Polamma did attack Parasayya. Did the Teddis ever prepare and present *mudupu*s to the Ramulus, and to their sister, Kutamma? (A *mudupu*, it will be recalled, is the cloth bundle containing a few coins that represents the client's intention to make offerings.) If the Teddis presented a *mudupu* for Sati Polamma, then a precedent clearly exists, and Danayya has proved his point.

The Teddi brothers all deny that Danayya's theory applies. Bandayya, one of the Teddi brothers, repeats the suggestion that reciprocal attacks may be involved ("The younger brother is there. When he said 'Are you quarreling?' she said, 'Don't you have loans; why do you quarrel?' "). Here the reference is not to the reciprocal goddess attacks, but to the reciprocal accusations leveled at each other by Kutamma and the Teddi brothers, which preceded the goddess attacks. When Jampayya (the younger brother) accused Kutamma of not repaying her loan to the Teddis, Kutamma rebuked him by asking if he had never owed anyone money. Of course he had! As far as the Teddi brothers are concerned, the fact that their accusations are mutual enhances the likelihood of reciprocal attacks by their respective household goddesses.

Danayya claims that the Teddis nevertheless possess the moral "high ground" if they argue that the attacking goddess is Sati Polamma and that this goddess attacked them only because Kutamma disliked being asked to repay a debt. The alternative to this, Danayya states, is to apportion the blame equally between brothers and sister, each side receiving some social disrepute (*grahacaram*). The first alternative—making Kutamma accept most of the blame—would result in a social break and some loss of prestige for both sides. The second alternative—distributing the blame between them—would result in the preservation of the cross-sex sibling relationship, although on a slightly different basis. They would have to give up trading fish with each other. But it would make it possible for both families to consider alliance marriage between their children—something both sides very much want. Danayya prefers, or seems to prefer, the first alternative and the Teddi brothers prefer the second, but as we shall see, their interests are in fact closely linked.

Section Two—Phase Three

Danayya insists that they postpone examination of the Ramulu household goddesses and consider the question of Sati Polamma's attack on another Jalari man with no direct connection to this case, a man called Gantodu. Apparently, Gantodu quarreled with Kutamma some time ago, and soon afterward both he and his son became ill. "Now the difficulty has affected us," Danayya concludes. He bases his claim on the similarity of the Gantodu case to the present one.

The Teddi brothers do not directly contradict Danayya but again try to shift the divination toward consideration of reciprocal goddess attacks. They repeat that a quarrel took place between Ramulu Kutamma and one or several of the Teddi wives. Jampayya says that ever since Kutamma accused the Teddi goddess of attacking and called the Teddis "*dayyam* (demon) people," the Teddis have been afflicted. Bandayya confirms that the quarrel took place and that he hit Kutamma, calling her "whore daughter." All of this should strengthen the Teddi brothers' assertion that their grievances against Kutamma, and Kutamma's grievances against them, are mutual; that she quarreled with them and that they quarreled with her, and that both sets of household goddesses attacked. The *dasudu* allows both propositions to stand, for the purpose of investigation—the first, that Sati Polamma did attack, and the second, that reciprocal goddess attacks did occur, implicating both the sister and her brothers.

Section Three—Phase Four

The Teddis want to investigate the causes of the reciprocal attacks by examining the relationship between Ramulu Kutamma and themselves. Interestingly, Danayya now assents by stating the case from the Teddi brothers' perspective: "If we hadn't asked for those ten rupees, we would have lived without any troubles—ask that." This is a cue to the *dasudu* to call up the affinal script, which will focus attention on the relationship between the Teddi brothers and their sister, Ramulu Kutamma. He asks Ellamma to confirm that "their goddess" (i.e., the Ramulus' goddess, Sati Polamma) attacked when "that child lowered her head" (i.e., when Kutamma felt angry) because "that child" (i.e., Teddi woman) asked her to repay the ten-rupee loan. This is a crucial step. The divination has now established that this problem is the prototypic affinal dispute, involving a conflict between brother and sister, and their allied families.

The next question is a counterfactual which restates the problem in contrary-to-fact form: "If we *hadn't* asked for those ten rupees, then that goddess wouldn't have come, would it?" The counterfactual question finalizes the argument structure. The scenario is stated from Kutamma's perspective, as if she herself is speaking: " 'OK, even though I am your sister, you did not love me. Those ten rupees she (Kutamma's brother's wife) saw them but she didn't see my face,' therefore, when her (Kutamma's) tears flowed, her goddess came to the Teddi people's household and attacked the son (i.e., Kutamma's brother's son), didn't she?" The premise states that a breach occurred in the normative relations between brother and sister, the prototypic source of difficulty between affinally related households, like the Teddis and the Ramulus. The relevant norm is the obligation of a brother to support and care for the sister, or, in this case, the obligation to recognize that preservation of the brother-sister bond transcends the maintenance of a strict reciprocity in business transactions. The Teddi brothers should have recognized the importance of that bond and not pressed Kutamma, their sister, to repay the ten rupees. They are guilty of "not seeing her face," i.e., of not seeing their relationship with her and the special obligations it imposed on them. The result is a causal scenario linking observed effect with precipitating breach of normative affinal relations, a breach which now threatens the end of the alliance relationship between the Teddi and Ramulu families. It is a problem almost all Jalari brothers and sisters are guilty of, sooner or later.

The next question is the beginning of several questions (all predictive) addressed to Sati Polamma, the attacking spirit called to life by Kutamma's anger toward her brothers. When the *dasudu* last tried asking Sati Polamma a diagnostic question, he received a negative response, indicating that she did not attack. That is why all of the evidence so far of Sati Polamma's attack has been obtained through the testimony of Teddi household goddesses, especially Ellamma. Now the *dasudu* feels confident that Sati Polamma will answer his question positively. She does, but why?

Outside goddesses do not readily admit attacking to the family of the victim. They must be "forced" by rigorous analysis and the testimony of the victim's household goddess. That is what happened here. The earlier attempt failed because the case had not developed far enough to be convincing. After the arguments developed, a stronger case was presented. Now when the *dasudu* asks Sati Polamma to confirm her role, she does so immediately. This is important, because the attacking goddess's testimony is necessary to complete the argument structure. She must acknowledge her act. Circumstantial evidence and the testimony of witnesses, though vital to the construction of the argument, are insufficient.

Section Three

The *dasudu* continues to interrogate Sati Polamma, the attacking goddess. He proposes that she accept a *sabha dandam* and specifies that the offering will be in lieu of a chicken sacrifice. The goddess accepts. A *sabha dandam* is the simple offering of verbal homage to the attacking goddess. Afterwards, social relations between the affinal household resume, and marriage relations can be considered. The chicken sacrifice, like any blood sacrifice, has different consequences. Relations between the two households are dissolved, and their members never speak or interact with each other again. Social bonds are cut, and the all-important alliance relationship breaks down. The Teddi brothers prefer a *sabha dandam,* and continued relations.

But Danayya wants to demonstrate that Sati Polamma requires the offering of a chicken, and that if she does not receive it, her attacks on the Teddis will continue. In any case, he argues, what harm can it do to make the *mudupu:* "no one will say no." Later, if Kutamma refuses to receive a chicken sacrifice, the Teddis can always renegotiate a *sabha dandam.* This is an interesting, and strategic, argument. According to Danayya, it makes sense to offer something they know the goddess and Kutamma will have to accept and then, if possible, bargain down to something more to their own liking —that something, of course, being the kind of offering that will ensure the preservation of affinal relations and the continuity of the alliance. Consequently, the *dasudu* revises his offer and proposes chicken sacrifices instead.

A specific time limit, two weeks, is set in which to resolve the troubles between the Teddi brothers and Ramulu Kutamma. Sati Polamma agrees.

Section Four

Briefly, the participants return to the issue of agnatic relations, the principal alternative to the affinal scenario they have been considering. Did Ellamma attack the Teddi brothers because internal disharmony (stemming from breach of agnatic norms) made them unable to make offerings? Ellamma answers negatively and the agnatic script is rejected, once again. What this goes to show is that the dialectic of agnatic versus affinal relations is never far removed and that in any divination it is easy to move back and forth between the two. Either may be to blame—and ultimately, of course, both are, since there is no way to fulfill both sets of obligations. But why does the *dasudu* return to this issue so late in the *kaniki,* since he already established that outside, not inside, spirits attacked?

Just before, one Teddi brother had remarked that "the children quarreled at the *peddillu.*" This is a formulaic reference to a state of fraternal disunity, and to the agnatic script. The *dasudu* takes this as his cue to instantiate the agnatic script. But why do the Teddi brothers reopen an issue effectively dismissed earlier in the *kaniki?* The reason is that the Teddi brothers are now in the midst of the second kinship "crisis moment." They are on the verge of splitting up, but they are not so far along in this process as the Teddi Ammori family, examined in the last section. Each brother is more concerned with his own family than he is with the maintenance of the patriline and his obligations to it. There may have been no one act of defiance, no one outstanding breakdown to raise the issue of patrilineal solidarity to prominence, as there was in the Teddi Ammori case. There is just a vague fear that family affairs are slipping in the direction of separation.

Meanwhile, a more dramatic and precipitous decline in affinal relations has taken place. That issue is now understood and soon, if everything goes right, it will be settled to the brothers' satisfaction. The issue of patrilineal unity—always lurking in the background as the other prototypic reason things go wrong—therefore reemerges, as the other side of the social dialectic that governs Jalari life. The *dasudu* proposes that if Ellamma helps to alleviate their present difficulties with "the goddess that came" (Sati Polamma), then they, the Teddi brothers, "will become birds" at her feet. The Teddis will surmount their differences and make offerings to Ellamma if she helps them through the present crisis. This is a kind of "preemptive" arrangement, meant to ensure both that Ellamma assists them now and that she does not attack in the future until they have had a chance to settle problems within the patrilineal group.

Section Five

Now the Teddi brothers return to the business at hand, which is their relationship with the estranged sister, Kutamma. If they can demonstrate that Ellamma, the Teddi goddess, attacked Kutamma *reciprocally*, then a possible basis for their future relationship with Kutamma exists. At this point in the *kaniki*, it finally becomes apparent that what they want is to end the financial relationship with Kutamma but preserve all other aspects of the brother-sister relation, especially since both sides depend on their alliance relationship to arrange the marriages of their children. Trading fish with Kutamma is not to their advantage, it seems. She demands extremely favorable terms and refuses to pay on time or in full for the fish she purchases. Her brothers are obligated to sell to her. But the *kaniki* offers them a way out, if they demonstrate that the attacks have been reciprocal. That will help to persuade Kutamma to accept a mutual *sabha dandam*, instead of a one-way chicken sacrifice offered by her brothers.

The client, Teddi Parasayya, tells the *dasudu* to confirm that the Teddi goddess attacked the Ramulus. After all, hasn't Kutamma's husband been ill recently? One of the brothers clinches the argument by recalling that Kutamma accosted one of the Teddi wives and called the Teddis "*dayyam* people." That's like saying they are guilty of provoking the spirit attack and proves that the Ramulu people *believed* that they have been attacked by the Teddi goddess. Why else would they have said it? Danayya is convinced, too. He instructs the *dasudu* to proceed on the assumption that an attack by Ellamma on the Ramulus is plausible. The next several questions confirm that the Teddi family goddess, Ellamma, attacked the affinally related Ramulu family.

But certain characteristics of the attack are at odds with what we know from earlier discussions. Consider the scenario. Kutamma's insult or "teasing" is the initiating cause. The outcome is attack by the Teddi goddess on Kutamma's family. Earlier, however, we learned that Kutamma's remarks caused fighting between her and one of the Teddi brothers or his wife. Teddi Bandayya claimed that he hit or slapped Kutamma, causing Kutamma's goddess to attack the Teddis. Are these two different accounts, and if so, which one makes the most sense?

Of the two accounts, the one constructed earlier in the *kaniki* made the most sense to me, as I compared the two at the time. First, why would

Kutamma call the Teddis "*dayyam* people" *before* the Teddi goddess had attacked her family? And if the Teddi goddess had attacked her family (as the Teddi brothers now claimed), why would Kutamma's so-called teasing have been understood as anything other than an appropriate response? Second, if the "insult" is given causal priority in explaining why the Teddi goddess attacked the Ramulus, then when did Kutamma's goddess, Sati Polamma, attack the Teddis? Accepting the later scenario seriously disorganizes the argument structure assembled earlier in the *kaniki*. Kutamma's culpability is demonstrated only by sacrificing the logic of the previous argument.

My assessment of the situation was not shared by the participants, who considered the "new" scenario a completely harmonious addition. Given what we know about Jalari divination, we cannot assume that the participants suddenly become unmindful or uninterested in observing correct form. Something else must be going on.

From conversations with the participants before and after the *kaniki*, we know that the scenario they accept is the one constructed earlier. To recapitulate, that version is as follows:
1. The sister owed her brothers money.
2. The sister refused to repay the money.
3. When the brothers asked for the money, they insulted the sister.
4. The sister's goddess, Sati Polamma, attacked the brothers.

The Teddis' goal is to confirm that their goddess attacked Kutamma. We now know that this account is to be incorporated as an intermediary scenario within, not in lieu of, the one outlined above, as follows:
1. The sister owed her brothers money.
2. The sister refused to repay the money.
3. The Teddi goddess attacked the sister's family.
4. When the brothers asked for the money, they insulted the sister.
5. The sister's goddess, Sati Polamma, attacked the brothers.

Kutamma's "teasing" is thus an enabling condition. When a Teddi accosted Kutamma and asked her for the money, he breached certain norms of Jalari behavior which prohibit open indications of bad feeling between affines. He insulted Kutamma. Kutamma responded by calling her Teddi brothers "*dayyam* people." Of course, the Teddi goddess had already attacked her family by that time, or so it is now believed, in order to punish Kutamma for not repaying the loan. But this has nothing to do with why Kutamma rebuked them in public. Rather, it expressed her feeling that the Teddis' insult—openly demanding the money to be repaid—showed disregard for her status as their sister. Kutamma was not upset at that point by the goddess attack but by the Teddis' public breach of the norms governing cross-sex sibling relations. Her emotional response to this insult then caused her goddess to attack her brothers.

The Aftermath

Two months after the *kaniki,* the Teddi brothers agreed on all major aspects of the scenario. Their sister owed them money for fish they had given her. When one Teddi individual (the brothers' mother, or, in some versions, a brother's wife) asked Kutamma for the money, Kutamma insultingly refused. The Teddi individual who asked for the money then "lowered her face" (*mukham dincu*), and the Teddi goddess, Ellamma, attacked Kutamma's family.

Later, Teddi Parasayya's wife met Kutamma in the street and demanded the money from her. Now, Parasayya's wife is not related to Kutamma except as sister-in-law (*kodalu*). Sisters-in-law are not supposed to address each other in this way. To do so is to give the other sufficient ground to feel insulted. That is why Kutamma in turn "lowered her face" and felt that her brothers had wronged her for allowing one of their wives (or, in one version, mother) to insult her.

There were two striking changes in the brothers' later accounts. First, they claimed that the attacking goddess was *not* Sati Polamma but Kutamma's own household deities. Second, they said that no offering of a chicken had been considered. Instead, the brothers told me that they had offered, and Kutamma accepted, a *sabha dandam.* As far as I knew, no subsequent divination had taken place to amend or revise the argument structure of the *kaniki* discussed here. So, what happened? Most probably, Kutamma and her family were as much terrified by the prospect of making a chicken sacrifice to Sati Polamma as were the Teddis, and they simply bargained down to a *sabha dandam.* This was what Danayya seemed to have had in mind all along, when he proposed the chicken sacrifice. Now that the matter had been resolved, the Teddi brothers remembered the matter as they preferred to, as one that had never involved the threat of dissolving the relationship to Kutamma.

We are now in better position to understand their reasons. The Teddi brothers are at the point in their development as a family when significant internal divisions have appeared. They are having difficulty meeting their agnatic obligations to each other, let alone their affinal obligations to their sisters and sisters' families. Altering their obligations to Kutamma, but preserving their relationship with her, was a stop-gap measure intended to take some of the pressure off the competing relational networks for some

period of time. They could then continue to balance their agnatic and affinal relationships. This kind of balancing act could be only a temporary
solution, however.

The issue involving a ten-rupee loan was not important in itself, but
as symbol of obligations to their sister which the brothers were no longer
prepared to meet. Getting rid of the financial arrangement (trading fish for
money) therefore became the means, symbolically, of altering their relationship with her, so that the brother-sister relationship itself no longer
exerted as much pressure on them. This was never a consciously expressed
goal. It was realized in a certain form after illnesses in the Teddi family directed attention to the money issue and hence to the precipitating crisis in
affinal relations.

All of this did not take place without the cooperation of Kutamma's
family, the Ramulus. They wanted a change as much as the Teddis. How
do we know this? Interviews with Cinnodu, Kutamma's husband, revealed
that he accepted the Teddis' argument structure but reversed it. The Ramulus did not owe the Teddis money, he said, but the other way around.
According to Cinnodu, his wife demanded money from the Teddis' mother.
Then the Ramulu household goddess (not Sati Polamma) attacked, afflicting the Teddis with illness. The Teddis paid homage to the attacking goddess and their illnesses abated. Then a Ramulu household member accosted
a Teddi in the street, demanding money. The directness of the demand,
together with making it in public, caused the Teddi individual to feel insulted. The principal Teddi household goddess, Ellamma, attacked and afflicted the Ramulus with illnesses.

The Teddi and Ramulu stories are identical—but reversed. Both point
to tension on the affinal axis as the locus of the present dispute. It is fair
to say that the questions, "Who owed whom the original money?" and
"Who actually insulted whom?" are unanswerable, if not uninteresting,
questions. Whatever happened, it fulfilled both families' desire to "have it
out" and reconstitute their affinal relationship on terms more agreeable to
both. In Jalari culture, recognition of a kinship problem and change take
place through the idiom of goddess attacks and by means of divination.

NORMATIVE CONFLICT AND THE PARADOXES OF EXPLANATION

The sibling relationship is the core of Jalari society, and from it emerge
the two ways of pursuing the culturally directive goal of unity, agnatically
(in fraternal solidarity) and affinally (in the solidarity among brothers and
sisters). The goal cannot be achieved because the two paths conflict, both

internally and with each other. That is why it is impossible to look at Jalari kinship as a formal system of relations and status markers. Jalari kinship is a set of enduring paradoxes which realize themselves over and over again in most organized knowledge structures, such as divination.

Lévi-Strauss does not define the dynamics of patrilineality as "elementary," something I find a bit odd. For example, in speaking of the opposition of nature and culture, and the first essentially cultural act, Lévi-Strauss refers to the incest prohibition and the resulting exchange of women. Marital exchange represents the dialectical resolution of the opposition, but only a partial one, and thus provides the impetus to a continuing dialectical movement that systematically generates all the major forms of marriage (Lévi-Strauss 1969). By resolving the opposition, the regulation of incest endows sexuality with a cultural nature, and the importance of this to the formation of cultural institutions is what concerns Lévi-Strauss.

The same point has been made in different ways by others, earlier by Freud and later by Parsons (1951) and Fox (1967). I do not wish to challenge it, but simply to pose a question: If the most basic (and widely distributed) form of descent is patrilineality, and if most patrilineal societies consist of patrilineal groups, then why doesn't this fact constitute a basic opposition in whose dialectical resolutions culture is made up? Lévi-Strauss (echoing Freud) asserts that culture is produced the moment men begin to deny themselves the women to whom they are most closely related. Freud conjectures that self-denial was preceded by prohibition, when the senior male denied access to the younger men and forcibly ejected them from the group. Now, for reasons that are probably peculiar to the West, "denial" has always seemed a much more powerful tool of civilization than anything else. But one could just as easily attribute importance to the exodus forced on the younger men by their genealogical superior. Why not consider descent-group segmentation the "birth" of culture?

Patrilineal fissioning is as elementary as the incest prohibition or the systems of exchange it prompts. The two always go together. In fact, the dynamics of patrilineality necessarily precede and condition the circumstances which give rise to the incest prohibition in the first place. A group that is patrilineally organized cannot survive in unlimited extension or genealogical depth. It would simply get too big. Such groups always break down, usually by the third generation, and rarely extend much beyond a group of uterine brothers. This being so, the logic of patrilineal succession could be considered the origin of group distinctions and the basis of the "discriminatory procedure" (Lévi-Strauss 1969:119) that sorts out kinship categories. The incest prohibition is simply the codification of a distinction *already* brought about through the consequences of patrilineality.

I do not wish to make strong claims for this argument, or dispute the importance of descent or alliance. My point is to suggest that patrilineality is fundamentally problematic and oppositional, and very likely constitutes social dialectics everywhere it arises. Robert Murphy discovered the same principle in his study of the Bedouin and said that the problem of patrilineal ideology had to arise. The ideology could be preserved against the realities of breakdown and separation only through "blind spots in the normative system" (Murphy 1971:219). If oppositions are basic to cultural evolution, as Lévi-Strauss argues, then patrilineality fits the bill.

The Jalaris already know this. Brothers must uphold the value of the group's integrity and know that by doing so they inevitably lead to the group's destruction through division into subgroups, the nuclei of new patrilineal groupings. The Jalaris are not the only patrilineally organized people to experience the force of this paradox firsthand. What is interesting is what they have done with it dialectically, building up such cultural institutions as myth and divination. On this point I agree with Lévi-Strauss in assigning to structures of kinship a central role in constituting cultural knowledge systems. In fact, I would go further. Kinship structures are often deeply paradoxical, and some cultures have chosen to elaborate these paradoxes dialectically, in the form of knowledge systems such as myth and divination.

In the evolution of a patrilineal group, crises will erupt which at certain times prompt the members of the group to seek resolutions in the form of divinatory explanations. Uniting all such crises is the paradox which is central to the patrilineal ideology itself. The group must remain united, but it cannot, therefore it must divide; but it must remain united, and so on. Divinations interrupt this process, providing temporary respites, but they do not stop it. To look in any detail at a divination is to see the process at a particular moment of its evolution. In some cases, the group is nearing the point of division but has not reached it. There are still a few more crises to go. The divination arrests the process for a moment, providing a breathing space, and preserving the family for a while longer. But in such a moment one can already see the tensions which will cause the same crises to erupt with greater fury the next time round. Throughout the process the goal of fusion is never lost. It expresses itself in a search for temporary divinatory solutions and, after the group's dissolution, in a wistful nostalgia for the state of fraternal togetherness.

Chapter Eight

Reflections on the
Anthropology of Knowledge

The progress of science turns not on the proliferation of mere speculation but on the proliferation of informed speculation. (McCauley and Lawson, "Who Owns Culture?")

This book has not presented an account that is either exclusively interpretive or explanatory. A strictly interpretive account is not adequate, because it denies the relevance of generalization over specific instances and therefore fails as a science. Some would say that cultural anthropology is not (and should not be) a science, anyway. At the same time, explanatory theory of the strictly nomothetic type is not completely serviceable, since cultural anthropology, no matter how scientific, rarely identifies clearly objective causes. There are usually no discrete and observable causal agents, like the ones mechanical physics (in the popular view) describes. In their absence, does that mean that explanation itself is impossible? At this point we must delve into the philosophy of explanatory theory, to consider the differences between types of explanation, and the advantages of a "structural" account which Lawson and McCauley (1990) and McMullin (1978) advocate.

In all disciplines which profess or pretend to scientific rigor, the question arises; What is the cause of the phenomenon described? If I explain the peculiar American fascination with government conspiracy as a result of a "paranoid national character," what is the warrant for this, and how can it be justified as an explanation? It is surely not the case that I can point to something called "American culture" and leave it at that. Then again, why not? Most of the scientific disciplines are beset with the same difficulty. In physics, for example, the most basic constituents of matter (subatomic particles) cannot be seen, yet their existence is posited and used to explain the

264

phenomena which follow from their interaction. Similarly unseen agents are posited in other disciplines, from biology (e.g., genes) to astrophysics (e.g., black holes). If it were the case that an explanation had to specify perceptually exigent phenomena in order to be scientific, then there would be no science.

Most explanations in science are of this type, which McMullin calls "structural." Structural explanations postulate a structure to account for the observed properties of the entity or process under investigation. The warrant for believing that the entity or process actually possesses this structure is the success of the explanation it enables one to give. The explanation is hypothetical, since a different structure could be posited to account for the observation.

> The function of the explanation is not only to help one understand these features but also to discover the intrinsic structure of the entity. When the astronomer explains the changing shadows on the lunar surface by postulating that they are cast by mountain peaks, he not only explains the shadows, he also tells us something about the moon we might not otherwise know, i.e., that it (probably) has mountains. (McMullin 1978:139)

Hypotheses that can be tested across a range of instances are called "theoretical." A theory is a set of propositions which is explanatory in its intent. Explanatory theories which are structural will contain as part of their content a description of the structure they posit.

Despite their ubiquity, structural explanations have not received much acclaim in the philosophical tradition of the West. Philosophers have tended to believe that if science is to furnish eternal and necessary truths, it must begin from premises derived by induction from the sense perception and, therefore, known with certainty to be true. Given that structural explanations do not rely on sense perception but postulate the existence of hypothetical structures, how can they possibly qualify as scientific?

The contrast isn't as great as it seems, in any case, because explanations with clearly specifiable causal agents are not all that they are cracked up to be. To take an example from the natural sciences: Most of the empirical "laws" which summarize the results of observational work are not of causal form, even though appearing to be. Boyle-Charles law relates the pressure, volume, and temperature of a body of gas. Chemical reactions within the gas are correlated with temperature, but the "law" which describes this correlation does not identify any one of the relevant variables (e.g., temperature, pressure, or volume) as "cause" in regard to the observed regularity. Nomothetic explanations of the strictly causal, nonteleo-logical type that science is supposed to prefer are actually quite limited, since the primary function of empirical scientific laws is not to explain but to organize experience in a way that makes it explicable.

Whether "natural" or "social," most scientific explanation is not nomothetic but structural, in the sense I have used the term. As McMullin notes, "structural explanations point to 'causes' which have not been observed, but which are postulated to be causally responsible for what *is* observed" (1978:145). That is what makes them so powerful.

It is easy to see why, when we consider in more detail the kind of inferences each type, nomothetic and structural, must involve. Nomothetic explanations are almost invariably inductive, going from the particular to the general; the transition from one to the other is simply one of extension. What McMullin refers to as "retroductive inference" introduces conceptual novelty, and thus the extension involved is much greater. The justification for the latter is the explanatory success of the hypothesis. In other words, the hypothesis is confirmed or disconfirmed only to the extent that it is shown to have explanatory power. Thus, a good structural explanation is not just the result of induction from the particular to the general. It is more, since it is not just a matter of inference but of imaginative extension into the realm of "suggestion." It may remain provisional at the same time that it provokes the search for new causal agents and mechanisms.

The upshot is that questions of causal agency which ask one to pinpoint or specify the precise form of the agency in question are misguided in psychological anthropology, and in most of science as well. To a large extent this is recognized, and scholars of both the social and physical long ago abandoned the attempt to specify cause as a necessary step in the analysis of something—although most also allowed that such a specification might follow from successful research. Astonishing, then, that is still possible criticize someone for not having located and specified, say, "culture" or "the unconscious," as if that is the sole criterion by which to judge the explanatory adequacy of a scientific hypothesis. Most of our work cannot meet this criterion. "Explanation" that reduces to empirical causal agents is simply not feasible in cultural anthropology, most of the time. But that does not make it any less a science.

If, then, structural explanation can be viewed as a successful and certainly much more common form of explanation, how can this fact be used to achieve an interactive synthesis of interpretivist and explanatory approaches?

Against the view that there is a necessary difference, I agree with Lawson and McCauley and proceed on the assumption that the two are intimately related *and must be so* when the kind of explanation is structural in orientation. The purpose of structural explanation is not to specify causal agents but to generate theories which account for the observed phenomena in the absence of immediately specifiable agents. This is what makes them sources of innovative understanding. Structural explanation generate platforms from which to make novel interpretations. The interpretations thus generated use the categories of theories and models already in place as explanatory structures. When these structures cease producing satisfying interpretations, the theory which frames them undergoes change, and new explanations are given. The production of new meanings facilitates the generation of new explanatory theories (while at the same time) prior explanatory discoveries inform all good interpretations. As Lawson and McCauley point out:

> When people seek better interpretations they attempt to employ the categories they have in better ways. By contrast, when people seek better explanations, they go beyond the rearrangement of categories; they generate new theories which will, if successful, replace or even eliminate the conceptual scheme with which they presently operate. (1990:29)

Knowledge tends to advance when better interpretations of existing data are not enough, because the existing conceptual structures which provide explanations do not suffice. Without interpretations, in other words, the progress of explanatory theory could not continue.

We tend to differentiate between explanation and interpretation, not because the two are opposed, but for rhetorical and polemical purposes. Ironically, the rhetoric is put to service in the justification of an explanatory approach which accounts for cultural forms as mystifications of the processes of power. One can hardly imagine a more reductive explanation. The failure to acknowledge the theoretical character of recent work on cultural anthropology, especially of the postmodernist variety, is responsible for a lot of misunderstanding.

Since explanation and interpretation are already linked, the best approach is to be explicit about both. How can we do that? The approach taken by Lawson and McCauley is extremely useful. The epistemological preeminence of science, they state, rests not in its ability to lay bare the ultimate causal structure of reality, but rather in its ability to generate systematic explanations of phenomena that are of interest to us. Such explanations are almost always structural, but the trick is to be explicit about this. Two criteria help in this regard. The first is that scientific explanations must operate by means of systematically related general principles that employ concepts at least one level of abstraction removed from the phenomena they purport to explain. Second, such systems of principles must be empirically tractable beyond their initial domain of application (Lawson and McCauley 1990:27).

The first criterion makes it possible for us to generalize across a range of phenomena deemed to be members of the same class. In the absence of explicit generalizability, one is left with particularistic description. But this is only a ruse: Every description involves some kind of theory, even if it amounts to no more than the assumptions which must be made in order to translate one term from another language into its assumed English equivalent. The point is to be explicit about the principles which inform the inevitable acts of generalization which accompany all ethnography. The more general the explanation's principles, the more likely it is that the explanation will count as scientific, and while this is not every ethnographer's goal, it *is* the goal of this account.

The second criterion follows from the first. The fact that an explanation is generalizable is what makes it empirically tractable, since opportunities for testing its applicability will be more numerous. A theory limited to the explanation of a single occurrence would not constitute a theoretical proposition, since the explanation could be tailored to fit the instance. This does not mean that historical explanations are not theoretical, or that science necessarily precludes interpretation of unique events. On the contrary, the point is not to eradicate specificity but to inform it with theories capable of extension to other domains. The explanation of why Booth assassinated Lincoln involves great specificity, but the theories which inform that specificity must be capable of generalization in order to make comparative analytic judgments. That is what would be needed if we wanted to develop, say, a model of political killing in the United States, or a framework for attributing responsibility to the perpetrators, or judgments on the relative effectiveness of direct action. However seemingly particularistic, all histories do this, to one extent or another: The point is to be explicit about *how* it is done.

Linking explanation and interpretation, and specifying their theoretical status, does not mean that we abandon the distinction. Interpretation assumes the existence of systematic knowledge, on which it depends, while explanation provides the springboard for the making of interpretation. The two are intimately related but involve different cognitive operations. "Interpretations uncover unexpected connections in the knowledge we already possess," as Lawson and McCauley say, while "the success of new explanatory theories establishes new vistas" (1990:30). This interaction is an unending dialectical process, and it will be productive scientifically to the extent we are willing to be explicit about its inner workings.

The explanation I have offered accounts for features of the observed phenomena by relating them systematically and at a level of generality higher than that of the phenomena themselves. It is therefore a "structural" explanation in the sense described above. Dialectically elaborated paradoxes become complex knowledge systems, rationalized toward culturally defined goals which they cannot achieve. Paradoxes generate ambivalence and the desire to resolve it, which motivates knowledge as well as the complex interactions that result in new knowledge. Cultures are problems that can never be solved, and problems are deeply motivating, shaping the knowledge systems which rationalize them. That is why we need an account of dialectical knowledge that is simultaneously cognitive and psychodynamic — to help us get at both the shape of knowledge and its deep motivations.

The importance of this book will be in its demonstration that valid interpretations follow from the conceptual structure employed and that the theory which informs this structure is empirically tractable in the form described. This is the standard by which it should be judged. Like all science, it is not a finished product, nor is it an account of everything. There is a great deal left out. It is a tentative exploration, based on a potentially useful synthesis, that will provide a new framework for asking questions about knowledge and desire.

PARADOX AS A STRUCTURE OF EXPLANATION

No doubt the idea of a structural theory of culture based on paradox appears strange. Most of us are accustomed to thinking of paradox as a source of vexation, and therefore to imagine any system based on paradox is difficult. One recalls the story of Philetas of Cos, said to have vexed himself to death from excessive contemplation of the famous Liar Paradox: "What I am now saying is false." Paradoxes of this kind are extremely frustrating. But this only indicates their power to motivate thinking, for just consider: If an explicitly stated paradox has that kind of power—which it does, to judge by its frequent citation ever since antiquity—then what kind of power must the paradoxes which are embedded in social formations or unconscious processes have?

Historically, paradoxes are associated with long-term philosophical problematics, such as the opposition of the real and the ideal (Lovejoy 1966) and revolutionary advances in systems which are dialectical, based on irreconcilable oppositions in values or ideals. Paradox drives or directs dialectical knowledge systems by ensuring that the integrations achieved are temporary and that change continues in pursuit of the goal of unity, however this is defined. Paradox is the essential starting point of this process, not merely a by-product of the system but the very thing which sustains it.

Looking at culture and mind as a paradox does not limit us to a view of either as essentially static or constantly changing. Nor does it confirm what LaBarre called "the melancholy fact that men persist in cherishing old errors in preference to new knowledge" (1972:633). On the contrary, if dialectics are fundamental to knowledge systems, then conflict, contradiction, and inconsistency are *absolutely fundamental* to what we call "culture." There can be no getting away from them. The point is that a knowledge system can represent a cultural dialectic motivated by a problematic opposition, or paradox, which cannot be resolved—*and must not be*, in order for the cultural dialectic to continue to be motivating. If culture is made up of problems that cannot be solved, then a very different analytic approach is called for, one which comprehends the dynamic of culturally constituted paradox.

The problem until now has been that most psychodynamic explanations focus on *why* something occurs rather than *how*, and this makes them less useful when it comes to matters of cognitive process and social practice, when the details of knowledge structure and the interpretation of social meaning are important. Most cognitive-style explanations suffer the equally serious defect of neglecting deep motivation, or worse, relegating it to rational intent or the desire for power. Each side needs the other. It is the historic antipathy between the two—reducible, in part, to the fear of each that the other means to swallow it whole—that forestalls the development of an integrated theory. The purpose of this book has been to develop a dialogue between cognitive and psychodynamic approaches, by showing that both are dialectical and begin in culturally elaborated paradox.

Ethnographically, I have focused on South India and on the neat categorical array based on cross-cousin marriage that presents an ideal of harmonious unity. Men must give up their mothers and sisters, and sisters must give up their fathers and brothers, but through cross-cousin marriage, a return of what was relinquished is promised. This ideal is never actually realized in practice, however. Categories create desires that cannot be fulfilled and thus conflict with the ideal of harmony and structural reduplication embedded in the kinship system. My point has been that desires are not extraneous to the category structure of South Indian kinship. That is because the longings and frustrations created by the gap between ideal and practice are not merely a by-product of the system. Cross-cousin marriage is sustained not simply because it is "there," the only kinship pattern available, but because it holds out for people the possibility of achieving the goal of unity. They pursue it, as Trawick (1990) has pointed out, not realizing that the quest for fulfillment is permanently fleeting.

COMPARING KNOWLEDGE SYSTEMS: AMERICAN PSYCHIATRY
AND JALARI DIVINATION

American psychiatry and Jalari divination are cultural institutions shaped by paradox and the desire to resolve it. The paradoxes that motivate cultural institutions are powerful, and this power is dependent on three things. The first is the nature of the paradoxes themselves. They must be based on values that are fundamental but mutually contradictory. The second is that the paradoxes cannot be solved as long as they exist in their present form. This means that they remain for long periods of time, shaping and constraining the knowledge forms which develop out of them, and constituting at least one important aspect of cultural continuity. The third is that paradoxes create cultural ambivalence as the result of the desire to resolve them in pursuit of a culturally defined goal.

Americans value "independence" and "dependence" as cultural norms, but find them exceedingly difficult to reconcile, because their competing normative demands pull in opposite directions. Writers from Tocqueville (1969) to Robert Bellah (1985) have noticed the opposition and traced its effects in institutional practices and personal experiences (see also Hsu 1963; LaBarre 1972; Lynd 1939; Stein and Apprey 1990). Americans respond to the contradiction in a variety of ways. One is by allocating the values of independence and dependence to men and women, respectively, then essentializing these values as inherent dispositions which psychiatric categories merely name but do not create. Thus the "problem," which is cultural, is converted into a medical issue, where it is then "solved" through translation into psychiatric categories that are assumed to be objectively real and natural (Nuckolls 1992b).

Consider this example: One of the "problems" of American psychiatry is that men are diagnosed much more often with the personality disorders of "independence" (e.g., paranoid and antisocial), whereas women are diagnosed much more often with disorders of "dependence" (histrionic and borderline). There is no obvious reason why there should be a difference in the first place, let alone one so marked. While it might be (and usually is) considered a real biophysical problem, and the difference in rates attributed to genetic differences, the problem is also *the solution* to a culturally constructed problem that is unrecognized, because it refers to the paradoxical opposition of deeply cherished but contradictory cultural values. The value of independence, transformed into a personality attribute, is assigned to men. For American men it is culturally normative to act independently. Normative independence, however, is only a standard, a marker which calibrates the scale according to which judgments of a certain kind are made. Yet there can be too much of a good thing. Men who are too independent become diagnosable with one of the disorders of independence, e.g., paranoia, antisociality, or narcissism. These disorders simply refer to different styles of being independent.

For example, the difference between paranoia and narcissism as disorders of independence is in their directedness, whether active and outward or passive and inward. Overly independent men who are passive—that is, men who seek and obtain reinforcement from within themselves—are narcissists. Overly independent men who are active—that is, men who seek and obtain reinforcement from others—are either paranoid or antisocial.

Similarly, dependence is culturally defined as a normative attribute of women. It is also a marker. Overly dependent women become diagnosable as dependent, histrionic, or borderline personalities, each representing a different style of dependence. The difference between them is in their directedness, active or passive, to possible sources of reinforcement. Actively dependent women are histrionic; They go out of their way to create dependency relationships. Passively dependent women are "dependent" (i.e., classified as having "dependent personality disorders") and simply wait and hope that a source of nurturance and support will appear. Borderline personalities are those which take to an extreme either the histrionic's active or the dependent's passive behavior style.

No paradox could sustain this kind of knowledge structure unless it were founded on a deeply felt and possibly defensive need. In this case, it is the "need" to avoid the ambivalence that results from contemplation of two cherished but antinomian values—independence and dependence. Bellah and his coauthors (1985) identify this cultural ambivalence as a defining feature of the modern American ethos. In a series of poignantly developed case studies, they note that Americans desperately want both the freedom of independence and the communitas of shared dependency. And they conclude:

> What this suggests is that there is profound ambivalence about
> individualism in America among its most articulate defenders. This

ambivalence shows up particularly clearly at the level of myth in our
literature and our popular culture. There we find the fear that society
may overwhelm the individual and destroy any chance of autonomy
unless he stands against it, but also recognition that it is only in relation
to society that the individual can fulfill himself and that if the break with
society is too radical, life has no meaning at all. (1985:144)

As Bellah et al. remark, "most Americans would prefer not to see the impasse as starkly as we have put it" (144). Undoubtedly, that is true. But it also raises a question: Just how do most Americans *avoid* seeing the impasse, even though, from all accounts, they experience its consequences deeply and constantly? If it all adds up to a "classic case of ambivalence" (151), as Bellah puts it, then the consequences are not difficult to anticipate. One of the consequences is the cultural construction of the personality disorders in the psychiatric nosology.

To avoid the ambivalence, and the unpleasant feelings it arouses, competing values are externalized and projected outward onto a "delegate group" who then "act out" the values which have been assigned to them. Moreover, such acting out is defined as a result of the delegates' natural and predisposing qualities. In this way, competing values are retained (because both continue to be valued) and the competition continues, albeit "externally" between representative surrogate groups. The personality disorders reprsent extremes in the values assigned to delegate groups. Their social function is to mark such extremes as dangerous and interesting. They are what LaBarre calls "social cynosures" (LaBarre 1956), which means that they stand out and attract attention as markers of social value. How do we identify them as such or, to put it differently, what are the criteria according to which social cynosures of this type can be identified?

A similar process in Jalari culture represents the paradox of agnatic and affinal solidarity, values which conflict both internally and with respect to each other. The divinatory system realizes this paradox in the form of knowledge about goddess attacks and resolves it, temporarily, in each new diagnosis. Resolutions in this form never last for long, because the goal toward which the system is directed—emotional fusion—cannot be achieved with either of the two classes of people with whom it is desircd: brothers and sisters. Eventually, the paradox reasserts itself in the next cycle of family development and disintegration, beginning the process all over again.

If Jalari divination and American psychiatric diagnosis are alike in some respects, they are also different in others, the result of differing explanatory goals. The American system seeks resolutions which represent progressively more complete realizations of its directive goal—abstract and objective generalization over a universe of facts. These realizations are the new theories, new codifications, and new perspectives which we have come to expect of science on a fairly regular basis. The fact that such realizations constitute no more (and no less) than moments in a constant dialectical movement is not recognized. Jalari divination is not rationalized toward the same goal. It does not seek progressive betterment of theory or practice, to bring itself into fuller accord with the processes of objective reality as "science" defines them. It therefore does not have the look of a progressive science, with its constantly revised explanatory paradigms. In fact, the paradigms remain fairly constant. So where are the resolutions or integrations which the dialectic is supposed to realize? They are in each new divinatory explanation.

A divinatory explanation which ends a precipitating social dispute in favor of a return to fraternal solidarity temporarily resolves the paradox inherent in relations between brothers. For a while the brothers achieve the state of group cohesion that is the ideal. But embedded in the very moment of resolution are the seeds of its own destruction. There is simply no getting around the fact that brothers have interests which can and do diverge, both among themselves and with respect to their married sisters. So the crisis repeats itself, culminating in the same resolution or in the decision to separate permanently. The same is true of affinal relations.

Whereas resolutions in science take the shape of formalized knowledge structures recognized as such, and believed to develop progressively, resolutions in Jalari divination are social formations that are specific to family context. They do not exist independent of this context, and there is no sense in which they are viewed as progress. As I said in chapter 3, we need the language of the primary process to understand knowledge systems that are rationalized with respect to goals of this kind. Failing to do so simply means that we end up comparing apples and oranges, thus contributing to the confusion known as the "rationality debate."

Another important difference between the two dialectical systems is that the American system reproduces itself in response to factors that are much more complex and include forces of political economy which operate transnationally. For example, women now work outside the home in unprecedented numbers, achieving parity in areas once considered exclusively male domains. Is that because the principle of democratic access, as it becomes increasingly rationalized and therefore more encompassing, finally included women in the workplace? Is it because women became progressively more intolerant of discrimination and organized against it? Or is it because, in a capitalist system, economics tend to compel people who were once outside wage labor to enter it? The present study has not addressed such questions, only the forms which, regardless of the answer, the development of one cultural institution takes.

By this I mean that various factors will determine the changing ways women will be considered dependent. But the logic of the system suggests that whatever these ways are they will be reduced to psychiatric categories and attributed to women as inherent traits—traits which, taken to an extreme, result in the diagnosis of a personality disorder. This analysis does not make predictions about revisions in the category structure. We know only that the process will continue, and that with each revision the paradox will realize itself, most probably in the allocation of conflicting values to gender.

FINAL THOUGHTS: THE PRIMACY OF PARADOX
IN CULTURAL DIALECTICS

> *The Unhappy Consciousness is the consciousness of self as a dual-natured, merely contradictory being. [It] is the gazing of one self-consciousness into another, and itself is both, and the unity of both is also its essential nature.*
> *(Hegel,* The Phenomenology of Spirit*)*

The history of thought in the West (especially in England and France) usually takes contradictoriness and dialectical thinking to be a weakness or failure. After all, to be at variance with what one also desires could be taken to be symptomatic of the irrational, the schizophrenic, the insane. The preferred alternative to dialectics is the positive view, which is that reality is a self-consistent and objective whole, and perception capable (in principle) of direct encounters with it. Let us call the position which holds that one should be consistent and objective the "monist" view. The monist position is the view that the ideal, proper, or best mode of thinking is one in which all propositions are consistent. Spinoza's *Ethics* is the classic presentation of a monism so complete that it insisted that, "No one can hate God." Monism is also characteristic of "positivism," and of the form of empiricism which holds that knowledge is restricted to the passive reception of sense data, a complex and endless stream of impressions. Monism is easily the most identifiable characteristic of the "empirical" social sciences, especially those which locate causal forces in the objects of sense impression and their techno-eco-demographic arrangement.

Against monism there stands a long tradition of dialectical thinking, beginning with Plato, which questions the existence of things in themselves in preference for complex relations, and the interaction between these re- lations and the perceiving consciousness. Socratic dialogue was the first "dialectic" in the most technical sense, through its use of *elenchus*—the methodological interrogatory testing of the interlocutor for contradictory presuppositions, in order to lead him through awareness of contradictions to a new realization. Rorty elevates it to the status of a paradigm. Philoso- phy is:

> a "voice in the conversation of mankind," . . . which centers on one topic
> rather than another at some given time not by dialectical necessity but as
> a result of various things happening elsewhere in the conversation (the
> New Science, the French Revolution, the modern novel) or of individual
> men of genius who think something new (Hegel, Marx, Frege, Witt-
> genstein, Heidegger), or perhaps the resultant of several such forces.
> (Rorty 1979:264)

In this expanded sense, dialectic refers to the coming together of different individuals with differing opinions, working together toward some kind of rapprochement. The purpose of the dialectical encounter is not to locate objectively verifiable facts by adjudicating claims to truth among the ad- herents of different positions. It is to create a dynamic movement in the interplay of these positions, so that when they clash they bring about some- thing new—a new form of knowledge—which contains within itself the seeds of its own supersession.

Kant argued that dialectically opposed opinions or positions represent an underlying characteristic of thought itself. Abstract perspectives natu- rally and inevitably veer into their opposite. Recognizing this imposes what Kant calls a "regulative" limit on thought, and acts as a safeguard against various forms of monism that generally tend to be overly optimistic about what they know, or can know. For Hegel this was only the beginning, since dialectics are not merely forms of thought but intrinsic properties of nature which thought merely represents. The concepts of understanding are not conditioned by the knower, but unconditioned universals which obtain in all things, everywhere, and at all times. They are not just applied to experience, Hegel said, but actually precede experience as its organiz- ing principles. And since it is the "I" that supplies these concepts, it is no longer to be viewed as primarily a receptor, but as an activity—the activity of providing rules and laws which govern everyday human experience.

What is the state, or condition, of this "I" in its awareness of itself and everything else as oppositional and conflict-ridden? Hegel describes it as *die verkehrte Welt,* the "upside-down" or "topsy-turvy" world, in which everything is the opposite of what it is: black is white, up is down, left is right. The supposedly real world of objective facts turns out not to be real at all; indeed, what is real is that there are no eternal or objective forms, which Hegel expresses as the idea that "we have to think pure change" (1977:160). What Hegel refers to as the Absolute is not static, therefore, but dynamic and based on "contradiction" (*Widerspruch*). Thus the world of the understanding, and of the transcendental ego, gives rise to consequences which, by its own standards, the "I" must find intolerable.

To this form or state Hegel gives the name "the unhappy consciousness." It is the consciousness of contradiction that is unending (Hegel 1977:208), a state of absolute dialectical unrest. It seems to me that what Hegel calls the unhappy consciousness is the state of dynamic conflict that is characteristic of both mind and culture. It is not necessarily "unhappy"; but neither is it capable of the quiet and full knowledge of experience that Aristotle described as ideal.

The danger of the unhappy consciousness is that it ends up insisting on a merely aesthetic viewpoint. That was Schelling's response. One simply gives up knowledge and concentrates instead on more refined judgments of taste, of "elegance," and even "beauty." Another possibility, chosen by Marx, is to attempt to restore the unhappy consciousness to a condition of wholeness and unity by locating the dialectic in the world of material forces, then foreseeing the day when that dialectic will complete itself in a moment of total resolution, ending all contradictions.

This book began by noting the impasse in anthropology that makes it difficult to discuss knowledge and motivation together, without reducing one to the other, or both to social structural imperatives. Motives are usually formulated in individualistic terms, with an emphasis on the agent's desire to master the environment, control his or her actions, seek self-realization, or manipulate power relations (Deci and Ryan 1985; Lutz 1988; Rodin 1990; Ryan and Connel 1989). Recently, there have been attempts to breach the impasse by locating motivation in the structures of cultural knowledge and calling it "goals." Such goals possess directive force, acting as motivators of behavior. While this represents a welcome departure from the utilitarian individualism of other approaches, the attempt to reconcile cognition and desire by locating motives in cultural models cannot be considered completely satisfactory. It is difficult to account for conflict between motives and for the fact that such conflict itself might be highly motivating. It is also developmentally superficial by failing to relate enduring motivational complexes to features of childhood experience that may be recurrent across broad sections of society.

Instead of arguing against the dualism constituted by cognitive and psychoanalytic perspectives, I have tried to build a synthesis, by showing that the dualism can be reconfigured as a dialectic necessarily involving both. I have argued for a return to the broadly integrative paradigms of the past, and to the philosophical tradition, beginning with Kant and culminating in Bateson, which unites them as dialectical theories. Seen thus, the synthesis I have proposed in this book does not look especially radical. But it does constitute a challenge to the cultural anthropology of the present, a discipline nearly devoid of theory, except when it reduces culture to power, and increasingly suspicious of itself and any claims it might make to being a science.

References

Index

References

Abu-Lughod, L. 1991. "Writing against Culture." In *Recapturing Anthropology*. Ed. R. Fox. Santa Fe, N.M.: School of American Research Press.

Adorno, T. 1973. *The Jargon of Authenticity*. Trans. Knut Tarnowski and Frederic Will. London: Routledge & Kegan Paul.

Agar, M. 1986. *Speaking of Ethnography*. Beverly Hills: Sage Publications.

Alexander, J. 1982. *The Antinomies of Classical Thought: Marx and Durkheim*. Berkeley: University of California Press.

Alexander, S. 1920. *Space, Time, and Deity*. vols. 1 and 2. New York: Humanities Press.

American Psychiatric Association. 1987. *Diagnostic and Statistical Manual of Mental Disorders III-R*. Washington, D.C.: APA.

Babb, L. 1983. "Destiny and Responsibility: Karma in Popular Hinduism." In *Karma: An Anthropological Inquiry*. Ed. C. Keyes and E. Daniel. Berkeley: University of California Press.

Barth, F. 1987. *Cosmologies in the Making*. Cambridge: Cambridge University Press.

Barth, F. 1995. "Other Knowledge and Other Ways of Knowing." *Journal of Anthropological Research* 51(1): 65–68.

Bartlett, F. 1932. *Remembering; A Study in Experimental and Social Psychology*. Cambridge: Cambridge University Press.

Bateson, G. 1958. *Naven*. 2d ed. Stanford: Stanford University Press.

Bateson, G. 1972. *Steps to an Ecology of Mind*. New York: Ballantine.

Bateson, G. 1979. *Mind and Nature: A Necessary Unity*. New York: Dutton.

Beck, B. 1981. "The Goddess and the Demon: A Local South Indian Festival in Its Wider Context." *Purusartha* (Paris) 5:83–136.

Bellah, R., et al. 1985. *Habits of the Heart*. Berkeley: University of California Press.

Ben-Amos, D. 1984. "The Seven Strands of Tradition: Varieties in Its Meaning in American Folklore Studies." *Journal of Folklore Research* 21:97–131.

Benedict, R. 1934. *Patterns of Culture*. New York: Houghton Mifflin.

Bennett, L. 1983. *Dangerous Wives and Sacred Sisters: Social and Symbolic Roles of High-Caste Women in Nepal*. New York: Columbia University Press.

Black, P. 1985. "Ghosts, Gossip, and Suicide: Meaning and Action in Tobian Folk

Psychology." In *Person, Self, and Experience: Exploring Pacific Ethnopsychologies*. Ed. G. White and J. Kirkpatrick. Berkeley: University of California Press.

Boas, F. 1940. *Race, Language and Culture*. New York: Macmillan.

Bond, J., J. Hansell, and H. Shevrin. 1987. "Locating Transference Paradigms in Psychotherapy Transcripts: Reliability of Relationship Episode Location in the Core Conflictual Relationship Theme (CCRT) Method." *Psychotherapy* 24:736–49.

Bourdieu, P. 1977. *Outline of a Theory of Practice*. Trans. R. Nice. Cambridge: Cambridge University Press.

Bowlby, J. 1969. *Attachment and Loss*. London: Hogarth Press.

Boyer, P. 1990. *Tradition as Truth and Communication*. Cambridge: Cambridge University Press.

Briere, J., and J. Conte. 1993. "Self-Reported Amnesia for Abuse in Adults Molested as Children." *Journal of Traumatic Stress* 6(1): 21–31.

Brook, J. 1992. "Freud and Splitting." *International Review of Psychoanalysis* 19: 335–50.

Caplan, L. 1984. *The Insanity Defense and the Trial of John W. Hinckley, Jr.* Boston: Godine.

Carstairs, G. M. 1958. *The Twice-Born: A Study of a Community of High-Caste Hindus*. Bloomington: Indiana University.

Casson, R. 1983. "Schemata in Cognitive Anthropology." *Annual Review of Anthropology* 12:429–65.

Chasseguet-Smirgel, J., and B. Grunberger. 1986. *Freud or Reich? Psychoanalysis and Illusion*. New Haven: Yale University Press.

Chodorow, N. 1978. *The Reproduction of Mothering: Psychoanalysis and the Sociology of Gender*. Berkeley: University of California Press.

Coburn, T. 1991. *Encountering the Goddess: A Translation of the* Devi-Mahatmya *and a Study of Its Interpretation*. New York: State University of New York Press.

Cole, M. 1983. "Intelligence as Cultural Practice." *Carmichael's Handbook of Child Psychology*. Ed. W. Kessen. vol. 1. New York: Wiley.

Commager, H. 1950. *The American Mind*. New Haven: Yale University Press.

Coser, L. 1976. "Authority and Structural Ambivalence in the Middle-Class Family." In *Sociological Theory*. Ed. L. Coser and B. Rosenberg. New York: Macmillan.

Cox, R., ed. 1973. *Religious Systems and Psychotherapy*. Springfield, Ill.: Thomas.

Crits-Christoph, P., L. Luborksky, C. Dahl, J. Popp, J. Mellon, and D. Mark. 1988. "Clinicians Can Agree in Assessing Relationship Patterns in Psychotherapy: The Core Conflictual Relationship Theme Method." *Archives of General Psychiatry* 45:1001–4.

Cummins, R. 1983. *The Nature of Psychological Explanation*. Cambridge: MIT Press.

D'Andrade, R. 1987. "A Folk Model of the Mind." In *Cultural Models in Language and Thought*. Ed. D. Holland and N. Quinn. Cambridge: Cambridge University Press.

D'Andrade, R. 1991. "The Identification of Schemas in Naturalistic Data." In *Person Schemas and Maladaptive Interpersonal Patterns*. Ed. M. Horowitz. Chicago: U of Chicago Press.

D'Andrade, R. 1992. "Schemas and Motivation." In *Human Motives and Cultural Models*. Ed. R. D'Andrade and C. Strauss. Cambridge: Cambridge University Press.

D'Andrade, R. 1995a. *The Development of Cognitive Anthropology*. Cambridge: Cambridge University Press.

D'Andrade, R. 1995b. "Moral Models in Anthropology." *Current Anthropology* 36:399–408.

D'Andrade, R., and C. Strauss, eds. 1992. *Human Motives and Cultural Models*. Cambridge: Cambridge University Press.

Danforth, L. 1988. *Firewalking and Religious Healing*. Princeton: Princeton University Press.

Daniel, E. 1983. "Conclusion: Karma, the Uses of an Idea." In *Karma: An Anthropological Inquiry*. Ed. C. Keyes and E. Daniel. Berkeley: University of California Press.

Deci, E., and R. Ryan. 1985. *Intrinsic Motivation and Self-Determination in Human Behavior*. New York: Plenum.

Desjarlais, R. "Healing through Images: The Magical Flight and Healing Geography of Nepali Shamans." *Ethos* 17(3): 289–308.

Dougherty, J. 1985. *Directions in Cognitive Anthropology*. Urbana: University of Illinois Press.

Dunn, J. 1988. *The Beginnings of Social Understanding*. Oxford: Blackwell.

Durkheim, E. 1965. *The Elementary Forms of the Religious Life*. Trans. J. Swain. New York: Free Press.

Durkheim, E., et al. 1964. *Essays on Sociology and Philosophy*. Ed. K. Wolff. New York: Harper & Row.

Egnor, M. 1984. "The Changed Mother or What the Smallpox Goddess Did When There Was No More Smallpox." *Contributions to Asian Studies* 18:24–45.

Eliade, M. 1962. *The Two and the One*. Tr. J. M. Cohen. Chicago: University of Chicago Press.

Elmore, W. 1925. *Dravidian Gods in Modern Hinduism*. 2d ed. Madras: Christian Literature Society for India.

Erikson, E. 1969. *Gandhi's Truth: On the Origins of Militant Nonviolence*. New York: Norton.

Erndl, K. 1993. *Victory to the Mother*. Oxford: Oxford University Press.

Evans-Pritchard, E. 1937. *Witchcraft, Oracles and Magic among the Azande*. Oxford: Clarendon Press.

Fazio, R., and Cooper, J. 1983. "Arousal in the Dissonance Process." In *Social Psychophysiology*. Ed. J. Cacioppo and R. Petty. New York: Guilford.

Festinger, L. 1957. *A Theory of Cognitive Dissonance*. Palo Alto: Stanford University Press.

Festinger, L. 1962. "Cognitive Dissonance." *Scientific American* 207:93–102.

Fiske, A. 1962. "Cognitive Dissonance." *Scientific American* 207:93–102.

Fiske, A. 1991. *The Structures of Social Life.* New York: Free Press.

Fox, R. 1967. *Kinship and Marriage.* Baltimore: Penguin.

Fox, R. 1994. "Myth as Evidence of Psychological Processes." In *Psychological Anthropology.* Ed. P. Bock. Westport: Praeger.

Freud, S. 1950. *Totem and Taboo.* Trans. J. Strachey. New York: Norton.

Freud, S. 1953. *The Interpretation of Dreams.* vols. 4 and 5 of *The Standard Edition.* Trans. J. Strachey. London: Hogarth.

Freud, S. 1955. "The Unconscious." In *The Standard Edition of the Complete Psychological Works of Sigmund Freud.* Trans. and ed. James Strachey. vol. 14. London: Hogarth.

Freud, S. 1960. *The Ego and the Id.* Trans. J. Riviere. Ed. J. Strachey. New York: Norton.

Freud, S. 1961a. *Beyond the Pleasure Principle.* Trans. and ed. J. Strachey. New York: Norton.

Freud, S. 1961b. *The Neuropsychoses of Defense.* Ed. and trans. J. Strachey. Vol. 3 of the *Standard Edition.* London: Hogarth.

Freud, S. 1963. *Civilization and Its Discontents.* Trans. J. Riviere. Ed. J. Strachey. London: Hogarth.

Freud, S. 1965. *New Introductory Lectures on Psychoanalysis.* Trans. and ed. J. Strachey. New York: Norton.

Freud, S. 1966. *Introductory Lectures on Psychoanalysis.* Trans. and ed. J. Strachey. New York: Norton.

Freud, S. 1991. "The Taboo of Virginity." In *On Sexuality,* by Freud. Ed. James Strachey. London: Penguin.

Gaes, G., V. Melburg, and J. Tedeschi. 1986. "A Study Examining the Arousal Properties of the Forced Compliance Situation." *Journal of Experimental Social Psychology* 22:136–47.

Gay, P. 1985. *Freud for Historians.* New York: Oxford University Press.

Gay, P. 1988. *Freud: A Life for Our Time.* New York: Doubleday.

Geertz, C. 1966. "Religion as a Cultural System." In *Anthropological Approaches to the Study of Religion.* Ed. M. Baton. London: Tavistock.

Gellner, E. 1970. "Concepts and Society." In *Rationality.* Ed. B. Wilson. Oxford: Blackwell.

Gertlach, L. 1974. "Pentecostalism: Revolution or Counter-Revolution?" In *Religious Movements in Contemporary America.* Ed. I. Zaretsky and M. Leone. Princeton: Princeton University Press.

Goodman, N. 1978. *Ways of Worldmaking.* Brighton: Harvester.

Grathoff, R. 1970. *The Structure of Social Inconsistencies.* The Hague: Nijhoff.

Guillaumaud, J. 1980. "Sauver la dialectique?" *Science et dialectique chez Hegel et Marx.* Ed. M. Vadée. Paris: Editions CNRS.

Heald, S. 1994. Introduction to *Anthropology and Psychoanalysis.* Ed. S. Heald and A. Deluz. London: Routledge.

Hegel, G. 1969. *Science of Logic.* Trans. A. V. Miller. Oxford: Clarendon Press.

Hegel, G. 1977. *The Phenomenology of Spirit.* Trans. A. V. Miller. Oxford: Oxford University Press.

Heraclitus. 1979. *The Fragments 75.* In *The Art and Thought of Heraclitus.* Trans. C. Kahn. Cambridge: Cambridge University Press.

Heuscher, J. 1974. *A Psychiatric Study of Myths and Fairy Tales.* 2d ed. rev. and enl. Springfield, Ill.: Thomas.

Hiebert, P. 1967. *Konduru: Structure and Integration in a South Indian Village.* Minneapolis: University of Minnesota Press.

Hiltebeitel, A. 1989. "Draupadi's Two Guardians: The Buffalo King and the Muslim Devotee." In *Criminal Gods and Demon Devotees.* Ed. A. Hiltebeitel. Albany: SUNY.

Hobsbawm, E., and T. Ranger, eds. 1983. *The Invention of Tradition.* New York: Cambridge University Press.

Hollan, D., and J. Wellenkamp. 1994. *Contentment and Suffering: Culture and Experience in Toraja.* New York: Columbia University Press.

Holland, D., and N. Quinn. 1987. *Cultural Models in Language and Thought.* Cambridge: Cambridge University Press.

Holland, D. 1992. "The Woman Who Climbed up the House: Some Limitations of Schema Theory." In *New Directions in Psychological Anthropology.* Ed. T. Schwartz, G. White, and C. Lutz. Cambridge: Cambridge University Press.

Hollis, M. 1982. "The Social Destruction of Reality." In *Rationality and Relativism.* Ed. M. Hollis and S. Lukes. Cambridge: MIT Press.

Hollis, M., and S. Lukes, eds. 1982. *Rationality and Relativism.* Cambridge: MIT Press.

Holmes, J., and J. Rempel. 1989. "Trust in Close Relationships." In *Close Relationships.* Ed. C. Hendrick. Review of Personality and Social Psychology vol. 10. Beverly Hills: Sage.

Horkheimer, M., and T. Adorno. 1972. *Dialectic of Enlightenment.* Trans. J. Cumming. New York: Herder and Herder.

Horowitz, M., ed. 1988. *Psychodynamics and Cognition.* Chicago: University of Chicago Press.

Horowitz, M., ed. 1991. *Person Schemas and Maladaptive Interpersonal Patterns.* Chicago: University of Chicago Press.

Horton, R. 1982. "Tradition and Modernity Revisited." In *Rationality and Relativism.* Ed. M. Hollis and S. Lukes. Cambridge: MIT Press.

Hsu, F. 1963. *Clan, Caste, and Club.* Princeton: Van Nostrand.

Hsu, F., ed. 1971. *Kinship and Culture.* Chicago: Aldine.

Hughes, H. 1958. *Consciousness and Society: The Reorientation of European Social Thought, 1890–1930.* New York: Vintage.

Hutchins, E. 1980. *Culture and Inference: A Trobriand Case Study.* Cambridge: Harvard University Press.

Hutchins, E. 1987. "Myth and Experience in the Trobriand Islands." In *Cultural*

References

Models in Language and Thought. Ed. D. Holland and N. Quinn. Cambridge: Cambridge University Press.

Hymbaugh, K., and J. Garrett. 1974. "Sensation-seeking among Sky-divers." *Perceptual and Motor Skills* 38:118.

Jarvie, I., and J. Agassi. 1970. "The Problem of the Rationality of Magic." In *Rationality.* Ed. B. Wilson. Oxford: Blackwell.

Jaspers, K. 1965. *Allgemeine Psychopathologie.* Berlin: Springer-Verlag.

Jay, M. 1973. *The Dialectical Imagination.* Boston: Little, Brown.

Jay, M. 1984. *Adorno.* Cambridge: Harvard University Press.

Johnson, M. 1987. *The Body in the Mind.* Chicago: University of Chicago Press.

Kainz, H. 1988. *Paradox, Dialectic, and System: A Contemporary Reconstruction of the Hegelian Problematic.* University Park: Pennsylvania State University Press.

Kakar, S. 1981. *The Inner World: A Psycho-analytic Study of Childhood and Society in India.* rev. and enl. Delhi: Oxford University Press.

Kakar, S. 1982. *Shamans, Mystics, and Doctors: A Psychoanalytic Inquiry into India and Its Healing Traditions.* New York: Knopf.

Kakar, S. 1989. "The Maternal-Feminine in Indian Psychoanalysis." *International Review of Psychoanalysis* 19:355-62.

Kakar, S. 1990. "Stories from Indian Psychoanalysis: Context and Text." In *Cultural Psychology: Essays on Comparative Human Development.* Ed. J. Stigler, R. Shweder, and G. Herdt. Cambridge: Cambridge University Press.

Kant, I. 1965. *Critique of Pure Reason.* Trans. Norman Kemp Smith. New York: St. Martin's Press.

Kant, I. 1951. *Critique of Judgment.* Trans. J. H. Bernard. New York: Hafner.

Kant, I. 1974. *Anthropology from a Pragmatic Point of View.* Trans. M. Gregor. The Hague: Nijhoff.

Kant, I. 1990. *Foundations of the Metaphysics of Morals.* 2d rev. ed. Trans. L. W. Beck. New York: Macmillan.

Kaplan, E., ed. 1990. *Psychoanalysis and Cinema.* New York: Routledge.

Kaplan, M. 1983. "A Woman's View of DSM-III." *American Psychologist* 38:786-92.

Kasler, D. 1988. *Max Weber: An Introduction to His Life and Work.* Cambridge: Polity.

Kass, F., R. Spitzer, and J. Williams. 1983. "An Empirical Study of the Issue of Sex Bias in the Diagnostic Criteria of DSM-III Axis II Personality Disorders." *American Psychologist* 38:799-801.

Kemp Smith, N. 1984. *A Commentary to Kant's Critique of Pure Reason.* 3d ed. Atlantic Highlands, N.J.: Humanities Press.

Keyes, C. 1983. Introduction to *Karma: An Anthropological Inquiry.* Ed. C. Keyes and E. Daniel. Berkeley: University of California Press.

Kinsley, D. 1988. *Hindu Goddesses: Visions of the Divine Feminine in the Hindu Religious Tradition.* Berkeley: University of California Press.

Kirkcaldy, B. 1982. "Personality Profiles at Various Levels of Athletic Participation." *Personality and Individual Differences* 3:321-26.

Kolenda, P. 1964. "Religious Anxiety and Hindu Fate." *Journal of Asian Studies* 23:71-81.

Kolenda, P. 1993. "Sibling Relations and Marriage Practices: A Comparison of North, Central, and South India." In *Siblings in South Asia: Brothers and Sisters in Cultural Context*. Ed. C. Nuckolls. New York: Guilford.

Kramrisch, S. 1975. "The Indian Great Goddess." *History of Religions* 14:235-65.

Kramrisch, S. 1988. *The Presence of Siva*. Varanasi: Motilal Banarsidass.

Kunda, Z. 1990. "The Case for Motivated Reasoning." *Psychological Bulletin* 108: 480-98.

Kunda, Z., and K. Oleson. 1995. "Maintaining Stereotypes in the Face of Disconfirmation." *Journal of Personality and Social Psychology* 68(4): 565-79.

Kunda, Z., and R. Sanitioso. 1989. "Motivated Changes in the Self-Concept." *Journal of Experimental Social Psychology* 25(3): 272-85.

Kurtz, S. 1992. *All the Mothers Are One*. New York: Columbia University Press.

LaBarre, W. 1972. *The Ghost Dance: Origins of Religion*. New York: Dell.

Ladrine, H. 1987. "On the Politics of Madness: A Preliminary Analysis of the Relationship between Social Roles and Psychopathology." *Psychology Monographs* 113:341-406.

Ladrine, H. 1989. "The Politics of Personality Disorder." *Psychology of Women Quarterly* 13:325-39.

Lakoff, G. 1987. *Women, Fire, and Dangerous Things*. Chicago: University of Chicago Press.

Langer, S. 1942. *Philosophy in a New Key*. New York: New American Library.

Langer, S. 1953. *Feeling and Form*. New York: Scribner.

Lash, S., and S. Whimster eds. *Max Weber, Rationality and Modernity*. London: Allen & Unwin.

Lawson, E. T., and R. McCauley. 1990. *Rethinking Religion*. Cambridge: Cambridge University Press.

Lawson, E. T., and R. McCauley. 1994. "Who Owns Culture?" Paper presented to Mellon Symposium, "Cognition and Religious Ritual," Department of Anthropology, Emory University, November 1994.

Lee, D. 1959. *Freedom and Culture*. Englewood-Cliffs, N.J.: Prentice-Hall.

Leeuw, G. van der. 1933. *Religion in Essence and Manifestation*. Tr. J. E. Turner. New York: Harper & Row.

Levine, F., and L. Luborsky. 1981. "The Core Conflictual Relationship Theme Method: A Demonstration of Reliable Clinical Inferences by the Method of Mismatched Cases." In *Object and Self: A Developmental Approach*. Ed. S. Tuttman, C. Kaye, and M. Zimmerman. New York: International Universities Press.

Lévi-Strauss, C. 1969. *The Elementary Structures of Kinship*. rev. ed. Trans. J. Bell, J. von Sturmer, and R. Needham. Boston: Beacon.

Lévi-Strauss, C. 1981. *The Naked Man*. Trans. J. and D. Weightman. London: Jonathan Cape.

Lévi-Strauss, C. 1985. *The View from Afar.* Trans. J. Neugroschel and P. Hoss. New York: Basic Books.

Lévi-Strauss, C. 1988. *The Jealous Potter.* Trans. B. Chorier. Chicago: University of Chicago Press.

Lindholm, C. 1982. *Generosity and Jealousy: The Swat Pukhtun of Northern Pakistan.* New York: Columbia University Press.

LiPuma, E. 1983. "On the Preference for Marriage Rules: A Melanesian Example." *Man* 18:766–85.

Loewenberg, P. 1985. *Decoding the Past: The Psychohistorical Approach.* Berkeley: University of California Press.

Loftus, E. 1992. "When a Lie Becomes Memory's Truth: Memory Distortion after Exposure to Misinformation." *Current Directions in Psychological Sciences* 1(4): 121–23.

Lovejoy, A. 1966. *The Great Chain of Being.* Cambridge: Harvard University Press.

Luborsky, L., et al. 1991. "Freud's Transference Template Compared with the Core Conflictual Relationship Theme (CCRT): Illustrations by the Two Specimen Cases." In *Person Schemas and Maladaptive Interpersonal Patterns.* Ed. M. Horowitz. Chicago: University of Chicago Press.

Lukes, S. 1982. "Relativism in Its Place." In *Rationality and Relativism.* Ed. M. Hollis and S. Lukes. Cambridge: MIT Press.

Luria, A. 1971. "Towards the Problem of the Historical Nature of Psychological Processes." *International Journal of Psychology* 6:259–73.

Lutz, C. 1988. *Unnatural Emotions.* Chicago: University of Chicago Press.

Lutz, C., and L. Abu-Lughod, eds. 1990. *Language and the Politics of Emotion.* New York: Cambridge University Press.

Lynd, R. 1939. *Knowledge for What?* Princeton: Princeton University Press.

Macdonald, W. 1976. "Preliminary Notes on Some Jhankri of the Muglan." In *Spirit Possession in the Nepal Himalayas.* Ed. J. Hitchcock and R. Jones. Warminster, Eng.: Aris and Phillips.

McGuire, M. 1988. *Ritual Healing in Suburban America.* New Brunswick, N.J.: Rutgers University Press.

McMullin, E. 1978. "Structural Explanation." *American Philosophical Quarterly* 15:139–47.

Mahler, M., F. Pine, and A. Bergman. 1975. *The Psychological Birth of the Human Infant.* New York: Basic Books.

Malinowski, B. 1954. "Myth in Primitive Culture." In *Magic, Science and Religion: and Other Essays.* New York: Doubleday.

Marcuse, H. 1955. *Eros and Civilization.* Boston: Beacon.

Marriott, M. 1976. "Hindu Transactions: Diversity without Dualism." In *Transaction and Meaning: Directions in the Anthropology of Exchange and Symbolic Behavior.* Ed. B. Kapferer. Philadelphia: Institute for the Study of Human Issues.

Marriott, M. 1989. "Constructing an Indian Ethnosociology." *Contributions to Indian Sociology* 23:1–39.

Marx, K. *Capital.* 1970. vol. 1. Trans. E. Aveling. London: Lawrence & Wishart.

Marx, K., and F. Engels. 1942. *Selected Correspondence.* Trans. D. Torr. New York: International Publishers.

Mayar, J., M. DiPaolo, and P. Salovey. "Perceiving Affective Content in Ambiguous Visual Stimuli." *Journal of Personality Assessment* 54(3–4): 772–81.

Merkur, D. 1988. "Adaptive Symbolism and the Theory of Myth: The Symbolic Understanding of Myths in Inuit Religion." In *The Psychoanalytic Study of Society.* Ed. B. Boyer and J. Grolnick. vol. 13. New York: Psychoanalytic Press.

Merton, R. 1976. *Sociological Ambivalence and Other Essays.* New York: Free Press.

Metz, C. 1980. "The Fiction Film and Its Spectator: A Metapsychological Study." In *Apparatus, Cinematographic Apparatus.* Ed. T. H. K. Cha. New York: Tanam Press.

Metz, C. 1982. *The Imaginary Signifier: Psychoanalysis and the Cinema.* Bloomington: Indiana University Press.

Mines, M. 1994. *Public Faces, Private Voices: Community and Individuality in South India.* Berkeley: University of California Press.

Minturn, L. 1993. *Sita's Daughters: Coming out of Purdah.* New York: Oxford University Press.

Mitzman, A. 1970. *The Iron Cage: An Historical Interpretation of Max Weber.* New York: Knopf.

Mommsen, W. 1987. "Personal Conduct and Societal Change." In *Max Weber, Rationality and Modernity.* Ed. S. Lash and S. Whimster. London: Allen & Unwin.

Morgan, L. 1871. *Systems of Consanguinity and Affinity of the Human Family.* Smithsonian Contributions to Knowledge no. 218. Washington: Smithsonian Institution.

Mortensen, C. D. 1987. *Violence and Communication: Public Reactions to an Attempted Presidential Assassination.* Lanham, Md.: University Press of America.

Murphy, R. 1971. *The Dialectics of Social Life: Alarms and Excursions in Anthropological Theory.* New York: Basic Books.

Nagel, E. 1961. *The Structure of Science: Problems in the Logic of Scientific Explanation.* New York: Harcourt, Brace & World.

Needleman, J., and G. Baker, eds. 1978. *Understanding the New Religions.* New York: Seabury.

Neufeldt, R., ed. 1986. *Karma and Rebirth: Post Classical Developments.* Albany: SUNY Press.

Nisbett, R., and L. Ross. 1980. *Human Inference: Strategies and Shortcomings of Social Judgment.* Englewood-Cliffs, N.J.: Prentice-Hall.

Noy, P. 1969. "A Revision of the Psychoanalytic Theory of the Primary Process." *International Journal of Psychoanalysis* 50:155–78.

Noy, P. 1979. "The Psychoanalytic Theory of Cognitive Development." *Psychoanalytic Study of the Child* 34:169–216.

Nuckolls, C. 1987. "Causal Thinking in Śakentala: A Schema-Theoretic Approach to Classical Sanskrit Drama." *Philosophy East and West* 27:286–305.

Nuckolls, C. 1991a. "Culture and Causal Thinking: Diagnosis and Prediction in a South Indian Fishing Village." *Ethos* 19(1): 3-51.

Nuckolls, C. 1991b. "Becoming a Possession-Medium in South India: A Psychocultural Account." *Medical Anthropology Quarterly* 5:63-77.

Nuckolls, C. 1991c. "Deciding How To Decide: Possession-Mediumship in South India." *Medical Anthropology* 13:57-82.

Nuckolls, C. 1992a. "Notes on a Defrocked Priest." In *Ethnopsychiatry: The Cultural Construction of Professional and Folk Psychiatries*. Ed. A. Gaines. Buffalo: SUNY Press.

Nuckolls, C. 1992b. "Toward the Cultural History of the Personality Disorders." *Social Science and Medicine* 35(1): 37-49.

Nuckolls, C. 1993a. "The Anthropology of Explanation." *Anthropological Quarterly* 66(1): 1-21.

Nuckolls, C. 1993b. "Structure of Emotions in Jalari Divination." *The Eastern Anthropologist* 46(2): 111-44.

Nuckolls, C., ed. 1993c. *Siblings in South Asia: Brothers and Sisters in Cultural Context*. New York: Guilford.

Nuckolls, C. 1995. "The Misplaced Legacy of Gregory Bateson: Toward a Cultural Dialectics of Knowledge and Desire." *Cultural Anthropology* 10:368-96.

Nuckolls, C. In press. "Spiro and Lutz on Ifaluk." *Ethos*.

Nuckolls, C. Forthcoming. *Motivated Knowledge*. University of Wisconsin Press.

Obeyesekere, G. 1981. *Medusa's Hair: An Essay on Personal Symbols and Religious Experience*. Chicago: University of Chicago Press.

Obeyesekere, G. 1984. *The Cult of the Goddess Pattini*. Chicago: University of Chicago Press.

Obeyesekere, G. 1990. *The Work of Culture*. Chicago: University of Chicago Press.

O'Conner, T. 1994. "Emergent Properties." *American Philosophical Quarterly* 31(2): 91-104.

O'Flaherty, W. 1975. *Hindu Myths*. New York: Penguin.

O'Flaherty, W., ed. 1980. *Karma and Rebirth in Classical Indian Traditions*. Berkeley: University of California Press.

Otto, R. 1923. *The Idea of the Holy*. New York: Oxford University Press.

Parsons, T. 1947. Introduction to *Max Weber: The Theory of Social and Economic Organization*. By M. Weber. Tr. A. M. Henderson and T. Parsons. Ed. T. Parsons. New York: Free Press.

Parsons, T. 1951. *The Social System*. New York: Free Press.

Peterson, I. 1986. "The Tie That Binds; Brothers and Sisters in North and South India." Paper presented at the Conference on Religion in South India.

Polanyi, M. 1968. "Life's Incredible Structure." *Science* 160:1308-12.

Radcliffe-Brown, A. 1924. "The Mother's Brother in South Africa." *South African Journal of Science* 21:542-55.

Ramanujan, A. 1980. "Is There an Indian Way of Thinking?" Manuscript, Department of South Asian Languages and Civilizations, University of Chicago.

Ramanujan, A. 1991. "Toward a Counter-System: Women's Tales." In *Gender,*

Genre, and Power in South Asian Expressive Traditions. Ed. A. Appadurai, F. Korom, and M. Mills. Philadelphia: University of Pennsylvania Press.

Ramanujan, A., V. N. Rao, and D. Shulman, ed. and trans. 1994. *When God Is a Customer.* Berkeley: University of California Press.

Rank, O. 1992. *The Incest Theme in Literature and Legend.* Baltimore: Johns Hopkins University Press.

Reichenbach, B. 1990. *The Law of Karma: A Philosophical Study.* Honolulu: University of Hawaii Press.

Reik, T. 1956. *The Search Within: The Inner Experiences of a Psychoanalyst.* New York: Farrar, Straus & Cudahy.

Richman, P. 1955. "Tamil Songs to God as a Child." In *Religions of India in Practice.* Ed. D. Lopez Jr. Princeton: Princeton University Press.

Robinson, D. 1993. "Toward the Application of Diagnostic Criteria to Personality-Disordered Psychotherapy Patients: Understanding Axis II of the DSM-III-R as It Has Never Been Understood Before." *Journal of Polymorphous Perversity* 10(1): 9–14.

Rodin, J. 1990. "Control by Any Other Name: Definitions, Concepts, and Processes." In *Self-Directedness: Cause and Effects throughout the Life Course.* Ed. J. Rodin, C. Schooler, and K. Warner Schaie. Hillsdale, N.J.: Erlbaum.

Rogoff, B. 1980. "Schooling and the Development of Cognitive Skills." In *Handbook of Cross-Cultural Psychology.* Ed. H. Triandis and A. Heron. vol. 4. Boston: Allyn & Bacon, 1980.

Roheim, G. 1974. *Children of the Desert: Western Tribes of Central Australia.* New York: Basic Books.

Roland, A. 1988. *In Search of Self in India and Japan.* Princeton: Princeton University Press.

Rorty, R. 1979. *Philosophy and the Mirror of Nature.* Princeton: Princeton University Press.

Ryan, R., and J. Connell. 1989. "Perceived Locus of Causality and Internalization: Examining Reasons for Acting in Two Domains." *Journal of Personality and Social Psychology* 57:749–61.

Samanta, S. 1994. "The 'Self-Animal' and Divine Digestion: Goat Sacrifice to the Goddess Kali in Bengal." *Journal of Asian Studies* 53(3): 779–803.

Sapir, E. 1921. *Language.* New York: Harcourt, Brace.

Scheper-Hughes, N. 1992. "Hungry Bodies, Medicine, and the State: Toward a Critical Psychological Anthropology." In *New Directions in Psychological Anthropology.* Ed. T. Schwartz, G. White, and C. Lutz. New York: Cambridge University Press.

Schluchter, W. 1987. "Weber's Sociology of Rationalism and Typology of Religious Rejections of the World." In *Max Weber, Rationality, and Modernity.* Ed. S. Lash and S. Whimster. London: Allen & Unwin.

Schneider, D. 1968. *American Kinship: A Cultural Account.* Englewood Cliffs, N.J.: Prentice-Hall.

Schrempp, G. 1992. *Magical Arrows: The Maori, the Greeks, and the Folklore of the Universe.* Madison: University of Wisconsin Press.

Scribner, S., and M. Cole. 1981. *The Psychology of Literacy.* Cambridge: Harvard University Press.

Seymour, S. 1993. "Sociocultural Contexts: Examining Sibling Roles in South Asia." In *Siblings in South Asia: Brothers and Sisters in Cultural Context.* Ed. C. Nuckolls. New York: Guilford.

Sharp, P., M. Cole, and C. Lave. 1979. *Education and Cognitive Development: The Evidence from Experimental Research.* Monographs of the Society for Research in Child Development. Ser. no. 178, vol. 44, nos. 1–2. Chicago: University of Chicago Press for the Society.

Shedler, J., M. Mayman, and M. Manis. 1994. "More Illusions." *American Psychologist* 80(2): 54–69.

Shils, E. 1981. *Tradition.* Chicago: University of Chicago Press.

Shore, B. 1991. "Human Ambivalence and the Structuring of Moral Values." *Ethos* 18(2): 165–79.

Shore, B. 1996. *Culture in Mind: Meaning Construction and Cultural Cognition.* Oxford: Oxford University Press.

Shulman, D. 1976. "The Murderous Bride: Tamil Versions of the Myth of Devi and the Buffalo-Demon." *History of Religion* 120–46.

Shulman, D. 1980. *Tamil Temple Myths.* Princeton: Princeton University Press.

Shweder, R. 1984. "Anthropology's Romantic Rebellion against the Enlightenment." In *Culture Theory.* Ed. R. Schweder and R. LeVine. Cambridge: Cambridge University Press.

Shweder, R. 1986. "Divergent rationalities." In *Metatheory in Social Science.* Ed. D. Fiske and R. Shweder. Chicago: University of Chicago Press.

Shweder, R. 1991. *Thinking through Cultures.* Cambridge: Harvard University Press.

Shweder, R., and E. Bourne. 1984. "Does the Concept of the Person Vary Cross-culturally?" In *Culture Theory.* Ed. R. Shweder and R. LeVine. Cambridge: Cambridge University Press.

Shweder, R., M. Mahapatra, and J. Miller. 1987. "Culture and Moral Development." In *The Emergence of Morality in Young Children.* Ed. J. Kagan and S. Lamb. Chicago: University of Chicago Press.

Simon, H. *Models of Bounded Rationality.* vols. 1 and 2. Cambridge: MIT Press.

Singer, J., ed. 1990. *Repression and Dissociation: Implications for Personality Theory, Psychopathology, and Health.* Chicago: University of Chicago Press.

Singer, M. 1972. *When a Great Tradition Modernizes.* Chicago: University of Chicago Press.

Slaatte, H. 1968. *The Pertinence of the Paradox: The Dialectics of Reason-in-Existence.* New York: Humanities Press.

Slater, P., and D. Slater. 1965. "Maternal Ambivalence and Narcissism: A Cross-cultural Study." *Merrill-Palmer Quarterly* 11:241–59.

Slotkin, R. 1992. *Gunfighter Nation: The Myth of the Frontier in Twentieth-Century America.* New York: HarperPerennial.

Smith, J. C. 1990. *Psychoanalytic Roots of Patriarchy: The Neurotic Foundations of Social Order.* New York: New York University Press.

Smith-Rosenberg, C. 1985. *Disorderly Conduct: Visions of Gender in Victorian America.* New York: Knopf.

Solomon, R. 1983. *In the Spirit of Hegel.* New York: Oxford University Press.

Sperber, D. 1975. *Rethinking Symbolism.* Tr. A. Morton. Cambridge: Cambridge University Press.

Sperber, D. 1985. *On Anthropological Knowledge.* Cambridge: Cambridge University Press.

Spiro, M. 1950. "A Psychotic Personality in the South Seas." *Psychiatry* 13:189–204.

Spiro, M. 1952. "Ghosts, Ifaluk, and Teleological Functionalism." *American Anthropologist* 54:497–503.

Spiro, M. 1953. "Ghosts: An Anthropological Inquiry into Learning and Perception." *Journal of Abnormal and Social Psychology* 48:376–82.

Spiro, M. 1984. "Some Reflections on Cultural Determinism and Relativism with Special Reference to Emotion and Reason." In *Culture Theory.* Ed. R. Shweder and R. LeVine. Cambridge: Cambridge University Press.

Srinivas, M. 1952. *Religion and Society among the Coorgs of South India.* Oxford: Clarendon.

Stein, H. 1985. "Alcoholism as Metaphor in American Culture." *Ethos* 73(11): 195–235.

Stein, H., and Apprey, M. 1985. *Context and Dynamics in Clinical Knowledge.* Charlottesville: University Press of Virginia.

Stein, H., and M. Apprey. 1987. *From Metaphor to Meaning: Papers in Psychoanalytic Anthropology.* Charlottesville: University Press of Virginia.

Stein, H., and M. Apprey. 1990. *Clinical Stories and Their Translation.* Charlottesville: University Press of Virginia.

Stierlin, H. 1973. "Group Fantasies and Family Myths—Some Theoretical & Practical Aspects." *Family Process* 12(2): 111–25.

Stigler, J., R. Shweder, and G. Herdt, eds. 1990. *Cultural Psychology: Essays on Comparative Human Development.* Cambridge: Cambridge University Press.

Straub, W. 1982. "Sensation-Seeking among High- and Low-Risk Male Athletes." *Journal of Sport Psychology* 4:246–53.

Strauss, C. 1992. "Models as Motives." In *Human Motives and Cultural Models.* Ed. R. D'Andrade and C. Strauss. Cambridge: Cambridge University Press.

Tambiah, S. J. 1990. *Magic, Science, Religion, and the Scope of Rationality.* Cambridge: Cambridge University Press.

Tarksi, A. 1969. "Truth and Proof." *Scientific American* 194:63 77.

Taylor, C. 1982. "Rationality." In *Rationality and Relativism.* Ed. M. Hollis and S. Lukes. Cambridge: MIT Press.

Thom, G. 1983. *The Human Nature of Social Discontent.* Totowa, N.J.: Rowan & Allanheld.

Thurston, E. 1909. *Castes and Tribes of Southern India*. 7 vols. Madras: Government Press.

Tipton, S. 1982. *Getting Saved from the Sixties: The Transformation of Moral Meaning in American Culture by Alternative Religious Movements*. Berkeley: University of California Press.

Tocqueville, A. de. 1969. *Democracy in America*. Ed. J. P. Mayer. Trans. G. Lawrence. Garden City: Doubleday.

Trawick, M. 1982. "The Changed Mother; or, What the Smallpox Goddess Did When There Was No More Smallpox." *Contributions to Indian Sociology* 18: 24–45.

Trawick, M. 1990. *Notes on Love in a Tamil Family*. Berkeley: University of California Press.

Triandis, H., and A. Heron. 1980. *Handbook of Cross-Cultural Psychology*. vol. 4. Boston: Allyn & Bacon.

Tulving, E., and D. Schacter. 1990. "Primary and Human Memory Systems." *Science* 247:301–7.

Turner, V. 1967. *The Forest of Symbols: Aspects of Ndembu Ritual*. Ithaca: Cornell University Press.

Turner, V. 1974. *Dramas, Fields, and Metaphors: Symbolic Action in Human Society*. Ithaca: Cornell University Press.

Turner, V. 1975. *Revelation and Divination in Ndembu Ritual*. Ithaca: Cornell University Press.

Turner, V. 1978. "Encounter with Freud: The Making of a Comparative Symbologist." In *The Making of Psychological Anthropology*. Ed. G. Spindler. Berkeley: University of California Press.

Tversky, A., and D. Kahneman. 1981. "The Framing of Decisions and the Psychology of Choice." *Science* 66(6): 11998.

Tyson, P., and R. Tyson. 1990. *Psychoanalytic Theories of Development: An Integration*. New Haven: Yale University Press.

Volkan, V. 1994. *The Need to Have Enemies and Allies: From Clinical Practice to International Relationships*. Northvale, N.J.: Aronson.

Volkan, V., D. Julius, and J. Montville, eds. 1991. *The Psychodynamics of International Relationships*. 2 vols. Lexington, Mass.: Lexington Books.

Wadley, S. ed. 1980. *The Powers of Tamil Women*. Syracuse: Maxwell School, Syracuse University.

Weber, M. 1946. "The Social Psychology of the World Religions." In *From Max Weber*. Ed. H. Gerth and C. W. Mills. New York: Oxford University Press.

Weber, M. 1958a. *The Rational and Social Foundations of Music*. Trans. and ed. D. Martindale, J. Riedel, and G. Neuwirth. Carbondale: Southern Illinois University Press.

Weber, M. 1958b. *The Protestant Ethic and the Spirit of Capitalism*. Trans. T. Parsons. New York: Scribner.

Weber, M. 1968. *Economy and Society*. 3 vol. Ed. G. Roth and C. Wittich. Trans. E. Fischoff et al. New York: Bedminster Press.

Weber, Max. 1991. *From Max Weber.* new ed. Trans. and ed. H. H. Gerth and C. W. Mills. New York: Routledge.

Weber, M. 1993. *Sociology of Religion.* Boston: Beacon.

Weigert, A. 1988. "Joyful Disaster: An Ambivalence-Religion Hypothesis." *Sociological Analysis* 50:73–88.

Weinberger, D., and M. Davidson. 1994. "Styles of Inhibiting Emotional Expression: Distinguishing Repressive Coping from Impression Management." *Journal of Personality* 62:587–613.

Weinberger, D., and G. Schwartz. 1990. "Distress and Restraint as Superordinate Dimensions of Self-Reported Adjustment: A Typological Perspective." *Journal of Personality* 58:381–417.

Weisner, T. 1993. "Overview: Sibling Similarity and Difference in Different Cultures." In *Siblings in South Asia: Brothers and Sisters in Cultural Context.* New York: Guilford Press.

Werner, H. 1978. *Developmental Processes.* 2 vol. Ed. S. Barten and M. Franklin. New York: International Universities Press.

Westen, D. 1991. "Social Cognition and Object Relations." *Psychological Bulletin* 109(3): 429–55.

Westen, D. 1992. "The Cognitive Self and the Psychoanalytic Self: Can We Put Ourselves Together?" *Psychological Inquiry* 3(1): 1–13.

Westen, D. 1994. "Is Freud Really Dead? Toward a Psychodynamically Informed Model of Personality." Manuscript, Department of Psychiatry, Harvard University.

Wexler, P. 1983. *Critical Social Psychology.* London: Routledge & Kegan Paul.

White, G. 1990. "Moral Discourse and the Rhetoric of Emotions." In *Language and the Politics of Emotion.* Ed. C. Lutz and L. Abu-Lughod. Cambridge: Cambridge University Press.

White, G. 1992. "Ethnopsychology." In *New Directions in Psychological Anthropology.* Ed. T. Schwartz, G. White, and C. Lutz. Cambridge: Cambridge University Press.

White, G., and C. Lutz. 1992. Introduction to *New Directions in Psychological Anthropology.* Ed. T. Schwartz, G. White, and C. Lutz. Cambridge: Cambridge University Press.

Whitehead, A. 1950. *Science and the Modern World.* New York: Macmillan.

Whitehead, H. 1921. *Village Gods of South India.* 2d ed. rev. and enl. Calcutta: Association Press.

Whorf, B. 1956. *Language, Thought, and Reality.* Cambridge: MIT Press.

Wicklund, R., and J. Brehm. 1976. *Perspectives on Cognitive Dissonance.* Hillsdale, N.J.: Erlbaum.

Wikan, U. 1990. *Managing Turbulent Hearts: A Balinese Formula for Living.* Chicago: University of Chicago Press.

Williams, L. 1995. "Recall of Childhood Trauma: A Prospective Study of Women's Memories of Child Sexual Abuse." *Journal of Consulting and Clinical Psychology* 63:343.

Wilson, B. ed. 1970. *Rationality.* Oxford: Blackwell.

Winch, P. 1970. "Understanding a Primitive Society." In *Rationality.* Ed. B. Wilson. Oxford: Blackwell.

Wuthnow, R. 1976. *The Consciousness Reformation.* Berkeley: University of California Press.

Wuthnow, R. 1979. *Experimentation in American Religion: The New Mysticisms and Their Implications for the Churches.* Berkeley: University of California Press.

Yinger, J. M. 1982. *Countercultures.* New York: Free Press.

Zanna, M., and J. Cooper. 1976. "Dissonance and the Attribution Process." In *New Directions in Attribution Research.* Ed. J. Harvey, W. J. Ickes, and R. Kidd. Hillsdale, N.J.: Erlbaum.

Zuckerman, M. 1971. "Dimensions of Sensation-Seeking." *Journal of Consulting and Clinical Psychology* 36:25–52.

Zuckerman, M. 1979. "Sensation-Seeking and Risk Taking." In *Emotions in Personality and Psychopathology.* Ed. C. Izard. New York: Plenum.

Zukow, P., ed. 1989. *Sibling Interaction across Cultures: Theoretical and Methodological Issues.* New York: Springer-Verlag.

Index

Abraham (biblical figure), 100
Abstractness, 97
Adam and Eve, 101–3
Addalu pettu, 127
Adi Sakti, 152–62, 177–79, 187, 190,
  192–93, 197
Adorno, Theodor, xxxvi–xxxviii
Adultery, 84–86, 96
Aesthetic judgment, in Kant, 35–36
Affinal relations, 47, 227–28, 231, 247
Aggression, 8, 34, 58
Agnatic relations, 47, 145, 213–14, 227–28,
  231, 233–48, 251
Ahankaram, 235
Alcoholism, 15–16, 22
Alexander, J., xxv–xxvi
Allgemeine Psychopathologie (Jaspers), 32
Althusser, Louis, xxxv
Ambivalence, 48, 108–9; and cultural cog-
  nitivism, 5–6, 10, 12, 15–16, 18; and
  goal-directed schemata, 12, 15–16; and
  Weber and Freud, synthesis of, 24, 28,
  32–37; paradoxical-dialectic of, 32–36;
  rationalization of, and dialectical paradox, 36–37; and the rationalization of
  directive goals, 79, 91; and dissonance,
  91; and the infant-mother bond, 109;
  elementary structure of, in Jalari kinship,
  120–44; and the father-daughter relation,
  189–90, 192; and the brother-sister relation, 209, 210; and divinatory resolution,
  227–28; and the brother-brother relation,
  243–44
Amma, 165, 169, 198–200, 247
Ammavallu, 47

Ammavari jabbu, 215
Ammavaru, 208, 209
Amnesia, 18–19. *See also* Forgetting
Andhra Pradesh, 37–45, 120, 163
Andreas-Salome, Lou, 33
Anger, 170, 171, 221
Anthropology from a Pragmatic Point of View
  (Kant), 34, 35–36
Antinomies, 25–28, 36
Anxiety: and the problem of motivation,
  17, 18, 20; in Freud, 58, 59, 65; and
  ethos, 65; and ambivalence, 118; and the
  mother-son relation, 168, 169, 172
Arapesh people, xxxix
Arini, 191, 193
Asceticism, 52
Asthma, 18
Astrophysics, 26
Attachment: and the mother-child rela-
  tion, 128–29, 131–33, 208–9; and the
  brother-sister relation, 139–40; and the
  father-daughter relation, 189, 192–93
Azande culture, 88–89, 104

Bachofen, Johann, xxxviii
Bacon, Francis, 92
Balinese culture, 104
Bartlett, F., 70, 72
Bateson, Gregory, xli–xlii, xliv, 22, 47–79,
  98, 278; *Naven*, 48, 51 52, 55–56, 59,
  66–67, 73–74; and Hegel, 49, 73–74, 76;
  and the standardization of emotions, 50–
  68; and Freud, 51, 58–59, 60, 63, 65–66;
  and *Unnatural Emotions*, 52; and Durkheim, 66–68; and the dynamics of eidos,

Bateson, Gregory *(continued)*
68–74; and *Remembering: Experiments in Social Psychology*, 68; and the paradoxical dialectics of desire and knowledge, 72–74; and directive goals, 80
Bay of Bengal, 38
Bedouin culture, 263
Bellah, Robert, 271, 273
Benedict, Ruth: *Patterns of Culture*, xliii–xliv, 50, 52, 76; and Bateson, 50, 52, 54, 76; and directive goals, 80
Bengali sacrifice, 106
Bentham, Jeremy, 8
Berlin Psychoanalytic Institute, xxxviii
Beyond the Pleasure Principle (Freud), 34
Bhakti, 133, 162
Blake, William, 111
Blue-collar workers, 10–11, 13, 17
Boas, Franz, xlii–xliii
Bohr, Niels, 26–27
Bourdieu, Pierre, 150
Bowlby, J., 129, 131
Boyle-Charles Law, 265
Brahma, 153, 156, 157
Breadwinner model, 11–14, 16
Breast-feeding, 129–31
Brother-brother relation, 137–38, 213, 230–33
Brother-sister relation, 144, 148–49; and cross-cousin marriage, 121; the paradox of unity and separation in, 139–42; and myth and the dynamics of desire in kinship, 152, 189–90, 193, 198–211; and ambivalence, 189, 190, 193; dialectic of, 213, 214, 247–48
Buddhism, 15

Caffeine consumption, 19
Calvinism, 32, 98
Cancer, 18
Capa rayi cupincadam, 215, 217–18, 220–21
Capital, Das (Marx), xxxv–xxxvi
Capitalism, 11, 31, 98, 108
Caplan, L., 83–84
Caste, Reddi, 163–64, 168, 169
Causality, 214–30
Chasseguet-Smirgel, Janine, 11, 145

Cholesterol levels, 18
Christianity, 77, 165; charismatic movements in, 15; Calvinism, 32, 98; Genesis myth of, 85, 99–103, 110–11; and the doctrine of karma, 94
Chronological/episodic formats, 70
Cinnamma, 129
Cinnola Papamma, 168, 169
Cognition: and the paradoxical dialectics of desire and knowledge, 72–74; the primary process as a mode of, 107–8
Cognitivism, 3–23; and ethnopsychology, 4–9; and goal-directed schemata, 9–17
Communism, 11
Complementarity, 26–27, 57
Compromise formation, 10, 22, 60; and goal-directed schemata, 16; and the problem of motivation, 18–19, 20; and the *naven* ceremony, 78
Configuration, use of the term, 49–50
Consistency, explanatory, 80–86, 96–98, 104
Copenhagen Interpretation, 26
Cornelius, Hans, xxxvi
Cosmology, 85, 98–104
Counterculture groups, 118
Covenants, 100
Creation myths: Christian (Genesis myth), 85, 99–103, 110–11; Hindu, 99, 110–13
Creative energy, 161
Crime: and the insanity defense, 83–84, 97; and adultery, 84–86, 96; and arrest procedures, 101; and punishment, in the Genesis myth, 102–3
Crisis moments, 145, 147
Critique of Judgment (Kant), 34–35
Critique of Pure Reason (Kant), xlii, 27n3, 79, 152
Cross-cousin marriage, 47, 144, 150; and ambivalence, 120–22; and the mother-son relation, 127, 132, 158, 161–62; and the father-daughter relation, 173, 175, 187, 188; and the brother-sister relation, 211; and the rationalization of paradox, in explanatory systems, 212, 214, 219–20, 227, 229, 247–48; in Lévi-Strauss, 247–48